Topical Index

SECOND EDITION

The MATH We Need to KNOW and DO in Grades 6-9

SECOND EDITION

The MATH We Need to KNOW and DO in Grades 6-9

CONCEPTS, SKILLS, STANDARDS, AND ASSESSMENTS

PEARL GOLD SOLOMON

CORWIN PRESS
A SAGE Publications Company
Thousand Oaks, CA 91320

For information:

Corwin Press
A Sage Publications Company
2455 Teller Road
Thousand Oaks, California 91320
www.corwinpress.com

Sage Publications Ltd.
1 Oliver's Yard
55 City Road
London EC1Y 1SP
United Kingdom

Sage Publications India Pvt. Ltd.
B 1/I 1 Mohan Cooperative Industrial Area
Mathura Road, New Delhi 110 044
India

Sage Publications Asia-Pacific Pte. Ltd.
33 Pekin Street #02-01
Far East Square
Singapore 048763

Printed in the United States of America.

Library of Congress Cataloging-in-Publication Data

Solomon, Pearl G. (Pearl Gold), 1929-
The math we need to know and do in grades 6-9 : concepts, skills, standards, and assessments / Pearl Gold Solomon. — 2nd ed.
    p. cm.
Rev. ed. of: The math we need to "know" and "do." c2001.
Includes bibliographical references and index.
ISBN 978-1-4129-1725-4 (cloth : acid-free paper) — ISBN 978-1-4129-1726-1 (pbk. : acid-free paper)
    1. Mathematics—Study and teaching (Middle school)—United States. 2. Mathematics—Study and teaching (Elementary)—United States. I. Solomon, Pearl G. (Pearl Gold), 1929- Math we need to "know" and "do."
II. Title.

QA135.6.S6246 2007
372.7—dc22

                                        2006035775

This book is printed on acid-free paper.

07 08 09 10 11   10 9 8 7 6 5 4 3 2 1

Acquiring Editor:	Faye Zucker
Editorial Assistant:	Gem Rabanera
Project Editor:	Astrid Virding
Copyeditor:	Gillian Dickens
Typesetter:	C&M Digitals (P) Ltd.
Proofreader:	Kevin Gleason
Cover Designer:	Rose Storey
Graphic Designer:	Scott Van Atta

Contents

Note to Teachers

The embedded concepts and their matching skills and performance indicators are presented in numbered table form in Chapter 2. Chapter 3 provides correspondingly numbered suggestions for the matching instructional dialogue, manipulatives, and sample problems that can be used by the teacher to help develop the concept or skill. If further clarification is needed, or the teacher needs suggestions for how to scaffold the concept with dialogue and problems to solve, there is a simple cross-check from Chapter 2 to the more comprehensive Chapter 3.

Preface to the Second Edition

WHAT THIS BOOK IS ABOUT ■

This book accepts the current climate of accountability by assessment and focuses both on the identification of the specific embedded concepts of mathematics—*what we need to know*—and the matching skill expectations—*what we need to be able to do*—to apply and demonstrate what we know. Using current national and state standards as a guide, it covers these elements of mathematics content for Grades 6 to 9, relates it to the current expanded pedagogical knowledge, and offers suggestions for instructional approaches and sequencing. Current curriculum standards documents include algebraic concepts at earlier grade levels than previously. Therefore, most of what was originally the elementary algebra of the ninth grade, as well as some intermediate algebra (such as quadratic equations), is addressed. We have also included advanced topics in geometry and probability and statistics because their introductions have been filtered down to earlier grades. Some topics, such as logic, that have not yet been commonly addressed in the eighth grade are not included. To show the conceptual sequence, we also show some topics that are introduced at the exploratory level in the fifth grade.

The book is designed as a resource for teachers to use as they

- Plan curriculum for a school, particular grade level, or specific lesson
- Assess their students' knowledge, both formally and informally
- Respond to individual conceptual or procedural problems among their students
- Review their own mathematical concepts

Since the publication of the first edition of this text, accountability for the achievement of high standards by educational systems was federally legislated in the form of required state-produced high-stakes assessments and improvement mandates by the No Child Left Behind (NCLB) legislation (NCLB, 2001). The legislation was initially responsive to heightened public attention and criticism of the problems of our educational systems. Not the least of that criticism was directed at the performance of our students in mathematics, especially when it was compared to that of students from other countries on international tests such as the Trends in International Mathematics and Science Study (TIMSS) (Schmidt, 2004; Schmidt, McNight, & Raizen, 1997). The NCLB legislation called for mandated assessments in literacy and mathematics from Grades 3 to 8 and identified specific sanctions for schools failing to show improvement in terms of adequate yearly progress. Although the tests are developed on a state level, the sanctions for school districts are powered by the mandatory reallocation of federal funds to remedies such as school transfers and tutoring for students when district schools or subgroups of students within them do not meet the criteria for adequate yearly progress.

A mixture of criticism and support continues to confront the assessments and their connected mandates. Most of the negative response is related to the sanctions imposed on poorly performing schools and the resulting stress on teachers and students. A recent report by the National Conference of State Legislatures (Dillon, 2005) says the law sets unrealistic expectations and defies commonsense notions of how to rate schools. State lawmakers also cite the conflict of NCLB with other legislation that protects the disabled. There has actually been some backtracking on previously instituted state-generated actions, as well as a push for more state control over NCLB criteria and sanctions. Unfortunately, despite evidence that the assessments have begun to improve student performance in some places, unresolved deficiencies or gaps in the overall achievement of specifically identified groups of students continue the calls for improvement.

Despite the varying opinions on the value of high-stakes assessments in the context of the stress and limitations they place on teachers and students and their possible misuse, it is my firm belief that assessment has a vital role in the educative process. It is most productive, however, when used as a tool through which the teacher manages instruction. When intensive professional development has accompanied careful curriculum construction and attention is paid to teacher ownership, assessments matched to that curriculum have contributed to improved student performance. I will address this issue further in Chapter 1, and for in-depth analyses, see Solomon (1995, 2002, 2003).

Although there are still a number of possible unproven reasons for the less than desired overall performance of U.S. students and the persistent gaps for certain groups of students, the first possibility that our educational community responded to was that our curriculum may have been an affecting factor. Comparisons of math curricula in our country to that in countries more successful on the international assessments revealed that ours covered too many topics repetitively and lacked intensity and focus. The initial response to this possible reason for failure, therefore, was to develop standards that outlined the necessary curriculum. Standards, initially published by the National Council for Teachers of Mathematics (NCTM, 1989, 2000), were then individually adapted by states to create state standards documents.

The state standards documents have helped to remedy some of the deficiencies in the curriculum, but some early versions of the state standards have been recently criticized for lack of clarity and specificity (Fordham Report, http://www.edexcellence.net/foundation/global/index.cfm). This book may provide some of what is missing. The first edition of *The Math We Need to Know and Do* was actually cited by the New York State Education Department as a key resource for its newly issued and much more explicit standards document.

My own observations of teachers in varying states and socially different schools reveal that, despite published curriculum documents, most of what is taught in schools today is still governed by published texts and workbooks. There is much that is worthwhile in today's textbooks for young learners; they provide drill and practice for operations and some good and varied application activities. New-generation technology, such as graphing calculators and computer software that allows for exploration and spatial problem solving, as well as access to data sets on the Internet, is even more hopeful, if used properly. The deficiency in the technology and some texts lies in the fact that they do not clearly delineate for the teachers or the students what exactly one needs to know to be an effective quantitative problem solver. Nor do they help teachers understand and build upon what research has taught us about how learning happens. Frequently, our students learn how to do the procedures in the books without constructing mathematical concepts that may be generalized to novel or real-life problems. The state curriculum documents try to define the skills but usually neglect to clarify the underlying or embedded mathematical concepts—and frequently are too general to override the day-to-day teacher-friendly comforts of text programs.

At the secondary level, where less attention has been paid to professional development, there is the added tendency of American mathematics teachers to teach complex procedures by example and practice with numbers, rather than by a focus on problem-solving approaches that encourage understanding of the concepts that underlie the procedure. Perhaps due to the great number of variables involved, the exact relationship between teaching method and student achievement is still unproven (Wang & Lin, 2005). Nevertheless, a recent analysis of results and teaching contexts of the international 1999 TIMSS assessment reveals that teachers in the United States are less likely to use the conceptual teaching methods that are used more frequently in high-performing countries and that this preference for procedural teaching is more prevalent with low-achieving students (Desimone, Smith, Baker, & Ueno, 2005). The authors of the TIMSS study suggest professional development programs for this group that focus on conceptual approaches. In the present stressful climate of high-stakes assessment, middle and high school teachers sometimes do not take the time to have students put an explanation for why and how procedure is applied into words or to state what the embedded concept is that makes the procedure work.

Pedagogical texts for teachers begin do this, but often they, too, neglect specificity in the concepts. Strangely, very old mathematics textbooks stated very clearly and simply what the necessary concepts were. *New Practical Arithmetic,* which was written by Benjamin Greenleaf (1872), brings the learner from the very elementary notations of single-digit numbers all the way to cube roots and the applications of stocks, bonds, taxes, principal, and interest, within 322 small (4 by 6 inch) pages. On these pocketbook-size pages are 465 paragraph sections that include precise definitions and succinct statements of the concepts as well as limited exercises. What Greenleaf did establish, for his time, was a clear mathematical knowledge base.

Although the world has gained much new knowledge since 1872, and topics such as probability, statistics, and mathematical modeling have to be added to help prepare our students for the technology-based modern world, the basic known content or knowledge base of elementary mathematics is not that different. The modern world, however, may not offer children the same kind of learning experiences. Hands-on real-life experiences are replaced with computer games as time spent on automatized facts and drill and practice is diminished by calculator computations. Nevertheless, our pedagogical knowledge base, especially our knowledge about how children learn, is much expanded. We use many new and better approaches to learning and teaching. Preoccupation with this new pedagogical knowledge has perhaps distracted us from the mathematics knowledge itself. For example, knowing that estimation skills and the ability to factor algebraic expressions with understanding and facility depend on quick mental retrieval of multiplication facts can lead us to value the automatization of facts. Knowing that automatization may be easier at earlier developmental stages may guide us into allocating that expectation to an early grade.

Like Greenleaf, we have tried to be parsimonious with words. For in-depth discussions of the background research, readers can refer to the literature cited in our references. This is also not a mathematics textbook, although it will provide some illustrative activities for students. Instead, it will compensate for the missing components of recent texts and curriculum guides—statements of the very specific concepts and procedures embedded in mathematical knowledge. These are phrased succinctly and precisely in Chapter 2 as the embedded concepts (what students need to know) and articulated skill or performance indicators (what students need to be able to do). These tell us more exactly what students need to solve the problems in their texts, the real world, and the state assessments. The skills and concepts tell us some of what they will need to know as adults in order to have lifelong comfort and ease with new mathematical problems and compete with others in a technological future. They will help teachers analyze whether their students have achieved the specifics of that knowledge and guide them in the correction of unsound or incomplete constructions of knowledge.

This book is a resource meant to be used by teachers in conjunction with other materials: texts, workbooks, manipulatives, and technology. It can also serve as an adjunct textbook for teachers in training—one that focuses more intensely on the content as it applies rather than generalizes the pedagogy. To accomplish our purpose of clarity in the presentation of the concepts, the embedded concepts and their matching skills and performance indicators are presented in numbered table form in Chapter 2. Chapter 3 then provides correspondingly numbered suggestions for the matching instructional dialogue, manipulatives, and sample problems that can be used by the teacher to help develop the concept or skill. The problems are designed to develop the embedded concepts but are also forms of "proximal" assessment. Proximal assessment (Solomon, 2002, 2003) is the informal form of assessment that teachers, who are close to those they assess, need to do in the classroom as they teach. With minor additions, however, the problems can be adapted for more formal forms of assessment.

There are clear purposes for this separation. Chapter 2 can be used to plan school curriculum from a multigrade or single-grade perspective. Teachers can use it as a daily assessment check and lesson planning guide, as well as an easy opportunity to look back at the grounding concepts from previous grades. If further clarification is needed, or the teacher needs suggestions for how to scaffold the concept with dialogue and problems to solve, there is a simple cross-check to the more comprehensive Chapter 3. However, no single activity or even set of activities is guaranteed to ensure the new knowledge for all students. Just doing a prescribed activity is not enough: the embedded concept has to be constructed by the student and assessed by the teacher.

Although suggestions are offered for the vocabulary and substance of the teacher-directed dialogues and peer interactive discourses that can help students construct new knowledge, this is far from a script. It is different from many curriculum guides produced by teachers in that it shows the sequential and specific development of concepts over the grades, rather than at a specific grade. The reason for this is so that teachers may check for prior knowledge and know where a particular concept can lead. It is hoped that this will make their curriculum more responsive to the individual differences among their students.

The concepts or content standards included are a composite from many sources. Many were identified over time by careful personal and shared collegial observation of students' thinking: within a range of elementary through graduate classes in math teaching methods. They reflect mathematics educators' most current research on how children learn mathematics as reported in the literature but also pull from resources as disparate and remote as Piaget, Greenleaf, and a comprehensive curriculum guide published by the Baltimore schools in 1952 (Baltimore Public Schools, 1952). They are functionally based on the ideas and organization of the 2000 version of the standards for mathematics developed by the NCTM (2000) and adaptations of these by state and local agencies. The original NCTM standards document may be more comprehensive in terms of the pedagogy rationale, and a recent document from NCTM (2006) also suggests grade-level focal points for the topics. The standards-based curriculum developed by the individual states is used as a framework for their mandated assessments. Therefore, the relevant state or local and NCTM documents should be consulted in tandem with this book. Most of these documents are, however, less specific and organized about the content knowledge, particularly the embedded concepts and definitions. This leaves much for the teacher to provide. For example, the standards statements are often framed in terms of understanding, such as, "Students will understand how to multiply a fraction by a fraction." Chapter 2 and certainly Chapter 3 are more explicit about what the students need to understand. Concept statements and scaffolds for building understanding would include ideas such as the following:

> The product of a fraction multiplied by a fraction less than one whole will always be less than the multiplicand. It is the same as finding the fractional part *of the fraction.*

This book will fill in some of the gaps, but certainly not every possible construction of knowledge. Others may be identified or newly constructed by teachers as they begin to teach in a different way: with a clearly identified concept or construct in mind. If they provide opportunities for their students to reason and solve problems creatively, new concepts for both teacher and student may be intersubjectively constructed.

The book is presented in three chapters, which should be considered in sequence. Chapter 1 provides a rationale for the suggested learning approach and explains the organization and sequence of the following chapters. Chapter 2 provides the actual content standards in numbered table form, showing median grade-level expectations for concepts and skills or performance indicators, as well as suggestions for mathematics vocabulary and usage of mathematics language. The content standards are organized to agree with the organization of the NCTM standards, with some exceptions that are explained in Chapter 1. Chapter 3 provides articulated illustrative activities and problems that can be used with students, either for concept development or assessment purposes. It also contains suggestions for using other than text materials: manipulatives, calculators, educational software and graphics programs (commercial and shareware), and Web sites.

Acknowledgments

For their inspiration and contributions to the additions and revisions of this second edition of *The Math We Need to Know and Do,* I would like to offer my gratitude to the teachers and administrators of the East Ramapo Central School District in Spring Valley, New York. I have worked with the dedicated faculty of this district as a consultant for the past ten years. Although the intent of our relationship was for them to learn from me, they need to know that I learned so much from them. It was this new knowledge that motivated me to update and revise what I had previously written. I would particularly like to mention David Fried, Assistant Superintendent, and Rhoda Fischer, Director of Curriculum, for their faith in me and their concern for the children of the district they serve. However, there is also a whole team of classroom teachers with whom I shared the task of writing curriculum and assessments for the K–12 program in mathematics. I do not think I would have continued my interest and endeavors in math education without their inspiration and knowledge.

The team at Corwin Press has been both inspirational and comforting in their diligence and guidance through the process of producing a worthwhile contribution to education. Editor Faye Zucker and her assistant, Gem Rabanera, played a vital role in getting this project started and brought to fruition. The structure of this manuscript was very complex, but copyeditor Gillian Dickens and senior production editor Astrid Virding were always patiently and expertly at my side as we strove for the best possible outcome.

As I have in the past, I would also like to thank my colleagues at St. Thomas Aquinas College and my husband, Mel, and grandchildren Joseph and Edward for their patience and support. Edward was particularly helpful as I bounced possible activities and scaffolds off his middle school student eyes, ears, and prior knowledge.

Corwin Press thanks the following reviewers for their contributions to this book:

Anne Roede Giddings
Assistant Superintendent
Ansonia Public Schools
Ansonia, CT

Mansoor Kapasi
Math Coach
Urban Education Partnership
Sepulveda Middle School
Los Angeles, CA

Mary Kollmeyer
Math Teacher

Lejeune High School
Camp Lejeune, NC

Edward C. Nolan
Mathematics Department Chair
Albert Einstein High School
Kensington, MD

Kimberly Puckett
Math Teacher
Tri-Village Jr/Sr High School
New Madison, OH

Mark Yates
Math Teacher
Northfield Mount Hermon School
Northfield, MA

Wesley Yuu
Educational Specialist
Instructional Services Branch—Mathematics
Hawaii Department of Education, Honolulu, HI

About the Author

Pearl Gold Solomon is Professor Emeritus of Teacher Education at St. Thomas Aquinas College in Sparkill, New York. She received a doctorate in educational administration from Teachers College, Columbia University. She has served as a public school teacher and administrator, director, and officer for professional organizations and as a consultant to many school districts, the New York State Education Department, and the U.S. Department of Education. She is the recipient of a number of special awards from the state and community for her work in science, math, health, and career education.

As director of the St. Thomas Aquinas Marie Curie Math and Science Center, her activities included authorship and management of Eisenhower, National Science Foundation, and Goals 2000 grants. As a private consultant, she has acted as a mathematics and science curriculum and assessment specialist and presenter for a number of school districts, including the cities of New York and Chicago. Present endeavors include contracts as consultant and evaluator of math- and science-funded programs for St. Thomas Aquinas College and Columbia University as well as an SBIR for the National Institutes of Health (NIH). She has also continued graduate-level teaching assignments on a part-time basis for both preservice and inservice teachers.

Dr. Solomon is a frequent speaker at professional conferences and the author of several books published by Corwin Press, including *No Small Feat: Taking Time for Change* (1995); *The Curriculum Bridge: From Standards to Actual Classroom Practice* (1998; 2nd ed., 2003), which was selected as an outstanding academic book for 1999 by the American Library Association's Choice Magazine; *The Math We Need to "Know" and "Do": Content Standards for Elementary and Middle Grades* (2001), which was selected as a finalist for the Outstanding Writing Award from the American Association of Colleges of Teacher Education; and *The Assessment Bridge: Positive Ways to Link Tests to Learning, Standards, and Curriculum Improvement* (2002).

1

Designing a Standards-Based Math Curriculum

KNOWLEDGE ∎

Education is preparation for life. Derived from the Latin, it also means *to lead forth*—perhaps to knowledge. But what is the knowledge that we educators must lead our students to? Knowledge is defined as an acquaintance with a fact, a perception, an idea. A suggested classification of knowledge divides it into procedural and conceptual components. The two categories are distinguishable and yet intersecting. They are not hierarchical; one does not necessarily come before the other. They differ in that procedural knowledge is more rigid and limited in its adaptability but highly efficient, especially when it is applied with meaning. Conceptual knowledge is more flexible—it reorganizes and stretches itself as it tries to connect new perceptions and previous generalizations. Conceptual knowledge may then reform itself as a new generalization. Reasoning requires conceptual knowledge (for an in-depth discussion of conceptual and procedural knowledge, see Hiebert & Lefevre, 1986; Hiebert & Wearne, 1986).

A chef following an often-used recipe is efficiently carrying out his procedural knowledge. He knows that it must be done in a certain order and with specific ingredients and quantities. Suppose one of his ingredients is unavailable. He has a problem. When he tries to innovate with a substitute ingredient, he calls upon his conceptual knowledge, reorganizes it, connects it to other concepts and perhaps to a new generalization, and then, with practice, connects it to a new procedure. The best procedures are those built with conceptual knowledge, those learned with meaning. Conceptual knowledge may, however, also come from procedural knowledge. An infant puts blocks one on top of the other; perhaps in a self-initiated procedure or perhaps copying an adult. Eventually, a concept is formed: the larger blocks need to be at the bottom. *The conceptual and procedural knowledge components that we expect our students to have—and that therefore we must lead them to— form our content standards.* Our expectations are based on our own knowledge, our experience, and our predictions about what our students will need. Content standards describe what we value and we want our students to know or be able to do.

The reason for the discussion above is that in the past, mathematics has often been taught as a set of specific procedures, sometimes disconnected from the real problems that will confront us in life. Doing mathematics requires a set of concepts and procedures that develop over time. Experiences with objects and verbalization—both monologic and interactive—help that development. The concepts enlarge our capability to solve problems; the procedures make us more efficient. An understanding of this dual nature of knowledge also provides a rationale for the organization of standards-based curriculum.

ORGANIZATION AND DESIGN OF CURRICULA

Although concepts and procedures develop individually for each student over time, it is useful for the teacher to know what the necessary ones are—the ones that can help the student do mathematics and solve mathematical problems. The common procedures we use and some of the concepts we share are in what has been called "the consensual domain" (Cobb, 1990). This shared knowledge is the content of our curriculum. The framework for curriculum content includes normed expectations for achievement or *standards.* The multiplication facts are shared knowledge in the consensual domain of mathematics. That we expect third and fourth graders to know their multiplication facts is a normed expectation or standard based on history, teachers' experience, and the average achievements of children in these grades.

Content standards organize and describe the curriculum. They serve as guides for instruction that are planned to help students achieve the knowledge of the consensual domain. They tell us what students should know or be able to do. Many state-developed documents label their content standards as *performance indicators* that emphasize what students should be able to do. Performance indicators that focus primarily on procedural knowledge are then used as a basis for matching measurement guidelines or *test expectations.* Embedded concept knowledge, which describes what students should know, is assumed necessary for the measured performance of procedural knowledge, but the concepts are rarely explicitly stated. Clearly stated mathematical concepts within curriculum documents may prove to be helpful in achieving consensus and guiding instruction. Moreover, it is important not to neglect separate measures of the embedded concepts. Test items that ask for explanations specifically seek concept knowledge and can be used as a diagnostic that determines why a procedure is not understood. When constructed, assessments should be reflections of the concepts and procedures they measure. An analogy that might help is to compare them to the two sides of your hand. The back of your hand defines its form and its potential, but the palm is the implement and measure of what your hand does. Content standards are the framework for the assessments we need to make to help guide our instruction and students, as well as provide accountability to our publics.

Standards can be very general statements of expectations at a terminal or commencement point or more specific and assigned to a particular stage in development or grade level. The upside-down tree in Figure 1.1 illustrates a design process for standards-based curricula (Solomon, 2003). Like the trunk of a tree, general standards lead to a widely reaching set of more specific branches, twigs, and leaves. Curriculum is *designed down* from more general *commencement* levels to the more specific *benchmarks* and then to the even more specific levels of the course, grade, and unit. But it must work both ways. Just as the leaves of a tree must manufacture food and nurture the trunk, the more specific "designed-down" content standards of every lesson must feed the general ones— they make the general ones happen. Curriculum is *delivered up*—up toward the general or commencement standards. None of this works if the connections of internal flow are impeded. The junctures where twigs meet branches and branches meet trunks are particularly important. The outcome of each lesson of the leaves is fed through a twig to the branch that is the unit and then into a larger one that is the grade level. Several grade levels may feed into a larger branch at a benchmark juncture, and this, in turn, finally meets the main trunk. The tree is shown upside down because the design is the beginning, and we think of the processes as "design down" and "deliver up." At the same time, there must be horizontal articulation. As the leaves turn toward the sun, the carbon dioxide must enter them. There must be a balance between the concepts and the procedures.

The preplanned design is only the first step. The settings and activities of well-planned classroom activities must have a reasonable probability for helping *all* students to be successful in these measures. They should encompass a wider scope of the variables of the classroom experience: the teacher's knowledge and carefully reviewed previous experience, the discourse, the materials, the allocation of time and space, and the cultural and social contexts of peers and adults.

Design Direction

Delivery Direction

Figure 1.1
Curriculum Planning

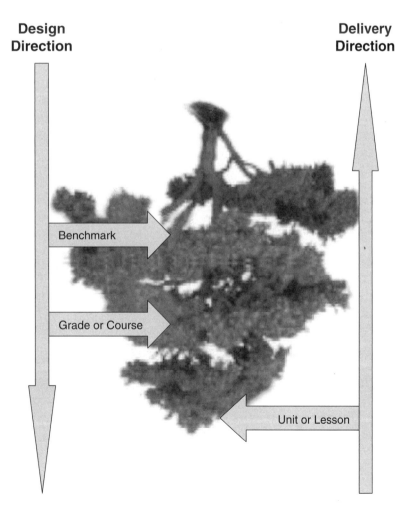

Benchmark

Grade or Course

Unit or Lesson

■ MATHEMATICS CONTENT STANDARDS: KEY IDEAS[1]

What kind of mathematical knowledge do we expect of all students when they enter the technological world of the third millennium? What are the steps for getting them there? Consider the upside-down tree for mathematics curricula. Beginning at the trunk, at the commencement level, we should expect that *all* students can do the processes of mathematics.

Nevertheless, the processes of mathematics are not performed in a vacuum. They depend on and produce a content set of conceptual and procedural knowledge about mathematics. However, before we address the specifics of the processes and content knowledge standards, some key ideas should be considered.

- In its traditional sense, mathematical *reasoning* includes both quantitative and spatial concepts, but it also has embedded *verbal constructs and a special language.* In addition, effective reasoning may also involve *metacognitive processes.* Thinking about what you are doing and purposely comparing problems and solutions may increase the power of reasoning (Kramarski & Mevarich, 2003).

- The special language of mathematical *communication* involves a system of *numbers and other symbols.* The symbols represent values and orders or something that changes the value. Not only do we need to use this language to communicate with others, but the symbols may also be necessary for our own internal concept formation. There is also a special language for sharing proof.

- A logical search for truth or *proof* requires reasoning and is a special power of mathematics (Herbst, 2002). Proof to oneself also strengthens the constructions of knowledge.

- As we observe, reason, connect, and communicate, we can develop and use an intuitive *number and spatial sense* that allows us to estimate values, judge relative size, visualize hidden parts of forms, decide on appropriate strategies for problem solving, predict the result of operations and transformations, and evaluate the reasonableness of our problem solutions.

■ MATHEMATICS CONTENT STANDARDS: PROCESSES AND DISPOSITIONS

Our expectations of students' ability to do the processes of mathematics reflect the way research has shown us that all learning happens; like all learning, doing mathematics involves connecting prior knowledge and new perceptions. The processes comprise strands of the mathematics curriculum or knowledge domain that describe what students need to be able to do. Doing mathematics requires and builds both conceptual and procedural knowledge. Doing the processes of mathematics means that students can

- *Perceive* and make observations of the world from a mathematical perspective, sensitive to similarities, differences, patterns, and change in size, value, time, and form
- *Connect* these observations to each other and to other concurrent observations and prior knowledge (e.g., the form of a sphere and a rolling ball)
- *Analyze problems* using mathematical *reasoning,* which is based on conceptual knowledge

- *Solve problems* and do this efficiently with meaningful procedures
- *Justify* and *defend* their solutions with logical *proofs* and *representations*
- *Represent* forms and number systems in multiple ways and models to help them visualize, construct concepts, organize data, prove, and communicate ideas
- *Communicate* what they perceive to others using multiple forms of representation and the special language of mathematics

Conceptual knowledge can also be knowledge about oneself; it can be an attitude, a value, or a goal (Anderson & Douglass, 2001). Attitudes, values, and goals control the learning process. Doing mathematics also requires that students

- Have *confidence* in their ability to do mathematics
- *Appreciate* the beauty and power of mathematics

A recent article in *The New York Times* (April 14, 2006) reminds us of the beauty and power of mathematics. It spoke of a phenomenon that developed as a result of a blog on the Internet (gottabook.blogspot.com) that discussed the Fibonacci sequence and applied it to the writing of "fibs" or short poems that follow the sequence in the number of syllables. As of this writing, more than 1,000 fibs have been contributed to the blog, and the following is another.

The

math

is great

when it says

something real and true

about your life or need to know

The processes and dispositions of mathematics are integral to the content set of mathematical knowledge. They guide us and provide a structure as we absorb the concepts of each of the content branches. And then, the increased knowledge of the content increases our skill in performing the processes while it strengthens our confidence and appreciation.

MATHEMATICS CONTENT STANDARDS: THE CONTENT SET OF DOMAIN KNOWLEDGE

For the purpose of description, we can organize the content set of the domain of mathematical knowledge into six major branches or strands. It is important to realize, however, that these strands are overlapping—both in their interdependence and in their function as we enact mathematical processes. For example, our operations are dependent on our number system, and our number system determines the form of our operations. We need knowledge of our number system, measurement, and data representation as we communicate to others what we have perceived. The content standards described in Chapter 2 include designed-down concepts and procedures from the following major commencement-level branches.

- *Number Systems.* The language of our common *number system* (which is based on our genetically and experientially determined sense of space and quantity and the number of finger or toe digits) allows us to perceive and communicate quantities in words and symbols. By making the left to right position of the symbols have different values, we are able to express all quantities with only ten symbols, including the placeholder zero. There are other number systems.

- *Operations on Numbers.* We can perform *operations on numbers.* Operations are systems that help us solve problems that involve change or comparisons. They allow us to determine values not directly counted or measured. Reasoning with our conceptual knowledge and using our number sense can help us predict the result of operations. The language of real-world problems needs to be translated into the language of mathematics so that we can solve the problems efficiently by performing operations.

- *Geometric Forms and Properties.* Defined two-dimensional surface areas and three-dimensional objects that take up space have different *geometric forms and properties.* Knowledge of the dimensions and properties of these forms, as well as the relationships among them, helps us solve problems and make use of the systematic relationship between the types of forms and their practical functions (e.g., the rolling sphere, the roman arch, the sturdy triangle).

- *Measurement.* We use our number system to *measure* the dimensions and characteristics of objects and areas as they exist or change in time and space. We also measure time itself and other values and phenomena such as money, light, wind, energy, votes, and the popularity of TV shows. Collections of *measurements* are called *data.*

- *Algebra: Expressions, Equations, Inequalities, and Functions.* We can express what we know and do not know using symbols within algebraic expressions that include the unknown terms or variables and the constants we know. When we need to find out what the values of the variables are and solve problems, we can use relationships between the terms that are equations or inequalities. Within the systems of numbers, forms, and data, there are recognizable patterns. Patterns help us reason, organize, and *automatize* (see ahead) concepts into more efficient procedures. We can use the *symbols* that represent either variable or constant values to show these patterns. When patterns are systems that describe relationships between variable values, they are called *mathematical functions* (as distinguished from practical functions). Conceptual and procedural knowledge of functions is very useful in complex problem solving and prediction.

- *Data Analysis, Statistics, and Probability.* We can use data to help us understand phenomena. Data can be analyzed to show patterns and trends that can help us make predictions. The systems for collecting and interpreting data are called *statistics.* Statistics are systems used to organize data and analyze them in many different ways. Predictions are based on the probability of the occurrence of an uncertain event. Some events are clearly predictable, but others are *uncertain. Probability* systems help us deal with uncertainty by giving us a way to have reasonable expectations about the occurrence of an event. We need to count the possibilities of an event before we can determine its probability.

Figure 1.2 represents an organization of the overlapping process and content strands of mathematics as well as the dispositions or attitudes that affect all of them. They are placed between the inclusive and articulated anchors of *embedded concepts* and *performance indicators.* Our distinction between these two anchors is that the content standards focus clearly on the embedded concepts and skills that our students need to know and do, while the performance indicators focus on how we can measure or assess what our students know and can do. Perhaps, as stated in another way, it is what our students need to know versus how we, their teachers, can know what our students know.

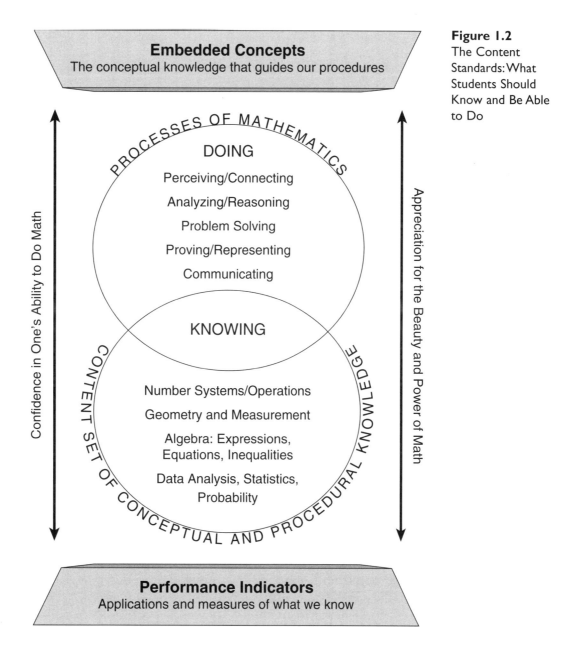

Figure 1.2
The Content Standards: What Students Should Know and Be Able to Do

The Presentation of Designed-Down Standards

As discussed previously, the mathematical processes and content branches are constantly overlapping. The presentation of the very specific content standards that are designed down from the branches in Chapters 2 and 3 is structured, however, with some sequential organization of the branches based on developmental expectations and traditional concentrations. For example, number and numeration are first and probability last. Nevertheless, the grade-level range within each branch demonstrates the gradual over-time development of complex concepts, and because of the interrelated nature of mathematical knowledge, the branches themselves need to be addressed as overlapping segments. The presentation also incorporates several critical premises about what students need, how learning happens, and how teachers use curriculum. The content and organization of these chapters responds to these premises in the specific manner as described below.

Premise 1. Inclusivity (see Note 1): Although Chapters 2 and 3 represent most of the topics typically included in math standards for Grades 6 to 9, they do not pretend to be all-inclusive—neither of the specific topics nor of the embedded concepts and procedures within them. In general, they are based on the expectations of published national and state curriculum guides and state assessments. These can also vary from state to state and year to year. Since the publication of the first edition of *The Math We Need to Know and Do,* state curriculum guides have changed to introduce many topics in the sixth- to ninth-grade math curriculum at earlier grade levels. For example, many topics that had traditionally been first introduced in high school algebra and geometry are now included at the seventh and eighth grades. Teachers and their students may discover needed additions or unnecessary inclusions and make some adjustments based on their particular needs. For example, we have included most of traditional high school elementary algebra and applied it to geometry. If a school has an accelerated eighth-grade class, the ninth-grade expectations can be shifted down. We have not, however, included all the topics in intermediate algebra for the ninth-grade classes. The concepts and expectations presented are comprehensive enough, however, to be a substantive starting place for designing and implementing local curriculum and assessments. The important outcome is to recognize the ideas for oneself, communicate them to others, and then reach a useful consensus about what is critical for us all to learn.

Premise 2. Developmental Timing: For some concepts and for some students, learning happens all at once. For many others, it is an iterative process that takes place over time as students develop meaning in a very individualized way. Sometimes this meaning is "buggy" or incorrect and is corrected by new perceptions. The grade-level expectations in Chapter 2 are therefore presented in three phases: exploration, concept mastery, and procedural or algorithmic mastery. In some cases, this sequence may all happen in one grade—even in one lesson; in others the span may be longer than three grades. The expectations listed are suggested medians based on observations of students and references to varied texts, assessments, and the state curriculum maps. Teachers should adjust these on a local basis. The idea behind the three phases is that as students engage in the mathematical processes, they begin with explorations: perceiving, observing, and trying to find solutions. At first, they may find solutions without crystallizing a concept that is permanently implanted as a schema in memory. They may need help from teachers and/or peers in the form of interactive dialogue to do this.

Premise 3. Algorithms: Once the concept is formed, further experience may *automatize* its retrieval from memory, and learners can incorporate it into strategies or procedures that can be efficiently employed. The common algorithms are an example of procedural strategies. The algorithms were invented over time as efficient procedures for solving common mathematics problems. Students should be able to use the algorithms in the consensual domain but be encouraged to invent and prove their own strategies as well. A good rule of thumb for the use of traditional algorithms by students is to evaluate the potential usefulness of the algorithm—as a tool for solving real problems in the current technological world, as a written record that might help organize concepts, and as a procedure, learned in its application to simple easily understood problems, that can then be extrapolated to more complex applications. In the past, much time has been spent by students in the process of developing skill, speed, and accuracy in using these algorithms—perhaps detracting from a focus on the more powerful ideas of mathematics and distracting students from interpretations of problems that would allow for quick mental solutions. These algorithms were most often learned without attention to understanding how and why they worked. Analysis of problems hinged on *key words* that told you which algorithm to use; the selected procedure was applied without conceptual understanding or recognition that sometimes the problem could be easily solved mentally.

Students should be encouraged to use their concept-based number or spatial sense to interpret a problem and estimate its answer before applying a procedure. They may, however, need the teacher's help and some practice to reach the third procedural mastery phase. In some cases, when the child's struggle with the construction of a concept is discouraging, it may even be necessary to move over the concept to a rotely learned procedure. But attempts to recursively revive the concept should continue. In general, moving to a procedure first should be avoided because there is some evidence that learning a procedure rotely—without the underlying concepts—may encumber concept development and handicap further development of mathematical processes.

Premise 4. Automaticity: In order to be able to estimate and use reasoning to solve problems, students need a repertoire of easily retrieved bits of conceptual and procedural knowledge. That repertoire includes related addition and subtraction facts for combinations up to 20 and multiplication and division tables to 12 as well as the standard unit equivalents for measurement. The need for automaticity may have been somewhat subsumed by the prevalent use of calculators, but a missing bank of automatized facts may be detrimental to the development of mathematical knowledge. My own experiences with children and other cognitive research have also demonstrated that the earlier the requirement or motivation for automatization, the easier it is to embed facts in long-term memory—and retain them there. As it does for the learning of a second language, the brain may have optimum development times for automatization of number facts.

We use the term *automatize* as an outcome descriptor to differentiate from the traditional term, *memorize,* to emphasize that the process of imprinting the facts should be a meaningful one, utilizing reasoning and pattern recognition. Automaticity implies fast retrieval from memory, but strengthened by reasoning and the conceptual knowledge of patterns, it also allows for fast reconstruction should a fact be temporarily lost.

Premise 5. Verbalization and Language: Although I have tried to use clear and simplified language, the words of the content standards are adult terms that express the consensual domain. It is not necessary for the children to use the exact words, as long as the teacher is convinced that the meaning has been correctly constructed. In some cases, students will only be able to demonstrate the concept by doing things with objects or giving examples, but verbalization of the concept in different ways should be encouraged and listened to. Verbalization of a concept helps place the concept in long-term memory. In order to verbalize, children need a shared language. The special language of mathematics, both in symbolic and word form, should be specifically attended to.

Premise 6. Embedded Assessment: The performance indicators and assessment expectations can be used for formal assessments, but they are also designed to be embedded in the informal assessments of everyday activities, the dialogues, and the questions and cues that teachers toss to students to help them construct new knowledge or correct preexisting concepts.

Premise 7. Representative Materials: Pictures and concrete materials, including real and representative manipulatives, increase the possibilities of mathematical perceptions. They provide useful, often indispensable, problem-solving strategies as they lead to concept formation. Manipulatives respond to individual differences in learning styles and forms of intelligence, increasing the feelings of self-efficacy for those who are more kinesthetic or tactile in their learning approach. They are sometimes neglected for middle and high school students, but they may even be necessary for adults whose concepts need to be redeveloped. I have found, for example, that the use of fraction tiles to help the understanding of division of a fraction by a fraction suddenly brings the light of understanding to my adult students who routinely performed the procedures without knowing what they were doing. We need, however, to remember that representative materials are in essence analogies for the real thing, and conscious connections have to be made. Further transitions have to be carefully constructed as students move from the concrete materials to the symbolic forms. Careful connections between the words of everyday language and the special language and symbols of mathematics are equally critical. There needs to be interactive dialogue connecting the spoken words that explain the concept, the manipulatives or graphic figures, and the written language of mathematics.

Learners vary in their need for manipulatives and sometimes reject them once the concept or efficient procedure has been developed. Manipulatives can become cumbersome when dealing with large numbers, and teachers need to use their best judgment about whether they are of value once the embedded concept is developed. A good rule of thumb is to use the materials to introduce concepts and abandon them for most students when they have made a conceptual shift to the symbolic form or operation. For some students, teachers will have to return to the concrete materials in remedial or small group sessions.

Premise 8. Problem-Solving Strategies: In addition to the use of representative materials, there are other problem-solving strategies that teachers may help students develop. In general, connections to real-life situations work as they retrieve prior knowledge and provide motivation. Other strategies include the following:

- Acting out the problem with physical movements (e.g., filling a sample space with alternative-bearing students to demonstrate combinations and permutations)
- Making a picture, concept map, or Venn diagram
- Individual and shared analysis of problems to identify given information and a desired objective
- Organizing given data on a table
- Generation, comparison, and evaluation of validity of different solution methods

Purposeful analysis of problems based on their underlying specific concepts may also be considered a general strategy, but one that is dependent on the concepts themselves. We will make specific suggestions for these concept-based strategies in Chapter 3, but they are also embedded in the content standards.

Premise 9. Technology: Calculators and computers are not substitutes for the conceptual and procedural knowledge needed for automaticity in the retrieval of basic facts, number and spatial sense, and process skills. Nor should they take away from the teacher-managed and peer-interactive discourse of doing mathematics. But they can help the students build knowledge. They are, in a way, our modern algorithms—short-cut procedures for complex computations—just as the wristwatch is a technological substitute for telling the time by looking at the positions of the sun. They should be considered as necessary and effective tools in learning and living, used like books, worksheets, manipulatives, balances, compasses, and protractors are now and like slide rules were in the past.

For some students, the motivation and immediate feedback of computer-managed drill and practice activities will be helpful if used in conjunction with other activities. Graphing calculators that allow for quick connections between equations and graphs, as well as graphic drawing programs that provide easy depiction, manipulations, and transformations of figures, are particularly useful. Real databanks retrieved from the Internet offer a fine supplement to the data collected by students themselves. Because of the almost universal existence of technology, it is no longer necessary for students to spend time building speed in completing multidigit addition, subtraction, multiplication, and division algorithms. As soon as the student provides evidence of automaticity in fact retrieval, an understanding of the algorithm strategy, and reasonable accuracy, multidigit problems should be estimated first and then done with a calculator. Some recursive practice with the algorithms can be done from time to time. But we cannot overlook the fact that being able to use technological tools is an important content standard in itself—necessary for survival in the third millennium.

HOW TEACHERS CAN USE THE FOLLOWING CHAPTERS

A Guide for Writing Grade-Level Curriculum

As previously explained, the process standards are not separately presented in Chapters 2 and 3 but continuously embodied in the performance indicators, as well as in the challenges of the exemplars in Chapter 3. The two listed disposition or attitude standards are similarly implied in the real-life applications of Chapter 3 and fostered by the careful attention to conceptual development in Chapter 2. The six major branches or strands of the content set are presented in an order that generally corresponds to the traditional level of concentration on that branch as students progress through the grades. As a consequence, the sequence of the branches also reflects an increasing degree of mathematical complexity. For example, counting number systems are presented first and the multiple representations of data at the end. However, each major branch has preparatory concepts at every grade level, and so teachers will find concepts that are appropriate for early grades in the final two branches. Within the major overlapping branches, each specific minor domain of the branch is presented in the order of a presumed developmental sequence.

When preparing grade-level curriculum, teachers should go through Chapter 2 and check off all standards appropriate for their own grade level, using the median expectations listed. Additional standards required by state documents or assessments may need to be considered, and some adjustments may be required by the particular group of students. The order in which the major branches are presented is optional. One branch can be presented at a time, or the teacher may choose to alternate between them. For example, the standards on statistics and probability might be a good supplement or review for fractions. Another alternative is to follow the order of a textbook, using all sections of this book as a side-by-side accompaniment and day-to-day reference as described below.

A Day-to-Day Reference Guide for Instruction and Informal Assessment

Once the curriculum sequence has been decided upon, teachers may use Chapter 2 as a daily lesson plan guide that begins with a reminder of what students need to know and attaches suggested indicators or assessments that measure acquisition of the knowledge. Having the desired concept and indicators clearly in mind will help teachers construct planned and unplanned dialogues and activities that incorporate *proximal assessment* opportunities (for an in-depth discussion on assessment, see Solomon, 2002). These are the probing questions and prompts that can uncover the chunks of knowledge already embedded in long-term memory, help transfer the knowledge from short- to long-term memory (Sousa, 2000), and uncover the needs of individual students. To help in the process, there are suggestions for these scaffolds or instructional-mapping dialogue and exemplar problems in Chapter 3. Each separate subdomain line-by-line listing of embedded concepts and indicators in Chapter 2 is numbered, and the line number matches the easily recognized number of the matching expanded instructional suggestions in Chapter 3.

These instructional supporting systems can facilitate the learning process, but individual students' prior knowledge, motivating goals, and the teacher's own experience with successful activities should also be considered. The exemplar problems can be used as they are presented and can also serve as models for the selection or creation of other, similar experiences that will help the student develop a concept or automatize a procedure. The topical index for Chapters 2 and 3 will provide easy access to these for a particular lesson or unit.

The performance indicators and assessment expectations will clearly delineate the forms and measures of the informal assessments that need to be an integral part of every day's activity because they provide the feedback necessary for reflective practice. Based on the responses of these informal assessments, teachers can make day-to-day and moment-to-moment adjustments in their instructional decisions. They can also form the basis for more formal assessments.

Formal Assessments

Formal assessments, for the purpose of program evaluation at critical grade benchmarks or at the end of a particular unit of study, can be constructed directly from the performance indicators and assessment expectations in Chapter 2 and from the exemplars in Chapter 3. Formal assessments can be prepared for analysis and individualized for students, as outlined below. (Examples of the analytical tools and reports may be found in the Resource section following Chapter 3.)

• Each item on the assessment (written test or other alternative form) should be articulated with a particular standard by number.

• If possible, items should be prepared in multiple forms that reflect the mastery levels. For example, students might be able to solve a problem conceptually with concrete materials or diagrams but be unable to translate the problem to algorithm form and solve it without materials. Clearly stated rubrics are needed for open-ended questions (see examples in the Resource section following Chapter 3).

• The expected level for each standard needs to be established. Is the expectation at the exploration level, or should the concept mastery or procedural mastery level be reached? Where is each student in reference to this expectation?

• An optional, above-standard mastery level, which is not listed in Chapter 2, could be added. This might assume, for example, that the student has reached a level of the particular concept where, in addition to solving problems presented by others, the student could create new problems that require that concept or apply the concept to other contexts or interdisciplinary connections.

- Comprehensive written assessment instruments should be constructed with a balance of short and extended responses, mental math (quick recall or calculation without need for written computation), and multiple-choice items. The instrument should also consider the sequence and number of items in terms of their cognitive demand or difficulty.

- When reporting to the students themselves and their parents, the standards should be shared. A report would list the number of the standard and a rubric that corresponds to the three or four developmental levels. The achievement level reached by the student for each standard would be noted, and there would be an indication of whether that level equaled or exceeded expectation.

- Individual student analyses and standard-by-standard analyses of class means can then provide knowledgeable direction for instruction. Several computer-based management programs can facilitate each of these analyses and reports. Examples of assessment items matched to standards are in Chapter 3. An example of a report to students or parents and a computer-based class analysis are in the Resource.

- An ultimate technology-based strategy that responds to assessment data would then provide teachers with interventions or instructional strategies designed to meet specifically diagnosed needs. For example, the technology would match a specifically diagnosed unfulfilled expectation or missing concept from Chapter 2 to a scaffolding dialogue or problem experience from Chapter 3. A data-based matching intervention (DBMI) system would place into the age of technology the best teaching strategies of individualized instruction—and perhaps finally make such instruction truly feasible in a classroom environment.

■ NOTE

1. The standards of the National Council of Teachers of Mathematics (2000) are the basis for the standards presented in this text, but the presentation differs in that it relates the standards to the forms of knowledge and its acquisition, presents the processes first and integrates them, adds perception and attitude standards, and includes succinct definitions of embedded terms. For greater elaboration and examples, see the standards themselves.

2

The Designed-
Down Content
Branches

*Embedded Concepts,
Performance Indicators,
and Expectations*

A GUIDE TO CHAPTER 2 ■

Chapter 2 takes the major strands of the mathematical *content standards* that are listed in Chapter 1 and designs them down to minor branches and some very specific things that students should know and be able to do. In response, however, to the integrated nature of process and content knowledge, there are no separate sections for the mathematical processes. Instead, they are embedded in the indicators and expectations of each content branch within the actions prescribed by such words as *solve, prove, analyze, describe, compare, connect, analyze, interpret, predict, construct, justify,* and *explain.* Illustrative teacher actions that are designed to engage students in the processes and help students develop the concepts are described in Chapter 3, in the form of scaffolding dialogues with probing questions and prompts, exploratory problems, and constructivist activities with manipulatives (also see Premises 5, 7, and 8 in Chapter 1 for initial generalizations).

In order to respond to traditional grade-level and developmental sequences of the content or domain branches, Chapter 2 and Chapter 3 organize the six major branches listed in Chapter 1 into nine sections as listed below:

- Number systems
- Number operations
- Operation patterns and properties
- Fractions
- Algebra: expressions, equations, and inequalities
- Algebra: functions, quadratics, and graphing

- Measurement
- Geometry
- Data analysis, statistics, and probability

These major domain sections are then designed down into topically organized groups of subdomain concepts, skills, and performance indicators that are numbered in decimal form. Each of the subdomain numbers in Chapter 2 corresponds to the numbers in Chapter 3. Page numbers for entries in both chapters are listed in the topical index.

The subdomain concepts and skills are designed to answer specific questions such as the following:

How do we multiply two binomials? *We use the FOIL method (first, outside, inside, and last).*

How and why does it work? *The FOIL method is an application of the distributive property. If you multiply by each term of the binomial multiplier separately and then combine the two products, the sum is the same as the result of the FOIL procedure. $(6 + 3) \times (6 + 3) = 6 (6 + 3) + 3 (6 + 3) = 6 \times 9 + 3 \times 9 = 27 + 54 = 81$, and that is the same as $(6 \times 6) + (3 \times 6) + (6 \times 3) + (3 \times 3)$ or $36 + 18 + 18 + 9 = 81$.*

What is the result of multiplying two binomials? *Multiplying two binomials may result either in a polynomial with three terms or a binomial.*

The suggested grade-level range for attainment of the subdomain concepts and indicators within each branch demonstrates the gradual over-time development of conceptual and procedural knowledge. The three levels represent the following stages of development: A, Exploration; B, Concept Mastery; and C, Algorithmic or Procedural Mastery. In addition, because of the interrelated nature of mathematical knowledge, the branches themselves need to be addressed as overlapping segments.

The specifics of the subdomains are stated in two sections. The *embedded concepts* are specific statements of the underlying mathematical constructs of conceptual knowledge that students need in order to understand mathematics and its procedures. Students should be encouraged to explain the concepts, orally and in writing, as they apply to the procedures and their observations. The designed-down *performance indicators* and *assessment expectations* tell the teacher what mathematical procedures the students must be able to do and how they must prove that they have constructed the concepts and achieved the content standards. If the indicator states that students should be able to *communicate* in their *analysis* with words and/or appropriate representations that they are able to distinguish whether a particular problem requires them to divide a whole group into a given number of parts and find out how large each part is, or whether it asks them how many parts of a given size will be in the whole, a matched assessment item should measure the ability to make this distinction (see the Resource following Chapter 3 for further suggestions for assessment).

Each section of concepts and expectations is also preceded by some basic vocabulary and language suggestions, but as teachers prepare to address the concepts and expectations listed, they should also refer to the explications of necessary transitions, suggested scaffolding dialogue, and activities that are presented in Chapter 3.

NUMBER SYSTEMS: 1. Place value/rounding/decimals; 2. exponential forms/scientific notation/zero/negative exponents; 3. square roots, perfect and nonperfect squares; 4. system definitions, sets and subsets
Vocabulary and Language: Exponent, exponential, base number; signed numbers; integers; natural, counting, whole and real numbers; rational and irrational numbers, imaginary numbers, terminating and repeating decimals, scientific notation

Content Branch	Suggested Grade-Level Timing*			Embedded Concepts	Performance Indicators/Assessment Expectations
	A	B	C		
Major/minor				See corresponding domain numbers in Chapter 3 for further development and exemplar problems.	
1.1 Place value: Whole numbers to one billion, one trillion	5 6	6 7	7 8	A right to left increasing-value place position of ten symbols (0–9) structures our number system. For the next value (10), a symbol (1) is placed in the next place to the left, the tens place. It requires zero as a placeholder. Numbers greater than (9) are assembled combinations of zeros and other values for each place they represent. Ten (tens) are represented by a (1) in the hundreds place and so on. Place value units over 1,000 are in groups of three: three units of thousands; one, ten, and hundred thousands followed by one million; and three groups of millions one, ten, and hundred millions followed by one billion. We use a comma to separate the groups.	Correct explanation of the system generalization. Correct reading and writing of numbers and regrouping of a value as separate components of system units (dissembling) (e.g., 1,007 ones are equal to [1] one thousand, [0] hundreds, [0] tens, and [7] ones). Addition and subtraction that requires place value regrouping
1.2 Systematic equalities to 1,000,000	6	7	8	Ten of any units in a place are equal to one unit in the next higher place to the left of it. 10,000 = (10) thousands, but it also equals (100) hundreds because each thousand is equal to (10) hundreds.	Renames and/or represents numbers as equal-value symbolic alternatives including other multiples of 10 (e.g., 6,000 = 60 hundreds or 600 tens)
1.3 Multiplying and dividing numbers by multiples of 10	5	6	7	Any number can be multiplied by a unit of 10 or more by simply shifting its place value to the higher left and adding needed zeros as placeholders. A multiple of 10 requires a shift of one place, a multiple of 100 a position shift of two places, a multiple of 1,000 three places, and so on. Any number can be divided by a unit of 10 or more by simply shifting its place value to the lower values to the right. A divisor of 100 requires a shift of two places to the right. Ones divided by 10 will require a shift to tenths, and a decimal point is needed to separate the whole numbers from the decimal fractions. (See Chapter 3 for alternate of shifting of decimal point.)	Multiplies and divides numbers up to one million by multiples of 10 using left or right place value shifts; explains how the process is related to the system

Content Branch	Suggested Grade-Level Timing*			Embedded Concepts	Performance Indicators/Assessment Expectations
Major/minor	A	B	C	See corresponding domain numbers in Chapter 3 for further development and exemplar problems.	
1.4 Decimals as extensions of number system place value to hundred thousandths	5 / 6	6 / 7	6 / 8	Decimals extend the whole-number system for values less than 1. We separate the symbols for wholes and decimals with a period or decimal point and the word *and* when reading. The number 25.23 is read "twenty-five and twenty three one hundredths" (avoid reading *point*). Each succeeding place value to the right is ten times smaller than the one to its left. Zeros replace empty digit values above the lowest decimal place that has a digit value.	Reads and writes decimals to the hundred thousandth place; *explains* the decreasing value of each digit as it shifts to the right; *compares* size of value for digits in different positions
1.5 Decimals as an alternate form of common fractions	6	7	8	Decimals are a subset of fractions written in an alternative representative form. They are fractions with denominators that are multiples of 10. For example, $\frac{1}{100}$ and $\frac{1}{1000}$ equation can be written as decimals or parts less than one whole by placing a decimal point after the ones place (3.1 is three wholes and $\frac{1}{10}$ of one whole, 3.01 is three wholes and $\frac{1}{100}$ of a whole, and 3.0001 is three wholes and $\frac{1}{10,000}$ or 3 $\frac{1}{10,000}$). Zero is used as a placeholder to correctly identify the place value of a digit (distinguish .01 from .1).	Renames and represents fractions with denominators that are multiples of 10 as decimals and vice versa; *explains* these forms as equal value symbolic alternatives Symbolically renames fractions with multiple of 10 denominators from 10 to 1,000,000 in decimal form; renames decimals as fractions: $\frac{2}{10,000} = .002$; $\frac{5}{10,000} = .0005$
1.6 Comparing, ordering, dissembling, and renaming decimals up to one hundred thousandth, one millionth	6	7	8	Hundredths are smaller than tenths and thousandths are smaller than hundredths and so on. Decimals can be dissembled and expressed as the sum of their components. One tenth is the same as (10) one hundredths or (100) thousandths. Fifteen thousandths is the same as one hundredth and 5 thousandths. Thousandths are one tenth as large as the same number of hundredths. We usually use the smallest place to express the number. The number .115 is expressed as 115 thousandths, but it is also equal to the sum of 11 hundredths and 5 thousandths.	Orders decimals from tenths to hundred thousandths; *compares* decimals and fraction forms in inequalities, for example, .002 > .0002 $\frac{2}{10,000} < .002$ Dissembles decimals and expresses them as the sum of their components

* NOTE: A = Exploration, B = Concept Mastery, C = Algorithmic or Procedural Mastery

Content Branch Major/minor	Suggested Grade-Level Timing* A	B	C	Embedded Concepts	Performance Indicators/Assessment Expectations
				See corresponding domain numbers in Chapter 3 for further development and exemplar problems.	
1.7 Converting fractions to decimals. Terminating, nonterminating, and repeating decimals	7	8	9	Fractions can be converted to their decimal form by dividing the numerator by the denominator. Sometimes that division results in a quotient that is a decimal without a remainder that needs to be regrouped. This would be a terminating decimal. If it does not end or keeps having a remainder that needs to be divided, it is nonterminating. Some nonterminating decimal forms just repeat the same digits and are called repeating decimals. We can use symbolic notation to show these decimal forms. We can also use a nonterminating decimal. We can also use $2.\overline{33}$ to show that the decimal (.33) keeps repeating.	Converts any fraction into a decimal by dividing the numerator by the denominator; identifies and gives examples of terminating, nonterminating, and repeating decimals; recognizes and uses the symbolic notations
1.8 Rounding whole numbers	5	6	7	Numbers can be rounded to the nearest hundred or thousand and so on. To the nearest hundred, for any value less than 50 or half the hundred, we round down and use zero placeholders; for 50 or more than half the hundred, we round up to the next hundred. To the nearest thousand, we round down for any value less than 500 or half the thousand and up for 500 or more than 500.	Correct conventional rounding of numbers up to the nearest 1,000,000; uses rounding in estimation, explains generalization, and justifies use or alternative in estimation
Rounding decimals and mixed numbers	6	7	8	Decimals can be rounded to higher digits in the rounding place value and digits to the right of the round-to digit dropped if the digit to the right of the round-to value is 5 or greater. Five tenths or more is rounded to the next whole number, five hundredths or more to the next tenth, and five thousandths or more to the next hundredth. A mixed number (3.4) with less than (.5) can be rounded to an existing whole number of ones (3). A mixed number with more than (.5)—for example, (1.53)—can be rounded to the next number of ones (2). A value of (.06) can be rounded to .1.	Correctly rounds decimals and mixed numbers to the nearest whole, tenth, hundredth, thousandth, and ten thousandth
1.9 Number system: signed numbers	5	6	7	Sometimes we need to think of a number line with values less than zero—for example, when the temperature is below zero or when you owe money to someone. Values less than zero are	Identifies positive and negative numbers, using the number line; describes examples and applications of positive and negative numbers

* NOTE: A = Exploration, B = Concept Mastery, C = Algorithmic or Procedural Mastery

(Continued)

Content Branch	Suggested Grade-Level Timing*			Embedded Concepts	Performance Indicators/Assessment Expectations
	A	B	C		
Major/minor				*See corresponding domain numbers in Chapter 3 for further development and exemplar problems.*	
				negative; values more than zero are positive. We use a high plus and minus sign before the number to indicate its value. (The high plus or minus sign distinguishes it from the operation sign.)	
2.1 Expressing exponential forms: base and exponent defined	6	7	8	You can use an exponent to show the repeated multiplication by the same multiplier. The exponential form of a number includes a base number followed by a raised smaller number, the exponent. The base number is a factor of the multiple it represents. The exponent tells how many times the base number is used as a factor to form the multiple. ($5^1 = 5$) because the base number must be used one time to show a value of 5. ($5^2 = 5 \times 5 = 25$) because the base number must be used as a factor two times for the value of 25.	Identifies base and exponent and explains what each represents
2.2 Expressing exponential forms: alternate expressions	6	7	8	Sometimes the exponent is expressed as "the power of" and the base is described as a number raised to the "power of." The *square of a number* is any real number multiplied by itself or raised to the power of 2. The *cube* of a number is the number raised to the power of 3 and represented in exponential form as 5^3. Five raised to the power of 3 is 5^3 or $5 \times 5 \times 5$ and equal to 125.	Uses and explains the expressions "square" and "cube" and "power of"; determines the value of exponential forms of positive numbers greater than one; translates multiples of the same number into exponential form; relates the expression to the figures of a square or cube
2.3 Powers of 10 related to place value	6	7	8	Our place value system groupings may be expressed as exponents of the base number 10. 10^1 is the number 10 itself, 10^2 is 100 or the next larger place to the left, 10^3 is 1,000 and so on, with the 1 shifting to the left and a zero added each time the exponent is increased, or the number is multiplied by 10 again. It is based on 10 because any multiple of 1 is still 1. The symbol (1) in the ones place can represent (1^1) or 1^3 or 1^0. A symbol (1) in the next place to the left, the tens place, requires zero as a placeholder and has a value of 10 or 10^1. Each position to the left corresponds to a base-10 exponential increase in value. For	Explains place value positions in terms of the number of base (10) multiples and relates these to increasing exponents; interprets exponential form of whole units of the system and writes as a number

* NOTE: A = Exploration, B = Concept Mastery, C = Algorithmic or Procedural Mastery

Content Branch	Major/minor	Suggested Grade-Level Timing* A	B	C	Embedded Concepts	Performance Indicators/Assessment Expectations
	Major/minor					*See corresponding domain numbers in Chapter 3 for further development and exemplar problems.*
					each higher multiple of 10 or increased exponent, we use the next place to the left. The symbol (1) in the hundreds place has a value of (100) or 10^2. A (1) in the next place to the left is the multiple of the 100, and 10 and has a value of 1,000 or 10^3.	
2.4	Exponential notation: negative integers	7	8	9	Negative integers raised to even-number powers (even exponents) are equal to positive integers. Negative integers with odd exponents are equal to negative integers.	*Predicts and computes the signed value of exponential forms of negative integers*
2.5	Expressing numbers as the sum of their exponential forms	7	8	9	We can express numbers that are not whole system units, such as 1,237, as the sum of exponential forms. $1{,}237 = 10^3 + 2(10^2) + 3(10^1) + 7$	Expresses numbers as the sum of their exponential forms
2.6	Scientific notation: positive exponents	7	8	9	Very large numbers, such as the distance to the moon, and very small numbers, such as the size of an atom, can be expressed in scientific notation. Scientific notation expresses a number as the product of two factors. The first factor is a number greater than or equal to 1 and less than 10, and the second factor is a power of 10. 200,000 can be expressed as 2×10^5, and 250,000 can be expressed as 2.5×10^5. We divide the standard number form by a multiple of 10, use the quotient as a factor, and use an exponential form of base 10 equivalent to the divisor as the other factor.	Writes very large numbers in scientific notation form; converts from one form to another Describes the distance of far-off real objects using scientific notation (e.g., shuttle from the Earth)
2.7	Exponential notation: exponent of zero	7	8	9	If we begin with 10^1 or the number 10 and shift the digit (1) to the right to make it ten times smaller, it becomes the number 1. In exponential form, we represent this as 10^0 or one less multiple of 10^1. For the same reason, any number raised to the zero power is equal to 1. 3^0 is equal to three times less than 3^1 or $3 \div 3$, which equals 1. (See Chapter 3 for further explanation.)	Explains why any number raised to the power of zero is equal to 1; uses the definition of any number raised to the zero power as equal to 1

* NOTE: A = Exploration, B = Concept Mastery, C = Algorithmic or Procedural Mastery

(Continued)

Content Branch Major/minor	Suggested Grade-Level Timing* A	B	C	Embedded Concepts	Performance Indicators/Assessment Expectations
					See corresponding domain numbers in Chapter 3 for further development and exemplar problems.
2.8 Exponential notation: numbers less than 1	7	8	9	If you continue a right shift of place value from the number 1, it becomes one tenth $\frac{1}{10}$ and may be expressed as 10^{-1}. Numbers less than 1 (fractions or decimals) can be expressed as negative powers of the base. 5^{-1} is five times smaller than 5^0 or 1 and equal to the fraction $\frac{1}{5}$; 5^{-2} is five times smaller than $\frac{1}{5}$ and is equal to the fraction $\frac{1}{25}$. $10^{-2} = \frac{1}{100} = .01$	Changes negative exponential notations into their fraction or decimal form Expresses unit fractions and decimals using exponential notations of the powers of 10 Compares and identifies real-life examples of linear and exponential growth
2.9 Scientific notation: negative exponents	7	8	9	Any number > 0 and less than 1 can be written in scientific notation using negative powers of 10. $.00252 = 2.52 \times 10^{-3}$	Changes large whole numbers, fractions, and decimals to scientific notation and explains the process
3.1 Square roots	5	6	7	The inverse of finding the square of a number is finding the square root of the number that is the square. It means finding a number that, when multiplied by itself, will equal the number whose square root is being determined. The square of 5 is equal to 25, and the square root of 25 is 5. We use a symbol to show the operation $\sqrt{25} = 5$.	Explains the meaning of the term *square root* and interprets it as the inverse of the square; uses the symbol for the square root of a number; evaluates expressions that contain it as a term
3.2 Perfect square numbers	6	7	8	There is a sequence of numbers that represents the squares of integers. They are 1, 4, 9, 16, 25, 36, 49, 64, 81, 99, 121, 144, 169, 196, 225,. . . . We call these numbers perfect squares. The sequence of these numbers forms an identifiable pattern.	Identification and automatization of perfect squares for integers 1 to 15; *analyses of sequences of perfect squares*
3.3 Nonperfect squares	7	8	9	The numbers in between the perfect square numbers are nonperfect squares. The square roots of nonperfect square numbers are irrational numbers. You can make estimates of the value of the square root of a nonperfect square by identifying the perfect squares between which it is located or enclosed.	Recognizes nonperfect square numbers and estimates the square roots based on the enclosing perfect squares; uses a calculator to determine more exact square root

* NOTE: A = Exploration, B = Concept Mastery, C = Algorithmic or Procedural Mastery

Content Branch	Suggested Grade-Level Timing* A	B	C	Embedded Concepts	Performance Indicators/Assessment Expectations
Major/minor				*See corresponding domain numbers in Chapter 3 for further development and exemplar problems.*	
4.1 Number system: sets and subsets	6	7	8	The set of the real number system consists of several subsets: The *counting/natural numbers* 1, 2, 3, 4 … are all the numbers we usually count with. They do not include zero. The *whole* numbers include all the counting numbers and zero. Rational and irrational numbers and integer subsets are defined below.	Distinguishes between the various subsets of real numbers; describes orally and in writing the relationship between the subsets of the real number system
4.2 Number system: integers defined	6	7	8	The integers include positive numbers (natural or counting numbers 1, 2, 3, 4 …), negative numbers (additive inverses of the positive numbers), and zero.	Reads, describes, and writes examples of the subsets of integers as positive (natural) numbers, negative numbers (additive inverses), and zero
4.3 Number system: rational numbers defined	6	7	8	Rational numbers include any number that can be represented by the fraction a/b, where (b) is not equal to zero. This includes all the integers because they can be represented as a/b with (a) as the integer and (b) as 1. Terminating or repeating decimals are rational numbers, but a nonterminating decimal is irrational.	Defines the rational and irrational subsets of the real number system; correctly identifies terminating, nonterminating, and repeating decimals as rational or irrational
4.4 Irrational numbers: examples	6	7	8	*Pi* (3.14…) is a nonterminating decimal and an example of an irrational number. The square roots of imperfect square numbers such as $\sqrt{2}$ are also irrational numbers.	Correct placement of rational numbers and irrational number approximations on a number line and *justification* of the placement of the numbers
4.5 Imaginary numbers	8	9	9	Imaginary numbers are numbers that do not belong to the real number system. They are recognized because certain operations will not result in a real number. For example, the square root of a negative integer is impossible or imaginary. The imaginary number that is $\sqrt{-1}$ is named (i).	Identifies and provides an example of an imaginary number

* NOTE: A = Exploration, B = Concept Mastery, C = Algorithmic or Procedural Mastery

(Continued)

NUMBER OPERATIONS: 5. Multiples/factors; 6. divisibility/factorization

Vocabulary and Language: Multiple, factor, composite, prime, least common multiple (LCM), lowest common denominator, greatest common factor (GCF), composite number, prime factor

	Content Branch	Suggested Grade-Level Timing*			Embedded Concepts	Performance Indicators/Assessment Expectations
		A	B	C		
	Major/minor				See corresponding domain numbers in Chapter 3 for further development and exemplar problems.	
5.1	Factors	5	6	7	Factors are all the whole-number values (referent and abstract operators) that can be combined in the multiplication process to give a particular value of the product. A number is a factor of a second number only if you can divide the second number by the first one with no remainder. Two is a factor of 6, but it is not a factor of 5. Dividing a multiple by one factor results in another factor.	Identifies all factors in a given number Given a number and a factor, correct identification of other factors Identification of quotients and dividends as factors
5.2	Multiples	5	6	7	Multiples are the products of factors.	Correct use of the term *multiple* in framing a problem
5.3	Common multiples	5	6	7	A common multiple is a computed value that is the same multiple for two different starting numbers. A balloon of size 4 blown up three whole times will be the same size as a balloon of size 3 blown up four times. Both balloons will now be size 12. So will a balloon of size 2 blown up six times, and so on. Twelve is a common multiple of the different numbers 3, 4, 2, 6, 12, and 1.	Identifies the common multiple of two or more numbers and proves that it is the common multiple
5.4	Least common multiple	5	6	7	The least common multiple (LCM) is the smallest value that is a multiple of each of two or more different values. If the original values are prime numbers, then the LCM is the product of the different values. If both values share common factors, the *least common multiple* will be less than their product.	Predicts and computes the least common multiple for different values
5.5	Common factors	5	6	7	Common factors are whole-number quotients that are the same for different multiples. 3 and 4 are common factors of 12. See Chapter 3 for scaffolds and illustrations.	Explains meaning of common factors; identifies common factors of two or more numbers and *proves* them correct
5.6	Greatest common factor	5	6	7	The greatest common factor (GCF) is the largest factor that is common (or the same) for two different numbers.	Defines, explains, predicts, and computes the greatest common factor

* NOTE: A = Exploration, B = Concept Mastery, C = Algorithmic or Procedural Mastery

Content Branch	Suggested Grade-Level Timing* A	B	C	Embedded Concepts	Performance Indicators/Assessment Expectations
Major/minor				*See corresponding domain numbers in Chapter 3 for further development and exemplar problems.*	
5.7 Prime numbers / Prime factors	5	6	7	A prime number is a whole number with exactly two factors: itself and one. *The number 1 is not a prime number because it does not have two factors.* / A prime factor is a prime number that is a factor of a multiple or composite number.	Identifies a prime number and *proves* what it is / Defines and identifies prime factors, using factor trees and repeated division
5.8 Composite numbers	5	6	7	A composite number is a whole number that has more than two factors.	Identifies a composite number and *proves that it is composite;* represents numbers in multiple ways (e.g., as a product of factors, as a product of prime factors, in exponential and scientific notation)
6.1 Divisibility tests	6	7	8	A number is divisible by another if the remainder is zero. There are certain tests we can use to determine divisibility. For example, any number where the ones digit is 0, 2, 4, 6, or 8 is divisible by 2. The number 324 is divisible by 2, but it is also divisible by 3 because the sum of its digits is divisible by 3 and by 4 because its last two digits (24) are divisible by 4 (see Chapter 3 for additional tests).	Applies divisibility tests to determine divisibility of multiples
6.2 Factoring composite numbers / Prime factorization	6	7	8	We can use factor trees and divisibility tests (see Chapter 3) to help us determine the prime factors of composite numbers. / A prime factorization of a composite number reveals only the prime factors whose product is equal to the composite number ($2 \times 3 \times 7$ are prime factors of 42).	Correct use of factor trees and application of divisibility tests to find prime factorization

OPERATION PATTERNS and PROPERTIES: 7. Patterns and sequences; **8.** properties/applications to algebra; **9.** division/zero and multidigit algorithm; **10–11.** decimal/percentage operations; **12.** integer operations
Vocabulary and Language: Inverse, commutative, identity, distributive, and associative properties; closure; reciprocal, absolute value, division by zero, arithmetic/geometric sequence

Content Branch	A	B	C	Embedded Concepts	Performance Indicators/Assessment Expectations
7.1 Whole-number base-10 unit	5	6	7	We know that $10 \times 10 =$ one hundred. Therefore, 20×30 is 6 hundred (600); $10 \times 100 = 1,000$, then 2 tens $\times$ 3 hundreds (20×300) = 6,000, $200 \times 300 = 60,000$, $200 \times 3,000 = 600,000$, $(20 \times 300) = 6,000,000$, $200 \times 300 = 600,000$,	Describes and applies whole-number base-10 unit multiplication patterns; *estimates* products of large whole numbers by rounding and applying the patterns

(Continued)

* NOTE: A = Exploration, B = Concept Mastery, C = Algorithmic or Procedural Mastery

Content Branch	Suggested Grade-Level Timing*			Embedded Concepts	Performance Indicators/Assessment Expectations
	A	B	C		
Major/minor				*See corresponding domain numbers in Chapter 3 for further development and exemplar problems.*	
multiplication and division patterns: to millions, estimations				and that therefore $204 \times 3{,}014$ is going to be a little more than 600,000. The patterns also may be applied to the inverse operation of division; hundreds divided by tens are tens, and thousands divided by tens are hundreds. For example, $24{,}000 \div 60$ (24 thousands divided by 6 tens) is equal to 4 hundreds (400).	
7.2 Arithmetic (addition) sequences: same and increasing addend or subtrahend	5	6	7	We can create number patterns or sequences by continuously adding the same number or a number that increases or decreases the same amount each time. 2, 5, 8, 11 is an arithmetic sequence. Each number is a term of the sequence.	Recognizes addition and subtraction patterns in sequences; reasoning with and then without concrete materials
7.3 Geometric sequences enlargement by the same multiplier	5	6	7	Sequences in which the numbers are increased in a pattern by the same multiplier (the ratio of the series) are called geometric. If we know the multiplication pattern in a sequence, we can predict the next number or any future number. Finding the common factor for the numbers helps us see the patterns.	*Analysis of geometric sequences with same multiple; generalization of function and expression in symbolic form* Identifies cardinal number given its ordinal position and explains the function equation
Expressed as a function	6	7	8	If the applied multiple is a fraction, the values will decrease. The patterns can be expressed in symbol form as a function. For example, for the three table, $N = 3 \times (n)$, where (n) stands for the ordinal position of the number in a series and (N) its cardinal value.	Writes an equation for a given geometric sequence; relates it to real-life examples
7.4 Exponential sequences	7	8	9	Number sequences that are created by continuously multiplying a previous product by a multiple equal to the first number are exponential. They are represented in exponential form as $N = B^n$, where B is the first (base) number and $n =$ the ordinal number of the term (see Chapter 3 for examples).	Identifies the cardinal number given its ordinal position and explains the function equation; writes an equation for a given exponential sequence; relates to real-life examples
7.5 Sequences other than	7	8	9	Not all sequences are arithmetic or geometric. We can write an expression or an equation that represents the sequence and use	*Analysis of nonarithmetic/geometric sequences; applies the equation for the*

* NOTE: A = Exploration, B = Concept Mastery, C = Algorithmic or Procedural Mastery

Content Branch	Suggested Grade-Level Timing*			Embedded Concepts	Performance Indicators/Assessment Expectations
	A	B	C		
Major/minor				*See corresponding domain numbers in Chapter 3 for further development and exemplar problems.*	
arithmetic or geometric				it to determine a number in the sequence. The letter n is used to represent the ordinal or sequence position of the term. The equation that describes the sequence, $N = n(n - 2)$, tells you that the fourth term ($n = 4$) in the series is the cardinal number 8.	sequence to identify the cardinal number given its ordinal position. Writes an equation for a given sequence; relates to real-life examples
8.1 Inverse properties: addition/ subtraction; applied to algebraic expressions	6	7	8	Addition is the inverse of subtraction and vice versa. If you add a number to a given number and then subtract the same number, you have not changed the original number or value of the number. The reverse is also true. -4 is the additive inverse of 4; $-a$ is named the additive inverse of a. $4 - 4 + 4 = 4 \quad a - a + a = a$	Names the additive inverse of a number and proves, using verbal and symbolic expressions, that combinations of a number and its additive inverse cancel each other
8.2 Inverse properties: multiplication/ division; applied to algebraic expressions	6	7	8	Multiplication is the inverse of division and vice versa. If you multiply a number by a given number and then divide the product by the same number, you have not changed the original number or value of the number. The reverse is also true. $2 \times 5 = 10, 10 \div 5 = 2$ $1 \div 5 = \frac{1}{5}$ and $\frac{1}{5} \times 5 = 1$ are inverse operations. $\frac{1}{5}$ is the multiplicative inverse or reciprocal of 1. $a \times b \div b = a \quad a \div b \times b = a$	Names the multiplicative inverse of a number and proves, using verbal and symbolic expressions, that combinations of a number and its additive inverse cancel each other
8.3 Reciprocals	6	7	8	Two numbers whose product is equal to 1 are reciprocals. $\frac{1}{8}$ is the reciprocal of 8. $\frac{1}{a}$ is the reciprocal of a.	Explains the reciprocal and proves the definition

Content Branch	Suggested Grade-Level Timing*			Embedded Concepts	Performance Indicators/Assessment Expectations
Major/minor	A	B	C		
				See corresponding domain numbers in Chapter 3 for further development and exemplar problems.	
8.4 Commutative property (law) addition and multiplication: applied to algebraic expressions	5 6	6 7	7 8	Changing the sequence or order of addends or factors does not change the sum or product. $a + b + c = b + a + c$ $a \times b = ab = b \times a = ba$	Applies and explains the commutative property of addition and multiplication to algebraic expressions *Proves the property by substituting numerical values for the variables*
8.5 Associative property of addition and multiplication: applied to algebraic expressions	6	7	8	Changing the grouping of addends does not change the sum. $(25 + 2b) + (c) = (2b + c) + 25$ Changing the grouping of factors does not change the sum or product. If the original value or referent is multiplied in separate steps or increments, and each time it is the previous product that is multiplied, the same end result can be obtained by multiplying the original referent by the product of each incremental step. For example, blowing up a balloon to two times the size and then making the new size balloon three times bigger is the same as blowing the original up two times and then three times more or six times all at once. $3 \times (2 \times N) = 2 (3 \times N) = 6 \times N$	Applies and explains the associative properties of addition and multiplication to numerical and algebraic expressions; *proves and justifies the property by substituting numerical values for the variables* *Analyzes* word problems and identifies the referent (multiplicand) and abstract operators (multipliers); provides alternate increments for reaching the same product or enlargement Simplifies equations and solves problems by applying the associative property
8.6 Distributive property of multiplication	6	7	8	If numbers are separated into parts and each part multiplied by the same multiplier, the sum of the products will equal the product of the whole number multiplied by that multiplier. $12 \times 16a = (12 \times 10a) + (12 \times 6a) = 120a + 72a = 192a$ $12 (10a + 6a) = 120a + 72a = 192a$	Applies the distributive property to algebraic expressions and explains it; *justifies the property by substituting numerical values for the variables*; explains the process of factorization as the inverse of the distributive property
8.7 Identity properties of addition and multiplication	6	7	8	The sum of any number and zero is equal to the number. $ab + 0 = ab$ The product of any number and 1 is equal to the number. $ab^2 \times 1 = ab^2$ The product of any number and zero is equal to zero.	Applies and explains the identity properties of addition and multiplication to algebraic expressions; *justifies the property by substituting numerical values for the variables*

* NOTE: A = Exploration, B = Concept Mastery, C = Algorithmic or Procedural Mastery

Content Branch Major/minor	Suggested Grade-Level Timing* A	B	C	Embedded Concepts	Performance Indicators/Assessment Expectations
					See corresponding *domain numbers in Chapter 3 for further development and exemplar problems.*
8.8 Law of closure	8	9	10	In a closed set of numbers, when a specific operation (such as addition or multiplication) is performed on any two numbers in the set, the result will always be a specific number in the set. For example, $4 + 5$ is always equal to 9 and 4×5 is always equal to 20. The set of rational numbers is closed for addition and multiplication but not for division because a number divided by zero is undefined.	Explains and illustrates the law of closure using Venn diagrams
9.1 Multiplication algorithm	5	6	7	The multiplication algorithm is an application of the distributive principle (see Number 8.6). We separately multiply the digits of the muliplicand by the separate digits of the multiplier and then combine them (see Chapter 3 for further development). If we need to multiply a multiplicand of (27) by a factor or multiplier of 26, we can multiply the 7 ones by (6), then the 2 tens or 20 by 6, regroup, and add them together.	Explains and applies the multiplication algorithm in terms of the distributive principle
9.2 Division of zero and by zero	5	6	7	Zero divided into 4 or any number of parts is still zero, and there are zero fours in zero; therefore, $0 \div 4 = 0$. However, the number of zeros in 4 is an undefined amount; therefore, $4 \div 0$ is undefined (any number with a zero denominator is irrational).	*Proof of generalization using verbal constructs or materials (sets of data with some zero readings are useful for explanations of an undefined amount)*
9.3 Division: multidigit patterns and estimations	5	6	7	When dividing by a two-digit number, you are dividing into groups of 20 or 30 (or 2 tens or 3 tens). It is useful to estimate first. Hundreds divided by tens are tens or 6 hundred (600) divided by 2 tens (20) = 3 tens or 30. Thousands divided by tens are hundreds	*Mentally computes division of unit multiples of 10 by divisors of 10, 20, 30, 40 (e.g., $200 \div 10$; $600 \div 20$; $1200 \div 30$; $8000 \div 40$)* Estimates quotients and identifies partial quotients and parts that have not yet been divided (see Chapter 3)
9.4 Division of three or more digit numbers by a two-digit	5	6	7	The division algorithms help us keep track of partial products and remainders. When doing the algorithm, round the divisor down to the digit with the largest place value. If you are dividing by 24 or 26, round to 2 tens. Do not round up. Numbers can be renamed and reorganized	Computes exact quotients and identifies partial quotients and remainders for word problems involving two-digit divisors and four or more digit dividends Correct use of algorithm and then calculator

(Continued)

Content Branch	Suggested Grade-Level Timing* A	B	C	Embedded Concepts	Performance Indicators/Assessment Expectations
Major/minor					
number: short- and long-form algorithms				so that division can be done or made easier. The final quotient is the sum of all the partial quotients (see Chapter 3).	*See corresponding domain numbers in Chapter 3 for further development and exemplar problems.*
10.1 Basic operations with decimals: addition, subtraction to ten thousandths to hundred thousandths	5 / 6	6 / 7	7 / 8	Decimals can be added and subtracted like whole numbers but, like denominations, must be added, or regrouping must be done (e.g., five tenths can be subtracted from one whole if the whole is regrouped for ten tenths). Ten hundredths = 1 tenth. Ten thousandths = 1 hundredth. Thousandths are one tenth as large as the same number of hundredths. Ten hundred thousandths equal one thousandth.	Renames ones, tens, and hundredths as thousandths (decimal and common fraction) Correct estimation and application of algorithm to multidigit decimal addition and subtraction problems. Correct use of calculator (after estimation) for these operations
10.2 Place value system: left or right shift for whole-number multipliers and divisors of decimals — Right shift for base-10 decimal unit multipliers	5 / 6	6 / 7	6 / 8	Each digit in a decimal place is ten times larger than the same digit in a place on its right and ten times smaller than one on its left. To make a decimal value ten times larger, shift it one place to the left; to make it ten times smaller (divide it by ten), shift it one place to the right. You can just move the decimal point one place in the opposite direction. Shifting the decimal point to the right moves the value to the left and increases it. When the multiplier is a decimal, you are making the number smaller. (.1) times any value is ten times smaller than that value. To multiply a number by .1, shift the number one place to the right. To multiply by .01, shift the number two places to the right and so on. To multiply any number by base-10 unit decimals, we can just shift each number place value to the right.	Multiplies and divides any decimal number by 10 or 100 mentally by shifting place (*Note:* Students may also choose the alternative of moving the decimal point, but only after understanding the connections to place value) Uses right shift or decimal point move to multiply by a base-10 decimal unit multiplier; explains the process
10.3 Decimals as parts of a whole	5	6	7	Parts of a single whole or area can be renamed as decimal parts and the exact measures determined by multiplying the whole by the decimal.	Describes parts of an area or single whole quantity in decimal terms (.50 of the field was planted with corn)

* NOTE: A = Exploration, B = Concept Mastery, C = Algorithmic or Procedural Mastery

Content Branch	Suggested Grade-Level Timing*			Embedded Concepts	Performance Indicators/Assessment Expectations
	A	B	C		
Major/minor				*See corresponding domain numbers in Chapter 3 for further development and exemplar problems.*	
Multiplication of decimals: concepts, whole numbers divided by tenths				Multiplying by a decimal is like multiplying by a fraction. The product of any number multiplied by a decimal is going to have a lesser value than the original number. Multiplying a whole number by $\frac{1}{10}$ or .1 results in the same value as dividing it by 10. Multiplying it by .2 is like multiplying it by $\frac{2}{10}$ (you multiply by 2 and divide by 10); .5 times a number is the same as $\frac{5}{10}$ or $\frac{1}{2}$ times the number.	Estimates multiplication of whole numbers by decimals, computes products
10.4 Multiplication of decimals by single-digit decimals; without regrouping; with regrouping	5 / 6	6 / 7	7 / 8	One tenth × one tenth equals one hundredth (.1 × .1 = .01) because $\frac{1}{10}$ of $\frac{1}{10}$ is $\frac{1}{100}$. Tenths times units = tenths; tenths times tenths = hundredths; hundredths times tenths = thousandths. 2 × 3 = 6; .2 × 3 = .6; .2 × .3 = .06 6 × 3 = 18; .6 × 3 = 1.8; .6 × .3 = .18 Decimals can be multiplied using an algorithm based on the one for whole numbers. When combining the partial products, only like denominations must be added, or regrouping must be done.	Explanation for generalizations for products of multiplication of decimals by decimals Correct computation using regrouping; analysis and solution of problems Correct placement of decimal points
10.5 Multiplication algorithm applied to decimals: two- and three-digit multipliers and multiplicands;	6	7	8	In the algorithm 19 × 28.2, the number (28.2) is multiplied nine times and then ten times. The total product is the sum of the partial products. *We can estimate that our answer is going be a little less than 28.2 repeated twenty times or a little less than 560.* In the algorithm 1.9 × 280, the number (280) is multiplied first .9 times and then one time. The total product is the sum of the partial products. *We can estimate that our answer*	Correct estimation and application of algorithm to multidigit decimal multiplication problems Correct application of algorithm Correct use of calculator *Uses calculators to demonstrate the partial products and sums* *Note: Comparisons such as the above may lead to the algorithm application of counting decimal*

Content Branch	Major/minor	Suggested Grade-Level Timing* A	B	C	Embedded Concepts	Performance Indicators/Assessment Expectations
	using the distributive principle with regrouping				*is going be a little less than 28 tens (280) repeated two times or a little less than 560.*	*See corresponding domain numbers in Chapter 3 for further development and exemplar problems.* *places—but begin with the understanding and explanations*
10.6	Decimals and percentage	5	6	7	Percentage and decimals can both be seen as ratios of a whole. If you divide one whole into 10 parts, each part is one out of ten parts, or .1 of the whole. Percentage is based on a whole of 100; thus, .25 is equal to 25 out of 100 parts ($\frac{25}{100}$) or 25% (see Numbers 13.4, 13.5).	Describes the equivalent relationships among representations of rational numbers (fractions, decimals, and percents) and uses these representations in estimation, computation, and applications Converts percentages to decimals and common fractions and vice versa
10.7	Percentage: finding the value of a given percentage of the whole	5 6	6 7	7 8	Percentage is commonly used to express the fractional part of a whole. If the percentage is less than 100%, the value will be less than the whole value; 100% of a value is the same as the whole, and more than 100% of a value is more than the whole value. Given the percentage or ratio of the whole that represents a part of that whole, we can find the actual size of the part by multiplying the whole by the decimal or fractional value of the ratio.	Correct estimates and computations of percentages of whole values Distinguishes between % of a value and the final cost—or result of adding the percent to the value or subtracting a percent from the value.
10.8	Finding percentages: 10% and 1%; other percentages	5 6	6 7	7 8	We can find 10% or $\frac{10}{100}$ or $\frac{1}{10}$ of a value by shifting the whole value to the next smaller place. One percent of a number is the whole value shifted two places to the right (or move the decimal point to the left to accomplish the same thing). Even multiples of 10% or 1% can also be mentally computed. For other percentages, change the percent to a decimal and multiply the whole number by it.	Mentally computes 10% and 1% of a number; mentally computes 20% and 2% of a number and makes other percentage estimates Computes the exact percentage of a number by changing to a decimal and multiplying

* NOTE: A = Exploration, B = Concept Mastery, C = Algorithmic or Procedural Mastery

Content Branch	Suggested Grade-Level Timing*			Embedded Concepts	Performance Indicators/Assessment Expectations
	A	B	C		
Major/minor				*See corresponding domain numbers in Chapter 3 for further development and exemplar problems.*	
11.1 Division of decimals by whole numbers that are multiples of 10. Estimating quotient size	5	6	7	For exact division of decimals by base-10 multiples of whole numbers such as 10, 100, and 1,000, you can use a right place position shift.	Divides or shrinks decimals by multiples of 10 using a right shift of place position
11.2 Division of decimals and whole-number dividends that are smaller than the divisor by whole numbers: algorithm with regrouping	5	6	7	We can divide decimal and whole-number dividends that are smaller than their divisors by whole numbers using the short- and long-form division algorithm. We regroup the whole-number or decimal dividends into their smaller size equivalents, which can be divided. Then we can use the division algorithm form to find the quotient. For the problem $3 \div 6$ or $.3 \div 6$, the dividend can be regrouped to $.30 \div 6$. For multidigit problems using the algorithm, we can also regroup remainders into smaller decimal units.	Uses the division algorithm for division of decimals by whole numbers; explains the regrouping process involved in the above
11.3 Division of whole numbers and decimals by decimals: concept generalizations and estimations	6	7	8	When we divide a whole number or a decimal by a smaller valued decimal or fraction, we get quotients more than one whole. Dividing a number by a decimal (or common fraction) is finding the number of parts in it that are of a size that is less than one whole, and therefore the quotient or number of parts in the dividend or number divided will be greater than the dividend. We get quotients less than one whole when we divide a whole number or a decimal number by a value that is larger	Explains why division by a decimal results in a quotient that is greater than the original dividend Conceptually estimates quotients for problems with one-digit decimal divisors and *predicts* whether answers will be more or less than one whole or more or less than the dividend

*NOTE: A = Exploration, B = Concept Mastery, C = Algorithmic or Procedural Mastery

(Continued)

Content Branch	Suggested Grade-Level Timing*			Embedded Concepts	Performance Indicators/Assessment Expectations
Major/minor	A	B	C		
				See corresponding domain numbers in Chapter 3 for further development and exemplar problems.	
				(e.g., 2.5 ÷ 1.2 is going to be more than one whole or about 2, but the quotient for 1.8 ÷ 2.0 is less than one whole or .9).	
11.4 Division of decimals by decimals: connections to equivalent fraction operations	6	7	8	When dividing by decimals, we remember that in the fraction form of numerator (dividend) over denominator (divisor), an equivalent fraction can be formed by multiplying the numerator and denominator by the same value. Dividing .8 by .2 is the same as dividing 8 by 2 or 80 by 20, or 800 by 200. Then 2.4 divided by 1.2 is the same as 24 ÷ 12.	Correct estimation, mental computations, and explanation of whole-number equivalents in decimal division problems
11.5 Division with decimals: algorithm avoiding decimal divisors by equal multiplication of dividend and divisor	6	7	8	The algorithm for division of whole numbers may be applied to division of decimals and mixed numbers by whole numbers. If we multiply dividend and divisor by the same multiplier or enlarge them both by the same multiple of 10, we can avoid decimal divisors and get the correct answer. The shortcut for this is equal left shifts of place value or moving the decimal point to the left (see Chapter 3). We can regroup remainders into their smaller decimal units.	Correct estimation and application of the algorithm to multidigit decimal division problems convert decimal divisors to whole numbers by equal enlargement of divisor and dividend; explains and applies division algorithm; uses calculator to compute exact answers for decimal division problems with higher values. Correct use of calculator (after estimation) for this operation
12.1 Integer operations: addition of like signs	6	7	8	An integer may be either positive or negative. A plus or minus sign is used to tell the direction. When we perform operations on integers, the outcomes depend on their positive or negative direction (positivity or negativity). Two positives or two negatives are simply added and retain the same sign or direction. If you earn $50 one day and $25 the next, you have earned $75 ($50 + $25 = $75). If you owe someone $50 and someone else $25, you owe $75 ($50 + $25 = $75).	Generalization of the concept that combinations of all positive or all negative values are cumulative and retain the same sign
12.2 Integer operations:	6	7	8	When integers that are additive inverses are combined, such as (−5) + (+5), one cancels the other. When combining or adding	Generalization of the concept that positive and negative equal values cancel each other when

* NOTE: A = Exploration, B = Concept Mastery, C = Algorithmic or Procedural Mastery

Content Branch	Suggested Grade-Level Timing* A	B	C	Embedded Concepts	Performance Indicators/Assessment Expectations
Major/minor				See corresponding domain numbers in Chapter 3 for further development and exemplar problems.	
addition of additive inverses and unlike signs				different negative and positive values, the result is the difference between the values. On the number line, we combine numbers by starting at zero and moving one value at a time to the right or left of zero. The final position is the result. We can also just find the difference between the two numbers. The sign of the difference will be the sign of the higher number.	combined or added; proves it on the number line or with other data and manipulatives Combines or finds the sum of positive and negative numbers using the number line and by finding the difference
12.3 Absolute value	6	7	8	The absolute value of an integer is the distance from zero on the number line, and it is always positive. The absolute value of (−4) is denoted as |−4| and is equal to 4. The distance between any two points (on a number line, map, or coordinate plane) is always an absolute value and positive.	Evaluates numerical expressions with the absolute value symbol Solves problems with absolute values
12.4 Integer operations: subtraction of a positive value	6	7	8	Subtracting or taking away a positive value is the same as adding a negative value. If you have $12 and give away $4, you only have $8 left. That is the same amount you really own if you have $12 and owe $4. Thus (⁺12 − ⁺4) is the same as (⁺12 + ⁻4). The difference is (8).	Explains and applies the concept that taking away a positive value is the same as adding a negative value; evaluates expressions and solves equations and problems that require the concept
12.5 Integer operations: subtraction	6	7	8	On the number line, to find the difference between (⁻6) and (⁻2), we must move (⁺4). If we owe $15 and someone takes away $5 of this debt, we only owe $10. From this, we can generalize that subtracting a negative integer from a negative integer changes the operation to the addition of a positive integer with the same absolute value. In the subtraction algorithm, we usually start with the higher value and subtract the lower value as in the equation below: (⁻2) − (⁻6) = ? If the subtracted number (⁻6) is changed to (⁺6) and the values are combined, the result (the difference) is +4. (⁻2) + (6) = ⁺4. The rule for subtracting negative values is to add its opposite value.	Generalization of concept and rule that two negatives equal a positive and proof on the number line; proves it on number line and with verbal logic (see Chapter 3) Finds the difference between positive and negative numbers using the number line and algorithm; evaluates expressions and solves equations and problems that require the concept

Content Branch	Major/minor	Suggested Grade-Level Timing* A	B	C	Embedded Concepts	Performance Indicators/Assessment Expectations
						See corresponding domain numbers in Chapter 3 for further development and exemplar problems.
12.6 Integer operations: multiplication		7	8	8	When a positive and negative integer are multiplied, the product is negative. The process can be viewed as the repeated addition of a negative value and increased negativity. The product of two negative integers is a positive value. The process decreases negativity (see Chapter 3).	Correctly evaluates expressions and solves equations that require multiplication operations with integers
12.7 Integer operations Squares and square roots		7	8	8	The square of any negative number will always be a positive number. The square root of a positive number could therefore be either a negative or a positive number.	Correctly determines the square of negative integers and explains the two roots of a positive number.
12.8 Integer operations: division		7	8	8	When a negative integer is divided by a positive integer (or vice versa), the quotient is negative. When a negative integer is divided by a negative integer, the quotient is positive (see Chapter 3 for explanations).	Correctly evaluates expressions and solves equations that require division operations with integers

FRACTIONS: 13. Definitions, division meaning, equivalents, common denominator; LCD, inequalities, lowest terms; 14. addition, subtraction, multiplication; 15. fractional parts of whole numbers and fractions, division of fractions, equivalents; 16. ratios, proportions, scale drawings, percentage, rates, unit cost
Vocabulary and Language: Rational number, common fraction, improper fraction, mixed number, unit and more-than-unit fractions, like and unlike fractions, least common denominator, lowest terms, equivalent fractions, ratio, proportion, percentage

Content Branch	Major/minor	A	B	C	Embedded Concepts	Performance Indicators/Assessment Expectations
13.1 Fraction: defined		5	6	6	A fraction is a value representation or expression in the form of a number or expression, placed over another number or expression, with a line in between. It can represent values less than, equal to, or more than one whole. If the fraction has a denominator that is not equal to zero, it is a rational number.	Defines and explains fraction notation; writes it as an expression from a verbal sentence / Applies the definition to real-world problems
13.2 Fraction: forms		5	6	7	A fraction that has a numerator smaller than the denominator is called a common fraction. A fraction with a numerator larger than the denominator is an improper fraction, and a fraction with an equal numerator and denominator is equal to one whole. A mixed number is a combination of a whole number and a fraction.	Distinguishes between and explains fraction forms; writes each form as an expression from a verbal sentence

* NOTE: A = Exploration, B = Concept Mastery, C = Algorithmic or Procedural Mastery

Content Branch Major/minor	Suggested Grade-Level Timing* A	B	C	Embedded Concepts	Performance Indicators/Assessment Expectations
				See corresponding domain numbers in Chapter 3 for further development and exemplar problems.	
13.3 Renaming mixed numbers and fractions greater than I (improper fractions)	5	6	7	Mixed numbers and improper fractions are different representations for the same value.	Interchanges the representation of mixed numbers and improper fractions
13.4 Fractions: as a form for division	5	6	6	A fraction can represent parts of a single whole, but the same fraction can also express division. If you divide two wholes into three parts, the size of each part is less than one whole. It is $1\frac{1}{3}$ of one whole plus $\frac{1}{3}$ of the other whole or $\frac{2}{3}$. Thus, $\frac{2}{3}$ also means two wholes divided into three parts and $\frac{9}{3} = 9$ wholes divided into three parts or a quotient of (3).	Forms fractions from division word problems; *predicts* whether the size of the part is smaller or greater than one whole Translates division problems and statements to fraction form and finds quotients for fractions; uses a calculator to get decimal value of fractions Applies the translation to real-world problems
13.5 Conversion of common fractions into decimals by dividing the numerator by the denominator	5	6	7	Any fraction can be converted to its decimal form through the process of dividing numerator by denominator. $\frac{24}{6}$ is the same as 24 wholes ÷ 6 or equal to 4. When we convert a common fraction such as $\frac{5}{6}$ to decimals, we use the division algorithm and regroup or trade indivisible digits and remainders for their smaller sized decimal equivalents. We can also use our calculators.	Uses the division algorithm for finding the decimal equivalent of improper and proper fractions Relates the conversion of fractions to decimals to the division meaning of fractions and explains the regrouping process involved
13.6 Comparing equivalent fractions; using patterns to compute equivalents	5	6	7	Equivalent fractions are fractions that represent the same value. They show relationship patterns. The greater the denominator, the smaller the size of each part, and the more parts are necessary for an equivalent fraction. Parts that are twice as small require twice as many parts to be equivalent. If the numerator is twice as large, the denominator is twice as large ($\frac{2}{3} = \frac{4}{6}$). If we enlarge or reduce the numerator of a fraction by multiplying or	Identifies patterns Explains the *generalization* of equivalent fractions; *proves* that value is not changed (uses manipulatives) Changes fractions to equivalents with common denominators Applies the *generalization* of equivalent fractions to real-world problems

Content Branch	Suggested Grade-Level Timing*			Embedded Concepts	Performance Indicators/Assessment Expectations
	A	B	C		
Major/minor				*See corresponding domain numbers in Chapter 3 for further development and exemplar problems.*	
				dividing it by a value (factor), we can form an equivalent fraction by multiplying or dividing the denominator by the same factor. $\frac{3}{4}$ is equal to $\frac{6}{8}$ because $2 \times (3) = 6$ and $2 \times (4) = 8$, and 2 is the factor (multiplier) by which both the numerator and denominator were enlarged.	
13.7 Least common denominator: changing fractions with unequal denominators to equivalents with equal denominators	5	6	7	To perform some operations on unlike fractions, we have to change them to equivalents with a common denominator. The least common denominator of a group of fractions is the least common multiple (LCM) of all the denominators. We can convert groups of fractions to their least common denominator by multiplying (or dividing) the numerator and the denominator of a fraction by the same factor because this does not change its value. See Number 13.6 and Chapter 3 for suggestions and calculator uses.	Identifies common denominators for fractions such as halves, fourths, eighths, thirds, sixths, tenths, and twelfths
13.8 Inequalities $\frac{3}{4} > \frac{1}{2}$ $\frac{1}{2} = \frac{1}{3}$	5	6	7	If fractions are not equivalent, you can use close equivalents to estimate their relative size (e.g., $\frac{3}{4}$ is more than $\frac{1}{2}$ because $\frac{1}{2}$ is equivalent to $\frac{2}{4}$). You can also compare the size of fractions by comparisons to one whole: 7/8 is more than 6/7 because it is only 1/8 less than a whole, and 6/7 is a greater amount, 1/7, less than the whole.	Orders halves, thirds, and fourths and solves inequalities $\frac{1}{2} < \frac{3}{4}$; $\frac{1}{4} < \frac{1}{2}$; $\frac{2}{3} < \frac{3}{4}$; $\frac{1}{3} < \frac{1}{2}$ Orders other fractions without converting to equal denominators (uses fraction number lines and concrete materials)
14.1 Addition and subtraction of like and unlike fractions: no regrouping	5	6	7	Like fractions can be added or subtracted by combining or finding the difference in the numerators and keeping the same denominator $\frac{5}{6} - \frac{2}{6} = \frac{3}{6}$. Unlike fractions cannot be added or subtracted before they are put into equivalent form with a common denominator. $\frac{5}{6} - \frac{1}{3} =$ $\frac{5}{6} - \frac{2}{6} = \frac{3}{6}$	Adds and subtracts unlike fractions (as above) without regrouping Applies the operation to real-world problems

Content Branch	Suggested Grade-Level Timing*			Embedded Concepts	Performance Indicators/Assessment Expectations
	A	B	C		
Major/minor					See corresponding domain numbers in Chapter 3 for further development and exemplar problems.
14.2 Addition and subtraction of unlike fractions with horizontal and vertical representation of fraction problems (with and without regrouping)	5	6	7	Once they have a common denominator, they can be added or subtracted by combining or finding the difference in the numerators. Regrouping from whole numbers to equivalent fractions allows us to solve some addition and subtraction fraction problems. For the problem ($1\frac{1}{6} - \frac{5}{6} = ?$), we can regroup the one whole to its equivalent fraction form of $\frac{6}{6}$ and then subtract. $1\frac{1}{6} = \frac{6}{6} + \frac{1}{6} = \frac{7}{6}$ and $\frac{7}{6} - \frac{5}{6} = \frac{2}{6}$	Adds and subtracts unlike fractions (as above) with regrouping from whole numbers Applies the operation to real-world problems
14.3 Multiplication of fractions by whole numbers	5	6	7	When a fraction is multiplied by a whole number, the fraction is repeatedly added or enlarged a whole number of times. The product is a fraction whose numerator is the product of the original (multiplicand) numerator and the whole-number multiplier, and the denominator is the same as that of the repeated (multiplicand) fraction.	Analyzes and solves real-world problems that require multiplication of fractions by whole numbers using the concepts of multiples of parts of wholes such as three pieces of pie that are each 1/4 of the whole, and enlargements of a single fraction such as the new size of a child who used to be 1/4 of his father's size but is now twice as big as he used to be.
14.4 Fractions: unit fractional parts of whole number or set	5	6	7	To find the size of one unit fraction of a whole number, you divide the number by the denominator.	Explains that finding the unit fractional part of a set is the same as dividing by the denominator; computes the value of unit fractional parts of multiple wholes from story problems
14.5 More-than-unit	5	6	7	When a whole number is multiplied by a fraction, it is the same as finding the fractional part of the whole number or set.	Explains that multiplying a number by a fraction is the same as finding a fractional part of it because it

(Continued)

Content Branch	Major/minor	Suggested Grade-Level Timing* A	B	C	Embedded Concepts	Performance Indicators/Assessment Expectations
	Major/minor				*See corresponding domain numbers in Chapter 3 for further development and exemplar problems.*	
fractional parts of a set Multiplication of whole numbers by more-than-unit fractions		5	6	7	$\frac{1}{2} \times 12$ is the same as $\frac{1}{2}$ of 12 because it means repeating the whole only half the time. $\frac{1}{3} \times 12$ is equal to 4, but $\frac{2}{3} \times 12$ is two times as much as $\frac{1}{3}$ of 12 or two times more than 4 and equal to 8. To find the size of more than one unit fraction of a whole number, you find the size of one unit by dividing by the denominator and then multiply by the number of unit parts, the numerator.	means repeating the number other than a whole number of times, and the product is equal to that fractional part of one whole multiple of the number Explains the algorithm of dividing by the denominator and multiplying by the numerator *Analyzes and solves problems that require the multiplication of whole numbers by fractions*
14.6 Unit fractions of unit fractions (multiplication of fractions by fractions)		5	6	7	Finding a unit fractional part of a unit fraction *value (or multiplying the value by the fraction as above)* has the same effect as dividing the unit fractional part into smaller parts. It makes the fraction a number of times smaller (the number of times is equal to the multiplier denominator). $\frac{1}{4}$ of $\frac{1}{5}$ is going to be four times smaller than $\frac{1}{5}$. $\frac{1}{5}$ will be divided into four smaller parts, and each part will only be $\frac{1}{20}$. You can see that the computed value has a denominator that is the product of the two denominators.	Explains why multiplying a unit fraction by a unit fraction results in a product of smaller value; also explains why the product is a fraction with a denominator that is the product of the two denominators, and the numerator is equal to (1), which is the product of the two numerators of (1)
14.7 Predicting products of fractional multiples of fractions Using number		6	7	8	The product of a fraction multiplied by a fraction less than one whole is always less than the multiplicand. It is the same as finding the fractional part of *the fraction.* $\frac{1}{2} \times \frac{1}{4} = \frac{1}{8}$ or $\frac{1}{2}$ of $\frac{1}{4} = \frac{1}{8}$ $\frac{1}{2} \times \frac{2}{3} = \frac{1}{3}$ and $\frac{1}{3}$ of $\frac{3}{4} = \frac{1}{3}$	*Predicts* whether the product of a value and a fraction will be more or less than the value; *proves* this with diagrams or manipulatives such as fraction bars Mentally computes some obvious fractional multiples of fractions

* NOTE: A = Exploration, B = Concept Mastery, C = Algorithmic or Procedural Mastery

Content Branch	Suggested Grade-Level Timing*			Embedded Concepts	Performance Indicators/Assessment Expectations
	A	B	C		
Major/minor				*See corresponding domain numbers in Chapter 3 for further development and exemplar problems.*	
sense to compute fractional multiples of fractions				$\frac{1}{2} \times \frac{1}{40} = \frac{1}{80}$ and $\frac{1}{5}$ of $\frac{5}{6} = \frac{1}{6}$ $\frac{1}{2}$ of $2\frac{1}{2} = 1\frac{1}{4}$	
14.8 Unit fractions of more-than-unit fraction Algorithm for multiplication of fractions	6	7	8	$\frac{1}{3}$ of $\frac{1}{7}$ would be $\frac{1}{21}$, but $\frac{1}{3}$ of $\frac{2}{7}$ is twice as much or $\frac{2}{21}$. You can see that for this problem, it was also necessary to multiply the numerators. A shortcut algorithm strategy is just to multiply the numerators and denominators.	Explains algorithm and computes unit fractions of fractions (see Chapter 3)
14.9 More-than-unit fractions of more-than-unit fractions: algorithm	6	7	8	To find more than one unit fraction of a unit fraction, you can find the smaller unit fraction value by multiplying the denominators; then, because it is more than one unit, multiply the numerators. $\frac{2}{3}$ of $\frac{1}{2} = \frac{2}{6}$ because $\frac{1}{3}$ of $\frac{1}{2} = \frac{1}{6}$ and $\frac{2}{3}$ of $\frac{1}{2}$ is twice as much as $\frac{1}{3}$ of $\frac{1}{2}$. $\frac{2}{3}$ of $\frac{3}{2}$ would be three times as much as $\frac{2}{3}$ of $\frac{1}{2} = \frac{2}{6}$. It equals 6/6 or one whole. The shortcut algorithm is to multiply numerators and denominators $\frac{2}{3} \times \frac{3}{2} = \frac{6}{6} = 1$.	Explains and applies the algorithm for multiplication of more-than-unit fractions of more-than-unit fractions Analyzes fraction of fraction problems and predicts the relative size of the product Uses number sense to compute and then prove answers to fraction multiplication problems Applies the commutative principle to explanations See Chapter 3 for examples
15.1 Multiplying mixed numbers	6	7	8	Multiplication of fractions by mixed numbers can be considered as an application of the distributive property. $2\frac{1}{2} \times \frac{1}{3} = 2 \times \frac{1}{3} + \frac{1}{2} \times \frac{1}{3} = \frac{2}{6} + \frac{1}{6} = \frac{1}{6}$	Multiplies mixed numbers by fractions and fractions by mixed numbers Explains answers using the distributive property and applies the algorithm

* NOTE: A = Exploration, B = Concept Mastery, C = Algorithmic or Procedural Mastery

(Continued)

Content Branch	Major/minor	Suggested Grade-Level Timing*			Embedded Concepts	Performance Indicators/Assessment Expectations
		A	B	C		
	Major/minor				The easier way is to change the mixed numbers to improper fractions and apply the algorithm. $\frac{5}{2} \times \frac{1}{3} = \frac{5}{6}$	*See corresponding domain numbers in Chapter 3 for further development and exemplar problems.*
15.2 Reducing fractions to lowest terms		5	6	7	In order to make our mathematical language and operations simpler we often change fractions to their equivalents with the smallest denominator. We know that dividing the numerator and denominator by the same value does not change the value, and so we try to find the largest value (factor) by which we can divide both numerator and denominator. This factor is called the greatest common factor (GCF).	Correct computation of lowest term equivalents. *Note:* Do not belabor this if it is not specifically required, but it may be helpful to note differences between invented strategies and algorithms. It is easy to understand that half of $\frac{2}{3}$ is $\frac{1}{3}$, but if you use the algorithm $\frac{1}{2} \times \frac{2}{3}$, it makes sense to change your answer of $\frac{2}{6}$ to $\frac{1}{3}$.
15.3 Division of fractions by whole numbers		5	6	7	Division of fractions by whole numbers is like division of whole numbers. We know the size of the whole, and we look either for the size of the parts (partition) or the number of parts (quotition). In partition, $\frac{3}{4}$ divided by 3 means the following: If I divide $\frac{3}{4}$ into three parts, how big will each part be? (1/4). In quotition, $\frac{3}{4}$ divided by 3 means how many parts of size (3) are there in $\frac{3}{4}$? There is less than (1) whole part of size 3 in $\frac{3}{4}$. There is only a part of size 3 in $\frac{3}{4}$. In both cases, $\frac{3}{4} \div 3 = \frac{1}{4}$.	Demonstrates the division of a fraction by a whole number using fraction bars or other objects; identifies divisor and dividend from a division of a fraction problem and tells what the quotient represents; mentally computes exemplars of the process. Applies the procedure and concept to real-world problems
15.4 Division of whole numbers by unit fractions		5	6	7	Whole numbers can be divided by fractions if we think about how many fractions of the given size are in the given wholes. There will always be more than one common fraction part in even one whole because the fraction is less than the whole. The	Demonstrates the division of a whole number by a unit fraction using fraction bars or other objects; identifies divisor and dividend from a division by a fraction problem and tells what the quotient

* NOTE: A = Exploration, B = Concept Mastery, C = Algorithmic or Procedural Mastery

Content Branch	Suggested Grade-Level Timing*			Embedded Concepts	Performance Indicators/Assessment Expectations
	A	B	C		
Major/minor				*See corresponding domain numbers in Chapter 3 for further development and exemplar problems.*	
				number of unit fraction parts in one whole is always equal to the denominator, and therefore the number of the unit fraction parts in more than one whole is equal to the denominator times the number of wholes. $3 \div \frac{1}{2}$ means how many parts of size $\frac{1}{2}$ are there in 3? (6) $\frac{3}{4} \div \frac{1}{4}$ means how many parts of size $\frac{1}{4}$ are there in $\frac{3}{4}$? (3)	represents; mentally computes exemplars of the process
15.5 Division of whole numbers by more-than-unit fractions	5	6	7	In any whole, there will be fewer more-than-unit fractions than there are unit fractions. If the fraction numerator is (2), then there will be half as many or the number of unit fractions divided by (2). To find more than the unit fraction of a number, we multiply the number by the denominator (to find the number of unit fractions) and divide the multiple by the numerator.	Demonstrates the division of a fraction by a more-than-unit fraction using fraction bars or other objects; identifies divisor and dividend and mentally computes exemplars of the process Uses the division by fractions algorithm
16.1 Fractions as ratios of part to whole or parts to parts; equivalent word and symbol expressions of ratio	5	6	7	The values of the numerator and denominator in a fraction can also express a pattern or relationship called a ratio. Ratios represent either a relationship between parts and the whole (or a given number of items in a group to the whole group of items) or a relationship between different parts of the whole. The fraction $\frac{2}{3}$ can represent two parts (items) out of a whole group of three parts (items). This ratio, expressed as $\frac{2}{3}$, can also be expressed in word form as 2 out of 3 or 2:3. The fraction 2/3 can also represent a ratio that means that for every two parts of one kind in a whole group, there are three parts of another kind. This ratio can also be expressed in word form as 2 is to 3, or 2 to 3, or symbolically as 2:3. If there were no other kinds of parts in this group, the size of the whole	*Analyzes word problems* that describe a part/whole or part/part ratio, distinguishes the forms, and expresses the ratio in words and as a fraction Applies the concept of ratio to simple probability problems and expresses probability as a ratio in word and fraction forms Distinguishes between part/whole and part/part ratios; converts part/part data into part/whole ratios

Content Branch	Suggested Grade-Level Timing*			Embedded Concepts	Performance Indicators/Assessment Expectations
	A	B	C		
Major/minor				*See corresponding domain numbers in Chapter 3 for further development and exemplar problems.*	
				would be 5 (or multiples of 5), and one kind of part would be $\frac{2}{5}$ of the whole, while the other would be $\frac{3}{5}$ of the whole (see Chapter 3).	
16.2 Ratios in algebraic form	6	7	8	Ratios can be expressed in algebraic terms as a/b, a out of b, or $a : b$. Ratios can be used in solving problems that compare part to whole relationships.	Correct translation of part/part ratio word problem statements into symbolic form
16.3 Proportions	5	6	7	Statements of equivalent ratios are called proportions. Five out of ten parts is the same as one out of two parts or half the total number of parts. The patterns of the proportions can be used to compute unknown parts and wholes. If we know one ratio, and that it is equal to a second, we can find a missing numerator or denominator for the second ratio by expressing them both as a proportion. Six out of ten books in the library are soft covered. If there were eighty books in the library, about how many would have soft covers? $$\frac{6}{10} = \frac{x}{10}$$	*Analyzes proportion word problems* and computes unknown quantities using common factors (multiples or divisors)
16.4 Proportions: algorithm for solving equations that represent them	5	6	7	For any two equivalent fractions, the product of the denominator of one fraction and the numerator of the second is equal to the product of the denominator of the second fraction and the numerator of the first. This is usually described as "the product of the means equals the product of the extremes."	Uses product of means = product of extremes algorithm and simple linear equations to solve real-world problems
16.5 Proportions in scale drawings	6	7	8	Sizes in scale drawings are proportional to the sizes in reality. Scale drawings such as maps are ratios with a scale unit that shows the relationship between a unit of distance on the map	Interpretation of scale drawings; construction of scale drawings

* NOTE: A = Exploration, B = Concept Mastery, C = Algorithmic or Procedural Mastery

Content Branch	Suggested Grade-Level Timing*			Embedded Concepts	Performance Indicators/Assessment Expectations
Major/minor	A	B	C		
				See corresponding domain numbers in Chapter 3 for further development and exemplar problems.	
				and the real distance. A proportion that compares the ratio of the scale to the measured distance on the map can be used to find the real distance. If the scale is 1 inch = 500 miles or a ratio of 1/500 and the measured map distance is 2 inches, the proportion is $\frac{1}{500} = \frac{2}{x}$. We can solve this by applying the algorithm. $500 \times 2 = x$ or $x = 1{,}000$ miles (product of the means equals the product of the extremes).	
16.6 Percentage as ratio	5	6	7	Percents are ratios that compare a number that represents a part of a whole to a whole, which is represented as 100. Percents therefore correspond to hundredths. Twenty-five percent of a whole is equal to .25 of the whole. In fraction form, this would be $\frac{25}{100}$ or 1/4 (see Numbers 10.6–10.8).	Changes percentages to decimals and common fractions Describes percentage as a ratio with 100 as the denominator Translates the equivalent relationships among representations of rational numbers (fractions, decimals, and percents) Uses the fractional representation of percent in ratio and proportion problems and expresses a ratio as a percent
16.7 Rate equivalents: converting between different standards of measure	7	8	9	Rates and proportions can also be used to convert measures from one standard form to another. One inch is equivalent to about 2.5 cm or expressed as a ratio 2.5:1 or $\frac{2.5}{1}$. How many inches would be equal to 175 cm? $\frac{2.5}{1} = \frac{175}{x}$ $2.5\, x = 175, x = 70$ inches	Converts rate measures from one standard form to another using a proportion; translates real data such as foreign money amounts and exchange rates from one standard to another using the unit rate equivalent
16.8 Comparing ratios: unit costs	7	8	9	We can also find the unit cost of items and compare them using ratios. If you pay $75 for three pairs of shoes, is this more or less per pair than paying $48 for two pairs? Is the ratio $\frac{75}{3}$ equal to, more than, or less than $\frac{48}{2}$? Does the product of the means equal the product of the extremes?	Compares the cost of multiple items by calculating unit costs for each; uses the proportion algorithm to compare them

Content Branch	Suggested Grade-Level Timing*			Embedded Concepts	Performance Indicators/Assessment Expectations
Major/minor	A	B	C	See corresponding domain numbers in Chapter 3 for further development and exemplar problems.	

ALGEBRA: EXPRESSIONS AND LINEAR EQUATIONS: 17. Algebraic expressions-forms; 18. evaluating algebraic expressions/operations; 19. factoring polynomials; 20. linear equations and inequalities; 21. solving equations, number series

Vocabulary and Language: Term, constant, variable, monomial, polynomial, binomial, trinomial, coefficient, expression, equation, inequality, order of operations, PEMDAS, FOIL, factorization, greatest common factor (GCF)

Content Branch	A	B	C	Embedded Concepts	Performance Indicators/Assessment Expectations
17.1 Algebraic and numerical expressions	5	6	7	In mathematics, an expression is a short way to describe a number (or amount) or to show a mathematical operation. A numerical expression has only numbers in it. An algebraic expression has both numbers and letters that represent numbers.	Distinguishes between a numerical and an algebraic expression
17.2 Terms: constants and variables	5	6	7	An expression may have one or more terms. Sometimes, the term is a specific number such as 6, and we call that term a constant. Sometimes, the term is a letter, such as (a) or (n), and we call that a variable. A variable is a symbol or letter that can represent different numbers.	Identifies the separate terms in an expression and describes the terms as variable or constant; correct translation of a verbal expression to a mathematical expression with different variable and constant terms
17.3 Operations in algebraic expressions	5	6	7	An expression can define an operation such as addition ($6 + n$), subtraction ($n - 6$), or multiplication ($6 \times n$ or $6n$).	Identifies the separate operations of addition and subtraction in an expression
17.4 Coefficients and fractions in expressions	6	7	8	The operation of multiplication in an expression can be shown by placing a constant multiplier in front of the variable. The constant number that is directly in front of a variable (e.g., $3r$ or $6b$) is called a coefficient. It indicates that the variable must be multiplied by the coefficient number. $3n$ means ($3 \times n$). When two variables are directly next to each other or side by side, that also means that they are multiplied (or are factors of a multiple). The expression (lw) in the equation $A = lw$ means ($l \times w$). Another form for this could be $l(w)$.	Correct translation of mathematical expressions, including coefficients to a verbal expression; correct translation of verbal expressions involving multiplication to mathematical expressions using coefficients

* NOTE: A = Exploration, B = Concept Mastery, C = Algorithmic or Procedural Mastery

Content Branch	Major/minor	Suggested Grade-Level Timing*			Embedded Concepts	Performance Indicators/Assessment Expectations
		A	B	C		
	Major/minor					*See corresponding domain numbers in Chapter 3 for further development and exemplar problems.*
17.5	Algebraic expressions: forms	6	7	8	Each separate variable or constant (or group of constants and variables within parentheses) that is separated from another individual or group by an addition or subtraction operation sign is a different term of the expression. A polynomial is an expression with one term or one that shows the sum or difference between two or more terms. A monomial expression is a polynomial with one term. A binomial is a polynomial with only two terms. A trinomial is a polynomial with three terms.	Identifies monomial and polynomial expressions and explains the classification Correct written creation of three forms of expression
17.6	Fraction form of division operation in expressions	6	7	8	The operation of division in an expression can be shown in its fraction form as $6 \div n$, which is the same as $\frac{6}{n}$, and $\frac{a}{b}$ is translated as (a) divided by (b).	Correct translation of mathematical expressions, including fractions to verbal expressions denoting division Correct translation of verbal expressions involving division to mathematical expressions using the fraction form
17.7	Operations in expressions	6	7	8	The operation signs $(+, -)$ indicate separate terms, but the multiplication and division operations may also be part of the same term. When a coefficient (with or without parentheses) is used to denote multiplication or the fraction form shows division of a term, it is part of the term. $3n$ is a single term, and $\frac{3}{4}n$ is a single term. A group of constants and variables within parentheses is a single term.	Translates given mathematical expressions that include operation signs into verbal expressions and vice versa Identifies the individual terms within the expression
17.8	Multiplying polynomials: parentheses	7	8	9	Any term (monomial or polynomial) in front of a parenthesis indicates that every term within the parentheses must be multiplied by the term in front of it (distribution property). $6(a + b + 3) = 6a + 6b + 18$	Explains and applies the distribution property as applied to the use of parentheses Proves the truth of the property by substituting number values for variables

*NOTE: A = Exploration, B = Concept Mastery, C = Algorithmic or Procedural Mastery

(Continued)

Content Branch	Suggested Grade-Level Timing* A	B	C	Embedded Concepts	Performance Indicators/Assessment Expectations
Major/minor				See corresponding domain numbers in Chapter 3 for further development and exemplar problems.	
17.9 Evaluating expressions: substituting known variables	6	7	8	When you evaluate an expression, you substitute numbers that you know or are given for any variable terms. Then you may be able to solve an equation that contains the expression and identifies the value of an unknown variable.	Correct substitution with a given value for a variable in an expression Correct evaluation of the expression Proves or disproves the truth of a particular substituted value
18.1 Evaluating expressions: adding and subtracting like monomials	6	7	8	Like terms have corresponding variables with the same exponents. $(6a)$ and $(3a)$ are like terms. $(6a^2)$ and $(3a^2)$ are like terms. The sum of like terms is equal to the common variable of the terms preceded by the sum of their coefficients. $6a + 3a = 9a$ and $6a^2 + 3a^2 = 9a^2$ The difference between like terms is similarly equal to the common variable of the terms preceded by the difference between their coefficients. $6a - 3a = 3a$ and $6a^2 - 3a^2 = 3a^2$	Identifies like and unlike terms and proves the choices (e.g., why $2a + 2a^2$ is not always equal either to $4a^2$ or $4a^3$); Adds and subtracts polynomials (integer coefficient)
18.2 Evaluating algebraic expressions: order of operations	6	7	8	When evaluating expressions, a specific order of performing operations allows us to communicate mathematically. The order corresponds to the acronym (PEMDAS). Operations attached to grouping symbols such as Parentheses and brackets are done first. Exponents come next. Multiplication and Division follow and are equal in status, but the operation that comes first from left to right is done first. This also holds true of the final Addition and Subtraction. When one grouping symbol is inside the other, perform the innermost operation first. For $3b + b(5 - 2) + 8$, subtract inside the parentheses first $(5 - 2)$ and then multiply by (b). $3b + 3b + 8 = 6b + 8$	Explains the order of operations as a human consensus of communication; automatizes the acronym and its meaning and correctly applies the order to polynomial expressions Note: P denotes parentheses, E denotes exponents, M denotes multiplication, D denotes division, A denotes addition, and S denotes subtraction

* NOTE: A = Exploration, B = Concept Mastery, C = Algorithmic or Procedural Mastery

Content Branch	Major/minor	Suggested Grade-Level Timing*			Embedded Concepts	Performance Indicators/Assessment Expectations
		A	B	C		
	Major/minor				*See corresponding domain numbers in Chapter 3 for further development and exemplar problems.*	
18.3	Evaluating expressions: multiplying like and unlike term monomials	7	8	9	The product of different powers of the same base is the sum of the exponents. The product of like and unlike term monomials is the composite product of the variables and their coefficients. $3a \times 6a = 18a^2$ $3a^2 \times 6a^3 = 18a^5$ $6ab = 18a^2b$	Correct multiplication of monomials
18.4	Evaluating expressions: multiplying binomials	8	9	9	We use a procedure called the FOIL method (first, outside, inside, and last) for multiplying two binomials. FOIL is an application of the distributive property (see Chapter 3). If you multiply by each term of the binomial multiplier separately and then combine the two products, the sum is the same as the result of the FOIL procedure. $(6 + 3) \times (6 + 3) = 6(6 + 3) + 3(6 + 3) = 6 \times 9 + 3 \times 9 = 27 + 54 = 81$, and that is the same as $(6 \times 6) + (3 \times 6) + (6 \times 3) + (3 \times 3)$ or $36 + 18 + 18 + 9 = 81$. Multiplying two binomials may result either in a polynomial with three terms or a binomial.	Applies and explains the FOIL procedure as an application of the distributive property
18.5	Evaluating expressions: division of a monomial by a constant	7	8	9	The division operation in algebraic expressions is usually represented by its fraction form. $6a \div 2$ is shown as $\dfrac{6a}{2}$ and is equal to $3a$. The quotient of a monomial divided by a constant is the quotient of the coefficient of the numerator divided by the constant and has the same variable as the numerator.	Divides monomials when the degree of the denominator is less than or equal to the degree of the numerator
18.6	Dividing monomials by monomials: same degree	8	8	9	The meaning of the fraction $\dfrac{12a}{3a}$ can be expressed as follows: How many units of $3a$ are there in $12a$? There are (4) units of $3a$ in $12a$. The quotient of like-term monomials is the quotient of the coefficient of the numerator divided by the coefficient of the	Divides monomials by monomials with the same degree and where the whole denominator is a factor of the numerator Explains application of the canceling algorithm

	Content Branch	Suggested Grade-Level Timing*			Embedded Concepts	Performance Indicators/Assessment Expectations
		A	B	C		
	and whole denominator is a factor of the numerator				denominator, and the variable of the numerator divided by the variable of the denominator is $\frac{12a}{3a} = 4$. A shortcut algorithm is to cancel the same term in the numerator and denominator because any number divided by itself is equal to 1.	*See corresponding domain numbers in Chapter 3 for further development and exemplar problems.*
18.7	Dividing monomials by monomials: dividing numerator and denominator by separate common factors	8	8	9	The coefficient and the variable are separate factors of a monomial. Dividing the numerator and denominator by the same factor can reduce a monomial division expression to a simpler fraction form. $\frac{6a}{2b} = \frac{3a}{b}$ and $\frac{7a}{9a} = \frac{7}{9}$	Reduces monomial fractions when the degree of the denominator is equal to the degree of the numerator; explains application of the canceling algorithm
18.8	Dividing monomials by monomials: numerator variable is a higher degree of the same variable than that of the denominator	8	9	9	To find the quotient of a monomial divided by a monomial with a lesser degree of the same variable, we put the expression into fraction form and perform the following operations: $18a^2 \div 3a = \frac{18a^2}{3b}$ 1. Divide the coefficient of the numerator and the coefficient of the denominator by the same factor (3) 2. Divide the variable of the numerator and the variable of the denominator by the same factor (a) Or combine the coefficient and variable and divide numerator and denominator by 3a. $\frac{18a^2}{3a} = \frac{6a}{1} = 6a$	Divides a monomial of higher degree by a monomial of lesser degree (integer coefficients); explains the process as separate divisions of the numerator coefficient and variable and the denominator coefficient and variable by the same values to find an equivalent value Combines coefficient and variable as a divisor and explains division of the numerator and denominator by the same combined value; explains and uses the canceling algorithm

* NOTE: A = Exploration, B = Concept Mastery, C = Algorithmic or Procedural Mastery

Content Branch	Suggested Grade-Level Timing*			Embedded Concepts	Performance Indicators/Assessment Expectations
Major/minor	A	B	C		See corresponding domain numbers in Chapter 3 for further development and exemplar problems.
18.9 Dividing polynomials by monomials	8	9	9	When dividing polynomials by monomials, each individual term of the numerator must be divided by the monomial term of the denominator: $\dfrac{6a^3 + 9a^2 + 12a}{3a} = 2a^2 + 3a + 4$	Divides a polynomial by a monomial (integer coefficients); explains the process as expressing the division problem in fractional form and dividing each term of the numerator and denominator of the fraction by the same value to find an equivalent
19.1 Factoring polynomials	8	9	9	Factoring an expression means representing a composite group of terms by their common factors. We can simplify a polynomial expression by dividing all the terms by the same factor and then expressing it with the divisor we used as a multiplier factor and the quotients for each divided term as the multiplicands. If you divide each term by x in the expression $(3x + 5x)$, it can be expressed as $x(3 + 5)$ or $8x$. In factored form, $6b + 3a$ is equal to $3(2b + a)$.	Factors polynomials by dividing each term by the same divisor and explains the process as the inverse of the distributive property
19.2 Factoring polynomials with greatest common factor (GCF)	8	9	9	When factoring polynomials, it helps to factor groups of terms by the greatest common factor (GCF) or the largest multiple of common factors. $(3x^2 + 6x)$ can be expressed as $3x(x + 2)$ if you divide by the GCF of $3x$ for the two terms and show it as a separate multiplier.	Factors polynomial algebraic expressions by removing (dividing by) the GCF and using it as a multiple for each of the resulting quotients Solves equations that require factoring by the GCF
19.3 Factoring before dividing polynomials by binomials	8	9	9	When dividing a polynomial by a binomial, it may be useful to factor the numerator and find a factor that is equal to the denominator: $\dfrac{a^2 + 6a}{a + 6} = \dfrac{a(a + 6)}{a + 6} = a$	Divides a polynomial by a binomial in a two-step process by factoring the numerator to separate a factor equal to the denominator and then dividing the numerator and denominator of the fraction by the same value to find an equivalent; explains the process
19.4 Factoring trinomials; quadratic form	8	9	9	Trinomials in the quadratic forms of $ax^2 + bx + c$, $ax^2 - bx + c$, $ax^2 + bx - c$, and $ax^2 - bx - c$ may be factored into the two root binomials by thinking of the FOIL procedure in reverse. The first term must be the product of the first terms of the binomials and the last term the product of the second terms of the binomials, while the middle term must be the sum of inside and outside terms.	Correct identification of the quadratic forms Factors trinomials in the quadratic function form by reversing the steps in the FOIL method

Content Branch	Suggested Grade-Level Timing*			Embedded Concepts	Performance Indicators/Assessment Expectations
	A	B	C		
Major/minor				See corresponding domain numbers in Chapter 3 for further development and exemplar problems.	
19.5 Factoring a trinomial: difference between two perfect squares	8	9	9	If we multiply any two binomials in the form of $(a + b) (a - b)$, we always get a binomial of two perfect squares $(a^2 - b^2)$; therefore, the factors of a binomial that is the difference between two perfect squares will be $(a + b) (a - b)$; $(x^2 - 16) = (x + 4) (x - 4)$.	Factors a binomial that represents the difference between two perfect squares
19.6 Factoring a trinomial: two-step process	9	9	9	Trinomials may also be factored in a sequence of steps by separating the greatest common factor first and then applying the reverse FOIL method. (See Chapter 3 for suggestions.)	Factors a trinomial in the form $ax^2 + bx + c$ by separating the GCF and then using reverse FOIL
20.1 Algebraic equations: showing relationships between algebraic expressions	6	7	8	An equation is a mathematical sentence that says that the expressions on each side of it are equal. Equations may have both constants and variables. A single variable in an equation will have a specific value that can be determined or solved for. When a specific value for the variable is substituted into an equation, it will make that equation either true or false. The total cost for an item ordered online equals the cost of the item (*n*) and a shipping charge of $5.00. If the total cost is $30.00, write an equation that can be used to determine the cost of the item. Could the item cost $10.00?	Identifies the constant and variables in an equation; substitutes a given value for a constant and proves the equation true or false for the value Writes an equation from a verbal problem that includes a variable and a constant
20.2 Inequalities: showing relationships between algebraic expressions	6	7	8	When we need to show a relationship between expressions that is not equal, we use an inequality sign to form an inequality. The different relationships are shown by the signs $(>, <, \geq, \leq, \neq)$. For inequalities, a variable may have more than one value. In the expression $(b - 2) < 7$, $(b - 2)$ could equal any number less than (5). The inequality $(6a > 3 + a)$ tells you that the expression $(6a)$ is greater than the expression $(3 + a)$.	Verbally interprets inequality expressions Identifies and gives illustrations of particular values or range of values represented by the expression Represents an inequality on a number line Translates verbal sentences into algebraic inequalities

* NOTE: A = Exploration, B = Concept Mastery, C = Algorithmic or Procedural Mastery

	Suggested Grade-Level Timing*				
Content Branch	A	B	C	**Embedded Concepts**	**Performance Indicators/Assessment Expectations**
Major/minor				*See corresponding domain numbers in Chapter 3 for further development and exemplar problems.*	
				We can also use these symbols to show that a variable may be equal to a range of numbers that are less or more than or equal to a given value. ($6b \le 30$) means that (b) could be any number less than or equal to (5).	
20.3 Equations: keeping both sides equal and the equation true	5	6	7	If we add the same quantity or subtract the same quantity to both sides of an equation, the sides are still equal or balanced. The equation is still true.	Explains and illustrates how to keep the equality or balance of an equation by adding or subtracting equal quantities on both sides; *proves that the equation is still true*
20.4 Solving simple equations by using number sense of an inverse operation (adding or subtracting)	5	6	7	If the equation shows subtraction, such as ($n - 6 = 12$), we can think backward or look at its inverse operation of addition. What number (n) would we have to start with to get 12 after we subtracted 6? We know that number is 18, so ($n = 18$). We can also do this by adding or subtracting a number from both sides. If the equation is $n + 6 = 16$, we can subtract 6 from both sides and isolate the variable. The result is the equation ($n = 10$). In the equation ($n - 6 = 12$), we can get to this number value by removing the −6 from one side (canceling the subtraction by adding 6) and also adding 6 to the other side.	Solves simple equations, using number sense of inverse operations Isolates the variable by adding or subtracting equal values from both sides and explains the algorithm in terms of inverse properties and proves it using a balance (see Chapter 3) Understands that a linear equation containing one variable will be true for just one value of the variable
20.5 Solving simple monomial equations by addition of additive inverse signed numbers (integers)	6	7	8	We need to isolate the variable to solve an equation. We can isolate the variable and solve the equation by adding the additive inverse (as a signed number) of any constant that is on the same side as the variable to both sides of the equation. This cancels the constant and isolates the variable. For the equation ($b - 12 = 9$), we can add (+12) to each side: ($b - 12 + 12$) = ($9 + 12$) and ($b = 23$).	Solves simple equations by isolating the variable; explains the algorithm in terms of addition of additive-inverse signed numbers and proves it using a balance (see Chapter 3) Proves solutions true by substituting for the variable

*NOTE: A = Exploration, B = Concept Mastery, C = Algorithmic or Procedural Mastery

(Continued)

Content Branch	Suggested Grade-Level Timing*			Embedded Concepts	Performance Indicators/Assessment Expectations
Major/minor	**A**	**B**	**C**	*See corresponding domain numbers in Chapter 3 for further development and exemplar problems.*	
20.6 Solving equations: combining like terms	6	7	8	You must combine like terms in order to solve the equation. $$2c + c - 28 + 4 = 12$$ $$3c - 24 = 12$$ $$3c = 36, c = 12$$	Solves equations that require combinations of like terms and explains how it is done
20.7 Solving simple equations: inverse multiplicative operations:				If an equation includes multiplication by a factor, we can isolate the variable by performing the inverse operation, which is the division by the same factor, on both sides of the equation so that they remain equal. $$6 \times n = 42$$ If you divide both sides by (6), you get $n = 7$.	Solves simple equations by isolating the variable; explains the solutions in terms of division as the inverse operation of multiplication and maintaining the equality by dividing by the same factor
Division of and by monomial	6	7	8	When there is more than one term, we isolate the variable by dividing all terms on both sides of the equation by the same factor (divisor). This keeps the sides equal. $$3n + 9 = 21$$ $$\frac{3n}{3} + \frac{9}{3} = \frac{21}{3} \quad \text{(Then } n + 3 = 7 \text{ and } n = 4\text{)}$$	Correct solution and explanation of equations that require division of both sides by the same factor: division of and by monomial; division of polynomial
Division of and by polynomial	7	8	9	$$3c(a + b) = 6(a + b) \text{ and } 3c\frac{a+b}{a+b} = 6\frac{a+b}{a+b} \text{ and } 3c = 6 \; c = 2$$	
20.8 Solving equations: two step and adding or subtracting coefficients	7	8	9	We can add the additive inverse of variables to both sides of the equation to help isolate the variable. If there are more than one same-term variables, we can combine them by just adding or subtracting the coefficients. Sometimes it is necessary to perform both the additive-inverse and multiplicative-inverse operation. $$7a - 16 = 3a + 4$$ $$7a - (3a) - 16 = 3a - (3a) + 4$$ $$4a - 16 (+16) = 4 + 16$$ $$4a = 20 \qquad a = 5$$	Solves equations that require adding additive inverses of constants and variables; explains and proves the algorithm in terms of inverse properties and substitution of calculated value Correct solution and explanation of equations that require two-step additive- and multiplicative-inverse operations

* NOTE: A = Exploration, B = Concept Mastery, C = Algorithmic or Procedural Mastery

Content Branch	A	B	C	Embedded Concepts	Performance Indicators/Assessment Expectations
Major/minor				*See corresponding domain numbers in Chapter 3 for further development and exemplar problems.*	
20.9 Solving equations: two related variables	7	8	9	We can solve an equation with two variables if we know of a relationship between them. The second variable is a function of the first. If you buy three pairs of socks for one price and another pair that costs twice as much and pay $10 for them, you can find the cost of the socks with this equation: $3x + 2x = 10$ or $5x = 10$ and $x = 2$. The cost of the cheaper pair is $2.00, and the other pair cost $4.00. We can find the value of two unequal numbers that we do not know if we know the difference between them and we know their sum. The relationship between the variables is the difference. If we subtract the difference between them from their sum, we are left with the sum of two equal values (see Chapter 3).	Writes an equation from a verbal problem that includes two related variables; solves the equation Analysis and solution of problems where two parts are unknown, but the difference between them and the whole is known
21.1 Solving equations: multiplying by the reciprocal	8	9	9	We can isolate the variable in an equation with a fraction by multiplying both sides of the equation by the reciprocal of the denominator and then canceling. $\dfrac{2a}{5} = 10$ $(\dfrac{2a}{5} \times \dfrac{5}{1} = 2a) = (10x\,\dfrac{5}{1} = 50)$ $2a = 50, a = 25$ See Chapter 3.	Correct solution and explanation of how equations with fractions can be solved by multiplying by the reciprocal
21.2 Solving two- and three-step equations by dividing all terms by the greatest common factor (GCF) as a first step	8	9	9	In the equation $12a + 36 = 84$, dividing all the terms by the (GCF) factor of 12 and then combining terms would solve the equation. $(12a \div 12) + (36 \div 12) = (84 \div 12)$, $a + 3 = 7, a = -4$ For the equation $2a^3 + 4a^2 - 4a = 12a$, both sides of the equation can be divided by $2a$ to get to the quadratic form: $a^2 + 2a - 2 = 6$ or $a^2 + 2a - 8 = 0$ See Chapter 3.	Correct solution and explanation of equations that require a first step of factoring by the GCF

Suggested Grade-Level Timing

*NOTE: A = Exploration, B = Concept Mastery, C = Algorithmic or Procedural Mastery

(Continued)

Content Branch	Suggested Grade-Level Timing*			Embedded Concepts	Performance Indicators/Assessment Expectations
Major/minor	A	B	C		
				See corresponding domain numbers in Chapter 3 for further development and exemplar problems.	
21.3 Equations with two variables	7	8	9	Equations with two variables (x and y) may have a set of possible solutions. Changing the value of one variable will change the value of the other. The solutions may be expressed as ordered pairs of x and y. A possible value of x is followed by the resulting value of y. The equation $2x + 3 = y$ could include the following ordered pairs in its solution set: 2, 7; 3, 9; 4, 1; –2, –1	Given a set of values for one variable, writes the solution set as ordered pairs Translates a real-world verbal problem into an equation with two variables Uses two variables and appropriate operations to write an expression, equation, or inequality
21.4 Solving inequalities	7	8	9	A linear equation containing one variable will be true for just one value of the variable, whereas a linear inequality will have an infinite solution set. You solve an inequality in the same way that you solve an equation by simplifying it and isolating the unknown quantity. The range of values for the solution set may be shown on a number line as an arrow pointing in the direction of its continuing values.	Solves inequalities, shows the solution as an inequality, and identifies the solution set on a number line Solves real-world inequality problems
21.5 Number patterns and series	7	8	9	Patterns such as number series that depend on a specific relationship between values may be expressed as equations. Number series may be either arithmetic or geometric.	Identifies and describes patterns from tables of ordered pairs and real life; represents them in algebraic form and extends them

ALGEBRA: FUNCTIONS, QUADRATICS, AND GRAPHING: 22. Functions/solving quadratic equations; 23. coordinate plane/graphing linear equations; 24. Slopes, intercepts, and quadratic equations
Vocabulary and Language: Function (domain and range), coordinate plane, ordered pair, quadrant, slope, x and y intercept, parabola

Content Branch	A	B	C	Embedded Concepts	Performance Indicators/Assessment Expectations
22.1 Function: defined as set of input and output values	6	7	8	A function is a relationship between two variables (x and y) in which for each value of x in a set, there is only one value of y in a second set. A change in the value of x results in a related change in the value of y. We sometimes relate to the function value sets as input and output.	Writes an equation from a verbal problem that includes two variables that represent a function; represents the values as a table of inputs and outputs Proves that a relationship or set of inputs and outputs is a function
Domain and range of function	7	8	9	The set of inputs or values of x that satisfy the function is called the *domain* of the function, and the outputs or values of y are called the *range* of the function.	Describes a function in terms of its domain and range

* NOTE: A = Exploration, B = Concept Mastery, C = Algorithmic or Procedural Mastery

Content Branch	Suggested Grade-Level Timing*			Embedded Concepts	Performance Indicators/Assessment Expectations
	A	B	C		
Major/minor					*See corresponding domain numbers in Chapter 3 for further development and exemplar problems.*
22.2 Functions: forms and applications	7	8	9	Functions may be written in the following forms: $y = x + b$ or $f(x) = x + b$. $f(x)$ is substituted for y because the value of y is a function of the value of x.	Writes an equation in function form from a verbal problem; applies function form to problems involving rate of change/distance, tax, discount, and simple interest problems Given a change in the value of x in a function, computes the new value of y
22.3 Function: linear	7	8	9	A function in the form $f(x) = mx + b$ is a linear function.	Identifies linear function form Given a verbal function description, writes a function in algebraic form
22.4 Quadratic equation: defined	8	9	9	A quadratic equation must have one term where the greatest power of the variable is 2. The general form of a quadratic equation is $y = ax^2 + bx + c$, where (b) and (c) are constants. Quadratic equations can represent relationships where the square of a variable is related to another variable. For example, the area of a square is related to the square of the measure of a single side of the square. $y = x^2$, where x equals the measure of the side. If you increase the measure of a side by 2, the equation that describes the relationship is $y = (x + 2)^2$ or $y = x^2 + 4x + 4$ and an example of a quadratic equation in general form.	Identifies a quadratic equation; explains how a quadratic equation differs from a linear equation
22.5 Quadratic functions	8	9	9	An equation in the form of $(y = ax^2 + bx + c)$ is a quadratic function. Because the value of (y) is a function of the value of (x), we can substitute (y) with the term $f(x)$, and thus $f(x) = ax^2 + bx + c$. We can also reverse the substitution and name $f(x)$ as another variable (y).	Recognizes the nonlinear relationship of a quadratic function Expresses and explains quadratic functions in alternate $f(x) =$ and $y =$ forms
22.6 Solving quadratic equations	8	9	9	A quadratic equation in standard form can be solved for two roots or possible values for the variables x and y. Possible values are determined by substituting a zero for the value of y, $ax^2 + bx + c = 0$, and factoring the trinomial. One of	Solves quadratic equations by reverse FOIL method and explanation of possible root values in terms of the zero multiplication principle

*NOTE: A = Exploration, B = Concept Mastery, C = Algorithmic or Procedural Mastery

(Continued)

Content Branch	Suggested Grade-Level Timing*			Embedded Concepts	Performance Indicators/Assessment Expectations
	A	B	C		
Major/minor				*See corresponding domain numbers in Chapter 3 for further development and exemplar problems.*	
				the two binomial factors must be equal to zero, so each factor can be separately solved for the two possible values of the variable (x) or roots of the equation.	Proves the root of a quadratic equation to be true by substitution Represents the roots in graphic form (see Numbers 24.5–24.6)
22.7 Quadratic equations: applied to problems	8	9	9	Standard-form quadratic equations can have two roots that represent possible solutions to the value of the variable. We can prove that a root is a true solution to the equation by substituting the root value. Sometimes, one root may be eliminated as a solution to a problem because it is impossible for the problem. For example, a negative value makes no sense for the measure of the side of a plot of land.	Writes a quadratic equation from a problem and solves it Evaluates the roots as true for the equation and problem
22.8 Quadratic equations: difference between two perfect squares	9	9	9	If we set the difference between two squares as an equation $(x^2 - 16) = 0$ and factor the binomial into $(x + 4)(x - 4) = 0$, we reach the roots of $x = +4$ or -4. We find the same possible solutions by shifting the value of the constant to form the equation $x^2 = 16$ and finding the square roots of both sides of the equation; $x = +4$ or -4.	Solves quadratic equations that show the difference between two perfect squares; proves the algorithm by example
23.1 Coordinate plane	5	6	7	A coordinate plane consists of two perpendicular reference lines intersecting at one point or origin and equally measured spaces from the reference lines that form a grid. The grid locates specific points in the plane. The location or value of the points is shown as *ordered pairs of* digits. The first digit shows the distance from the vertical line (y-axis) and is the value of the x coordinate. The second digit is the distance from the horizontal line (the x-axis) and is the value of the y coordinate. Lines connecting the points form graphs on the coordinate plane that show how two variables are related—for example, how a variable changes over time.	Locates points on a grid from an ordered pair of coordinates Writes the ordered pair location for a given point on a grid Translates data tables showing two related variables into coordinates and line graphs

* NOTE: A = Exploration, B = Concept Mastery, C = Algorithmic or Procedural Mastery

Content Branch	Suggested Grade-Level Timing*			Embedded Concepts	Performance Indicators/Assessment Expectations
	A	B	C		
Major/minor				*See corresponding domain numbers in Chapter 3 for further development and exemplar problems.*	
23.2 Coordinate plane: quadrants	6	7	8	The coordinate plane can show both positive and negative values of the variables. The plane is divided into four quadrants that are numbered in a counterclockwise order. Quadrant I is where a (positive x, and positive y) point is located. Quadrant II is where a (negative x, positive y) point is found. Quadrant III is where a (negative x, negative y) point is located. Quadrant IV is where a (positive x, negative y) point is located.	Locates the quadrant of a point given the coordinates; draws a graph of a line with positive and negative values
23.3 The coordinate plane as a map	6	7	8	The coordinate plane can also be used as a map from a point of origin with the x-axis representing east and west intervals and the y-axis north and south intervals. The horizontal and vertical straight-line distance between points is the difference between the matching coordinates.	Calculates straight-line map distances on the coordinate plane
Diagonal distance between two points	7	8	9	The diagonal distance between two points can be determined using the Pythagorean theorem or the distance formula.	Calculates shortest (diagonal) distance between two points on the plane
23.4 Using coordinates to locate points on the graph of a linear equation	7	8	9	The ordered pairs of the possible solutions of a linear equation with two variables in the form $y = mx + b$ may be represented in table or graph form. The ordered pairs represent points in the coordinate plane because every value of x determines a specific value of y. The points may be connected to form a line. A graph of a linear equation forms a straight line.	Translates a table of ordered pairs that represent possible values of x and y in a linear equation to graphic form on the coordinate plane; explains how the graph was constructed
23.5 Defining and graphing linear equations	7	8	9	A linear equation is one whose graph is a straight line. It can be represented in the form $y = mx + b$. The terms (m) and (b) are constant values. Additional solutions may be determined by extending the line on the graph. A linear equation only has variables to the power of 1.	Recognizes the linear equation form Reorders equations to the linear form Constructs a graph of a given equation and determines whether it is linear

Content Branch	Suggested Grade-Level Timing*			Embedded Concepts	Performance Indicators/Assessment Expectations
Major/minor	A	B	C	See corresponding domain numbers in Chapter 3 for further development and exemplar problems.	
23.6 Extending solution sets by extending the graph of a linear equation	8	9	9	Since only two points are needed to form a straight line, the solution set of a linear equation can be extended from a set of only two ordered pairs that represent possible solutions. The line is extended and passes through all the possible points that represent the set.	Extends the graph of a linear equation and identifies additional ordered pairs of coordinates from the graph
23.7 Horizontal and vertical lines	8	9	10	Horizontal and vertical line equations have only one variable. A graph of a vertical line does not cross the y-axis and has a constant value of x. The equation for a horizontal straight line s simply the unchanging value of y —for example, (y = 3). The equation for a vertical line is the unchanging value of x (x = 3). The equation is represented by a vertical line in Quadrants I and IV. A graph of a horizontal line does not cross the x-axis and has a constant value of y. The equation y = 3 is represented by a horizontal line in Quadrants I and II.	Identifies the form of a single-variable equation as a horizontal or vertical line and, given the line, writes the equation
24.1 The slope of a straight line: defined Graphed in the coordinate plane	8	9	9	The relationship between the variables in a linear function is the slope of the line. Slope is defined as the change in y over (or divided by) the change in x. The rate of change is a constant. If y (the numerator) changes very quickly compared to x, the slope is greater. The slope is like the steepness of a hill or staircase. The faster the rise (value of y) compared to the run (value of x), the steeper the hill. The slope can be determined from the graph of the line or from a table of ordered pairs by finding the difference between two values of y and two values of x. $$\text{Slope} = \frac{y_2 + y_1}{x_2 - x_1}$$	Explains the meaning of slope as a constant that describes the relationship between x and y, and as the change in y over (or divided by) the change in x; determines the slope of a line from a graph

* NOTE: A = Exploration, B = Concept Mastery, C = Algorithmic or Procedural Mastery

| Content Branch | Suggested Grade-Level Timing* | | | Embedded Concepts | Performance Indicators/Assessment Expectations |
	A	B	C		
Major/minor				*See corresponding domain numbers in Chapter 3 for further development and exemplar problems.*	
24.2 Graph of linear function	8	9	9	If we write a linear function in the form of $f(x) = mx + b$ or as the equation $y = mx + b$, the coefficient of $x(m)$ will be equal to the slope of the graphed line, and b will be equal to the y intercept or the y coordinate of the point where the line crosses the y-axis.	Creates a graph given a description or an expression for a situation involving a linear relationship; determines the equation of a line given the slope and the y intercept; determines the equation from a graph of the line
24.3 x and y intercepts	8	9	9	The y intercept of the graph of a straight line in the coordinate plane is the value of y where the line crosses the y-axis ($x = 0$). The x intercept is the value of x where the line crosses the x-axis ($y = 0$).	Identifies x and y intercepts from graphs and equations
24.4 Horizontal and vertical lines: slopes	8	9	9	The equation for a horizontal straight line is simply the unchanging value of y—for example, ($y = 4$). The equation for a vertical line is the unchanging value of $x(x = 5)$. A horizontal line has a slope of zero (there is zero change in y and zero divided by any number is still zero). A vertical line has no slope (the change in x is zero, and any number divided by zero is undefined).	Identifies the equations of horizontal and vertical lines and writes them from a graphic representation Describes the slope of horizontal and vertical lines; relates the concept to graphic form and the definition of slope
24.5 Graph of a quadratic function	8	9	9	The graph of a quadratic function is a nonlinear open curve called a parabola. When the parabola crosses the x-axis at two points, the intersect points are two roots of the equation. The parabola may intersect only once or not at all. If it intersects once, it meets the x-axis at its vertex. If it does not cross the x-axis, the roots of the equation of the function are imaginary numbers.	Identifies a graph of a quadratic function Identifies roots of the equation from the graph Explains the lack of intersect in terms of imaginary numbers
24.6 Graph forms of quadratic functions	8	9	9	The parabola of a graph of a quadratic function may face in different directions. When the coefficient of x^2 in the general equation $y = -x^2 + mx + b$ is negative, the parabola will face downward with its vertex on top.	Identifies sign of coefficient of x^2 in the general equation for a downward-facing graph; predicts position of graph from equation

(Continued)

Content Branch	Suggested Grade-Level Timing*			Embedded Concepts	Performance Indicators/Assessment Expectations
	A	B	C		
Major/minor				*See corresponding domain numbers in Chapter 3 for further development and exemplar problems.*	

MEASUREMENT: 25. Forms, equivalents, standards, general applications for measures of length; 26. equivalent conversions/within and across standards; 27. mass/weight, density, capacity, volume, time; 28. money, temperature, time
Language Check: Inch (in), foot (ft), yard (yd), centimeter (cm), meter (m), liter (l), millimeter (mm), gram (g), milligram (mg), kilogram (kg), customary system, metric system, significant figures, longitude

Content Branch	A	B	C	Embedded Concepts	Performance Indicators/Assessment Expectations
25.1 Standards of measure	5	6	7	Measurement standards help us communicate quantitative properties. They are decided by governments or informal human consensus. Government standards are based on carefully maintained representations of the measures. Different governments have different systems of measures. The U.S. customary system differs from the metric system used in much of the rest of the world.	Names, explains, and gives examples of measurement standards; explains why they are necessary
25.2 Customary standards of linear measure	5	6	7	The customary units of the length of lines (or distance between points) are the inch, foot, yard, and mile. The multiples of the units within the customary system are usually based on their utility for the measurement process and containment of factors. The foot is divided into 12 inches because the number 12 has factors of 1, 2, 3, 4, 6, and 12. There are 36 inches in the 3 feet of a yard. The number (36) has factors of 1, 2, 3, 4, 6, 9, 12, 18, and 36. Three inches are therefore exactly $\frac{1}{4}$ of a foot and $\frac{1}{12}$ of a yard.	Automatizes the equivalent units of customary units of length; explains the use of multiples of 12 and 36
25.3 Metric standards of measure	5	6	7	The advantage to the metric system is its relationship to the place value system and the consistent vocabulary for unit subdivisions. The prefixes describe the sizes. A decimeter is one tenth of the meter, a centimeter is one hundredth, and a millimeter one thousandth. The same prefixes apply to the gram and liter. The kilometer is 1,000 meters, and the kilogram is 1,000 grams.	Automatizes the equivalent units of metric units of length; explains the use of prefixes and the relationship to place value

* NOTE: A = Exploration, B = Concept Mastery, C = Algorithmic or Procedural Mastery

	Content Branch	Suggested Grade-Level Timing*			Embedded Concepts	Performance Indicators/Assessment Expectations
		A	B	C		
	Major/minor				See corresponding domain numbers in Chapter 3 for further development and exemplar problems.	
25.4	Accuracy and precision in measurement	5	6	7	Measures are sometimes not precise. The accuracy of measures is dependent on the measurement instrument and the recorder of the measures. The necessary precision in measurement depends on what is being measured. The weight of a truck of garbage demands less precision than the size of a needle hole or the eye of an insect. The smaller the unit, the greater the need for precision. Measurement instruments with smaller units are used to measure more precise quantities.	Explains the limitations of measure and instruments; explains the applications of smaller and larger units to the size of the object measured
25.5	Significant digits	7	8	9	Significant digits represent actual measures. All the digits in positive integers except zeros between the actual measured digit and the decimal point (the placeholders) are considered significant. All decimal digits except zeros used as placeholders that precede them are significant. Zeros following the decimal digit are also significant. If the length is reported as 230.050 meters, only the last zero representing zero hundred thousandths of a meter and the nonzero digits are significant.	Explains the meaning and applications of significant digits; denotes significant digits in measures that include zeros and decimal places
25.6	Within customary standard unit conversions	6	7	8	When converting larger units into smaller ones, there will be more of the smaller ones. You therefore multiply by the equivalent. When converting smaller sized units into larger ones, there will always be a fewer number of larger ones. You therefore divide by the standard equivalent. Remainders are the smaller unit. We can use function equations: If $y = $ # of oz and $x = $ # of lbs, then $y = 16x$, and $x = y \div 16$.	Explains conversion generalization; applies the generalization of conversions between customary units
25.7	Within standard metric conversions	6	7	8	Metric conversions can be made by multiplying or dividing by the multiple of 10 that represents the unit relationship. Remainders are the smaller unit. 1 kg = 1,000 g, therefore 2 kg = 2,000 g, 2.2 kg = 2,200 g, 2,002 g = 2.002 kg	*Explains conversion generalization; converts metric measurements from smaller to larger and larger to smaller units*

* NOTE: A = Exploration, B = Concept Mastery, C = Algorithmic or Procedural Mastery

(Continued)

| Content Branch | Suggested Grade-Level Timing* | | | Embedded Concepts | Performance Indicators/Assessment Expectations |
	A	B	C		
Major/minor				*See corresponding domain numbers in Chapter 3 for further development and exemplar problems.*	
26.1 Equivalent measures: estimates across common systems	6	7	8	A meter is a little more than 3 feet. There are about 2½ cm in an inch and a little more than 2 km in a mile. A kg is a little more than 2.2 lbs. One ounce equals about 28 g.	*Estimates* metric and customary equivalents
26.2 Cross-standard conversions Single units	6	7	8	Conversions of equivalent measures across standards are based on calculated tables of unit equalities. For example, a single kilogram is equal to about 2.2 pounds. We can use proportions and function equations to make the conversions. A shortcut for making approximate conversions from one standard unit to another is to multiply the number of the larger units by the cross-standard equivalent of smaller units for a single larger unit. The single-unit equivalent of the kilogram is approximately 2.2 pounds. Therefore, 5 kilograms would equal about 5 × 2.2 pounds.	Makes simple single-unit conversions from the larger to smaller unit
26.3 Conversions between different standard systems Multiple units	7	8	9	A kg is a little more than 2.2 lbs $\left(\frac{2.2\,\text{lbs}}{1\text{kg}}\right)$. We can use proportions to convert across standard systems by comparing a measured quantity to the unit rate. A customary scale measured the weight of the baby as 8.8 lbs. How many kilograms did the baby weigh? $\frac{22}{2} = \frac{88}{x}$　　$x = 4$ kg	Correct *estimations* from metric to customary standards and exact across standard system conversions with and without a calculator
27.1 Mass/weight: defined	5	6	7	Mass is a measure of the amount of matter in an object. Gravity exerts a force on mass that varies directly with the amount of mass. The force of gravity increases with mass. We measure mass by measuring the force of gravity on the mass. This force is weight.	Defines mass in terms of the amount of matter and the effect of gravity

* NOTE: A = Exploration, B = Concept Mastery, C = Algorithmic or Procedural Mastery

	Content Branch	Suggested Grade-Level Timing*			Embedded Concepts	Performance Indicators/Assessment Expectations
		A	B	C		
	Major/minor				*See corresponding domain numbers in Chapter 3 for further development and exemplar problems.*	
27.2	Mass/weight: measures	6	7	8	We measure mass by balancing an unknown mass with the standard measure determined by the government. The standard of measure for mass is the pound (lb) or kilogram (kg). One pound or kilogram is equal to the force of gravity on the matter in the government's standard sample for that amount.	Names standard and abbreviation for mass; estimates weight of common objects based on pound or kilogram standard; compares pound and kilogram as an inequality
27.3	Mass/weight differences	6	7	8	The measures of mass and weight are used interchangeably even though they have different meanings because our standards for mass are based on their weight on Earth. The mass of objects stays the same in space, but weight varies with gravity (see Chapter 3).	Explains weight differences due to force of gravity; recognition of mass as unaffected by gravity
27.4	Measuring mass in ounces and pounds, grams, kilograms	5	6	7	When using a balance scale, we balance the unknown quantity with a known on a fulcrum. These can then be used on a simple balance. Spring scales measure weight based on the pull on a spring and a scale that measures the pull. They are easier to use but may not be as accurate as a balance.	Estimates and orders measured masses; *proves* measures with the balance; predicts relative give of spring for different standard weights; accurate use of the balance and spring scale
27.5	Equivalent standard conversions: oz ↔ lbs ↔ tons kg ↔ g ↔ mg	6	7	8	Standard units can be combined into larger units. The equivalent heavier units are better for measuring heavier objects. 1 lb = 16 oz, 1 ton = 2,000 lbs, 1 kg = 1,000 g	Makes exact correct equivalent conversions from grams to kilograms or ounces to pounds using equations and solves problems that require it
27.6	Density	7	8	9	Density is the amount of matter for a given volume. It is based on the mass of the matter in one cubic centimeter. Water has a density of 1.0 or one gram per cubic centimeter (1 g/cc). The closer the molecules are, the greater the density. Gases have a lesser density than liquids or solids.	Describes density in terms of the amount of mass in a given volume

* NOTE: A = Exploration, B = Concept Mastery, C = Algorithmic or Procedural Mastery

(Continued)

	Content Branch	Suggested Grade-Level Timing*			Embedded Concepts	Performance Indicators/Assessment Expectations
		A	B	C		
	Major/minor				*See corresponding domain numbers in Chapter 3 for further development and exemplar problems.*	
27.7	Capacity/volume	5	6	7	Although capacity and volume are related, they use different measures. Volume is applied to solid objects that have firm and measurable dimensions. Capacity is applied to liquids and small grains that assume the shape of their containers. It follows, therefore, that we measure capacity by filling a standard measure and not with a ruler.	Distinguishes between capacity and volume; provides physical examples
27.8	Capacity: measures	6	7	8	Equations describe conversions: 1 cup = 16 fluid ounces, 2 cups = 1 pint, 4 quarts = 1 gallon, 2 pints = 1 quart = 4 half pints, 2 quarts = 1 half gallon, 1 liter = 1,000 ml A quart is just a little less than a liter. A half-gallon or 2-quart milk container is slightly less than a 2-liter soda.	Uses equations to convert units within systems. Estimate only for across standards conversions or use a calculator
27.9	Money: Cross-standard references	6	7	8	Different countries use different money standards; exchange rates vary from day to day. The euro is the common standard unit used in most of Europe.	Uses equations with proportions to convert euros to dollars and vice versa based on current exchange rate, with and without calculator
	Cross-standard conversions	7	8	9	We can use proportions to find the values we need to know using the current rates.	
28.1	Time: relative to rotation of the Earth	5	6	7	Because the Earth rotates, the standard time of day is different at different places on the Earth. Since the Earth rotates toward the east, places to the west are behind in the time of day as compared to places to their east. We lose time when we travel to the east faster than the Earth moves. It takes the Earth about 365¼ days to rotate around the sun, so every four years we add an additional day.	Explains the variations in time around the world Explains why there are changes in standard time as the Earth rotates

* NOTE: A = Exploration, B = Concept Mastery, C = Algorithmic or Procedural Mastery

	Content Branch	Suggested Grade-Level Timing*			Embedded Concepts	Performance Indicators/Assessment Expectations
		A	B	C		
	Major/minor				See corresponding domain numbers in Chapter 3 for further development and exemplar problems.	
28.2	Time: zones and dates	6	7	8	Standards of time depend on the lines of longitude that are drawn from the North to South Pole. There is a 15° difference between each line, and the space between defines a different time zone. When it is midnight at one point on Earth, the place on the completely opposite side, or 180° of longitude away, is at noon. The actual distance between each line varies, with the greatest distance at the equator and the least at the poles. A new date begins at midnight at the international date line (180° longitude), which is directly opposite the meridian of Greenwich in England at 0° of longitude.	Computes the standard time of day in a different zone when given the time in a specific zone and the zone difference and direction; computes differences in time when given longitude differences
28.3	Time: daylight saving time	6	7	8	Because the Earth is tilted on its axis, and the hours of daylight change, we change the clocks at different times of the year to add more daylight hours.	Explains shifts in time decided by governments such as daylight saving time
28.4	Temperature: comparing Fahrenheit/ Celsius readings	6	7	8	Standard units of measure for temperature are degrees Fahrenheit (F) or Celsius (C). Water freezes at 32°F (0°C) and boils at 212°F (100°C). Room temperature is about 70°F (21°C). Each degree Fahrenheit is about 5/9 of a degree Celsius. Each degree Celsius is 9/5 of a degree Fahrenheit.	Reads and records temperature from a thermometer to the nearest degree and has automatized the common temperatures (freezing , boiling, room); calculates temperature differences, including difference between negative and positive values Estimates seasonal averages, as well as conversions between systems, and uses a calculator for exact conversions

* NOTE: A = Exploration, B = Concept Mastery, C = Algorithmic or Procedural Mastery

(Continued)

Content Branch	Suggested Grade-Level Timing*			Embedded Concepts	Performance Indicators/Assessment Expectations
Major/minor	A	B	C	**GEOMETRY: 29.** Definitions and relationships of lines, curves, planes; 30–31. angles (definitions, construction of special angles and relationships); 32. two-dimensional figures, congruence, polygons, quadrilateral subsets; 33. triangles (definitions and construction); 34. circles (definitions and construction); 35. measures of area of two-dimensional spaces; 36. three-dimensional objects (definitions, volume, and surface area); 37. symmetry, transformations; 38. similarity, proof of congruence, similarity, algebraic applications, and symbolic representations **Vocabulary and Language:** Horizontal, vertical, perpendicular, collinear, polygon (and derivatives such as hexagon), simple curve, closed curve, symmetry, bilateral, radial, transform, flip, rotation, slide, congruent, plane, angle, vertex, circumference, radius, diameter, bisector, midpoint	*See corresponding domain numbers in Chapter 3 for further development and exemplar problems.*
29.1 Terms: defined and undefined	6	7	8	Mathematicians do not always agree on the exact definitions of some terms such as *point, line, curve,* and *plane,* and so they are classified as undefined. We can, however, use common meanings that help us understand and describe them.	Explains why some geometric terms are classified as undefined
29.2 Terms: point, line, collinear	5 6	6 7	7 8	A *point* is a particular location in space. A *line* is determined by connected points that follow a straight path and go on infinitely (endlessly) in only two opposite (mirror image) directions. A line can be determined by any two points. We can show that it goes on endlessly by drawing arrows in its continuing direction. Points on the same line are collinear.	Describes points and lines; constructs a line from two given points / Draws arrows to show that the line extends beyond the points / Correctly identifies collinear points
29.3 Terms: line segment, ray	6	7	8	A *ray* is the part of the line that is going in one direction from one point on the line. The point where it begins is the endpoint. A *line segment* is part of a line between two particular points. It includes all the points in between the two particular ones.	Defines and constructs line segments, rays
29.4 Terms: horizontal vertical, perpendicular lines	5	6	7	Horizontal lines are like the horizon—they go from left to right or right to left. Vertical lines go up and down from the horizon. When two lines meet and form a right angle (see below), we say the lines are *perpendicular.*	Constructs horizontal, vertical, and perpendicular lines; identifies them in the environment and makes connections to architecture

* NOTE: A = Exploration, B = Concept Mastery, C = Algorithmic or Procedural Mastery

Content Branch Major/minor	Suggested Grade-Level Timing*			Embedded Concepts	Performance Indicators/Assessment Expectations
	A	B	C		
				See corresponding domain numbers in Chapter 3 for further development and exemplar problems.	
29.5 Symbolic notation	6	7	8	The symbol for a line is a notation of two points with a double-pointed arrow pointed in $\overleftrightarrow{AB}$. A ray is denoted with an overbar of a single arrow pointed in the direction in which it continues: $\overrightarrow{AB}$. The symbolic notation for a line segment is $\overline{AB}$.	Identifies a line, ray, and line segment from its notation; uses the notation in explanations and equations
29.6 Lines: intersecting and parallel	5	6	7	When two lines meet, the point at which they meet is the intersection, and the lines are *intersecting lines.* *Parallel lines* are two separate lines that go in the same directions in the same plane and never cross (intersect).	Explains and draws intersecting lines; relates the term to common uses such as "traffic intersection" Construction and identification of parallel lines, parallelograms
29.7 Terms: midpoint, perpendicular bisector	6	7	8	The midpoint of a line segment is the point halfway from either point of the segment. The midpoint of a line segment can be located by drawing two equal arcs—one from each point—and then drawing a second line between the intersections of the arcs. The second line will be the perpendicular bisector of the first line and intersects it at the midpoint.	Locates the midpoint of a line using a compass
29.8 Term: curve	5	6	7	A curve is determined by connected points that do not follow a straight path. If the first and last points are connected to each other, it is a closed curve. If the path of the points does not cross over itself, it is a simple curve. A circle is a closed curve.	Describes a curve and distinguishes between open and closed curves
29.9 Term: plane	5	6	7	A *plane* is a surface determined by three points on that surface that are not on the same straight line. A line between any two points on the determined plane will be on that surface. A tabletop is often thought of as a plane surface, but the plane on which it lies goes on infinitely. The legs of the table are on different planes.	Determines whether a surface is a single plane; identification of different planes in three-dimensional objects
Parallel plane	6	7	8	*Parallel planes* are two separate planes that never intersect.	Identification in models and construction of models of parallel planes

(Continued)

NOTE: A = Exploration, B = Concept Mastery, C = Algorithmic or Procedural Mastery

* NOTE: A = Exploration, B = Concept Mastery, C = Algorithmic or Procedural Mastery

Content Branch	Suggested Grade-Level Timing* A	B	C	Embedded Concepts	Performance Indicators/Assessment Expectations
Major/minor				*See corresponding domain numbers in Chapter 3 for further development and exemplar problems.*	
30.1 Definition: angles	5	6	7	When two rays come from the same endpoint, they form an *angle*. That common endpoint is called the vertex. The rays are the *sides* of the angle. The larger the opening between the rays, the larger the angle. Larger angles will have a greater difference between the rays than smaller angles at the same distance from their endpoint. The size of the angle determines the direction from the endpoint.	Demonstrates and explains variations in angle size and relates them to differences in direction from an endpoint; draws or constructs and compares smaller and larger angles using a protractor and compass
30.2 Adjacent angles	6	7	8	When two angles share a vertex (come from the same endpoint), they are called adjacent angles. Adjacent angles have a common side.	Explains and illustrates use of term; makes connection to use of term in everyday language (e.g., "The fence was shared by the adjacent homes.")
30.3 Measures of angles	5	6	7	If you rotate a duplicate of a ray away from the original, you form angles of increasing size. The more you rotate, the larger the angle. If you keep rotating to return to where you started, every point on the ray has described a circle. The measure of an angle is the same as the part of the circle the ray has described. We therefore measure the size of angles or the opening between the rays in degrees like a circle. The higher the number of degrees, the greater the distance between the rays.	Demonstrates angle formation by physical rotation of a straight edge while compared to a baseline; compares relative size of angles
30.4 Measures of circles and angles	6	7	8	Measures of angles and circles are related. The standard decided by mathematicians for the total rotation of a ray to form a circle is 360 units, called degrees. A symbol for the unit (°) is used for both angles and circles (360°). The number 360 has many factors, which makes it easy to describe fractional parts of a circle. The total measure of a circle is 360°. A half circle (semicircle) is 180°. A quarter circle is 90°. The largest angle can be any measure less than 360°.	Makes the *connections* between the measures of angles and circles by drawing and explaining; identifies degrees in full circle, semicircle, quarter circle *Connects* the structure of circles to their radial symmetry and makes transformations of circles

* NOTE: A = Exploration, B = Concept Mastery, C = Algorithmic or Procedural Mastery

Content Branch		Suggested Grade-Level Timing*			Embedded Concepts	Performance Indicators/Assessment Expectations
		A	B	C		
Major/minor					*See corresponding domain numbers in Chapter 3 for further development and exemplar problems.*	
30.5	Straight angles: measuring angles with protractors	6	7	8	If you rotate a ray halfway around to form a semicircle, the duplicate ray and the original have formed a straight line or straight angle. It measures 180° or half the total distance of 360° that, when rotated, would form the circle. A protractor can be used to draw and measure the rotation and size of the angle (see Chapter 3).	Uses a protractor to draw and measure angles; draws congruent angles
30.6	Using compasses to construct circles	5	6	7	The compass allows you to draw a set of points all equally distant from the center, which forms a circle.	Uses a compass to construct a circle; uses a compass to construct and bisect an angle
	Construct and bisect angles	7	8	9	It can also be used to construct an angle and to divide an angle into two equal parts or bisect an angle.	
31.1	Special angles; right angles	6	7	8	A *straight angle* of 180° has two rays coming from one point in opposite directions. If we rotate one ray of the straight angle half of the way to 180°, the two rays are perpendicular and form an angle of 90°. The 90° angle is also called a *right angle.*	Identification of straight and right angles; makes right angle transformations; Draws and measures right and straight angles
31.2	Acute and obtuse angles	6	7	8	An angle that measures more than 0° and less than 90° is an acute angle, and an angle that measures more than 90° but less than 180° is an obtuse angle.	Identification of acute and obtuse right angles; draws and measures acute and obtuse angles
31.3	Supplementary angles	6	7	8	Two angles that form a straight angle or add up to 180° are supplementary angles.	Identification of supplementary angles; computation of unknown measure of the supplement of a known angle
31.4	Complementary angles	6	7	8	Two angles that form a right angle or add up to 90° are complementary angles.	Identification of complementary angles; computation of unknown measure of the complement of a known angle

* NOTE: A = Exploration, B = Concept Mastery, C = Algorithmic or Procedural Mastery

(Continued)

Content Branch	Suggested Grade-Level Timing*			Embedded Concepts	Performance Indicators/Assessment Expectations
	A	B	C		
Major/minor				See corresponding domain numbers in Chapter 3 for further development and exemplar problems.	
31.5 Vertical angles	6	7	8	The two opposite angles formed by intersecting lines are called vertical angles. They are congruent.	Explanation and illustration of use of term Identifies vertical angles in figures and solves problems that seek the size of an angle that is vertical to a known angle
32.1 Congruent: use of term	5	6	7	When figures are the same size and shape, they are called congruent. Individual sides or angles may also be congruent. We use the term congruent instead of equal because congruent figures may be in different positions on a surface or in space.	Explanation and illustration of use of the term congruent
32.2 Definitions: polygons	6	7	8	Polygons are two-dimensional closed figures on a surface. They are formed by connected line segments, which form the sides and angles at the connections. Polygons have different numbers of segments (sides) and different angles. Polygons with all congruent sides and angles are called regular polygons.	Describes and draws a polygon; identifies number of sides and angles Distinguishes a regular polygon
32.3 Definitions: triangle, square, rectangle, pentagon, hexagon, heptagon, octagon, nonagon	6 7	7 8	8 8	Polygon names are derived from their properties. Different combinations of them can form different patterns and figures. Familiar items in the environment are named after polygons (e.g., Pentagon building).	Identifies shapes on paper and in the environment, finds patterns, reproduces shapes; explains prefix-suffix meanings
32.4 Definitions: quadrilaterals: sets and subsets; parallelogram, rhombus, square, rectangle	6	7	8	Polygons with four straight-line sides are quadrilaterals. If the sides are all congruent, the quadrilateral is a rhombus. If the figure has two pairs of opposite parallel sides, it is a parallelogram. If it has only two opposite parallel sides, it is a trapezoid. If it is a parallelogram with four right angles, it is a rectangle. A square has four right angles, four equal sides, and two pairs of opposite parallel sides. Therefore, it is a quadrilateral, a rectangle, a rhombus, and a parallelogram.	Distinguishes between and explains the differences and similarities of the sets and subsets of quadrilaterals

* NOTE: A = Exploration, B = Concept Mastery, C = Algorithmic or Procedural Mastery

Content Branch	Suggested Grade-Level Timing*			Embedded Concepts	Performance Indicators/Assessment Expectations
Major/minor	A	B	C		
				See corresponding domain numbers in Chapter 3 for further development and exemplar problems.	
32.5 Polygons: total measure of angles	7	8	9	There is a pattern between the total number of sides of a polygon and the total measure of the interior angles. The total measure of the angles is equal to $(n - 2) \times 180°$, where (n) = the number of sides (see Chapter 3 for proof).	Computes the total measure of the angles of a polygon from the number of sides; proves the formula
32.6 Parallelogram	6	7	8	The parallelogram has two pairs of opposite sides that are parallel. Although any side can be considered the base, it is usually the bottom of the figure. The altitude (height) of the parallelogram is the right-angled distance (it must be perpendicular to the base) between the base and the opposite side.	Describes and draws different parallelograms; identifies and draws the altitude (height) Explains the use of the term *base*
33.1 Definitions: triangle altitude, and base	5	6	7	A triangle is a polygon with three sides and three angles. Any side can be considered the base of the triangle (usually it is the side on the bottom). The height or altitude of the triangle is the distance from the vertex of the angle opposite the base to the base (the line of distance must be perpendicular to the base).	Describes and draws different triangles; identifies and draws the altitude (height); explains the use of the term *base* Computes the measure of an unknown angle in a triangle given the measures of each of the others or the sum of the others
Angle total	6	7	8	The total measure of the angles of a triangle is equal to 180°.	
33.2 Classifying triangles: right, obtuse, acute, scalene equilateral, isosceles				Triangles are classified according to the congruence of their sides and the types of angles. The classifications or names can overlap. A right triangle can also be an isosceles triangle, and an equilateral triangle is also an isosceles triangle.	Identifies, describes, and draws different triangle forms
33.3 Equilateral triangle	6	7	8	An equilateral triangle has three congruent sides and angles. Each angle, therefore, measures 60°.	Identifies and draws an equilateral triangle
33.4 Isosceles triangle	6	7	8	An isosceles triangle has at least two congruent sides.	Identifies and draws an isosceles triangle

(Continued)

* NOTE: A = Exploration, B = Concept Mastery, C = Algorithmic or Procedural Mastery

Content Branch	Suggested Grade-Level Timing*			Embedded Concepts	Performance Indicators/Assessment Expectations
Major/minor	A	B	C		
				See corresponding domain numbers in Chapter 3 for further development and exemplar problems.	
33.5 Angles and sides: proportions and equalities	6	7	8	The angles and sides of a triangle are in proportion to each other. The largest angle is opposite the largest side. In equilateral or isosceles triangles, the angles opposite the congruent sides are congruent.	Given measures of the sides and angles of a triangle, matches them in a figure drawing
33.6 Right triangle: unknown angles Naming sides	5 6	6 7	7 8	A right triangle has one angle that is a right or 90° angle. The other two angles, therefore, must add up to another 90°. The side opposite the right angle in a right triangle is called the hypotenuse and is always the largest side. A side opposite or e of the other angle is called the opposite side. The other side of the angle (not the hypotenuse) is called the adjacent side.	Identifies and draws a right triangle, computes the measure of an unknown angle in a right triangle given the measure of one other angle Names the sides
33.7 Right triangle: Pythagorean theorem	7	8	9	The proportional relationship between angles and sides of a triangle is very useful in determining unknown values such as the height of a tower without climbing it. The Pythagorean theorem tells us that for any right triangle, the square of the hypotenuse is equal to the sum of the squares of the other two sides. If a = hypotenuse and b and c are the other sides, then $a^2 = b^2 + c^2$. We can determine the measure of the sides of a right triangle using this formula.	Determines the measure of the unknown sides of a right triangle using the Pythagorean theorem and known sides
33.8 Right triangle: ratios between the sides	8	9	10	We can also determine the size of the angles other than the right angle using the ratio between the sides and the measures of the angle. The ratio of the opposite side of an angle to the hypotenuse is called the sine, and the ratio of the adjacent side of an angle to the hypotenuse is called the cosine. The ratio of the opposite side to the adjacent side is called the tangent. These ratios are functions of the size of the angle. If we know the sine, cosine, or	Determines measure of the unknown angles of a right triangle from known measures of sides; the ratios of sine, cosine, and tangent; and tables or calculators

* NOTE: A = Exploration, B = Concept Mastery, C = Algorithmic or Procedural Mastery

Content Branch	Suggested Grade-Level Timing*			Embedded Concepts	Performance Indicators/Assessment Expectations
	A	B	C		
Major/minor				*See corresponding domain numbers in Chapter 3 for further development and exemplar problems.*	
				tangent of an angle, we can determine the size of the angle, and if we know the size of the angle, we can determine the ratios. $\text{Sine} = \frac{opposite}{hypotenuse}$ and $\text{Cosine} = \frac{adjacent}{hypotenuse}$ $\text{Tangent} = \frac{opposite}{adjacent}$	
34.1 Circle definitions: center, closed curve, radius, diameter	5	6	7	A circle (closed curve) is a set of points in which all the points that form the circle are the same distance from a given point that is the *center* of the circle. The distance around the closed curve is the circumference of the circle. The distance from the center to any point on the curve is the radius, and the distance from any point on the circle through the center to the opposite point is the diameter. The length of the diameter is always twice the length of the radius.	Describes and compares circles using the terms *diameter, radius,* and *circumference*; draws the radius and diameter of a given circle; traces the circumference
34.2 Circle definitions: arc, central angle	6	7	8	An arc is part of a curve or part of the closed curve that is the circumference of a circle. Two points on the circumference identify two arcs, a major and minor arc. An angle whose vertex is at the center of a circle and whose sides are radii is a central angle. A central angle defines an arc.	Identifies an arc given two points Identifies and draws a central angle
34.3 Value of pi	6	7	8	If we measure the diameters and circumferences of several circles and look for the relationship between the measures, we discover that the circumference of a circle is always about 3.14 times larger than the diameter. It is a constant value represented by a Greek letter called pi (π). The circumference of a circle is therefore expressed as $C = \pi d$, where C represents the size of the circumference and d the size of the diameter of the circle.	*Predicts relative size of circumference from given diameters; estimates and then computes circumference from diameter (see Chapter 3 for activities that construct the meaning and value of pi)*
35.1 Perimeter: defined Circumference	5	6	6	The perimeter of a figure is the total distance around it. The perimeter of a polygon is the sum of its sides. The perimeter of a circle, which is the distance around it, is called its circumference.	Describes and calculates the perimeter of polygons; describes the circumference of a circle

Content Branch	Suggested Grade-Level Timing*			Embedded Concepts	Performance Indicators/Assessment Expectations
Major/minor	A	B	C	*See corresponding domain numbers in Chapter 3 for further development and exemplar problems.*	
35.2 Area: defined	5	6	7	Area is the amount of space on a flat surface. Area is measured in square units on a two-dimensional surface (multiples of the product of length times width). Squares and rectangles have repeated similar square units, and the area is the product of their length and width.	Defines area and measures area of squares and rectangles
35.3 Area of a parallelogram	6	7	8	Not all areas have repeated similar groups of units, but we can use our geometric knowledge to help us measure these areas. The area of a parallelogram is equal to the product of its base times its altitude (height).	Defines area and measures area of a parallelogram
35.4 Area of a triangle	5	6	7	The area of a triangle is half the area of a parallelogram that can be formed by putting together two of the same triangles—or ½ the base times the height.	Describes how the area of the triangle is half the area of the rectangle formed; computes area of given right triangle
35.5 Area of a circle	6	7	8	The area of a circle is equal to pi (π) times the square of the radius. $A = \pi r^2$	Measures area of a circle given the radius or diameter
35.6 Area of regular polygons (5 or more sides)	6	7	8	The areas of regular polygons can be calculated by dividing the polygon into congruent measurable triangles. The area of a hexagon is equal to ½ hp, where h = the height of each triangle and p equals the perimeter of the polygon (see Chapter 3).	Applies formula to measure the area of regular polygons with five or more sides Explains formula by partitioning the polygon into congruent triangles
35.7 Area: measures of irregular space on surfaces	6	7	8	Irregular spaces can be measured by separating the whole space into measurable areas and combining or removing measured areas.	Measures area of irregular spaces by combining and/or subtracting areas calculated using given measures (two- and three-step problems)

* NOTE: A = Exploration, B = Concept Mastery, C = Algorithmic or Procedural Mastery

Content Branch		Suggested Grade-Level Timing*			Embedded Concepts	Performance Indicators/Assessment Expectations
	Major/minor	A	B	C		
					See corresponding domain numbers in Chapter 3 for further development and exemplar problems.	
35.8	Area of a trapezoid	7	8	9	The area of a trapezoid can be calculated by partitioning the polygon into measurable figures (triangles or triangles and a rectangle). It is equal to ½ the height times the sum of the parallel sides (the base and its opposite). $A = \frac{1}{2} h(b_1 + b_2)$ (See Chapter 3).	Applies formula to measure the area of a trapezoid Explains formula by partitioning the trapezoid
36.1	Naming and comparing shapes of solid forms (three-dimensional objects) that take up space	5	6	7	Solid forms are three-dimensional (3-D) figures that take up space. Solid forms have faces, edges, and corners. Different forms have different numbers of sides (edges), faces, and corners. The size of the edges of a solid form may be the same as or different from each other. There are patterns between the number of faces and the number of corners.	Identification of solid forms: cube, cylinder, sphere, prism, cone; count faces, edges, corners; recognize patterns
36.2	Three-dimensional figures: defined	7	8	8	A cube has twelve congruent edges, six congruent faces, and eight congruent corners. A prism has two congruent bases that are parallel and lateral faces that are parallelograms. The prism is named after the shape of the bases. A rectangular prism has a rectangle as a base. A cylinder has two congruent circular bases and a single curved lateral face. A cone has a single circular base and a single curved lateral face that merges in a vertex opposite the base. A pyramid has a single base and is named after its polygon shape. The number of lateral faces corresponds to the number of sides of the base figure. The lateral faces merge in a vertex opposite the base.	Describes and compares solid forms: cube, cylinder, sphere, prism, cone, pyramid; finds patterns Uses computer programs to convert two-dimensional figures into three-dimensional shapes

(Continued)

Content Branch	Suggested Grade-Level Timing*			Embedded Concepts	Performance Indicators/Assessment Expectations
	A	B	C		
Major/minor				*See corresponding domain numbers in Chapter 3 for further development and exemplar problems.*	
36.3 Volume	5	6	7	The volume of a three-dimensional object that takes up space is the product of its three dimensions: length, width, and depth. Three-dimensional volume is measured in cubic units (multiples of the product of single units of length × width × depth, such as 1 cubic inch [I^3 inch] or [I^3 centimeter]).	Applies and explains the formula for measures of the volume of cubes and rectangular prisms Given one measure (l, w, or h) for the cube, computes the volume Given the three measures (l, w, and h) or the area of the base and the height of a rectangular prism, computes the volume
36.4 Volume of cube and rectangular prisms	5	6	7	The volume of a cube or a rectangular prism is equal to the area of the base times its depth or height.	Applies and explains the formula for measures of the volume of a cylinder
36.5 Volume of a cylinder	6	7	8	The volume of a cylinder is equal to the area of its circular base times its depth or height.	Uses the compass to construct a circle and protractor to draw and measure angles
36.6 Surface area of three-dimensional figures	5	6	7	The surface area of three-dimensional figures is the sum of the areas of all planes. Different figures have different relationships of volume to surface area.	Analysis and comparison of relative size of surface areas for three-dimensional objects (e.g., cube vs. flat cylinder, sphere vs. cone); computes surface area of cube and cylinder
37.1 Bilateral (mirror) or reflective symmetry	5	6	6	The same pattern in reverse on either side of a line creates mirror or reflective symmetry. Reflections can be created with a flip from right to left across a line or from top to bottom.	Identification and proof of reflective symmetry
37.2 Radial symmetry	5	6	6	If you can rotate a form in any way and it still is the same, it has radial symmetry.	Identification of radial symmetry; construction of forms with radial symmetry

* NOTE: A = Exploration, B = Concept Mastery, C = Algorithmic or Procedural Mastery

Content Branch	Suggested Grade-Level Timing*			Embedded Concepts	Performance Indicators/Assessment Expectations
	A	B	C		
Major/minor				*See corresponding domain numbers in Chapter 3 for further development and exemplar problems.*	
37.3 Symmetry in number tables: triangular and square numbers	5	6	6	Number tables or objects can be constructed with symmetry and/or in shapes (e.g., triangular numbers [3, 6, 10] or square numbers [1, 4, 9, 16, 25]).	Recognizes symmetry in a table or constructs an object triangle from triangular numbers
37.4 Transformations	6	7	7	When you flip (reflect) or rotate a figure, or move it to the side (translation), it has been transformed in its position on a plane, but the original figure and the one you transformed have the same dimensions and attributes. Transformed figures with the same dimensions are congruent (use computer software to demonstrate and prove this).	Draws transformed figures and identifies congruent triangles and parallelograms; solves problems that require reference to congruent objects; proves congruence using computer-based transformations or cutouts
37.5 Transformations: dilation Similar figures	7	8	9	A transformation in which a figure is proportionately enlarged or reduced is called a dilation. The size of the change is called the scale factor. All dimensions are proportionately changed by the same scale factor. The new and original figures are similar figures. All circles are similar to each other.	Draws dilated figures Uses the scale factor in a proportion to compute dimensions of the transformed figure
38.1 Similar figures: using proportions to determine unknown measures	7	8	9	Polygons that have congruent corresponding angles and sides in the same ratio (in proportion to each other) are similar polygons. When polygons are known to be similar, we can determine the measure of unknown dimensions by using a proportion that compares the corresponding sides of the two figures. If you know the measure of two corresponding sides or the ratio of the relationship between the sides, you can find the measure of an unknown side using the known value of a corresponding side in the proportion (see Chapter 3).	Identifies similarity given the dimensions of figures Sets up a proportion
38.2 Corresponding parts of congruent figures	7	8	9	The matching angles and sides of congruent figures are corresponding parts.	Identifies corresponding parts of congruent figures

* NOTE: A = Exploration, B = Concept Mastery, C = Algorithmic or Procedural Mastery

(Continued)

Content Branch	Suggested Grade-Level Timing* A	B	C	Embedded Concepts	Performance Indicators/Assessment Expectations
Major/minor				See corresponding domain numbers in Chapter 3 for further development and exemplar problems.	
38.3 Proving congruence: squares, rectangles	7	8	9	If all the corresponding parts of a figure are congruent, then the figures are congruent. Nevertheless, it is possible to prove congruence without knowing all the measures. For example, just knowing that the length and width of two rectangles are congruent proves that the figures are congruent.	Proof or disproof of congruence of two squares or rectangles by completion and measure of figures when only given measures of congruent sides Judges congruence of figures given partial corresponding measures
38.4 Proving congruence: triangles	8	8	9	There are several options for proving that two triangles are congruent. Knowing that: • All three sides are congruent (SSS) • Two connected sides and the angle in between are congruent (SAS) • Two angles and the side in between are equal (ASA)	Proof or disproof of congruence of two triangles by completion and measure of figures when given measures of congruent sides and/or angles Judges congruence of figures given partial corresponding measures
38.5 Definition: transversal	7	8	9	A transversal is a line that intersects two other lines.	Identifies and draws a transversal that intersects two parallel lines
38.6 Definitions: corresponding angles and alternate interior angles	8	8	9	When a transversal intersects two parallel lines, there are certain congruent angles formed. These are identified as corresponding and alternate interior angles. Corresponding angles are congruent to each other. Alternate interior angles are congruent to each other.	Identifies corresponding and alternate interior angles
Congruent angles				If the corresponding or alternate interior angles formed by a transversal that connects two lines are congruent, then we know that the lines are parallel. And vice versa, if we know that the lines intersected are parallel, then we know that the corresponding or alternate interior angles are congruent (see Chapter 3 for diagrams and problems).	Calculates the ungiven measure of angles formed by a transversal based on given measures

* NOTE: A = Exploration, B = Concept Mastery, C = Algorithmic or Procedural Mastery

(Continued)

| Content Branch | Suggested Grade-Level Timing* | | | Embedded Concepts | Performance Indicators/Assessment Expectations |
	A	B	C		
Major/minor				See corresponding domain numbers in Chapter 3 for further development and exemplar problems.	

DATA ANALYSIS, STATISTICS, AND PROBABILITY: 39. Central tendency, distributions; 40. graphs and plots; 41. probability/possibility: combinations; 42. permutations/applications of counting principle/symbolic notation; 43. experimental/theoretical probability, probability of multigroup choices, effects of replacement or nonreplacement, proof of inferences

Vocabulary and Language: Mean, mode and median, percentile, quartile, bar, histogram, line graph, line plots, stem-and-leaf plot, scatter plot, distribution of data, measure of central tendency, trend, theoretical and experimental probability, random choice, combination, permutation, counting principle

Content Branch	A	B	C	Embedded Concepts	Performance Indicators/Assessment Expectations
39.1 Data gathering organization; tallying	5	6	7	Data are a collection of measures. When recorded and organized it can be analyzed and compared. A data table helps us organize measured attributes or events. It helps us see patterns more clearly and plan for other models. Data gathering is subject to error.	Organizes loose data; uses tallies and interprets them Constructs data tables, *analyzes* data (recognizes patterns, trends) and predicts errors in gathering
39.2 Measures of central tendency forms: mean, median, and mode	5	6	7	To understand data, we can look at the measures of central tendency. In addition to the *mean* or the average, we can look at the *median* or the point at which half of the scores or events are above and the other half below. The *mode* is the score or event that occurs most frequently.	Explains applications of central tendency estimate and calculates mean, locates mode, and determines median from tables of values and graphic representations (number lines, histograms, line graphs, line plots)
39.3 Range of data	6	7	8	The range of the data or set of scores is the difference between the greatest and least value.	Calculates and explains the range of a set of scores
39.4 Measures of central tendency: mean definition and representation	5	6	7	The mean score is the average and is equal to the sum of the scores divided by the number of scores. In symbolic form, the letter x with an overbar, $\overline{x}$, represents the mean; (n) represents the number of scores; and $\sum$ represents the sum of the scores. $$\overline{x} = \frac{\sum}{n}$$ To raise the mean of a set of scores one point, an additional score must be equal to the original mean score plus one more than the original number of scores.	Estimates and computes means and explains them Expresses the mean equation in symbolic form Predicts how the mean score will be affected by additional scores

* NOTE: A = Exploration, B = Concept Mastery, C = Algorithmic or Procedural Mastery

(Continued)

Content Branch	Major/minor	Suggested Grade-Level Timing*			Embedded Concepts	Performance Indicators/Assessment Expectations
		A	B	C		
	Major/minor				*See corresponding domain numbers in Chapter 3 for further development and exemplar problems.*	
39.5	Outliers raised and lowered score effects	7	8	9	Sometimes, a single score that is very different (much higher or lower) can affect the mean. That event or score is called an outlier. The greater the number of scores, the less the effect of an outlier or a single additional score.	Identifies outliers; explains how outliers affect mean (see Chapter 3)
39.6	Data distributions: percentiles	8	9	9	In order to understand data, we can look at the percentiles. They tell us what percent of all the scores or events below that score or number. A score in the 90th percentile is higher than 90% of all the scores. A city that is in the 90th percentile in terms of traffic accidents has more accidents than 90% of the other cities recorded.	Explains a percentile score; calculates percentile of a single score when given the set
39.7	Data distributions: quartiles	8	9	9	Scores can also be grouped into four quartiles. A score that is in the 75th percentile or above is in the top or first quartile, and a score below the 25th percentile is in the lowest or fourth quartile. The median, which as the 50th percentile divides all the scores into equal halves, also divides the scores between the lowest and highest quartiles into two middle second and third quartiles.	Explains the four quartiles; Identifies the position of a single score when given the percentile or quartile
40.1	Choosing appropriate representations	5	6	7	Different graphs and representations are used to show data. The choice depends on the relationships or trends you wish to take note of or the ideas you wish to communicate.	Explains and *justifies* choice of a graph; *connects* use of different graphs to different sets of data and purposes
40.2	Graphs: bar, histogram	5	6	7	Graphs can be used to show data. Bar graphs use two perpendicular lines as labeled reference lines but differ from the coordinate plane used for line graphs in that the intervals on the axes may be different and separate from each other. Bar graphs show data distributions well. A histogram is a special bar graph that has equal intervals without spaces.	Constructs, *analyzes*, and compares quantities from bar, histogram graphs; Uses computer programs to translate data tables into graphs

* NOTE: A = Exploration, B = Concept Mastery, C = Algorithmic or Procedural Mastery

Content Branch	Suggested Grade-Level Timing*			Embedded Concepts	Performance Indicators/Assessment Expectations
Major/minor	A	B	C		
					See corresponding domain numbers in Chapter 3 for further development and exemplar problems.
40.3 Graphs: circle and line	6	7	8	Bar graphs show data distributions well. Line graphs show the relationships between variables such as variations over time.	Constructs, *analyzes*, and compares quantities from circle and line graphs Compares applications of bar, histogram, circle, and line graphs
40.4 Line plots, stem-and-leaf plots, and scatter plots (construction-interpretation)	5	6	7	Line plots and stem-and-leaf plots show groupings of data and can be used to find the measures of central tendency and distribution. Scatter plots show paired data and identify trends well.	Constructs and interprets line plots, stem-and-leaf plots, and scatter plots; identifies relationships and trends
40.5 Time lines and scatter plots	5	6	7	Events can be recorded on time lines in order of their occurrence either from left to right or bottom to top. Distance between events should relate to the time between their occurrences. Scatter plots on time lines can show how two different events may be coincidental or occur at the same time.	Constructs and interprets an event sequence from a time line; constructs a time line from a story and/or real-life adventure Uses a time line to construct a scatter plot and interprets the occurrence of events
40.6 Box-and-whisker plots	7	8	9	Box-and-whisker plots identify clusters of scores and recognize outliers. They are organized into the four quartile distributions and can help students understand the applications of quartiles.	Constructs and interprets box-and-whisker plots
41.1 Certainty/uncertainty	5	6	7	Events and choices can be either certain or uncertain. A sequence of day followed by night about every twenty-four hours is certain at the equator of the Earth but uncertain at the poles. If you only have white socks, it is certain that you will pick white socks, but white socks are uncertain if you have several different colors. Probability is a measure of how close an event is to being certain.	Explains with illustration the concept of certainty and uncertainty; relates uncertainty to probability Describes a range of probabilities using words (*certain, likely, unlikely, possible, sometimes impossible*)

* NOTE: A = Exploration, B = Concept Mastery, C = Algorithmic or Procedural Mastery

(Continued)

Content Branch		Suggested Grade-Level Timing*			Embedded Concepts	Performance Indicators/Assessment Expectations
	Major/minor	A	B	C		
					See corresponding domain numbers in Chapter 3 for further development and exemplar problems.	
41.2	Probability/possibility	5	6	7	The probability of the occurrence or outcome of an event is dependent on the possibility that a particular event or outcome can occur. Unless there is a major catastrophe on Earth, there is only one possibility at the equator: Day follows night. It is therefore certain, and the probability of a new day is 100% because there are no other possibilities. Knowing the extent of the possibilities or *counting* them has to come before estimating the probability of the event. If you consider the three possible alternatives of rain, clouds, or sunshine for most of the day, however, the probability of one of these events is not certain and is less than 100%.	Explains the relationship between possibility and probability and the need to count the possibilities to determine the probability
41.3	Counting possibilities	6	7	8	The number of possibilities for a single event depends on the total number of possible alternative outcomes, including the one desired. The number of possibilities for a single event is simply equal to the number of choices. There are seven possibilities for it to be a particular day of the week.	Recognizes the relationship between the number of alternative choices and the possibility for a particular one
41.4	Combined events/same set: order does not matter Combinations	6	7	8	Sometimes choices or events are combined. If the *order* of selection and the arrangement of events or choices from a single set *do not matter*, we call these events combinations. They are order-independent choices.	Distinguishes between combinations (order independent) and permutations (order dependent)
41.5	Counting possibilities: combinations (order does not matter)—use of tree diagrams and sample spaces	6	7	8	Combinations of events and choices have more possibilities than single events. There are seven possible days of the week, but combined with the two alternative choices of rain or no rain, there are fourteen possibilities—two for each day. We can calculate the number of possible combinations of events or choices by constructing a tree diagram, a table of possible events, or filling a sample space. You need to check to make sure there are no repetitions.	Calculates the possible number of combinations of events or choices from single sets by constructing a tree diagram or filling a sample space

* NOTE: A = Exploration, B = Concept Mastery, C = Algorithmic or Procedural Mastery

Content Branch	Suggested Grade-Level Timing*			Embedded Concepts	Performance Indicators/Assessment Expectations
	A	B	C		
Major/minor				See corresponding domain numbers in Chapter 3 for further development and exemplar problems.	
41.6 Counting possibilities: different ways to consider the set or sets of choices	6	7	8	The possibilities for a particular event can be considered in alternate ways: • As a single set of different choices (the days of the week) • As more than one separate set of alternatives or events that are to be combined (a set of shoes and a set of socks)	Distinguishes between a single set of choices or events and a combination of alternatives or events
41.7 Possibilities: combinations of events from the same set	6	7	8	The number of possibilities for a particular combination of events chosen or happening from the same set depends on the following: • The number of alternative choices in the set • The number of choices made	Calculates the possible number of combinations of events or choices from single sets by constructing a tree diagram or filling a sample space; compares and predicts relative number of possibilities from the alternatives and number of choices
41.8 Combinations: order-independent patterns for number of choices	7	8	9	Four individually and randomly selected items (A, B, C and D) from a group of A, B, C and D can be arranged in only one combination. As long as the number of choices made is equal to the total number of alternative outcomes and order does not matter, there is only one possible combination. You just pick and have them all. The probability of your choice is 100% If the total number of items to choose from remains the same, the number of possible combinations grows larger as the size of the combined choices gets smaller. There are four possible combinations if you randomly pick three out of four choices, but 6 different possible combinations of two choices out of four	Compares and predicts relative number of possibilities from the alternatives and number of choices; explains why the probability of four choices out of four is 100% for a combination Recognizes and explains the pattern of the inverse relationship between the number of choices and the number of possibilities
41.9 Possibilities and probability: combined events/ different sets or categories	6	7	8	A tree diagram will show you that the total number of possible combinations of events or choices from two different sets is the product of the number of choices in one set multiplied by the number in the other. If you have a set of three different pairs of shoes and six different pairs of socks, there are eighteen different possible combinations of shoes and socks. The probability of	Calculates the possible number of combinations of events or choices from more than one set by constructing a tree diagram or filling a sample space; explains and uses the algorithm for the probability of choices from more than one set

*NOTE: A = Exploration, B = Concept Mastery, C = Algorithmic or Procedural Mastery

(Continued)

	Suggested Grade-Level Timing*				
Content Branch	A	B	C	Embedded Concepts	Performance Indicators/Assessment Expectations
Major/minor				See corresponding *domain numbers in Chapter 3 for further development and exemplar problems.*	
				choosing any one of the pairs of shoes is 1/3, and the probability of choosing any one of the pairs of socks is 1/6, but the probability of one particular match of shoes and socks is 1/18 (see Chapter 3 for examples such as menu choices).	
42.1 Permutations: order-dependent combinations of two objects	6	7	8	If the order or sequence of random choices or events matters, we call the possibilities *permutations.* There are more possibilities for permutations than there are for combinations. A group of three individually selected items (A, B, and C) can be selected (or arranged) in six different ways if the order matters.	Explains that objects can be differently arranged; computes number of sets of two from three or four different objects using real objects and tables; constructs a tree diagram or table of possible events
42.2 Using the counting principle algorithm for total number of possibilities: order counts (permutations)	7	8	9	Filling a *sample space* will demonstrate that after you pick your first item, the number of possibilities for the next item diminishes by one and so on until the last one is left. For this one, there is only one possibility. The counting principle can therefore be used to determine the total number of possibilities. For a group of four items, when order matters, there are $4 \times 3 \times 2 \times 1 = 24$ possible arrangements of the four items. The factorial notation is a way of denoting and applying the counting principle. $4! = 4 \times 3 \times 2 \times 1 = 24$	Explains and uses factorial notation and the counting principle algorithm for calculating the number of permutations of a set; proves it by filling the sample space or vice versa; generates the concept from the sample space
42.3 Selecting from a group: order matters	7	8	9	When a *specific number of choices* are selected *from a group of possibilities* and order matters, sample space records of permutations will prove that the factorial is again useful. For example, if we choose only three choices out of the five, we only go as far as the first three steps of the sample space. Only three items of the five would result in $5 \times 4 \times 3 = 60$ possibilities.	Explains and uses the factorial notation and counting principle algorithm for calculating the number of combinations of a set; proves it by filling the sample space or vice versa; generates the concept from the sample space

* NOTE: A = Exploration, B = Concept Mastery, C = Algorithmic or Procedural Mastery

Content Branch	Suggested Grade-Level Timing*			Embedded Concepts	Performance Indicators/Assessment Expectations
Major/minor	A	B	C		
				See corresponding domain numbers in Chapter 3 for further development and exemplar problems.	
42.4 Permutations: symbolic notation of selected choices from a group	8	8	9	The possibilities of selected choices may be expressed in symbolic notation form as $_nP_r$ or $_5P_3$, where the subscript (n) in front of the P represents the size of the whole group, and (r) represents the number of picks or choices from the group.	Explains and uses the symbolic notation for permutations
42.5 Order-independent combinations: symbolic notation	8	8	9	We can also represent combinations in symbolic notation form as $_nC_r$, where n = the total number of possibilities and r = the number of picks or choices. $_5C_3$ means three picks out of a group of five.	Explains and uses the symbolic notation for combinations
42.6 Order-independent combinations: algorithm using the counting principle				When order does not matter, there are fewer possibilities. Sample space examples show that the total number of possibilities is equal to a fraction of the total number calculated by the counting principle for a permutation. The numerator would start with the counting principle of the total number of possibilities but only continue the number of times that is equal to the number of choices. The denominator would be the counting principle for the number of choices.	Explains and uses the factorial notation and counting principle algorithm for calculating the number of combinations of a set; proves it by filling the sample space or vice versa; generates the concept from the sample space
42.7 Using the counting principle for combinations of choices: symbolic notations	8	8	9	The number of different possibilities for picking an unordered group of four out of five possible items would be $\dfrac{5 \times 4 \times 3 \times 2}{4!}$ $= \dfrac{120}{24}$ or the number of permutations divided by the factorial of the number of choices. Symbolically, we can also write this as $_nC_r = \dfrac{1}{r!} \times _nP_r.$	Applies the counting principle to combinations of choices from a group Explains that because the order does not matter, the number of possibilities will be less *Note that, as discovered above, when using the formula for choosing five items of the five and order does not matter, there will only be one possibility for the five items*

(Continued)

Content Branch	Suggested Grade-Level Timing* A	B	C	Embedded Concepts	Performance Indicators/Assessment Expectations
Major/minor					*See corresponding domain numbers in Chapter 3 for further development and exemplar problems.*
43.1 Probability: as a random prediction of uncertain events	6	7	8	We can predict the occurrence of uncertain events based on the probability that they will occur. Probability tells us what the chances are that something will happen. When we calculate probability, we assume that the event we are predicting is a random event and not certain or impossible. When we pick something we cannot see, feel, or smell as different from anything else in a group, it is a random choice.	Explains the meaning and application of probability in terms of chance or random choice
43.2 Theoretical probability	6	7	8	If the number of possibilities is certain, the probability of the occurrence of a desired outcome is determined theoretically. It is *the number of the desired outcomes in a set divided by the total number of possible outcomes in the set.* If a group of seven marbles has three desired red ones, the probability of choosing a red one is 3/7.	Defines and represents theoretical probability; expresses probabilities as fractions, decimals, or percents
43.3 Experimental probability	6	7	8	If the number of possibilities is uncertain, we can make estimates and predictions. We can then prove our predictions by collecting sample data.	Recognizes when an estimate is appropriate *Predicts* outcomes and conducts experiments with independent events (combinations); compares the results with the prediction *Proves* prediction by collecting and collating data
43.4 Probability expressed as a percentage or fraction; zero and 100%; connections to words	5	6	7	We can describe the range of probability using words. The words for the top and bottom of the range are *certain* and *impossible.* In between these extremes, we use words and phrases such as *possible, probable, likely, unlikely, less likely, more likely, most likely, least likely,* and *equally likely.* We can also describe a range of probability using fractions and percents that represent parts of the whole. If an event is certain, its probability is 100%. Anything less than 100% and greater than zero is uncertain. An event with zero probability is impossible.	Relates the words that express probability as fractional or percentage equivalents (e.g., "An event with a 1% probability is very unlikely to occur.")

* NOTE: A = Exploration, B = Concept Mastery, C = Algorithmic or Procedural Mastery

Content Branch	Suggested Grade-Level Timing*			Embedded Concepts	Performance Indicators/Assessment Expectations
	A	B	C		
Major/minor				*See corresponding domain numbers in Chapter 3 for further development and exemplar problems.*	
43.5 Probability of single events: expressing probability in fraction form	5	6	7	If there are four possible choices or outcomes for a single independent event, the probability of one of these occurring is 1/4 or 25%.	Expresses the probability of a single event as a fraction and percent when there is only one possibility for the desired event
43.6 Probability: more than one of a kind in a set	6	7	8	If a set of five objects has two objects of one kind and three of another, there are only two possibilities. The probability of one kind is 2/5 or 40%, and the probability of the other kind is 3/5 or 60%.	Expresses the probability of a single event as a fraction and percent when there is more than one possibility for the desired event
43.7 Probability: replacement and independent or dependent events	7	8	9	The probability of an event is altered if the size of the group changes. Not replacing a chosen item changes the size of the whole group and the probability. It is a *dependent event* and depends on how the whole group was changed. If a desired red marble has already been chosen and removed from a group of seven that originally had three red ones and a probability of $\frac{3}{7}$, the probability for another red one is now only $\frac{2}{6}$ or $\frac{1}{3}$.	Explains replacement and the difference between independent and dependent events; calculates the probability of dependent events when given the sequence of previous choices
43.8 Experimental probability: conducting experiments, sample polls	7	8	9	Experimental probability is determined by conducting experiments. A sample of possible outcomes or trials should be randomly chosen and recorded. The experimental probability of a particular or desired event of the trial is equal to the *number of times the desired event occurs divided by the total number of trials.* We can also use experiments to prove that our predictions based on theoretical probability are incorrect and prove the effect of a particular variable on the outcome.	Distinguishes between theoretical and experimental probability; conducts experiments such as polls, records results; predicts the results of a series of trials once the probability for one trial is known; explains that the larger a well-chosen sample is, the more likely it is to represent the whole and that there are many ways of choosing a sample that can make it unrepresentative of the whole
43.9 Probability: single choices combined	7	8	9	The probability of two independent events occurring at the same time is equal to the product of the probability of each event. If the probability is that it will rain once every four days in April, the probability for rain is $\frac{1}{4}$. Since there are seven days in a week the probability for a Monday is $\frac{1}{7}$, but the probability that it will rain on a Monday is $\frac{1}{28}$.	Calculates the probability of combined independent and then dependent events
Independent or Dependent	8	9	9		

3

Scaffolds for Teachers and Problems for Students

A GUIDE TO CHAPTER 3 ■

Chapter 3 is designed as a supplement to Chapter 2. It provides some of the instructional ideas for achieving the concepts listed by number in Chapter 2. The ideas presented are based on the work of many mathematics education researchers (some of whom are listed in the references), my own observations of students in the grades addressed and preservice teachers as they learned, as well as those of the experienced teachers with whom I work. The item numbers in Chapter 3 correspond to the Chapter 2 domain groupings of whole numbers, with subdomain decimal notations of the skills and concepts within each whole-numbered group. As in Chapter 2, the concepts within each group whole-number heading of the domain span several grade and developmental levels. The specific item number-matched presentations of scaffolding ideas and illustrative developmental problems are sometimes consolidated into inclusive groups in order to further demonstrate a clear sequence of concepts. This format is also intended to provide a basis for needed review, connections to prior knowledge, and possible acceleration.

Each separate or grouped number item entry begins with a section on the developmental transitions and scaffolds. This is a discussion of the skills and concepts presented within the group in Chapter 2 and an analysis of the challenges of helping students learn them. These challenges are the commonly occurring "bumps in the road of understanding" that I, and other researchers, have uncovered as we watched many children learn. There are specific suggestions for scaffolding dialogue and manipulatives to help in the process. The discussion is accompanied by articulated exemplar problems that can be used for both concept development and proximal (classroom) assessment purposes. Because of their developmental learning and embedded sequential assessment purposes, the exemplars may be somewhat different from problems found in textbooks. They may be culminating problems that have diagnostic subtasks and questions that take students over several development levels and connect the current task to other concepts. The exemplars were designed to be used as an interactive support in the scaffolding process as the teacher guides and proximally, or informally, assesses the progress of students in the construction of new knowledge. Within each subgroup, they are presented in order of increasing levels of difficulty. Final problems in the group are usually culminating accumulations of the concepts within previous ones. With minor adjustments, they can, however, be used for more formal assessments.

Teachers may wish to copy the exemplar problems as presented for use with their students, but they may need to adapt some of them to the developmental level of their students. Many of the exemplars involve group activities. They represent only a limited sample of the kinds of problem-solving challenges teachers will need to present in order to help students develop a wide range of concepts and skills. Teachers should consult the many additional scaffolding ideas and sample problems in the National Council of Teachers of Mathematics (NCTM, 1989, 2000) standards documents and other sources listed in this book's reference section. Mathematics textbooks meant for use by children also have many problems and activities that can be used along with these examples for further practice and challenges. The Web is another source from which teachers can select appropriate materials. Whenever possible, the selection of practice material should be tailored to both the individual diagnoses of student needs and the common "bumps in the road" that are addressed in the discussions ahead.

As discussed in Chapter 1, calls for curriculum reform to meet the needs of an increasingly technological society have resulted in some downshifting of the curriculum. We have responded by including most of the traditional high school content of elementary algebra as well as some of the traditional high school geometry. On the other hand, my attention has been called to an apparent gap in the ability of students to be able to quickly retrieve (automatize) some basic facts. Cognitive research tells us that memorization is easier at younger ages, and automatized facts enable a better focus on the understanding of algorithms. Although appropriate use of calculators is an important skill for complex calculations, students who still demonstrate a gap in the automatization of basic facts by the sixth grade should be particularly encouraged to use the facts to make estimates of their calculations before using the calculator.

The algorithms for which scaffolding is suggested are, for the most part, the standard algorithms. Technology makes many algorithms less important, but they are fast, accurate, and powerful, and they provide a written record (Usikin, 1998). We also need to recognize that different algorithms are standards in other places or have been the standard form at different times. Learned with meaning, algorithms may also help students understand relationships and patterns. Concurrently, students should be encouraged to try to develop their own algorithms and perhaps share them with others. The value of student-invented algorithms is that the process of invention firmly constructs mathematical concepts. This value is further enhanced by opportunities to describe the invented procedure. Even if the invention is not as efficient as the standard procedure, it should be recognized as valid. Student attention, however, should be called to the relative efficiency of standard algorithms. In any case, teachers should avoid spending too much time on drill and practice with algorithms—there are too many other useful mathematics ideas that students have to learn.

I have also discovered that even the adults I teach benefit from the use of manipulatives. Procedures originally learned and performed by rote suddenly become meaningful. Most of the concrete manipulatives suggested are among those in most common use, available from educational supply companies, and there are many additional forms that are useful. One of the common complaints from students at this level is that the math has no meaning or purpose for them. Therefore, wherever possible, we have tried to use real-life applications.

The suggested technology applications are just the tip of the iceberg. A basic standard for all is the ability to perform operations with scientific calculators. Many of the new-generation software applications can be used as supplements to help provide additional experiences. Using common drawing applications, students can construct their own chips, as well as duplicate and manipulate them. They can create figures, rotate them, and transform them. They can use interactive probes to collect original data on temperature or light, organize the data into tables, plot graphs, and perform operations with graphing calculators. Over the Internet, students can retrieve data such as seismographic readings, temperature, distances, and annual rainfall from all over the world.

The overriding concept, however, is that we all learn by "doing" mathematics.

NUMBER SYSTEMS ■

1.1–1.3 Place Value Systems: Whole Numbers

See also Chapter 2, pages 17–20, for embedded concepts and performance indicators/assessment expectations.

Developmental Transitions and Scaffolds

Place value concepts are very critical for the understanding of our number system but often incompletely developed. The additive equivalent relationships between the units—for example, that there are ten ones in (10) or ten hundreds in (1,000)—are introduced at the lower grades and then extended to place value concepts that recognize that each digit in a position or place is ten times greater than the one to its right. Extensions to the larger billions place can be a useful review before proceeding to the decimal concepts. Connections to exponential forms (see below) will help reinforce and extend previous concepts as well as provide an expression algorithm. A suggested developmental sequence of concept constructions that help smooth the necessary transitions includes the knowledge that

- Each symbol in a position represents one or up to nine units of a specific size.
- There can only be nine whole-number units of a size in any place position.
- Numbers of more than (9) units are assembled combinations of zeros and other values for each place they represent.
- The value of a symbol can *change with its position.*
- The size of the units increases from right to left and vice versa.
- Except for the ones, the whole-number units are multiples of 10 or positive exponents of 10.
- Any number may be written as a composite of different size units: 110,056 is a composite of one hundred thousand (100,000) plus one ten thousand (10,000) plus five tens (50) plus six ones (6). Alternatively, using exponential form where possible, it is equal to $10^5 + 10^4 + (5 \times 10) + (6 \times 1)$.
- The progression of named place value units over 1,000 is in groups of three: three units of thousands one, ten, and hundred thousands followed by one million and three groups of millions one, ten, and hundred millions followed by one billion.

Begin with a recursive review of whole-number place values. Try using sectioned boxes drawn on paper with units represented by chips, beans, or any other accessible set of identical objects and have students increase and decrease the value by multiples of 10 or increased exponents. Make the connections between the manipulative and the place value and exponential concepts.

What happens to the value of a chip when it is moved from the hundreds box to the thousands box? What happens when it is moved from the hundreds to the ten thousandths? How do we represent empty boxes? Show the numbers 10,000 and 10 million. Write them in standard symbol form. Write the numbers 100 and 1,000 in exponential form. What do you notice about the exponents and the number of empty boxes?

The multiplication and division of numbers by units of 10 should be immediately connected to place value concepts. A digit of 5 in the tens place expresses a value of 50. Ten times 50 or a number that is ten times greater than 50 is 500. All we have to do is shift the 5 digit one place to the higher left.

Exemplar Problem

Complete the following table:

1. *Multiply the number in row A by 1,000. Show the product in row B.*

2. *Divide the number in row B by 100. Show the quotient in row C.*

3. *Multiply the number in row C by 100. Show the product in row D.*

4. *Multiply the number in row E by 100. Show the product in row F.*

The number in row A can be separated into its component units. There are nine ones in row A. Write the number in row A as its separate components of ten thousands, thousands, hundreds, tens, and ones.

_____ ten thousands   _____ thousands   _____ hundreds   _____ tens   _9_ ones

Hundred Millions	Ten Millions	Millions	Hundred Thousands	Ten Thousands	Thousands	Hundreds	Tens	Ones	
				6	7	5	8	9	A
									B
									C
									D
			9	0	0	3	0	5	E
									F

Describe what happened when the nine ones in row A were multiplied by 100 in row B.

How many columns would we have to add to show the 100 billions?

How many columns would we have to add to show the 100 trillions?

Write the number in row F on this line. Use commas where needed _____.

Explain where you put the commas.

1.4–1.6 Place Value System: Decimals

Developmental Transitions and Scaffolds

Decimal place value concepts should follow review activities with whole numbers as above. Construction of the meaning of decimals can be introduced as less than one whole extension of the whole-number place value systems or fractional parts of a whole.

- Decimals are extensions of the place value system to values less than one whole.
- They are, therefore, fractions.

The decimal units also may be expressed as their equivalent smaller units. Five tenths is the same as 50 hundredths, 500 thousandths, and 5,000 ten thousandths.

The question of how to divide ones by 10 should lead to the concept of decimal fractions and the extension of the place value system to values less than one whole.

What fraction is one tenth of one whole?

What fractional part of a whole is ten times smaller than the whole?

How can we show values less than one whole?

What happens when we shift one place to the right?

Why do we need a decimal point?

How do we make the number 57 ten times larger?

- We have to make both the five tens larger and the seven ones larger by shifting both to the left.

What do we need in the ones place now?

How do we make the number 576 ten times smaller?

- We change the five hundreds to five tens and the seven tens to seven ones, and the six ones have to become a decimal fraction of six tenths.

Why do we need a decimal point?

- We need to show a number that is less than 1 or a decimal fraction. The decimal point separates the whole numbers from the fractions in a mixed number.

When using words to describe mixed whole numbers and decimals, avoid the use of the term *point* to mark the decimal point terminus for whole numbers. Read the decimal point as *and,* and the decimal values as the smallest place (read 25.23 as "twenty-five and twenty-three hundredths"). The use of this language works to embed greater meaning than when the value is just read as digits after the decimal point. It also reinforces the concept of the mixed whole number/decimal number as a whole number and a fraction.

The concept of decimal place values can also be concurrently connected to the division application of fractions (partition form).

Dividing a number by 10 is like finding what fractional part of it?

How can we find one tenth of a number by shifting places?

How can we find 10% of a number by shifting places?

Once the concept of place shifting is clear, it may be practical to introduce movement of the decimal point as an alternative, but the connections should be clear.

What happens to the decimal point when we multiply a mixed number such as 23.46 by 10?

- The decimal point moves one place to the right when the digits move one place to the left.

The common notations for money (the whole dollar, dime, and cent) or manipulative representations (base-10 blocks) can be used in a triad that also includes the descriptive words and the symbolic forms to construct and strengthen the concepts of the place value system. Students should discover that the need for zero as a placeholder is opposite that for a whole number, where a zero is not needed for values larger than the largest digit value. In decimal notation, it is not needed for values less than the smallest digit value. We do not need zeros at either end, but we need them in between the largest and smallest digits. Additionally, needed transitions and scaffolds include the following:

Why do we need a decimal point?

- The decimal point separates whole numbers from decimal fractions of the value of (1).

What makes one position of a number different from another?

- Each similar-sized unit in place is ten times smaller than the one to its left or one tenth of the value.

How do we name the decimals?

- The decimal place number names are derived from their size relative to one whole; one tenth is one tenth the size or 1 divided by 10, one hundredth is one hundredth the size or 1 divided by 100, and so on.

What does a number such as 1.026 mean?

- The number (1.026) is a composite of one whole plus two hundredths plus six thousandths, with a zero in the tenths place.

Alternately, use the equivalent fractional representation to reinforce the meaning. The number .026 can also be expressed as $\frac{26}{1,000}$. If one tenth means one whole divided by 10, then $\frac{26}{1,000}$ means twenty-six wholes divided by 1,000. This leads to the understanding that any fraction can be changed to its decimal form by dividing the numerator by the denominator.

As a manipulative connection, you can begin by using the same boxes and chips that were used for whole numbers, but separate the whole numbers and decimals with a dark line or section divider to represent the decimal point. Connect the tactile use of the manipulatives to problems using the written symbolic form. The concept that decimals can represent fractional parts of different-size wholes can then be reinforced here. Five tenths of a dollar is different from five tenths of a euro. One tenth of an inch is different from one tenth of a yard. See Number 10.3 for decimal parts of an area.

Exemplar Problems

Make this value a hundred times smaller. Write it in the box.

H	T	O
4	3	2

→

H	T	O	tenths	hundredths

Make this value ten times larger. Write it in the box.

H	T	O	tenths
	3	6	5

→

H	T	O	tenths

Find one tenth of this value. Write it as a decimal in the box.

   Write it as a mixed number _____

H	T	O	tenths
6	5	3	

→

H	T	O	tenths	hundredths

———————— ✄ ————————

Follow these directions for completing the table on the next page.
   Multiply the number in row A by 10. Show the product in row B.
   Divide the number in row B by 1,000. Show the quotient in row C.
   Write the number in row C in fraction form as a mixed number. _____

   Multiply the number in row C by 100. Show the product in row D.
   Divide the number in row E by 100. Show the product in row F.
   Write the number in row F on this line. Use commas where needed. _____

   The number in row C can be separated into its composite units. Write the number in row C on this line as a decomposed number of hundreds, tens, ones, tenths, hundredths, and thousandths.

Ten Millions	Millions	Hundred Thousands	Ten Thousands	Thousands	Hundreds	Tens	Ones	Tenths	Hundredths	Thousandths	
			6	7	5	8	0				A
											B
											C
											D
		9	0	0	3	0	5				E
											F

1.7 Converting Fractions to Decimals

Developmental Transitions and Scaffolds

Review the division meaning of fractions—that $\frac{2}{3}$ can mean two wholes divided into three parts as well as two out of three parts of a single whole. If you divide two wholes into three parts, each part will be $\frac{2}{3}$ of a single whole. Fractions can be converted to their decimal form by dividing the numerator by the denominator. Begin with easily understood improper fractions greater than 1. Connect the mixed number and decimal equivalents. $\frac{3}{2} = 1\frac{1}{2} = 1.5$. Then move to the proper fractions, which require more complex applications of division of decimals (see Numbers 11.1–11.5 and 13.3–13.5).

Sometimes the division of whole numbers or decimals results in a quotient that is a decimal without a remainder that needs to be regrouped. Why do we call this a terminating decimal?
   If it does not end or keeps having a remainder that needs to be divided, it is nonterminating.

Some nonterminating decimal forms just repeat the same digits. What do we call these?
   They are called repeating decimals.

How do we show that a decimal is nonterminating? How many digits do we have to show?
   We can use symbolic notation to show these decimal forms. (2.256…) shows a nonterminating decimal. We can also use $2.\overline{33}$ to show that the decimal (.33) keeps repeating.
   The number of digits we show depends on what we are measuring. Significant digits are those that are actually measured (see Number 26.5).
   Be careful about the fact that the set of nonterminating decimals includes repeating decimals.

Exemplar Problems

Explain the decimal set inclusions in the following figure. Give an example of each.

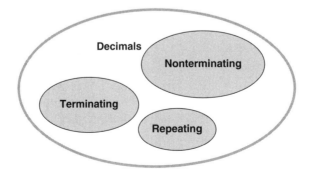

Convert the following fractions to their decimal equivalents. Identify each decimal equivalent as terminating or nonterminating by putting a check in the right column. Put a circle around the repeating decimals.

Fraction	Decimal Equivalents	Terminating Decimals	Nonterminating Decimals
$\frac{2}{5}$			
$\frac{2}{3}$			
$\frac{2}{7}$			
$\frac{2}{16}$			
$\frac{5}{6}$			

1.8 Rounding

Developmental Transitions and Scaffolds

When we round numbers to a particular size unit, we use half of the next smaller unit to determine whether to round up or down. If the value is half or more, we round up; less than half, we round down. Some of the difficulty students have had with the rounding convention for larger numbers may be because of the traditional focus on just the number 5 rather than on the concept that five tens are half of one hundred and five hundreds are half of one thousand. Scaffolding can help.

For rounding a number such as 36,340 to the nearest thousand ask, *How many hundreds for half a thousand? Do we have more or less than five hundreds? What do we do with less than five hundreds?*

For rounding numbers more than one place, such as a frequently mishandled quantity like 26,638 to the nearest hundred, ask these probing questions:

What is the next smallest place after the hundreds?

How many tens for half a hundred?

Do we have more or less than five tens?

Since we have less than half a hundred, what should we do with the tens and ones?

What should take their place?

What do we have to think about when we round to the millions place?

If we think of half a million or 500,000, how would we round the number 2,498,087 to the nearest million?

In some test items, the place to which a number is to be rounded is underlined. *Round each number to the underlined place value and explain how you did it.*

18,24<u>3</u>2   290,<u>4</u>98   3,465,<u>0</u>07

3<u>9</u>,018   382,<u>0</u>56   5,40<u>6</u>,789

Rounding of decimals is an extension of the same pattern. The inclusion or exclusion of zeros is, however, a variation of the pattern but related to understanding of the place value system. The concepts listed below are often a challenge.

- If the digit to the right of the round-to place value is less than 5, decimals can be rounded by just dropping the values to the right of the round-to place value.
- If the digit to the right of the round-to place value is greater than 5, the digit in the round-to place is made one digit higher.
- Rounded to the nearest tenth, the decimal value .63789 is simply .6.
- When rounding to the nearest tenth, .52 is rounded to .5, but because five hundredths are half of one tenth, (.56) is rounded to .6.
- Zeros to the right of the rounded numbered digit are not necessary, but those to its left are needed.
- Five tenths or more is rounded to the next whole number; five hundredths or more to the next tenth, and five thousandths or more to the next hundredth. The decimal .2006, rounded to the nearest thousandth, would be .201, but to the nearest tenth, it would simply be .2.
- Rounding to the nearest whole number, (3.52) is more than 3.5, so we round to 4.0.
- To the nearest ten thousandth, the value .00529 is rounded to .0053.

Round each number to the underlined place value and explain how you did it.

457.24 _____

78.062 _____

.3980 _____

.25000 _____

Conventional rounding is an important number sense skill, but it needs to be considered in the context of other estimation approaches. The kinds of estimations we make depend on the purpose of the computation or use of the value. Sometimes, just front-ended estimation (using the highest place value) is good enough. If the attendance at a series game is 10,346 on day 1 and 12,765 on day 2, it may be good enough to estimate 10,000 and 12,000 for a 2,000 difference—even though conventional rounding would produce a different figure. If I were estimating the sum of 1,438 and 1,247 to the nearest hundred, I would estimate it as 2,700, quickly noting that the sum of the tens and ones would be close to one hundred and adding that to the sum of the hundreds without thinking of rounding. If the numbers had been routinely rounded to the nearest hundred first, the estimate would have been 2,600 and further from the exact answer of 2,685.

1.9 Number System/Positive and Negative Numbers

Developmental Transitions and Scaffolds

Awareness of the increased smallness of nonterminating decimal notations as they approach zero can be used to illustrate the need to use alternate notation to show values less than zero. An introduction to negatively signed numbers as a way of showing values less than zero, such as below-zero temperatures or below-sea-level measures, is a practical approach. Use of negative decimal values on a number line should help to clarify the demarcations between positive decimal values, zero, and negative values. Use a raised plus or minus sign to distinguish the number sign from the operation. See Numbers 12.1 to 12.6 below for further operations with signed numbers and 20.2 for the inequality symbols that can be used to show a range of values.

Exemplar Problems

*In Fairbanks, Alaska, the low temperature to the nearest whole degree on Monday was ⁻5°
Fahrenheit. On Tuesday, the low was 2° Fahrenheit. How much warmer was it on Tuesday than
on Monday?*_____

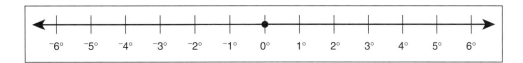

    *On Wednesday, the low temperature was (⁻.5°). Put an (x) on the number line to show that
value.*
    On Thursday, the low was (⁺2.5°). Put a (y) on the number line to show that value.

———————————— ⚜ ————————————

*You are in the process of climbing up a mountain. When you begin your climb at the base of the
mountain, the temperature is ⁺15° Fahrenheit. For every increase in elevation of 500 feet, the temperature decreases about 5° Fahrenheit.*
    *Correctly label the intervals on the number line below and plot the change of
temperature.*
    *Approximately what would you expect the temperature to be when you reach an
elevation of 3,000 feet?*

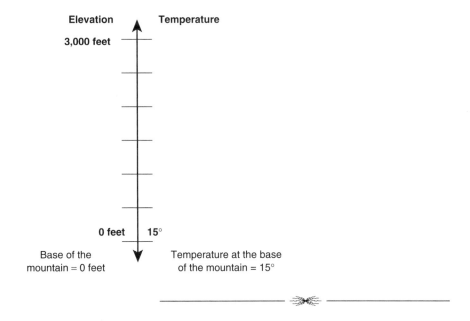

———————————— ⚜ ————————————

Write the inequality sentence that is represented on the number line below.

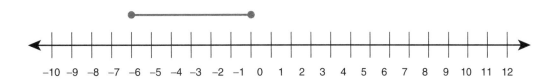

2.1 Exponential Forms: Base and Exponent

See also Chapter 2, pages 20–22, for concepts and expectations.

Developmental Transitions and Scaffolds

The use of exponential notation forms is a natural follow-up or accompaniment to the review of standard forms of whole and decimal number representation. It should be presented as a useful alternative shortcut expression of numbers that avoids long sequences of zero digits, makes multiplication and division of large numbers easier, and is actually based on the standard base-10 system. A review of the form of base and exponent as symbols for repeated multiplication should come first. In the earlier grades, the use of the term *square* is related to the repeated addition or multiplication of units in the area of a square, and *cube* refers to the volume of a cube. The concept of square root as the inverse action is appropriately connected here, and a progression to perfect and nonperfect square numbers is a useful preparation for the concept of irrational numbers. Necessary subconcepts include the following:

What is a shortcut way of expressing numbers?

- Numbers can be expressed in exponential form as a base number (3) with a raised exponent such as 3^2.

What do we call the form of these numbers, and what do they mean? How many factors of 3 are in 3^2?

- The base number is a number that is repeatedly multiplied by itself. The raised number is the exponent. It represents the number of times the base number is repeatedly multiplied or how many factors of the base number there are. *It may be helpful to use the mnemonic that the <u>b</u>ase is the <u>b</u>ottom number and the <u>exp</u>onent is the number of times the base is repeated and multiplied in <u>exp</u>anded form.*

What happens in repeated multiplication?

- In repeated multiplication, each previous product is successively multiplied by the same base number.

  $3^4 = 3 \times 3 \times 3 \times 3$, which equals 81 because $3 \times 3 = 9 \times 3 = 27 \times 3 = 81$.

What happens as the exponent gets larger and smaller?

If we place exponential notations of the same base on a number line sequence to see the pattern, the values increase to the left and decrease to the right just like our number system, which has a base number of 10. In our base-10 number system, 10^3 or 1,000 is ten times larger than 10^2 or 100, and 10^1 or 10 is ten times smaller than 10^2 or 100.

The number 4^3 is four times *larger* than 4^2, the number to its right on the number line. 4^3 is the product of multiplication of 4^2 by the base-value factor of 4. The number to the right of 4^2 on the number line is 4^1, which is four times smaller or the quotient of division by the base-value factor. 4^2 is four times *smaller* than 4^3, and 4^1 is four times smaller than 4^2. The exponents and expanded values increase to the left and decrease to the right. See Numbers 2.7 to 2.9 for extensions to zero and negative exponents.

2.2 Alternate Expressions for Exponential Forms

Developmental Transitions and Scaffolds

What are some other ways to describe exponential notations?

- We sometimes express the exponential form in words such as "(x) to the power of (n)," where (x) is the base and (n) stands for the exponent number. (6^5) can be expressed as six to the power of five.
- Bases with exponents of 2 are usually called square numbers because they are just the base number multiplied by itself—and the area of a square figure is the measure of one side multiplied by itself.
- Bases with exponents of 3 are called cubed because they correspond to the three repeats of the measures of a side of a cube to determine its volume.

2.3 Number System/Place Value: Related to Exponential Forms

Developmental Transitions and Scaffolds

How is our standard number system related to exponential forms?

- Our number system is organized using exponents of a base of 10. Starting with the number 10, each place value is an increasing or decreasing exponent of 10. *There may be a slight hump to overcome with the realization that the system begins with a base of 10 rather than 1. However, students can quickly pick up the concept that we can't use a base of (1) because it is impossible to get the progression of increasing values we need with a base of 1.*

How can we express large numbers in exponential form?

- Large single-unit numbers (numbers that do not have any digits after the whole place value unit) may be expressed in exponential form as multiples of the powers of 10.

   100,000 is equal to $10 \times 10 \times 10 \times 10 \times 10$ and may be expressed as 10^5 because there are five factors of 10 in the number.

Is there an easy way to know this?

- There is a pattern in the relationship of the exponent and number of zeros in the standard form of the unit number. The number of placeholder zeros is equal to the exponent. This is because 10^1 has only one factor of 10 and 10^2 has two factors of 10 ($10 \times 10 = 100$). Therefore, 100,000 would have five zero placeholders and can be expressed as 10^5.

Relate again to place value:

- The number 1 has an unrepeated value of (1) or 1^1 or 1^0.
- The next place to the left of the (1), the tens place, has a value of 10 or 10^1 and requires *zero as a placeholder.*

- The symbol (1) in the hundreds place has a value of (100) or 10^2. A (1) in the next place to the left is the multiple of the 10 and the 100 and has a value of 1,000 or 10^3.
- Each position to the left corresponds to a base-10 exponential increase in value.
- The number 9 in the hundreds place represents nine hundreds. It has an additional factor of 9 or $(9 \times 10 \times 10)$ or 9×10^2.

Exemplar Problems

Exponents are used to indicate repeated multiplication. The number machine problem below investigates numbers in exponential notation. Use what you know about multiplication to help you see the patterns of exponential notations.

Problem: Richard is a new employee at Exponents 'r Us. His job duties are to change exponential notations into expanded number form. Richard's inputs are recorded in the Number Machine tables below. Complete the tables to show the patterns.

NUMBER MACHINE: TABLE A

INPUT	5^1	5^2	5^3	5^4	5^5	5^6
OUTPUT		25		625		

NUMBER MACHINE: TABLE B

INPUT	10^1	10^2	10^3	10^4	10^5	10^6	10^7
OUTPUT	10		1,000				

1. *What pattern did you observe in the outputs for Table A?*

2. *What pattern did you observe in the outputs for Table B?*

3. *What similarities did you observe in the outputs for both Tables A and B? Use mathematical reasoning to explain your results.*

4. *How is our place value system related to exponential notation?*

5. *Express the number 100,000,000 in exponential notation.*

6. *The richest people in this country are billionaires. How many factors of 10 are in one billion? If you started with $10, how many times would you have to multiply your money by 10 to become a billionaire? Express your net worth as a billionaire in exponential notation.*

2.4 Negative Integers

Developmental Transitions and Scaffolds

The recognition that negative integers raised to even exponent powers will result in positive values and that negative integers raised to odd powers will be negative values can be recognized (we commonly use the terminology *pattern recognition*) as a pattern. See Numbers 12.6 and 12.7 for preparatory concepts on the multiplication of positive and negative integers.

Exemplar Problem

A	$(-3)^2$	$(-3)^3$	$(-3)^4$	$(-3)^5$	$(-3)^6$	$(-3)^7$
B	9	−27	81	−243	729	−2,187
A	$(-4)^2$	$(-4)^3$	$(-4)^4$	$(-4)^5$	$(-4)^6$	$(-4)^7$
B						

Compare the exponential forms (row A) of negative three (−3) and the signs (row B) of the expanded value. Use your calculator to find the expanded values of the same exponents of (−4). What pattern do you see?

2.5 Composed Numbers

What about a number that is not a single-unit number?

- 3,000 is equal to $3 \times 1,000$, and 1,000 can be expressed as 10^3 or $10 \times 10 \times 10$, so we can express 3,000 as 3×10^3, and 26 million can be expressed as 26×10^6.
- 3,650 is composed of $3 \times 10^3 + 6 \times 10^2 + 5 \times 10^1$.

Exemplar Problem

Express the number 463,050 as its separate components of factors and exponents of 10.

2.6 Scientific Notation

An efficient way to express very large and small numbers is in scientific notation. The number 3,650 can also be expressed as 3.65×10^3.

What do we do to find the equivalent expression that is called scientific notation?

- Separate the number into two factors, one of which is an exponential notation of base 10. The other factor will be the number divided by a multiple of 10 that is equal to the value of the exponential notation. For 3,650, we can use 10^3 to express a factor of 1,000 and then divide 3,650 by 1,000 by shifting the number three places to the right (or moving the decimal point to the left). The product of this division is 3.65. Since we divided by a thousand, we can get back to the same value by multiplying by the 1,000 or 10^3. The result is two factors that equal (3,650) or (3.650×10^3). These two expressions have equal values.

Express the number 42,000 in scientific notation.

2.7–2.9 Zero and Negative Exponents

Developmental Transitions and Scaffolds

Although mathematicians have offered varying versions, explanations for zero and negative exponents are best connected to the logic of sequence patterns on a number line (see Number 2.1). If you think of each increasing exponent of the expression and expanded value to the left as requiring multiplication by an additional factor of the base, then moving to the right corresponds to a decreasing value of the exponent and division by a factor of the base. At the level of an exponent of (b^1), the expanded value is the unrepeated or unmultiplied base number. Moving one step further to the right of the unrepeated base number to an exponent of zero (b^0) requires that the base number be divided by itself for a value of (1). The expanded value for all bases to the zero power equals (1), $b^0 = 1$. The next value of the exponent to the right of an exponent of zero has to be (−1) and the expanded value a fraction: the value of (1) divided by the base.

$$3^2 = 9, \ 3^1 = 3, \ 3^0 = 1, \ 3^{-1} = \frac{1}{3}$$

Exemplar Problem

The values of numbers with exponents of zero and a negative number can be related to a pattern that decreases from left to right like our place value system.

Look at the patterns of exponents and expanded values in the following table.
Complete the table over and under the line.
Show the base-10 numbers with negative exponents in decimal form.
Show the base-4 numbers with negative exponents in fraction form.

10,000	1,000	100	10	1				
10^4	10^3	10^2	10^1	10^0	10^{-1}	10^{-2}	10^{-3}	10^{-4}

4^4	4^3	4^2	4^1	4^0	4^{-1}	4^{-2}	4^{-3}	4^{-4}
254	64	16	4	1				

What is the pattern of the expanded values of numbers with positive number exponents? What happens each time you move to the right and the exponent is decreased by 1?

- The expanded value to the right is the base number of times smaller (divided by the base number).

What is true about 4^1 and 10^1?

- $4^1 = 4$ or 4 one time and 10^1 is equal to 10.

What is true about any base number with an exponent of 1?

- Any base with an exponent of 1 is just the value of the base number.

What happens in the pattern if you continue to the right?

- If you continue to the right, the notation to the right of 4^1 is 4^0 and the value is four times smaller than 4 or equal to 1. 10^0 is also equal to 1 because it is ten times smaller than 10^1.

What is true about base number with an exponent of zero?

- Any base raised to the zero power is equal to 1.

What happens to the value if you continue further to the right?

- If you continue further to the right, the next value must be four times smaller than 1 or equal to $\frac{1}{4}$. The exponential notation for the value of $\frac{1}{4}$ is 4^{-1}. The next value to the right is four times smaller than $\frac{1}{4}$ or $\frac{1}{16}$, and the exponential notation is 4^{-2}. Bases with negative exponents will always have values less than 1. If you look at the pattern, you will see that the value of the base with a negative exponent is the inverse of the value of the base with a corresponding positive exponent.

If $4^3 = 64$, then what is the value of 4^{-3}?

$$4^{-3} = \frac{1}{64}$$

The utility of exponential forms to express small fractions and decimals in notations, including scientific notation, can be elucidated with examples such as the size of cell parts and sections of DNA, minor variations in the world populations, and the Earth in comparison to the universe. Operations are also easier.

Exemplar Problems

About 57,230,000 square miles of the Earth's surface is land. Write this in scientific notation.

———————————— ✁ ————————————

There are 8.64×10^4 seconds in a day. Write the fraction that represents the part of a whole day for a second.

———————————— ✁ ————————————

A raisin weighs 4×10^{-2} oz. What is this weight as a decimal?

3.1–3.3 Square Roots, Perfect, and Nonperfect Square Numbers

See also Chapter 2, page 22, for concepts and expectations.

Developmental Transitions and Scaffolds

What is the square root of a number?

- The square root of a number is the number that must be multiplied by itself to get a product that is that number. The square root of 36 is 6 because 6×6 is 36. In symbol form, $\sqrt{36} = 6$.

What are perfect square numbers?

- The numbers that have whole-number square roots are called perfect squares.
- The perfect square numbers include 1, 4, 9, 16, 25, 36, 49, 64, 81, 100, 121, 144, 169, 196, 225, and many others.

Do you see a pattern in the sequence of these numbers?

- The sequence of these numbers forms an identifiable pattern (an increase by the sequence of odd numbers starting with 3).
- The numbers in between are nonperfect squares.
- The square roots of nonperfect squares are irrational numbers.

For developing some facility with geometry and other real-life problems, it may be a good idea to aim for automatization of the sequence of perfect square numbers through 225 or the square of 15. Students can then make estimates of nonperfect numbers when necessary and appropriate and also use the estimates as a check when they use their calculators to get the exact value.

Recognition of the numbers in between the perfect square numbers as nonperfect squares is useful in understanding geometric measures. Basic concepts include the following:

- The square roots of nonperfect square numbers are irrational numbers because they are nonrepeating, nonterminating decimals.
- *If they terminated, they would be perfect squares.*
- You can make estimates of the value of the square root of a nonperfect square by identifying the perfect squares between which it is located or enclosed.

Exemplar Problem

Between which two consecutive whole numbers does $\sqrt{61}$ lie?

4.1–4.4 Number System Sets and Subsets

See also Chapter 2, page 23, for concepts and expectations.

Developmental Transitions and Scaffolds

The various terminologies and overlapping sets that identify and discriminate between the number system sets can be confusing to students—at times even to teachers. For example, the term *rational number* is not just an alternate term for *fraction,* even though most ordinarily used numbers in fraction form are rational numbers. The basic definitions, however, may be necessary for understanding later applications. A Venn diagram will help develop the understanding of the set inclusions of number systems.

- The real number system includes all whole numbers, integers, and rational and irrational numbers.
- The whole-number system includes the positive counting numbers and zero.
- The integers include all the whole positive numbers and their inverses or opposites (negative numbers) and zero.

- The rational numbers are numbers that can be represented in the form *a/b*, where *b* is not zero. Integers are rational numbers because they can be represented in this form (e.g., 6/1).
- The irrational numbers cannot be represented in the form *a/b*, and there are many of them, including nonterminating decimals, nonrepeating decimals (such as the value of pi), and the square roots of nonperfect squares.

4.5 Imaginary Numbers

There is, in contrast to the real numbers, a set of imaginary numbers. They are recognized because certain operations will not result in a real number. For example, the square root of a negative integer is impossible or imaginary. The imaginary number that is $\sqrt{-1}$ is named (*i*).

Exemplar Problem

Use the Venn diagram below to help you locate the sets within which you would find each of the following numbers. Check each box that applies.

Number	Real Number	Whole Number	Counting Number	Integer	Rational Number	Irrational Number
24						
25.5						
−3						
$\sqrt{5}$						
Π (Ω)						

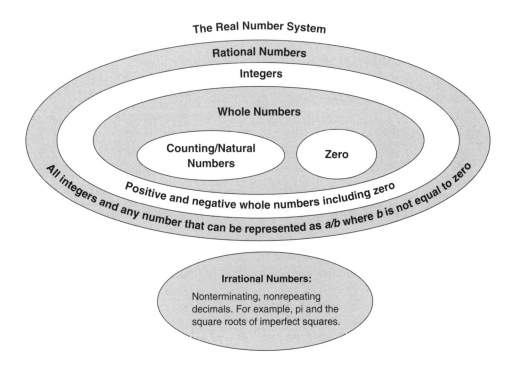

■ **NUMBER OPERATIONS**

5.1–5.2 Factors and Multiples

See also Chapter 2, pages 24–25, for concepts and expectations.

An understanding of multiples and factors should precede the introduction of complex operations with fractions. The concept of the associative principle of multiplication is a first step. Let students explore this with arrays of color tiles or computer drawing programs. When they realize that enlarging a value three times and then two times results in the same outcome as multiplying it six times or the product of the separate increments, you can introduce the concept of the common multiple as it relates to the associative principle. A difficulty observed for some sixth graders is in the distinction between the greatest common factor (GCF) and the least common multiple (LCM). Try using the balloon-shrinking reversal of the associate principle (see number 5.5) to begin to clarify this. The rectangle building activity described on page 113 may also help. The basic concepts include the following:

- Factors are all the whole-number values (referent and abstract operators) that can be combined in the multiplication process to give a particular value or multiple of the product.
- The products of factors are called multiples.
- A number is a factor of a second number multiple only if you can divide the multiple by the first one with no remainder.
- Two is a factor of 6, but it is not a factor of 5.
- Dividing a multiple by one factor results in another factor.
- One or more factors can be common for two or more different multiples (e.g., 2, 4, and 5 are factors of 10, 20, and 40).
- Different sets of more than two factors may have common multiples (e.g., a set of factors 3, 2, and 6 and a set of 4, 3, 1, and 12 have a common multiple of 12).

5.3 Common Multiples

Use arrangements of color tiles in rectangles to demonstrate the concept of a common multiple. A rectangle of 30 tiles can be formed with sides of 5 and 6 tiles, 15 and 2 tiles, 3 and 10 tiles, and 30 and 1 tile. The lengths of the sides are the factors. Each rectangle for the same multiple of 30 has the same number of repeated units of area, 30 square tiles. This can also be related to the associative principle, as demonstrated below.

$$(3 \times 5) \times 2 = 15 \times 2 = (3 \times 2) \times 5 = 6 \times 5 = 30 \times 1$$

Developmental Transitions and Scaffolds

What is the final product when you begin with a factor of 3 and multiply it by a factor of 4 and then multiply the product by a factor of 2?

What is the final product when you begin with a factor of 2 and multiply it by a factor of 12?

Why did you get the same multiple?

What is a common multiple for the factors 2, 3, 4, and 12?

Write what you did as equations:

$$3 \times 4 \times 2 = ?; \quad 2 \times 12 = ?$$

Can you rewrite the second equation so that it has the same factors as the first?
Are there other ways to reach a multiple of 12?

5.4 Least Common Multiple

The common multiple concept can be extended from the rectangle building activity on page 113 to illustrate that although there are other possible multiples for the factors of (1, 2, 3, 5, 6, 10, 15, 30), the smallest possible rectangle that is a multiple of all of these factors is their *least common multiple* (LCM). This can later be related to the *least common denominator* needed for fraction operations.

Showing its utility in measures can enhance the common multiple concept. I like to call multiples that have many factors "Happy Numbers."

Developmental Transitions and Scaffolds

Why do we divide our day into 24 hours or 12 before noon and 12 after noon, and why did we decide that 12 eggs are a dozen?

- Because the multiples of 12 and 24 have many factors. We can divide 12 into 2, 3, 4, and 6 or 12 *equal whole-number parts.*

Why do we divide a circle into 360°? What makes 360 a "Happy Number"?

- It has many factors, including 15 and 24. The whole circular sphere of the Earth is divided into 360 degrees and lines of longitude every 15 degrees. It takes the Earth one hour or 1/24 of the day to rotate these 15 degrees. The number 360 is a common multiple of 15 and 24.

5.5 Common Factors

Developmental Transitions and Scaffolds

What are the common factors of 12 and 24?
A balloon of size 3 can grow four whole times to size 12, a balloon of size 2 can grow six whole times to size 12, and a balloon of size 1 can grow twelve whole times to size 12. Therefore, 1, 2, 3, 4, 6, and 12 are factors of the multiple of 12. A balloon of size 3 can grow eight whole times to size 24, a balloon of size 4 can grow six whole times to size 24, a balloon of size 2 can grow twelve whole times to size 24, and a balloon of size 1 can grow twenty-four whole times to size 24. 1, 2, 3, 4, 6, 8, 12, and 24 are factors of the multiple of 24. A balloon of size 12 can also shrink three whole times to size 4, twelve whole times to size 1, or six whole times to size 2. A balloon of size 24 can shrink six whole times to size 4, two whole times to size 12, twenty-four whole times to size 1, and eight whole times to size 3. Therefore, 1, 2, 3, 4, 6, and 12 are common factors of the multiples of 12 and 24.

What factors of 24 are not factors of 12?

- A balloon of size 24 can shrink twenty-four whole times to size 1 or eight whole times to size 3. A balloon of size 12 cannot shrink twenty-four whole times or eight whole times. Therefore, 8 and 24 are not common factors of 12 and 24.
- A balloon of size 8 can shrink four whole times to 2, two whole times to 4, or eight whole times to 1, but it cannot shrink three whole times to a whole number. Two and 4 are also common factors of 8, but 3 is not because there is not a whole number of threes in 8.

5.6 Greatest Common Factor

The relationships between factors and their multiples can be explored with tiles and then organized into tables. It is also useful to find the *greatest common factor (GCF)*.

Reverting to the factors that form the sides of the rectangles above, try building different rectangles using one of the same-side measures (just add to either the length or width without touching the other). Each multiple or rectangle formed has a *common factor that is the untouched side*. Common factors are factors that are common to different multiples. Each of the multiples with a common factor can be equally divided into whole-number parts. This relationship between multiples and factors is needed for reducing fractions to lowest terms. Using the GCF simplifies the process. Some texts refer to the *greatest common divisor*, which is the operational terminology for the *greatest common factor*. We can reduce fractions to simplest terms by dividing numerator and denominator by the GCF or greatest common divisor, and we simplify algebraic expressions by dividing all terms by the GCF.

Developmental Transitions and Scaffolds

Some multiples have *common factors*.

Look at your color tile rectangles with multiples of 12 and 24.

1. What are the *common factors* of multiples of 12 and 24?
   There are whole groups of twelve, six, four, three, two, and one in 12 and 24. They are common factors of the different multiples, 12 and 24.

2. What are the factors of 24 that were not factors of 12?

3. What is the *greatest common factor* of 12 and 24?

4. Why isn't 8 or 24 the *greatest common factor* of 12 and 24?

5. How many different rectangles can you build with a multiple of 18 tiles?

6. What are the factors of 18?

7. What factors are common for multiples of 12, 18, and 24?

8. What is the *greatest common factor* of 12, 18, and 24?

Find the factors of 12 and 24. Then find the factors of 18. Make a table of factors and common factors. Explain any difference.

Exemplar Problems

Match each equation with a picture and your tiles.

$$5 \times 3 = 15 \quad\quad 2 \times 3 = 6$$
$$2 \times 15 = 30 \quad\quad 5 \times 6 = 30$$

How many groups of three tiles are in both final multiples of 30?
Complete the equation to show these: (? × 3 = 30).
How many single tiles result in a multiple of 30?
Complete the equation: (? × 30 = 30).
30 is a common multiple of the factors (5, ?, ?, ?, ?, ?, ?, and ?).
Are there other common multiples for these factors?
What would be the least common multiple (LCM)?

Build these rectangles with your color tiles.

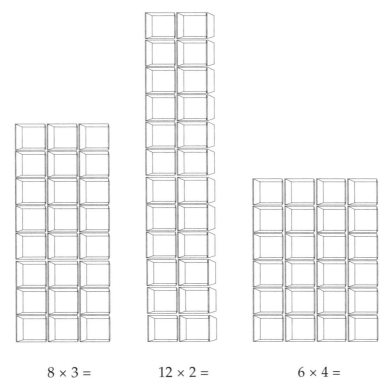

$$8 \times 3 = \quad\quad 12 \times 2 = \quad\quad 6 \times 4 =$$

1. Count the total number of color tiles in each rectangle.

2. What is the common multiple of the color tile lengths and widths?

3. Make a list of all the different lengths and widths (in color tiles).

4. Why can we call the lengths and widths factors of the multiple of 12?

5. What are the factors of 12?

6. Can you build a larger rectangle, with a multiple of 24, using all of the factors of the multiple of 12?

7. *What are all the factors of the larger multiple?*

8. *What is the* least common multiple *for the factors of 1, 12, 2, 6, 3, and 4?*

9. *What is the* least common multiple *for the factors of 1, 12, 2, 6, 3, 4, 8, and 24?*

10. *What are the common factors of multiples of 12 and 24?*

11. *What are the factors of 24 that were not factors of 12?*

12. *What is the* greatest common factor *of 12 and 24?*

13. *Why isn't 8 or 24 the* greatest common factor *of 12 and 24?*

14. *How many different rectangles can you build with a multiple of 18 tiles?*

15. *What are the factors of 18?*

16. *What factors are common for multiples of 12, 18, and 24?*

17. *What is the* greatest common factor *of 12, 18, and 24?*

If you divide multiples of 12 and 24 tiles into groups that are the size of each factor, what is the number of groups that you will have for each factor?

Multiples of 12	**Multiples of 24**
Groups of size 1 ____	Groups of size 1 ____
Groups of size 2 ____	Groups of size 2 ____
Groups of size 3 ____	Groups of size 3 ____
Groups of size 4 ____	Groups of size 4 ____
Groups of size 6 ____	Groups of size 6 ____
Groups of size 12 ____	Groups of size 8 ____
	Groups of size 12 ____
	Groups of size 24 ____

What relationship do you see between the size of the multiples and the number of groups of each common factor size?

––––––––––––––––––– ✳ –––––––––––––––––––

Use your color tiles to find the least common multiples for these factors. Construct the smallest rectangle that contains whole groups of each factor.

Factors	Least Common Multiples
3, 4, 2, 12	
7, 3, 1	
7, 3, 6, 21	

Multiple	All Factors	Common Factors of 12 and 24	Common Factors of 12 and 18	Common Factors of 12, 18, and 24
12				
24				
18				

Some multiples have common factors.
Circle the greatest common factor in each common factor column.
The concept of factors and common factors is critical as a basis for solving complex algebraic equations, and practice will be needed for this. Use the color tiles and tables as above, but factor trees can also work. Try relating factors to measures.

Use exchanges in money to make the concept real. A dime and a quarter are common factors of the dollar because you can change the dollar for only dimes or quarters. But the dime is not a factor of the quarter because the quarter cannot be exchanged for a whole number of dimes. It is a factor of a half dollar. Nickels and pennies are common factors of the quarter, the dime, and the half dollar.

5.7–5.8 Prime Numbers, Prime Factors, and Composite Numbers

Developmental Transitions and Scaffolds

Use the same rectangles made from color tiles to construct other multiples and define the factors. Let them discover that some rectangle multiples can only have two factors—the multiple and 1—and therefore form only one kind of rectangle, with one side = 1. *These are prime numbers.* Prime numbers have only two factors: themselves and (1). Factors of a multiple that are prime numbers because they cannot be further equally divided into whole numbers are *prime factors. Composite numbers* are not prime because they have more than two factors. Mathematicians have agreed that the number (1) itself is neither prime nor composite since it fits neither definition.

1. How many different rectangles can you build with 3, 5, 7, and 9 tiles?

2. What was true of the multiples of 3, 5, and 7 that was not true of 9?

3. What are some other multiples that can only form one rectangle?

Let students use color tiles to discover the generalization that although for two prime numbers, the (LCM) is always the product of the two, other LCMs may be less than the product of the factors.

6.1 Divisibility Tests

See also Chapter 2, page 25, for concepts and expectations.

Developmental Transitions and Scaffolds

Divisibility tests are useful patterns for factorization problems. A multiple number is divisible by another if the remainder is zero, or it can be divided into equal whole-number parts. There are certain tests we can use to determine divisibility by possible factors. Divisibility confirms that the divisor is a factor of the multiple.

- Any number where the ones digit is zero is divisible by 10.
- Any number where the ones digit is (5) or (0) following a digit in the tens place is divisible by (5).
- Any number where the ones digit is 2, 4, 6, 8, or 0 following a digit in the tens place is divisible by 2.
- Any number where the sum of its digits is divisible by (3) is divisible by 3.
- Any number where the last two digits are divisible by 4 is divisible by 4. The number 324 is divisible by 2, but it is also divisible by 3 because the sum of its digits is divisible by 3, and it is divisible by 4 because its last two digits (24) are divisible by 4.

Exemplar Problem

Quickly judge what numbers are factors of these multiples and therefore divisible by the number. Put a check in all the possible columns for divisibility and factor confirmation. Can you find a number that would have a check in every column?

Number	Divisible by 2	Divisible by 3	Divisible by 4	Divisible by 5
30				
124				
261				
332				
372				
540				

6.2 Factoring

Developmental Transitions and Scaffolds

When we factor a number, we try to find all the possible factors. We can use factor trees to help guide us. A *prime factorization* takes us all the way to prime factors—we keep finding the smaller factors until we hit a prime number. Sometimes we may end up with more than a single event of the same prime number. We can represent these in exponential form. Remember that the product of all the factors must equal the multiple you begin with.

Exemplar Problems

Complete the following factor tree by writing the correct numbers in empty boxes.
Explain why there are no branches coming from the double-lined boxes.
What prime number is repeated?
How many times is it repeated?
How do we represent these prime factors in exponential form?
Write an equation that shows all the prime number factors of 40.

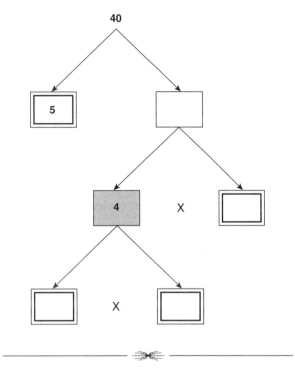

Compute the prime factorization of 32.
Write the prime factors of 32 in exponential form.

A restaurant owner was arranging tables for a party for thirty-six people. He needed to place an equal number of people at each table. His largest table could seat eighteen people, and the smallest table seated just two people.

A. What are all the different equal seating arrangements that he could make? Complete the chart below to show them.

Number of Tables	Number Seated at Each Table
	18
	2

B. The owner said that he could not arrange for equal seating if there was one more person (37), but that he could equally seat a group of one less person (35). Use what you know about prime and composite numbers to explain this.

⸻ ✳ ⸻ ⸻

Find the prime factorization of 6, 12, 24, and 48.

Number	Prime Factorization
6	
12	
24	
48	

Notice the pattern of the numbers and factors for 6, 12, 24, and 48. If this pattern continues, what would be the prime factorization of the next two numbers in the pattern?

■ OPERATION PATTERNS AND PROPERTIES

7.1 Multiplication and Division Patterns/ Estimation

See also Chapter 2, pages 25–27, for concepts and expectations.

Patterns are very useful in estimations. To help develop estimation skills, play games like "Beat the Calculator," in which a multidigit problem is estimated in different ways (such as front-end or rounding), checked with the calculator, and differences analyzed. It may be helpful for students to review the concept that 20 times a quantity is twice as much as 10 times that quantity and that we can either make the quantity ten times larger and then make it twice as large or make it twice as large and then ten times larger (the associative principle): $3 \times 10 \times 2$ is equal to $3 \times 2 \times 10$, and $(2 \times 10) \times (2 \times 10)$ is equal to 4×100 or 400. Therefore, we can generalize that 2 tens × 2 tens will be 4 hundreds, and because tens times hundreds are thousands, 20×300 will be 6,000, and by extending the concept, $200 \times 300 = 60,000$, $300 \times 6,000 = 1,800,000$, and $3,000 \times 6,000 = 18,000,000$.

We can also generalize the inverse division patterns: Hundreds divided by tens will equal tens, and therefore 600 (6 hundreds) ÷ 20 (2 tens) = 30 (3 tens). Similarly, 24,000 ÷ 60 (24 thousands divided by 6 tens) is equal to 4 hundreds (400). Millions divided by thousands equal thousands, and 18,000,000 ÷ 3,000 = 6,000.

Exemplar Problems

Number of times a group is repeated		$0\times$	$10\times$	$20\times$	$30\times$	$40\times$	$50\times$
	0	0	0	0	0	0	0
	10	0	100	200	300	400	500
	20	0	200	400	600	800	1,000
	30	0	300	600	900	1,200	1,500
Size of the group (unit)	40	0	400	800	1,200	1,600	2,000
	50	0	500	1,000	1,500	2,000	2,500
	60	0	600	1,200	1,800	2,400	3,000
	70	0	700	1,400	2,100	2,800	3,500
	80	0	800	1,600	2,400	3,200	4,000
	90	0	900	1,800	2,700	3,600	4,500
	100	0	1,000	2,000	3,000	4,000	5,000
	1,000						

How much is 3 tens times 6 tens? How much is 4 tens times 5 tens?
Do you see a pattern? Think about larger numbers that are not on the table.
How much would 4 tens times 5 hundreds be?
$60 \times 300 = ?$
$400 \times 30 = ?$
Finish the last row of this table. Add a 200$\times$ column.

Size of part or number of parts		10	20	30	40	50
	100	1,000	2,000	3,000	4,000	5,000
	200	2,000	4,000	6,000	8,000	10,000
	300	3,000	6,000	9,000	12,000	15,000
	400	4,000	8,000	12,000	16,000	20,000
Size of part or number of parts	500	5,000	10,000	15,000	20,000	25,000
	600	6,000	12,000	18,000	24,000	30,000
	700	7,000	14,000	21,000	28,000	35,000
	800	8,000	16,000	24,000	32,000	40,000
	900	9,000	18,000	27,000	36,000	45,000
	1,000	10,000	20,000	30,000	40,000	50,000
	2,000	20,000	40,000	60,000	80,000	100,000

Look for the patterns: What products do you see when you multiply tens × hundreds? What happens when you multiply tens × thousands?
Use this table to estimate the following multiplication problems:

The library shelves held many books. Each shelf in a shelf section held 485 books. There were nineteen shelves in one section. About how many books were there in this section? Use your calculator to get an exact answer and check your estimate.

Another room in the library had 42 sections with 610 books in each. About how many books was that? Use your calculator to get an exact answer and check your estimate.

Cover the table and try this estimate:

A room in the library had 39 sections with 510 books in each. About how many books is that?

Use this same table to help estimate the following division problems:

5,976 books were placed on thirty library shelves. About how many books were on each shelf?

59,045 books were stacked in the library with 2,000 books in each section. About how many sections were filled?

Use your calculator to get an exact answer and check your estimate.

What patterns do you see for dividing thousands by tens?

What patterns do you see for dividing ten thousands by thousands?

Try this without looking at the table.

About how many shelves would you need for 12,400 books if each shelf held 30 books?

7.2 Arithmetic Sequence Patterns

Recognition and practice with arithmetic and geometric sequences are excellent and interesting ways to practice concepts and skills. A recent popular Web site blog published a poem using the Fibonacci sequence. In this sequence, each successive term is the sum of the previous two numbers (0, 1, 1, 2, 3, 5, 8…). The poem had an increasing number of syllables in each line that corresponded to the sequence. As reported by *The New York Times* (April 14, 2006), within days, there were Fibonacci poems or "Fibs" all over the Internet. The relationships of mathematics to other subjects and real-life applications can make the math more meaningful and fun. They can bring important life skills to computations such as compound interest or sequential nonadditive discounts. Each number in the series is called a term, and three dots indicate that the series continues. The rule explains the relationship between each successive term. Sequences may be arithmetic, geometric, or neither. Arithmetic sequences add the same value to the preceding term each time to create the next term. Geometric sequences multiply the preceding term by the same value each time. The Fibonacci sequence is neither arithmetic nor geometric.

Begin with the arithmetic sequences, adding only positive integers at first, and then try adding negative integers. The temperature decline illustrated in Number 1.9 can be written as an arithmetic series adding negative integers.

Exemplar Problems

What are the next two terms in this series? 5, 12, 19, 26, . . .
   What is the rule that determines each subsequent term?

What are the next two terms in this series? 1, 3, 6, 10, 15 . . .
   What is the rule that determines each subsequent term?

Find the next two terms in this series: 18, 13, 8, 3, –2, . . .
   Explain the rule for the series.

Your new job pays $8.00 an hour, but every month, there is an increase of $.50 per hour. How much would you be earning at the end of 6 months?
   Try more complex series. Build geometric forms to match the series to see the pattern connections. *Build a series of triangles with your blocks. Make the bottom row one block larger each time. What happens to the total number of blocks each time?*

7.3 Geometric Sequences: Function Expressions

Geometric series that involve rules that are multiplicative functions should follow understanding of the arithmetic series. Each succeeding term is a multiple of the preceding one. The multiplier by which it increased is called the series ratio.

Developmental Transitions and Scaffolds

The rules for geometric series can be expressed as functions. Try the function notation for Susan's garden, $N = n \times (10)$, where N = the size of the garden for a particular term or year and n is the ordinal number of the term in the series (the fourth year).

$$N = 4 \times 10 = 40$$

Exemplar Problem

Susan had a garden that she kept. Each year she made her garden three times larger than it was in the first year. If the garden was 10 square feet in the first year, how large was it in the fourth year? Show the series and explain the rule.

7.4 Exponential Sequences

Sequences may also be exponential. An exponential series is simply an exponential expansion in which the starting term is the base number, and the number of the terms is equal to the exponent ($N = B^n$). The fourth term of a series that begins with 3 is $N = 3^4$ or $N = 81$.

Susan bought a special plant that always produced three bulbs in the fall. She planted the bulbs and they grew into healthy plants. Every year, she planted all the bulbs from each plant, and they all grew into new plants. How many bulbs did she have by the fourth year? Write the series and express the rule as a function.

$$N = n^4$$

7.5 Other Sequences

Like the Fibonacci sequence, some sequences are neither arithmetic nor geometric. We can write an expression or an equation that represents the sequence and use it to determine a number in the sequence. The letter (n) is used to represent the ordinal or sequence position of the term. The equation that describes the sequence, $N = n(n - 2)$, tells you that the fourth term ($n = 4$) in the series is the cardinal number 8. Some of these series, such as compound interest, affect our everyday lives.

Exemplar Problems

Use your calculator to help solve these problems.

Janine had a bank savings account that paid 8% interest quarterly or every three months. The bank divided the interest into four quarters, paying 2% for each quarter. She deposited her birthday gift checks that totaled $1,000 and expected to have $1,080 at the end of the year. To her surprise, she had $1082.62 at the end of the year. Explain the rule for the quarterly interest series that gave her this amount. What were the terms for each quarter? How much would she have at the next quarter? Write an equation that represents the rule for this series.

The store had a big sale on clothing. Chris bought a jacket that was originally $100. The sign on the ticket said it would be 25% off, but Chris also had a coupon for another 25%. He expected to pay only $50 for the jacket, but it rang up for $56.25. Was the register wrong? Explain the rule for series of discounts. Write an equation for the rule.

8.1–8.2 Inverse Properties: Addition/Subtraction and Multiplication/Division

See also Chapter 2, pages 27–29, for concepts and expectations.

An understanding of inverse properties is essential to algebraic problem solving. Apply the property first to simple constant values and then to variables.

Developmental Transitions and Scaffolds

Addition is the inverse of subtraction and vice versa. If you add a number to a given number and then subtract the same number, you have not changed the original number or value of the number. The reverse is also true.

-4 is the additive inverse of $+4$, $4 - 4 + 4 = 4$.

$-a$ is the named additive inverse of a, $a - a + a = a$.

Multiplication is the inverse of division and vice versa. If you multiply a number by a given number and then divide the product by the same number, you have not changed the original number or value of the number. The reverse is also true. If you divide a number by a given number and then multiply the quotient by the same number, you have not changed the original number or value of the number.

$$a \times b \div b = a \qquad a \div b \times b = a.$$

$1 \times 5 = 5$, $1 \div 5$ is an inverse operation and equal to $\frac{1}{5}$.

$\frac{1}{5}$ is the multiplicative inverse if 1 and the two numbers, 1 and $\frac{1}{5}$, are reciprocals.

8.3 Reciprocals

Two numbers whose product is equal to 1 are reciprocals. $\frac{1}{8}$ is the reciprocal of 8 because $\frac{1}{8} \times 8 = 1$. $\frac{1}{a}$ is the reciprocal of a.

8.4 Commutative Property (Law)

Changing the sequence or order of addends or factors does not change the sum or product.

$$a + b + c = b + a + c$$

$$a \times b = ab = b \times a = ba$$

The commutative property does not apply to subtraction or division.

8.5 Associative Properties of Addition and Multiplication

In addition, changing the grouping of addends does not change the sum. $(25 + 2b) + (c) = (2b + c) + 25$.

Changing the grouping of factors does not change the product of multiplication.

If the original value or referent is multiplied in separate steps or increments, and each time it is the previous product that is multiplied, the same end result can be obtained by multiplying the original referent by the product of each incremental step. For example, blowing up a balloon to two times the size and then making the new size balloon three times bigger is the same as blowing the original up two times and then three times more or six times all at once.

$$3 \times (2 \times N) = 2 (3 \times N) = 6 \times N$$

8.6 Distributive Property of Multiplication

If numbers are separated into parts and each part multiplied by the same multiplier, the sum of the products will equal the product of the whole number multiplied by that multiplier.

$$12 \times 16a = (12 \times 10a) + (12 \times 6a) = 120a + 72a = 192a$$

$$12(10a + 6a) = 120a + 72a = 192a$$

8.7 Identity Properties of Addition and Multiplication

The sum of any number and zero is equal to the number: $ab + 0 = ab$.
The product of any number and 1 is equal to the number: $ab^2 \times 1 = ab^2$.
The product of any number and zero is equal to zero.

8.8 Law of Closure

In a closed set of numbers, when a specific operation (such as addition or multiplication) is performed on any two numbers in the set, the result will always be a specific number in the set. For example, $4 + 5$ is always equal to 9, and 4×5 is always equal to 20. The set of rational numbers is closed for addition and multiplication but not for division because the quotient of a number divided by zero is undefined and not included in the set of rational numbers.

9.1 Multiplication Algorithm

See also Chapter 2, pages 29–30, for concepts and expectations.

A review of the multiplication algorithm for whole numbers may be a useful preparation for applications to decimals. The critical concept is that if each digit is repeatedly added separately and then the products are combined, the total is equivalent to repeated addition of both digits. Essentially, adding (23) four times to get 92 is the same as adding (20) four times to get 80 and (3) four times to get 12 and then combining the partial products to get 92. This is the distributive principle of multiplication.

Regrouping or trading in the algorithm as an alternative to separately added sub-products should not be a problem if the concept has been developed in previous grades. Begin by showing each partial product separately and then move to consolidating them. When necessary, use base-10 blocks as a manipulative and the triad connections of manipulative, words, and symbols.

If some students have not yet automatized the multiplication facts, encourage and help them to do this as soon as possible. Familiarity with the algorithm's application of the distributive principle will also help in algebraic applications. If students are resorting to their calculators to avoid the automatization challenge, stress the importance of mental estimation as a critical skill needed to check calculator entries and for understanding what you are doing.

Developmental Transitions and Scaffolds

Shanequa had a collection of CDs. She kept them on racks. Each rack held twenty-four CDs. About how many CDs would fourteen racks hold?

Exactly how many CDs would the fourteen racks hold?

Let's distribute the repeated additions or multiplications and write them as separate number sentences.

$$14 \times 24 = (4 \times 4) + (4 \times 20) + (10 \times 4) + (10 \times 20)$$

Let's do the multiplication in the parentheses first and then add.

$$14 \times 24 = 16 + 80 + 40 + 200 = 336$$

Now let's try the vertical algorithm.

Alan used an algorithm (A) to solve Shanequa's problem. Steve said he could simplify the algorithm and did (B). Were both algorithms correct? Can you explain what Steve did to get to B?

A   **B**

```
      2    (4)                              24
  ×  /1\  (4)                             × 14
  _____                                  96
       1    6                               240
       8    0                               336
       4    0
   2   0    0
   3   3    6
```

Now try this.

Write a number sentence for the product of the values in the hexagon and the circle.
Write a number sentence for the product of the values in the square and hexagon.
Write a number sentence for the product of the values in the triangle and the circle.
Write a number sentence for the product of the values in the triangle and the square.

9.2–9.5 Division

Just as subtraction presents the first great hurdle for students in the early elementary grades, division presents a challenge for the upper grades. Part of the difficulty lies in the variations of the division concepts and the tendency to overlook these concepts and move too quickly to a difficult algorithm. If we think of multiplication as repeated addition, division could also be conceptualized as repeated subtraction. This does not come easily from the earlier grade experiences, which introduced the operation as the concept of sharing. The sharing concept form for division is termed *partition*. Given real problems and manipulatives, students readily solve partition problems. In a partition problem, we know the whole value and we know the number of parts. What we do not know is the size of each part. Partition division is directly related to fractions. Dividing something into four parts is like finding 1/4 of it. The connection should be made as soon as possible.

In *quotition* division (some texts refer to it as measurement division), we know the size of the group but not the number of groups. Quotition is the inverse of repeated addition and can be explained on a number line as repeated subtraction. We start with the whole group and repeatedly subtract the equal parts to discover how many there are in the whole. Quotition problems are also a good way to understand the inverse relationship between division and multiplication. Finding out how many groups of size (5) there are in 30 is *the inverse* of finding out how much six groups of (5) is equal to. Quotition problems are less common to the child's experience, but the standard division algorithm is traditionally taught in the frame of reference of a quotition problem (e.g., How many 5s are there in 25?). Another important reason for recognizing the different forms is that it is impossible to apply the partition concept using fractional divisors. You cannot have a fractional number of parts. You cannot divide six wholes into .5 or 1/2 number of parts, but you can find out how many parts of size .5 are in six wholes.

Another division concept that needs clarity is that division of a number is not always going to result in an equal number of whole parts. Sometimes there are remainders. If it makes sense in the problem, remainders can be shown as fractional parts of the whole. The denominator of the fraction is the size of a whole group or part (the divisor), and the numerator is the remaining undivided pieces.

The automatization of division facts is just as critical as the multiplication facts and should be presented as the inverse of the multiplication facts, but in the frame of reference of both quotition and partition. There should also be clarity of the fact that, like subtraction, division is not commutative when considering the whole that is divided or grouped. $12 \div 3$ is not the same as $3 : 12$. However, the size of the group and the number of groups are alternate meanings for the same answer. $12 \div 3$ could mean either how many groups of size 3 are there in 12, with an answer of 4, or how large would each group be if you divided the 12 into three groups. Automatization of division facts is a precursor to the mastery of a division algorithm. Once the facts are automatized, estimation of quotients for multidigit divisor problems is both possible and useful. Allow students to use a variety of approaches to the estimation process, but an inverse generalization of the one for multidigit multiplication is very useful. If tens times hundreds are thousands (e.g., 2 tens times 3 hundreds are 6 thousands), then thousands divided by tens are hundreds and thousands divided by hundreds are tens ($21,000 \div 70 = 300$ and $21,000 \div 700 = 30$). Twenty-one thousand divided by 7 tens = 3 hundreds, and 21 thousands divided by 7 hundreds = 3 tens. Manipulatives and tables such as those in Number 7.1 will help students recognize the patterns.

Developmental Transitions and Scaffolds

Use a variety of manipulatives and the calculator to develop the division concepts.

Partition/Quotition:

> We had seventy-two candy bars and divided them among twelve of our friends. How many candy bars did each one get?

> We had seventy-two candy bars and gave twelve of them to each of our friends. How many friends could get the twelve bars?

> What does each problem tell us? Are we trying to find out the number of parts (quotition) or the size of each group (partition)?

Repeated Subtraction:

> Angelo had 156 pieces of gum for his party. The gum came in packages of twelve. How many whole packages did he have? Did he have any loose ones? Enter the whole number of gum pieces into your calculator. Subtract twelve at a time. How many times did you subtract twelve before you got to zero? How many twelves are there in 156?

Remainders:

Now try to find out how many whole packages there would be if he had 245 pieces.

Will there be more or less than twenty packages? How do you know? How many pieces in ten packages, in twenty packages? How many loose pieces do we have? What fraction of a whole package would that be?

Division of and by Zero

It is easy for students to understand that zero divided into any number of parts is still going to be zero or that there are no other quantities in zero. However, dividing a number value by zero is more of an abstraction and difficult to understand. When any number is divided by zero, the quotient is undefined. Although the most number of threes in 24 is always eight, there could be any number of zeros in 24.

Exemplar Problem

The following table shows the number of runs batted in (RBIs) for each baseball team that was the total for preseason games. For each team, decide what is the greatest number of innings where there could have been two RBIs, the greatest number of innings where there could have been three runs, and the greatest number of innings where there could have been zero runs.

Team	Total RBIs	Most Possible Innings With Two Runs	Most Possible Innings With Three Runs	Most Possible Innings With Zero Runs
Team A	24			
Team B	36			

How did you get your answer for the greatest number of innings with two runs and three runs?

Why was it impossible to get an answer for the greatest number of innings with zero runs?

Give some possibilities for how different numbers of zero RBI innings could be scored in one game with a score of twelve runs.

Why is any number divided by zero undefined?

Short- and Long-Form Algorithm

The division algorithm has always been a challenge for elementary students. The prevalence of calculators has made it less significant, but understanding of the processes involved enhances understanding of the numerical division process and prepares students for algebraic division problems. The division algorithm should be developed within a triad of problem words, manipulatives, and symbols in reference to both partition and quotition problems. The problem may lie in the way we describe the division problem.

Developmental Transitions and Scaffolds

From the quotitive perspective, when we ask, "How many twos are there in 6?" we infer "the most" number of twos. There could, for example, be (1) group of 2 and (1) group of

4 or (2) groups of 2 and (2) single ones in 6, but the most number of groups of two in 6 is (3). There is really no limit to the number of zeros in a sum value of 6, and so we say that 6 divided by zero is undefined. Real data such as that below are useful.

Even though we traditionally use quotition terms in teaching the algorithm, teachers may find themselves switching back and forth between the meanings. For example, partition thinking works easily for the regrouping or trading concepts needed for the algorithm. In the division of 201 by 3 (201 ÷ 3), we think partition when we say, "We cannot divide two hundreds into three equal parts of hundreds, and so we regroup the 2 hundreds into 20 tens." Then we switch to quotition and say, "How many threes are there in 20?" When we get to larger numbers, a switch from partition to quotition seems expedient. In addition to regrouping, use of the algorithm requires organization and careful step-by-step recording of the partial quotients, remainders, and final quotient. Try to connect this process directly to the meaning of the problem.

As in multiplication, estimation is important. Equally important is the understanding of the composite nature of a number and the patterns in whole-unit divisions. Knowing that 1000s divided by 10s results in 100s will enable the student to recognize the place in which the quotient of 3,000 ÷ 60 belongs. What we do in the division algorithm is separate the number into its whole-unit components and then try to divide these equally. As a review, begin with a single-unit divisor and the long-division form.

Suppose Angelo did not have a calculator and wanted to equally divide 135 pieces of gum that came in packages of ten pieces among his nine friends.

How many whole packages of ten could he equally give each friend?

How many pieces would that use up?

How many single pieces would be left?

If he divided these single-pieces (ones) equally, how many would each friend get?

How many pieces of gum did each friend get in all?

Indivisible remainders in the earlier grades are usually handled as notations ($r - 2$), especially if a fractional remainder does not make sense in the problem. By the sixth grade, students should be able to convert remainders to fraction form.

Money problems are useful because they visualize the need to change remainders that are unequally larger denominations for the smaller ones.

Exemplar Problems

Keshawn and his three friends teamed up to earn money by making deliveries for the store. They earned $96 one day and divided it equally among themselves. How much did each one earn? Show this problem as a number sentence and as an algorithm.

$$96 \div 4 = ? \qquad 4\overline{)96}$$

Estimate your answer and then see how to get the exact answer using an algorithm that is used for division problems such as Keshawn's. Explain it to your group. Look at the questions in the boxes. Use them to help explain the algorithm.

(A) How much money has to be divided?

(B) How many of the tens can each of the four friends get?

(C) How much of the whole amount of money will giving the tens use up?

(D) How many ones and tens are left?

(E) How much money is that?

(F) How can the remaining money be divided among the friends?

(G) What do you have to do with the remaining ones?

(H) How many of the ones will each friend get?

(I) How many ones does this use up?

(J) How much money is left to divide?

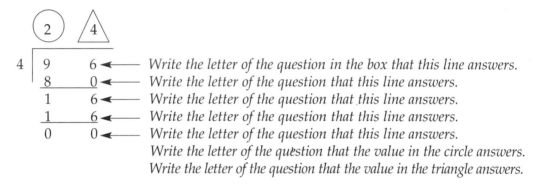

2	△4	

4) 9 6 ⟵ *Write the letter of the question in the box that this line answers.*
   8 0 ⟵ *Write the letter of the question that this line answers.*
   1 6 ⟵ *Write the letter of the question that this line answers.*
   1 6 ⟵ *Write the letter of the question that this line answers.*
   0 0 ⟵ *Write the letter of the question that this line answers.*
          Write the letter of the question that the value in the circle answers.
          Write the letter of the question that the value in the triangle answers.

Keshawn said he could do this in a shorter way. Explain what he did.

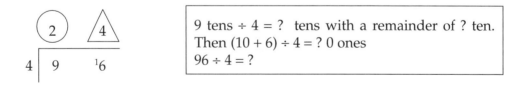

9 tens ÷ 4 = ? tens with a remainder of ? ten.
Then (10 + 6) ÷ 4 = ? 0 ones
96 ÷ 4 = ?

If Keshawn and his friends had earned $98, they could not divide the eighteen $1 bills equally. How many $1 bills would have remained? What could they do with these? Use a written algorithm to solve the problem.

Show the quotient of (98 ÷ 4) as a mixed number of whole numbers and fractions.

Show the quotient in decimal form. Check your answer with your calculator.

————————— ✳ —————————

A two-place divisor is the next hurdle. Begin again with estimation. The multiplication patterns will help identify the place of the each separate digit of the quotient.

Developmental Transitions and Scaffolds

The scouts collected used toys to give away at Christmas. They collected 546 toys and needed to put them in boxes of 26 each. How many boxes could they fill?

We are trying to find out how many groups of 26 there are in 546. Why would it be better to round down 20 and then to round up to 30?

If we use the higher number of whole groups, we may get fewer groups than we can really get. If we use the lower number and get a remainder, we can then divide the remainder into smaller units (boxes) or leave them aside until we have more. *Always round the divisor down.*

Estimate first: About how many groups of 2 tens (20) would there be in 546?
Now let's do the algorithm.

- Round the 26 down to 2 tens.
- Divide the 5 hundreds by 2 tens.
- How many groups of 2 tens (20) are in 500?
- There can only be 20 (hundreds divided by tens are tens) because 30 would be 600 and too much.
- Write the 20 as a partial quotient of 2 in the tens place.
- How many toys have we used for 26 groups of 20?
- Multiply the 26 by the 2 tens? Remember that tens times ones is tens.
- How many ones do we have left after we have used up 20 groups of 26?

```
            2 1
    26 | 5 4 6
         5 2 0      Write a number sentence that shows how you got this number.
           2 6      Write a number sentence that shows how you got this number.
           2 6      Write a number sentence that shows how you got this number.
           0 0
```

What if the scouts had 5,200 toys? Try the algorithm.
Check your answer with your calculator.

Once students can use and explain the standard algorithm as above and estimate answers with ease, it may be unnecessary to spend a great deal of time practicing multi-digit long-division algorithms. My suggestion for algorithm practice is a set of ten problems—all estimated first. The first three should then be completed without a calculator. If the answers are all correct, then the rest should be done with the calculator. If there is a mistake on the first three, then the student should correct it and do three more without the calculator. Any additional mistakes should be followed by three problems without the calculator until three problems are done correctly.

Developmental Transitions and Scaffolds

For the division problem 24,345 ÷ 81, will the answer be closer to 3,000, 300, or 30? Think: thousands divided by tens are hundreds, and therefore 24 thousands divided by 8 tens would be 300. Explain your estimate. Suppose the divisor was 89. Would the answer be more or less than 300, or more or less than 200? Why?

10.1 Decimals: Addition and Subtraction

See also Chapter 2, pages 30–32, for concepts and expectations.

Because decimals are an extension of our number system, addition and subtraction operations with decimals can be handled in the same way as whole-number multiples of 10. Only like things can be added and subtracted, and when we have too many of one kind to fit into our system or not enough, we trade. Start with money and then use other real data that are reported in decimal form such as rainfall amounts and batting averages. Compare decimal data by making graphs and using spreadsheet computer programs to translate data lists into graphic representations. Get data from the Internet. Analysis of inequalities will also help develop the relationships.

Exemplar Problems

The least average yearly rainfall in the world is recorded in Arica, Chile. It is only .03 of an inch. The least annual average rainfall in the United States is recorded at Death Valley, California. It is 1.63 inches. What is the difference between the average rainfall in these desert communities? The average rainfall for the entire world is about 34 inches. How much more is that than the rainfall in Death Valley? The most rainfall in the United States occurs in the Pacific Northwest, which gets about 100 inches. Find the difference in average rainfall between the greatest and least rainy places in the United States.

For the following inequality, choose a number that would make the inequality true for the variable X. Find the difference between your number and the larger value of the inequality.

$$19 \tfrac{1}{2} < X < 20.7$$

10.2–10.5 Multiplication of and by Decimals

Whole-Number Multipliers

Multiplication of decimals by *whole numbers* is a simple extension from whole-number operations. For single-unit base-10 multipliers, use the place value shift.

Developmental Transitions and Scaffolds

- Each digit in a decimal place is ten times larger than the same digit in a place on its right and ten times smaller than one on its left.
- To make a decimal value ten times larger, shift it one place to the left; to make it ten times smaller (divide it by 10), shift it to the right.

For whole-number multipliers that are not single-unit base-10, review the distributive principle and relate to multiplication by a fraction.

- $3 \times .009$ is the same as $3 \times \frac{9}{1,000}$ and equal to .027.
- $30 \times .009$ is the same as $(3 \times 10) \times .009$ or $(10 \times .009)\,(3)$. We can multiply by 10 first to get .09 and then by 3 to get .27.

Practice with the above should precede the use of the algorithm for multidigit multipliers of decimals and mixed numbers.

Evan grew 2.4 inches one year. If he grew at the same rate, how many inches would he grow in fourteen years? Try using your multiplication algorithm to multiply this mixed number. Explain the shortcut.

```
       tens | ones | tenths
              2. 4
            × 1 4
```

```
           1   6     Write a number sentence for this partial product.
           8   0     Write a number sentence for this partial product.
         2 4   0     Write a number sentence for this partial product.
         ---------
         3 3.  6
```

Shortcut ⟶

```
      2. 4
    × 14
     9. 6
    24. 0
    33. 6
```

Decimal Multipliers

Developmental Transitions and Scaffolds

Important distinctions to make between whole-number multipliers of decimals and less than whole-number (decimal) multipliers are the following:

- Multiplying any value, whole number or decimal, by a decimal multiplier will result in a value that is less than the original.
- Multiplying by a decimal fraction (as recalled from common fractions) is the same as finding a fractional part of it. Finding the product of .5 times a value is the same as finding $\frac{5}{10}$ or $\frac{1}{2}$ of the value.

Another review generalization is the following:

- The size of the part depends on the size of the whole. Therefore, .5 of 70 is not the same as .5 of 80.

Begin developing concepts related to multiplication by decimals with decimal values of given wholes. Area problems can help students visualize varying sized wholes and their decimal or common fraction equal parts.

Exemplar Problems

The population older than age 50 in most cities is .25 (or 25%). About how many people older than 50 would there be in a city of about 12,000?

What decimal part of the grid is shaded?
  If the grid represented an area of 200 square feet, what would be the area of the shaded part?

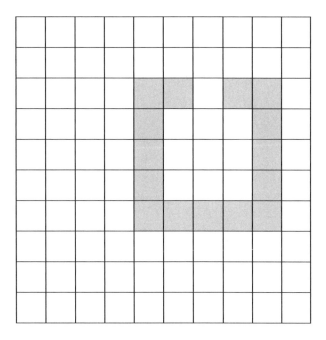

Developmental Transitions and Scaffolds

Multiplication by single decimal units of tenths, hundredths, and so on can be simply connected to the place value system. If you wish to make a value ten times smaller, you shift it one place to the right. .1 × 5 = .5, and .1 × .5 = .05 (later note the concurrent movement of the decimal point as a possible shortcut). Develop the patterns that tenths × tenths will equal hundredths and tenths × hundredths = thousandths and so forth. Then apply the distributive principle (.2 × .2 = .04) (.2 × .02 = .004).

Alternating between the decimal and common fraction should help students emerge with the generalization that when multiplying by a decimal, just as in multiplication by fractions, we multiply by the numerator and divide by the denominator to find the fractional value.

- If we are multiplying the whole-number value (5) by .6, which is the same as finding $\frac{6}{10}$ of it, we multiply the 5 by the numerator of 6 and divide by the denominator of 10. The product of the whole numbers is 6 × 5 = 30, but for .6 × 5, we have to then divide the intermediate product of 30 by 10 to get a quotient of 3. We can use the shortcut of a right shift to do this.
- This leads to the shortcut of just multiplying by the decimal digit and then dividing the product by the place value of the digit, which is the denominator of the corresponding common fraction. As an example, .06 × 5 would be .30 because the digit 6 in this place represents 6/100. The product is then 30/100 or in decimal form (.30). Pattern generalizations can help.

Once the generalization for multiplication by a decimal is clear (multiplying by the digit and dividing the product by the denominator of its place value), students can quickly progress to more than single-digit decimal multipliers. They will realize that they can proceed with the partial products and regroup as though they were dealing with whole numbers. Then, for the final result, they will need to divide by the place value of the operator or multiplier (the same as the denominator of its corresponding common fraction). This can be done with a simple right shift past the decimal point. Some students will suggest the counting of decimal places for this. Teachers should get them to explain why this works. It will also lead into the algorithm for multiplying decimals by decimals.

Once there is clarity in the place value of the partial products, the pattern and short-cut of counting decimal places in the multiplicand and multiplier for a similar total in the product can be applied. Allow students to use their calculators to check the patterns for large numbers.

$$\begin{array}{r} 2\ 4 \\ \times 1.\ 4 \\ \hline 1.\ 6 \\ 8.\ 0 \\ 24.\ 0 \\ \hline 33.\ 6 \end{array}$$

How did we get a partial product of 1.6?
How did we get a partial product of 8.0?
How did we get a partial product of 24.0?
How did we get a product of 33.6?

Shortcut $\longrightarrow$

$$\begin{array}{r} 2\ 4 \\ \times 1.\ 4 \\ \hline 9.\ 6 \\ 24.\ 0 \\ \hline 33.\ 6 \end{array}$$

Note that there was one decimal place in the multiplier and none in the multiplicand. How many decimal places are in the product?
Try multiplying 2.4 by 1.6 and see if you can find a useful pattern.
Try larger numbers with your calculator to prove the pattern.

Exemplar Problems

The library charges $0.25 per day for the first five days a book is overdue. After five days, the fine for each day is doubled. How much will the library charge for a book overdue for nine days?

Gina went to the store and bought 2 lbs of chopped meat at $1.98 per lb and 5 lbs of potatoes at $0.54 per lb. She gave the clerk $20. How much change did she receive?

Developmental Transitions and Scaffolds

The next step to reach is the understanding of what happens when both the multiplicand and the multiplier are decimals. Go back again to the multiplication of common fractions to demonstrate that multiplying tenths times tenths will result in hundredths as the denominators are multiplied. This should lead to the realization that in the algorithm, multiplying .6 × .6 will result in .36 and needs to be so recorded in the partial products.

Extend the concept to the following: *tenths time hundredths are thousandths and .06 × .6 is therefore .036 or 2 + 1 = 3 decimal places.*

The smallest place value in the product will be the result of multiplying the denominators of the two smallest decimal digits. Sometimes the product of the digits (numerators) will be a multiple of 10, and then because it is a decimal, we reduce to lowest terms. .6 × .5 = .30, but 30/100 is the same as 3/10. *In decimal form, therefore, we ignore zeros to the right of the smallest place value that has a nonzero digit.*

Eventually, this should lead to recognition of the pattern that the final total of decimal places in the product is equal to the sum of the decimal places in the multiplicand multiplier. The counting decimal places shortcut has an explanation!

Exemplar Problems

The average annual rainfall in the northwestern United States is 99.7 inches. How much rain would fall (on the average) in 3.3 years?

1. *Round the rainfall data to the nearest whole number.*

2. *Estimate your answer in whole numbers.*

3. *Predict how many decimal places there will be in the exact answer.*

4. *Compute an exact answer using the multiplication algorithm.*

5. *Explain how the algorithm worked to get you an exact answer. Does it agree with your estimate?*

Steven wanted to plant a garden. He marked off a plot that was 6 meters by 8 meters. What was the area of his plot? He wanted to carefully lay out parts of the garden and constructed a wire grid to help. He first divided it into two equal halves. What common fraction and decimal fraction would represent half of the plot? How much area would that be? How did you get your answer?

Steven then decided that he would like to grow vegetables in a little more than half of his garden. He used more wire to divide his garden into 100 equal parts. The part for vegetables is shaded on the picture below.

What decimal fraction of the whole garden plot does this represent?

Rename this decimal in common fraction form.

Can you reduce the common fraction to lower terms?

How much of the whole area would be vegetables?

Explain how you found this out.

Steven also wanted some herbs and decided on just .04 of the plot. Shade the part that would be herbs. What would be the area of the herb part? Express your answer as a decimal and as a common fraction in the lowest terms.

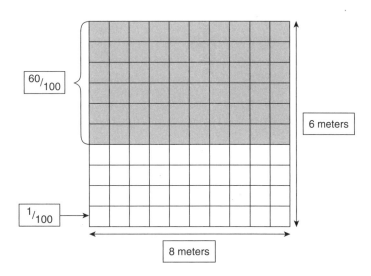

10.6–10.8 Decimals and Percentage

Developmental Transitions and Scaffolds

Because the percentage application of decimals is in such common use in our culture, it may be wise to approach percent problems in tandem with multiplication by decimals.

Finding the percent of a number and describing change in terms of percent is the everyday application of this operation—usually with the decimal rounded off to the nearest hundredth as the percent sign takes the place of the decimal point. Percentage and decimals can both be seen as ratios of a whole. If you divide one whole into ten parts, each part is one out of ten or .1 of the whole. Percentage is based on a whole of 100; thus, .25 is equal to 25 out of 100 parts ($\frac{25}{100}$) or 25%.

The development of number sense in the application of percent concepts may be one of the most important preparations for full participation in the mathematical communications of our present culture. Spatial perceptions of objects accompanied by quantitative descriptions in both percent and common fraction form will help students achieve the necessary concepts. Students should be able to mentally visualize and estimate how large 50%, 25%, $33\frac{1}{3}$%, 75%, and 10% of an object is. *Connections to the corresponding common fractions in lowest terms for these should be computed and then automatized.*

Using their previously developed fraction and decimal concepts, students should be encouraged to automatize the common fractional and percentage equivalents, including the following: $[\frac{1}{2}] = 50\%$, $25\% = \frac{1}{4}$, $\frac{3}{4} = 75\%$, and $33\frac{1}{3}\% = \frac{1}{3}$.

Other useful automatizations or mental computations are as follows:

Right shifting one place for 10% and two places for 1%

Doubling the result of a one place right shift for 20%

Adding half of 10% to 10% to compute a 15% tip. Use a number line and tables to show the relative values in different forms.

Exemplar Problems

On each of the following number lines, plot a point as directed.

Place point Q on $5\frac{1}{8}$ and point R on 6.25.

Place point R on 25%, point S on 2.75, and point T on $3\frac{1}{2}$.
The same value can be represented as a percent, as a fraction, and as a decimal. Fill in the missing boxes in the conversion table below.

Write the Percent	Write the Fraction	Write the Decimal
	$\frac{1}{4}$	
200%		
		.05
	$\frac{110}{100}$	

Put the following values in order from the smallest to the largest.

$\frac{1}{10}$, .09, 23%, .20, $\frac{1}{100}$, $\frac{6}{10}$, $33\frac{1}{3}$%

Developmental Transitions and Scaffolds

Beyond the automatizations, the computation of a percentage of a given value should be addressed as finding the equivalent decimal fraction of the value, which is multiplication by the decimal.

How can we find 27% of $380?
   We multiply 380 by .27.
   An important functional skill in problem solving with percentages is the language distinction between 20% off and *20% of a value.* Scaffolding questions to ask include the following: What part of the whole are you looking for when you take 20% off? Explain the difference between 20% of and 20% off. Twenty percent off a value is the same as what percentage of the value?
   Another data analysis and cultural survival skill is the realization that sequential percentage diminutions or accretions of a value are not additive. Taking 50% off a value and then taking 20% more off the product is not the same as taking 70% off the original. The concept to connect back to is that the value of fractional parts depends on the size of the whole. The larger the whole, the larger the value of the percentage or decimal fraction. After you shrink a value by 50%, 20% of the result is less than 20% of the original value.
   This concept has other applications besides department store sales. If the crime rate goes down an even 10% a year, the actual number of crimes it goes down gets smaller each year. On the other end, if you measured your growth over a five-year period and discovered that you grew an even 10% a year, when did you grow the most?

Exemplar Problems

Evan kept a record of how much he grew each year. He showed it to his friends and said that he grew 5% each year. He always rounded his new height to the nearest inch. His friends said that he was wrong because he did not grow the same amount each year. Who was right: Evan or his friends? Explain your answer. If he continued at the same rate, would he ever grow 5 inches in one year? Predict when that would happen. Is it likely to happen? Can you find a pattern for his increase in size?

Year	Height	Percent Change
1	46 in	
2	48 in	5
3	50 in	5
4	53 in	5
5	56 in	5
6	59 in	5
7	62 in	5
8	65 in	5
9	68 in	5
10	71 in	5
11	75 in	5

Compare the pictures of the home and the lighthouse. About what percentage of the height of the lighthouse is the height of the home? Choose from 33%, 50%, 10%, or 75%.

Draw another house that is about three fourths the size of the lighthouse. What percentage of the lighthouse would that be?

11.1–11.2 Division of Mixed Numbers and Decimals by Whole Numbers

See also Chapter 2, pages 33–34, for concepts and expectations.

Developmental Transitions and Scaffolds

Division of mixed numbers and decimal values by whole numbers can be explained both from a partition and quotition view, such as division of the corresponding fraction—just dividing the numerator and maintaining the same denominator. For example, .6 of a candy bar divided into three parts is equal to .2 of a candy bar, and 1.2 of a candy bar divided into three parts is .4—or there are three parts of size .4 in 1.2 of a candy bar. For more complex dividends, the traditional division algorithm may be required. As in the division of whole numbers and common fractions, an important concept is that we can regroup numbers for their smaller size equivalents so that division is possible. Any remainders of indivisible whole numbers or larger decimals can be regrouped into their smaller sized decimal. Money or base-10 blocks can help develop this concept, translating the manipulative to the symbolic decimal form step by step.

Cindy had to share her three tenths of a package of paper among five friends. She knew she could not divide 3/10 into five equal parts. How could she change the three tenths into smaller parts to divide equally? Explain what she can do with your base-10 blocks.

You just learned that .3 ÷ 5 is the same as .30 ÷ 5.
The quotient for .30 ÷ 5 = ?

What part of the package will each friend get?
Explain your answer.
How can Cindy find out how many sheets to give each friend?

Division by Whole-Unit Multiples of 10

Division of decimals by whole-number unit multiples of 10 (base-10 expansions) can be done by right shifting place value. This is a good opportunity to compare the similar operation for multiplying by a decimal and dividing a decimal by a whole number. Dividing by the whole number 10 is finding (.1) of the number and the same as multiplying it by (.1).

11.3–11.5 Division of Decimals by Decimals

Developmental Transitions and Scaffolds

For divisors that are smaller than the dividend and where the dividend can be equally divided, number sense from the quotition view reveals the concept. The number of parts of size (.2) or how many $\frac{2}{10}$ are there in $\frac{6}{10}$ is the same as the number of 2s in 6. There are three whole (.2) in (.6).

Then we can approach division in its fraction form to apply the process of multiplying the numerator and denominator—or dividend and divisor—by an equal multiplier of 10. The result is that $(.6 \div .2)$ or $\frac{.6}{.2}$ when the numerator and denominator are multiplied by 10. $\frac{.6 \times 10}{.2 \times 10}$ becomes $\frac{6}{2}$ or $(6 \div 2)$, which is equal to 3. Use base-10 blocks to help students see this.

For uneven or larger divisors, we may need to apply the algorithm.

The division problem $.6 \div .8$ or $\frac{6}{10} \div \frac{8}{10}$ can be represented in the fraction form of $\frac{.6}{.8}$. We can change the fractional numerator and denominator to whole numbers by multiplying each by 10, and we end up with $\frac{6}{8}$ or $6 \div 8$. We can leave this as a fraction and reduce it to $\frac{3}{4}$, or we can proceed with the division algorithm to convert to decimal form.

```
        .7 5      Write an equation that shows this division problem and quotient.
   8 ⟌ 6. 0 0
        5 6   →  Write an equation that shows how we got this number.
        4 0   →  Write an equation that shows how we got this number.
        4 0   →  Write an equation that shows how we got this number.
        0 0
```

The quotient of .75 is equal to the fraction $\frac{3}{4}$, and this proves the algorithm.

In the algorithm, we can change a decimal divisor (which is the denominator) to a whole number by multiplying it and the dividend (which is the numerator) by the same multiple of 10. If the denominator of the divisor is in the hundredths, then we multiply it and the dividend by 100.

A difficulty that sometimes arises with this process in applying it to problem solving is in interpreting any remainder. In the problem below, the algorithm finds the number of (.75) of a whole dollar in (10.00) dollars by finding the corresponding number of (75) dollars in 1,000 dollars. The answer to the problem is that there are 13 (.75) of a dollar in 10.00, not 13 groups of 75 whole dollars. And the remainder is not 25 whole dollars but .25 or 25 cents. When applying the algorithm to problem solving, therefore, it may be a good idea to label the quotient and remainders carefully. They also must make sense. The remainder in the problem is .25 or 1/3 of 75, but you cannot buy 1/3 of a token.

Exemplar Problems

Serena had a $10 bill to buy some subway tokens. Each token cost 75 cents (.75). How many tokens could she get with the $10? How much change would she get? Estimate your answer and then try the division algorithm.

1. *Explain how to get from A to B.*

2. *Explain the steps in C.*

3. *Explain what the remainder in C means.*

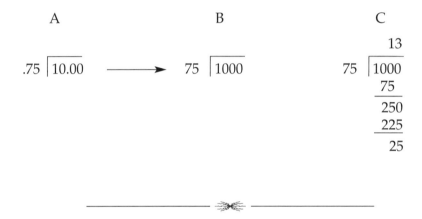

During the summer, people love going to the movies. Imagine that your neighborhood theater is selling special summer passes for $80.00. The pass can be used by anyone to see any movie at the theater for the summer weeks. Without a pass, tickets cost $7.70 each. If you did not have a pass, how many times would you have to go to the movies to spend $80.00?

Jerry is building shelves for his room. Each shelf has to be 4.6 feet. How many shelves can he get from 20.7 feet of wood? Would he have any wood left? How many feet or inches of wood would that equal? What could he do with it?

12.1–12.3 Integer Operations

See also Chapter 2, pages 34–36, for concepts and expectations.

Developmental Transitions and Scaffolds

Conceptual understanding of our algorithms for combining or adding negative and positive integers can be strengthened by demonstrating the values and operations on a number line with zero at the center. Positive values go toward the right of zero and negative values to the left. Movements in one direction cancel movements in the other direction.

Other demonstrations of the canceling concept may be helpful in understanding what happens when integers are combined. Some of the tracking systems in the new video games can be used for motivation here. If you gain six lives and lose two, how many do you have left? If you win three dollars and lose two, how many do you have left? Both of these problems can be translated to the number line and demonstrated with two-sided chips to show positive and negative values. The result may easily be seen as positive or negative, depending on what you had more of. If the two combined figures are additive inverses, they cancel each other completely.

$$^+6 + {}^-6 = 0$$

Exemplar Problems

In a card game, a pulled diamond card takes away a spade. How many spades would you have left in your hand if you pulled six spades and four diamonds from the deck?

$$^+6 + {}^-4 =$$

———————————— ✳ ————————————

John has $10 in his wallet. He already owes his friend $6 and then borrows $3 more. The white and gray chips below represent these amounts.

What value does each white chip represent? What is the total value of the white chips? What value does each gray chip represent? What is the total value of the gray chips?

12.3–12.5 Absolute Value/ Subtraction of Negative Integers

Developmental Transitions and Scaffolds

Demonstrations of the subtraction of integers on the number line are more difficult but useful in understanding how they work. If we think of subtraction as finding the difference or distance between any two values, that distance is an *absolute value*. In the common vertical subtraction algorithm, we usually place the higher value on top and, in order to get a positive value, count up from the lower positive value to the higher value, so that the difference is positive. On the number line, starting from the lowest value to find the difference always makes us move in a positive direction. When we subtract a negative value in the algorithm for combining integers, we are finding the difference or distance between the values. Therefore, a change in sign for the subtracted negative integer to the positive one is necessary before combining the values to get the absolute value of the total distance or difference between them. We represent the absolute value of a number in the following form, $|-5|$. Even if there is a negative sign for the integer, it is treated as positive. If there is an operation within the absolute value brackets, it must be done first. The absolute value of $|-7+2|$ is 5.

The temperature one morning was –3 degrees. In the afternoon, it was +4 degrees. What was the total change in temperature?

As an example, the difference between 3 degrees below zero and 4 degrees above is 7 degrees. To find the difference, we add the degrees below zero to those above zero. The operation $4 - (^-3)$ then becomes $4 + 3$ and equals 7. The confusing thing in the algorithm is that we use the same sign to show both a negative value and the subtraction operation. It is useful, therefore, to show the negative value with a superscript to distinguish it from the operation sign. On the number line, to find the difference between two negative integers (‾2) and (‾6), we count up +4 from the lower (–6) value. In a combining integers algorithm, starting with the higher value, (‾2) – (‾6), means the difference between them. It will = ⁺4 only if we change the negative integer sign to positive and the operation sign to a plus sign (‾2 + 6 = 4).

We can then make the generalization that when we subtract a negative number, the negatives cancel each other, and we add a positive value. This generalization that two negatives become a positive can also be reinforced with verbal logic. "I do not not have the right time" means that I have it.

Exemplar Problems

What would be the value of x in this equation?

$$12 + \left|-5\right| = x$$

―――――――――――― ✳ ――――――――――――

Sam thinks that for all real numbers, the following equation is always true.

$$\left|3 + {}^{-}5\right| = \left|3\right| + \left|{}^{-}5\right|$$

Do you agree with Sam? Use mathematical reasoning to explain your answer.

―――――――――――― ✳ ――――――――――――

A minivan travels 4 miles in one direction from the starting place (0) and then turns around and travels 6 miles in the opposite direction. Where does it end up in relation to where it started? (⁺4) + (‾6) =

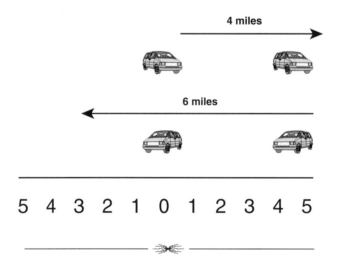

―――――――――――― ✳ ――――――――――――

The low temperature in Fairbanks, Alaska, was 5 degrees below zero on Monday and 2 degrees below zero on Saturday. How much warmer was it on Saturday?
    Why do we start the algorithm with Saturday's temperature?

Finish the equation: (‾2) – (‾5) = ‾2 + 5 = ?

	MON.			SAT.							
6	5	4	3	2	1	0	1	2	3	4	5

Fred and Alex play a chip game that gives you a green side when you answer a question correctly and a white side when you make a mistake. No chips are given for unanswered questions. The most greens win, but whites cancel greens. Decide who is the loser in this game. How many extra right answers are needed by the loser to tie the game? Does it pay to guess answers?

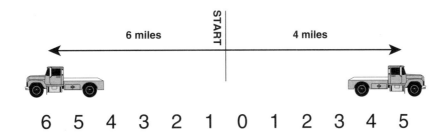

Finish the equation: $(^+7 + {}^-3) - (^+7 + {}^-5) = ?$ *Why did we start with Alex?*

Two pickup trucks left a rest stop at the same time. They traveled in opposite directions. One traveled 6 miles in one direction from the starting place, and the other traveled 4 miles in the opposite direction. What is the distance difference between them?

Finish the equation: $(^+4) - (^-6) =$

The sum of two integers is –3. The distance between them is 9. What are the two integers? Show them on the number line.

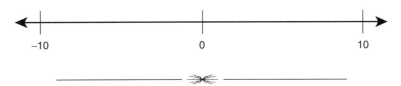

The daily low temperature readings in a town in North Dakota for six days in January were as follows: 5°C, –1°C, 0°C, –2°C, 3°C, and 7°C.

What was the average low temperature for the six days?

12.6 Multiplication of Negative Integers

Developmental Transitions and Scaffolds

Even mathematicians have struggled with explanations for the results of multiplication and division of signed numbers. Different-colored chips that represent the positive and negative values will help. If we think of multiplication as repeated addition, it is easy to understand that a negative number repeated a positive number of times will have increased negativity. (–3) repeated twelve times is going to add up to (–36). Therefore, 12 (–3) = –36. A negative value multiplied by a positive value will always result in a negative product.

If, however, the multiplier is a negative number, it implies the inverse, which is repeated subtraction of the negative value. If you have a debt of $36, you own (–$36.00). But if you repeatedly cancel or subtract that debt by paying $3.00 for twelve times, your debt is then zero. –36 + 36 = 0. The positive (36) came from the repeated subtraction for twelve times of –3. Therefore, –12 (–3) = 36. A negative value times a negative value will always result in a positive product.

The rules are as follows:

- When a positive and negative integer are multiplied, the product is negative. The process increases negativity.
- The product of two negative integers is a positive value. The process decreases negativity.

Exemplar Problems

Justin borrowed two dollars from his friend Allan for five days in a row. At the end of the week, he got his allowance and paid him back. Which of the two equations (a or b) can be used to find the loss from his allowance?

$$\text{(a) } x = 5\,(-2) \quad \text{(b) } x = 5(2)$$

What is wrong with the answer and form of the incorrect equation? How does the solution process for the correct equation prove the rule for multiplying positive and negative integers?

Justin owed Allan some money and paid him back by taking $3.00 from his allowance five times. Which of the two equations (a or b) could be solved to find how much money Allan got?

$$\text{(a) } (-5)\,(-3) = x \quad \text{(b) } 5\,(-3) = x$$

What is wrong with the answer of the incorrect equation? How does the answer for the correct equation prove the rule for multiplying two negative integers?

Justin owed Allan $15 and paid him back by taking $3.00 at a time from his allowance. Which of the two equations (a or b) could be solved to find how many times he would have to pay him the $3 and remove his debt?

$$\text{(a) } -15 - x\,(-3) = 0 \quad \text{(b) } -15 + x\,(-3) = 0$$

What is wrong with the answer of the incorrect equation? How does the solution process for the correct equation prove the rule for multiplying two negative integers?

Shannon and her friend played a quiz game in which right answers earned positive green chips and wrong answers earned negative red chips. The score was the sum of the chips. If she answered a really hard question, she could remove two red chips. How many times would Shannon have to remove two red chips to add 16 points to her score? Which equation (a or b) shows what she did?

$$(a) \ (-x) \ (2) = -16 \quad (b) \ (-x) \ (-2) = 16$$

What is wrong with the answer of the incorrect equation? How does the solution process for the correct equation prove the rule for multiplying two negative integers?

12.7 Exponential Expansions of Negative Integers

Developmental Transitions and Scaffolds

Since a negative value multiplied by a negative value will equal a positive value, the square of a negative number is going to be a positive number, and therefore the square root of any number may be either positive or negative.

For an exponent of 3 or any other odd-numbered exponent, however, the expanded value will be a negative number. It will be the product of the positive expansion of the square times the negative base number and result in a positive product or expansion.

Exemplar Problem

What is the expanded value for each of the following exponential expressions?

$$(-4)^2 \text{ and } (-4)^3 \ (-3)^4 \text{ and } (-3)^5$$

What pattern do you see?

12.8 Division of and by Negative Integers

Developmental Transitions and Scaffolds

We can consider division of integers similarly from either the partition or quotition perspective (see Numbers 9.2–9.4), but both do not always apply. It is not possible to consider division by a negative number from the partition perspective (the whole divided by the number of parts) because we cannot have a negative number of parts. From the quotitive perspective, the expression $-36 \div -3$ can mean how many groups of size (-3) are in (-36) or how many \$3.00 debts are there in a debt of \$36.00. There are twelve of them! A positive number 12 is the quotient and therefore $-36 \div -3 = 12$. A negative number divided by a negative number will always result in a positive number. On the other hand, dividing a negative number by a positive one can be considered from the partition perspective. If we think from the partition division perspective, a group of size -36 divided into twelve parts will result in parts that are size (-3). Therefore, $-36 \div 12 = -3$, and a negative number divided by a positive number or vice versa will always result in a negative quotient.

The rules are as follows:

- When a negative integer is divided by a positive number and when a positive number is divided by a negative number, the quotient is negative.
- When both dividend and divisor are negative, the quotient is positive.

Exemplar Problem

Some students in Mr. Brown's class bought a case of water to share at a game they attended. They each drank 2 pints of water. By the middle of the game there were 10 fewer pints in the case. Which of the two equations (a or b) can be used correctly to find the number of students who drank the water? What is wrong with the incorrect equation? How does the solution process for the correct equation prove the rule for dividing negative integers?

$$\text{(a) } \frac{-10}{-2} = x \quad \text{(b) } \frac{-10}{2} = x$$

If 15 pints of water were missing from the original case by the end of the game, which equation would tell you how many pints of water each of five students took away from the case?

$$\text{(a) } \frac{-15}{5} = x \quad \text{(b) } \frac{-15}{-5} = x$$

■ FRACTIONS

13.1 Fractions: Defined

See also Chapter 2, pages 36–38, for concepts and expectations.

Developmental Transitions and Scaffolds

Children develop beginning concepts of fractions at a relatively early age. There is a necessary shift in thinking about a fraction as part of a single whole to thinking about the form as part of a set of objects. Sometimes, there may be fuzziness about the class inclusion definitions of the total set. It is easy to visualize ten computers as a whole set or group, but there is a conceptual leap to considering an aquarium with different fish as a whole group of fish and the individual kinds of fish as parts of that whole. After all, the fish are different! Examples of both kinds of wholes or sets are needed. This may also serve as an introduction to set theory. The different kinds of fish are subsets of the whole set but also can be described as fractional parts of the whole.

There may also be difficulty in translating common experiences such as the pizza problems below to the fraction meaning of division as described below. By the sixth grade, the following concepts should be in place.

- A fraction is an expression that describes a quantity of parts in relationship to a whole, rather than a definitive quantity.
- The actual amount described depends on the size of the whole and the number of parts into which the whole has been divided.
- The whole can be a single item or a set of items.
- The denominator represents the number of parts the whole has been divided into.
- The numerator is the number of parts in the quantity described.
- The relative quantity of one part of the same whole decreases with the number of parts, as represented by an increasing denominator.
- A fraction expression can represent values less than, equal to, or greater than one whole.

13.2–13.3 Fraction Forms

Developmental Transitions and Scaffolds

The definitions and examples of the terms *common fraction, improper fraction,* and *mixed number* need to be reviewed as follows:

- A fraction that has a numerator smaller than the denominator is called a common fraction.
- A fraction with a numerator larger than the denominator is an improper fraction, and a fraction with an equal numerator and denominator is equal to one whole.
- A mixed number is a combination of a whole number and a fraction.

Connections to the number line and real problems are best for these definitions and concepts.

Exemplar Problems

Put these numbers in the right order and place them on the number line.

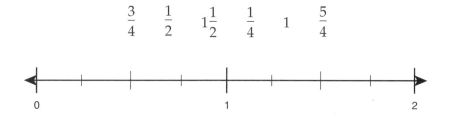

$$\frac{3}{4} \quad \frac{1}{2} \quad 1\frac{1}{2} \quad \frac{1}{4} \quad 1 \quad \frac{5}{4}$$

Identify one fraction in each form:

Common fraction _____

Improper fraction _____

Mixed number _____

These fractions show the part of a twenty-four-hour vacation day that some friends spent playing games on their computers. Put the fractions in order from least to greatest.

$$\frac{1}{2} \quad \frac{1}{4} \quad \frac{2}{8} \quad \frac{1}{3} \quad \frac{3}{4}$$

What fraction shows the most time? What fraction shows the least time? What was the least amount of hours spent? What was the most amount of time spent?

13.4 Fractions: As Division

Developmental Transitions and Scaffolds

The generalization that the fraction form represents the division process is best if taught as an extension of parts of a single whole to parts of more than one whole. This transition to an understanding of fractions as a representation of parts of a group or set where the number of parts into which the set is to be divided is more than the number of wholes is often overlooked. The first step in this transition is an understanding that when there is more than one whole in a set, each part of the set may be more or less than one whole. The numerator should be identified as the dividend and size of the whole set and the denominator as the divisor that represents either the number of parts or the size of each part.

We have three cupcakes to divide among the four of us. Will we each get more or less than a whole cupcake? Explain your answer.

We can't divide the three whole cupcakes evenly, so what will we have to do with them? If we divide the three cupcakes into the four parts we need, how big a part of each cupcake will each of us get? But we have three cupcakes, so how much cupcake will each of us get in all? Suppose we had six cupcakes divided into four parts. How much of a single cupcake would we each get? Would it be more or less than one whole cupcake?

This should lead to the generalization that any fraction can represent the operation of the numerator divided by the denominator.

An extension of this is that a whole number can be expressed as a fraction with a denominator of 1.

Exemplar Problems

Four friends went for pizza. They bought three large unsliced pizza pies. Could each one get a whole pizza? What fractional part of a whole pizza could each one get?

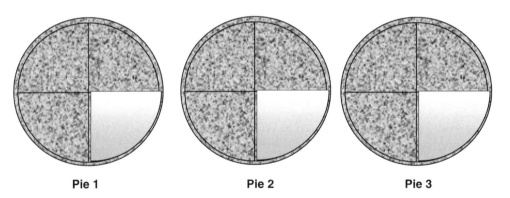

| Pie 1 | Pie 2 | Pie 3 |

Each friend got ☐ of each pie. All together, it was the same as ☐ of a single pie.

Three wholes divided into four parts = ☐.

How much would they each get if there were five friends?

Three wholes divided into five parts = ☐.

───────────── ✖ ─────────────

A group of friends went for pizza. They bought three pies and each got $\frac{3}{8}$ of a pie. How many friends were there?

───────────── ✖ ─────────────

A group of six friends went for pizza. They each got $\frac{5}{6}$ of a pie. How many pies did they buy?

Developmental Transitions and Scaffolds

Relating fractions to everyday life sometimes runs into problems because of custom. We are used to thinking of pizza in terms of a set of pieces rather than parts of a whole pie.

The problem below should help with the understanding of the shift from the fractional part of the single pie for two pieces as $\frac{1}{4}$ or $\frac{2}{8}$ of the pie to the fraction meaning of division as eight pieces of a set divided into four parts or $\frac{1}{4}$. In one case, the pie is the whole, and in the other case, each piece is treated as a single whole of the set of eight.

Four friends went for pizza. The pizza pie came sliced into eight pieces. How many pieces of pizza could each one get from the whole pie?

First let's think of the pizza as a whole pie.

Each piece = $\frac{1}{8}$ of a single whole pie.

Each friend will get $\frac{?}{8}$ or $\frac{?}{4}$ of a single whole pie.

Now let's think of each piece of the pie as a whole.

If a single piece of the pie was divided into four parts or $\frac{4}{4}$ of one piece, how many $\frac{1}{4}$ would there be in two whole pieces?

$\frac{1}{8}$ of one piece = $\square$ whole pieces.

8 pieces ÷ 4 parts = $\square$ pieces, and therefore $\frac{8}{4}$ means the same as 8 ÷ 4, and it is also equal to $\frac{1}{4}$ of eight pieces = $\square$ pieces.

Each friend will get $\frac{8}{4}$ of a piece or two pieces of pizza. The two pieces are equal to $\frac{1}{4}$ of a single whole pie of eight pieces.

13.5 Converting Fractions to Decimals

Developmental Transitions and Scaffolds

An extension of the fractions as a form of division is the conversion of any fraction to its whole number or decimal form by dividing the numerator by the denominator (see Number 11.2). Once there is a clear understanding of the application and ability to apply the division process with reasonable accuracy, calculator use for this purpose should be allowed following *estimation*. The number line can be used for comparisons of the alternate forms. Automatization of common equivalents from fraction to decimal and, inversely, to fraction form—for example, $\frac{3}{4} = .75$, $\frac{1}{2} = .5$, $\frac{1}{3} = .33\overline{3}$, $\frac{2}{5} = .4$—should also be encouraged and *assessed with mental math*.

Put these numbers in the right order and place them on the number line.

$$\frac{3}{4}, .25, \frac{1}{3}, 1.5$$

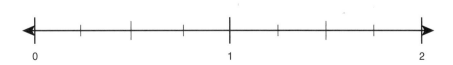

13.6 Comparing and Finding Equivalents

Developmental Transitions and Scaffolds

The concept of simple equivalents can be easily constructed by using real materials. Fraction bars and circles are useful manipulatives to develop and review these concepts when necessary. I prefer the bars for equivalents because the pieces are ordered so that the equivalents are all clearly recognizable as equal parts of the same-size whole that can be seen as a referent. Paper folding is also helpful. Students can actually produce equivalents as they fold equal-sized paper sheets into smaller and smaller parts.

Empty egg cartons filled with cubes, pom-poms, or color tiles are another manipulative to help students overcome the limitation of only seeing the whole as a single unit, and they can also work for better understanding of equivalents. Students can see the whole as a unit—the whole-dozen carton and, at the same time, the set of twelve individual units that comprise it. One half the whole carton is also six eggs, and $\frac{6}{12}$ of the whole carton is the same number of eggs as $\frac{1}{2}$ the carton or $\frac{2}{4}$ the carton. A combination of the fraction bars and the cartons may be the best. Also try sets of fraction bars and papers.

Several important generalizations should come from experiences with equivalent fractions:

1. First students need to understand that the larger the number of parts a whole has been divided into, the more parts you need for the same amount of the whole.

2. This generalization can be extended to the proportional relationship between equivalents for the number of parts in the whole and the number of parts required. If there are twice as many parts for the same whole, then you need twice as many of them for the same amount of whatever is being divided.

3. Then move to the symbolic algorithm for finding equivalents: that multiplying or dividing the numerator and denominator by the same *operator* forms an equivalent fraction.

Exemplar Problems

Luis and his three friends went for pizza. They ordered a large pie and divided it equally into four pieces. Angelo came in with seven friends, and they ordered two large pizzas. They divided each pie into eight parts, and each of them had two pieces. Angelo bragged that he had more pizza than Luis. Was he right? Explain your answer. Suppose Angelo had shared the two pies among six friends. Would two pieces be the same as Luis's one piece? Use your fraction parts to help you think of other compare fraction problems in the pizza store.

ONE WHOLE LARGE PIE							
1/2				1/2			
1/4		1/4		1/4		1/4	
1/8	1/8	1/8	1/8	1/8	1/8	1/8	1/8
1/3			1/3			1/3	
1/6		1/6		1/6		1/6	1/6

Jenny and Inge had equal numbers of pages in their notebooks. Jenny had hers divided into eight chapters, and Inge had hers divided into four chapters. What part of the whole was each of Jenny's chapters? What part of the whole was each of Inge's? They each counted the number of pages in two chapters of their notebooks. Which one had more pages? Whose chapters were smaller parts of the whole? How many of Jenny's chapters would be the same as two of Inge's? How many of Inge's would be the same as six of Jenny's? Jenny had her book divided into _____ as many parts of the whole as Inge, so she needed _____ as many of these parts to equal Inge's.

The fraction that describes two of Inge's chapters is 2/4, and the one that describes four of Jenny's chapters is 4/8, and we found that these were equal: 2/4 = 4/8. Look at the two numerators and then look at the two denominators. Do you see a pattern? Can you find another fraction that follows the same pattern? Use your fraction bars to prove that this fraction is equal to the others.

———————————— ✄ ————————————

Look at the A egg carton. *Find the halves. How many eggs in one half of a dozen?* $\frac{1}{2}$ = __ *eggs?*

Find the twelfths. How many of these in $\frac{1}{2}$ *dozen?* $\frac{1}{2} = \frac{6}{12}$ = __ *eggs.*

Look at the B egg carton. *Find the sixths. How many eggs in* $\frac{1}{6}$ *of a dozen?*

$\frac{1}{6} = \frac{?}{12}$ *(how many twelfths).* $\frac{1}{6} = \frac{?}{12}$ = __ *eggs.*

Look at the C egg carton. *Find the thirds. How many thirds in the whole carton? How many eggs in one third? How many* $\frac{?}{12}$'s *of the whole is that?*

How many eggs in $\frac{2}{3}$ *of the whole carton? How many* $\frac{1}{12}$'s *is that?*

$\frac{2}{3} = \frac{?}{12}$ = ____ *eggs.* $\frac{2}{3} = \frac{?}{12}$ = ____ *eggs.*

Look at the D egg carton. *How many eggs? What part of the whole is that?*
$\frac{?}{12} = \frac{?}{6}$ = __ *eggs.*

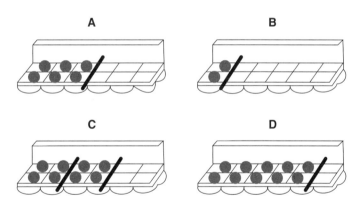

All of these fractions represent of $\frac{1}{3}$ *of the whole:* $\frac{1}{3}, \frac{2}{6}, \frac{4}{12}, \frac{8}{24}$ *. Look at the numerators. Do you see a pattern? Look at the denominators. Do you see a pattern? Supply the missing denominator for the next fraction in this series:* $\frac{16}{?}$.

Find the missing numerator or denominator for the following fractions that are equal to $\frac{1}{3}$.
$\frac{1}{3} = \frac{?}{33} = \frac{8}{?} = \frac{120}{?}$.

———————————— ✄ ————————————

How could you change 3/15 to an equal fraction with 5 in the denominator?

$$\frac{☎☎☎}{☎☎☎☎☎☎☎☎☎☎☎☎☎☎☎} \quad \begin{array}{c} \div \ ? \ = \\ \div \ ? \ = \end{array} \quad \frac{☎}{☎☎☎}$$

Three parts out of 15 are the same as one part out of _____.

13.7 Least Common Denominator

Developmental Transitions and Scaffolds

The concepts of equivalent fractions can be quickly followed with the need to find them for the purpose of performing addition and subtraction operations on unlike fractions. We can add and subtract like parts. Equal denominators of the same whole or group of objects represent parts of the same relative size of that whole or like parts of the whole. They can be added or subtracted by adding or subtracting the numerators.

I drank $\frac{1}{4}$ of a glass of milk with my breakfast and $\frac{3}{4}$ of a glass just after breakfast. How much of the glass of milk did I drink altogether? How much more did I drink after breakfast than I did with my breakfast?

The challenge is to perform the operation with fractions that have unlike denominators. We first need to find equivalent fractions with common denominators. In order to do that, we have to find a common multiple for the denominators. An important connection to make here is that the least common multiple (LCM) is the least common denominator (LCD) of the denominators. See Number 5.5 for the pertinent activities.

I drank $\frac{1}{4}$ of a glass of milk with my breakfast and $\frac{5}{6}$ of a glass just after breakfast. How much of the glass of milk did I drink altogether? How much more did I drink after breakfast than I did with my breakfast?

What are the two denominators? We need to find a common multiple. Look at the largest denominator. Is it a multiple of the other one? If not, what would be the smallest multiple of the larger denominator? Is it also a multiple of the smaller denominator?

We can therefore make the following changes:

$$\frac{1}{4} = \frac{3}{12} \text{ and } \frac{5}{6} = \frac{10}{12}, \text{ and to solve the problem, we add } \frac{3}{12} + \frac{10}{12} = ?$$

The purpose in using the LCM or LCD is to find the simplest equivalents. An efficient approach is to list the successive multiples of the greatest denominator until you come to one that is also a multiple of the smaller one. The fraction operations may, however, be successfully accomplished with greater multiples as the common denominator for the equivalent fractions or with decimal equivalents. Students also need to know that simply multiplying the denominators will provide a common denominator, and this is always the LCD for prime number denominators. Once the processes are understood and done with accuracy, the alternative of decimal equivalents obtained by using calculators should be allowed.

Exemplar Problems

Maria ate $\frac{1}{4}$ of a candy bar before lunch and $\frac{1}{3}$ of a candy bar after lunch. How much of a whole candy bar did she eat? Use your fraction tiles to help solve this problem. Add the pieces by putting them together. Do you see an equivalent fraction that is equal to their sum? In order to add the two different fractions, we had to change them into fractions that had the same denominator. How can we do that without changing the value of the fraction?

Look at the denominators of $\frac{1}{4}$ and $\frac{1}{3}$. Can you find their least common multiple? That will be your least common denominator. Now, for each fraction, find the numerator for that denominator that makes it an equivalent. Remember that the numerator has to be enlarged as much as the denominator because the greater the number of parts of a whole, the more parts you need for the same amount.

$$\frac{1}{4} = \frac{3}{12} \text{ and } \frac{1}{3} = \frac{4}{12}$$

Now add them together.

$$\frac{3}{12} + \frac{4}{12} = \underline{\qquad} \text{ and therefore } \frac{1}{4} + \frac{1}{3} = \underline{\qquad}$$

(12) is the least common multiple of the numbers ___ and ___.
It is also the least common denominator of the fractions ___ and ___.

ONE WHOLE											

1/2						1/2					

1/4			1/4			1/4			1/4		

1/8	1/8	1/8	1/8	1/8	1/8	1/8	1/8

1/3				1/3				1/3			

1/6		1/6		1/6		1/6		1/6		1/6	

$\frac{1}{12}$	$\frac{1}{12}$	$\frac{1}{12}$	$\frac{1}{12}$	$\frac{1}{12}$	$\frac{1}{12}$	$\frac{1}{12}$	$\frac{1}{12}$	$\frac{1}{12}$	$\frac{1}{12}$	$\frac{1}{12}$	$\frac{1}{12}$

1/3				1/4							

Use your fraction tiles to find these sums and differences:

$$\frac{1}{3} + \frac{1}{5}, \qquad \frac{3}{4} + \frac{5}{6}, \qquad \frac{5}{6} - \frac{1}{3}, \qquad \frac{3}{4} - \frac{1}{6}$$

Why can't you use these tiles to show how to add $\frac{1}{3} + \frac{1}{8}$?
What would be the LCD for $\frac{1}{3}$ and $\frac{1}{8}$?
Find the equivalents with common denominators for $\frac{1}{3}$ and $\frac{1}{8}$, and then add them to find the sum.
What would be the LCD for $\frac{1}{3}$ and $\frac{3}{8}$ and $\frac{3}{4}$ and $\frac{1}{6}$?
Find the equivalents with a common denominator for these fractions, and then add them to find the sum.

13.8 Inequalities

Developmental Transitions and Scaffolds

Finding the common denominator and then equivalents also works for solving problems of comparison or inequalities.

Is the following inequality true? $\frac{3}{4} > \frac{5}{6}$

If $\frac{3}{4} = \frac{9}{12}$ and $\frac{5}{6} = \frac{10}{12}$, then it is not true.

Nevertheless, fractional inequalities should be explored in several ways in addition to finding the least common denominator. Begin with inequalities that compare fractions to one whole. This approach makes the applications more meaningful and useful estimations possible.

Is 9/8 more or less than a whole? Is 9/10 more or less? Explain why 9/8 is more than 9/10.

For the problem above, try this approach. $\frac{3}{4}$ is $\frac{1}{4}$ less than a whole, but $\frac{5}{6}$ is only $\frac{1}{6}$ less than a whole, so $\frac{5}{6}$ is greater than $\frac{3}{4}$.

After students have developed familiarity with the common equivalents of $\frac{1}{2}$ and realize that any fraction where the denominator is twice the numerator will be equal to $\frac{1}{2}$, inequalities can be solved by comparisons to $\frac{1}{2}$.

Is $\frac{5}{9}$ smaller or larger than $\frac{8}{17}$?

$\frac{5}{9}$ is more than $\frac{1}{2}$, and $\frac{8}{17}$ is less than a half (there are alternative ways to reason this), so $\frac{5}{9}$ is more than $\frac{8}{17}$.

A final approach can be to treat the inequality as a proportion and see what happens when it is cross-multiplied (means × extremes).

Is this inequality true? $\frac{7}{8} > \frac{3}{4}$

Is $7 \times 4 > 3 \times 8$?　　　$28 > 24$, and the inequality is true.

14.1–14.2 Addition and Subtraction of Fractions

See also Chapter 2, pages 38–41, for concepts and expectations.

Developmental Transitions and Scaffolds

Practice with both the horizontal and vertical algorithm forms for addition and subtraction of unlike fractions should be attached to real problems. Following the critical generalization that finding the least common denominator comes first and students develop skill in finding the LCD, more complex addition and subtraction operations than those addressed above should be connected to the algorithms for whole-number operations. I suggest not using the traditional shortcut form of separately recorded common denominators and numerators at first. This may be disjunctive to the reasoning process. Convert each individual fraction to its common denominator form and do the operation. Then gradually introduce the algorithm as a way of organizing the process. The algorithm is less critical in the age of universal calculator use because eventually the process of changing unlike fractions to their decimal equivalents and performing the operations with the calculator will replace the algorithm. It is important, however, for students to understand the way it works. Consider the following difficulty sequence transitions.

1. Present only problems with proper fractions and easily computed LCDs that do not add up to more than one whole.

2. Present problems that add up to more than one whole, using vocabulary for *improper* fractions and *mixed numbers*, and practice changing in either direction. Compare the process to regrouping with whole numbers.

3. Present problems that require finding the difference between common fractions.

4. Present problems that require finding the difference between improper fractions but do not require regrouping or trading.

5. Present subtraction problems with fractions of all types that require trading.

Steve's problem below is a complex multistep problem that represents a change-unknown-subtraction problem (or finding the before-and-after difference) involving unlike fractions. The algorithm presented by Rhonda varies from the traditional in that the equivalent fractions are shown with both the numerator and denominator. Students may then suggest shortcuts and share these.

Exemplar Problems

Steve went trick or treating on Halloween. By the end of the evening at 9:00 p.m., he had collected seven of his favorite chocolate bars, but didn't have all of them left. He couldn't resist eating them, and by 7:00 p.m., one of them was half gone. At 9:00 p.m., he only had $4\frac{3}{4}$ bars left. How much more candy had he eaten between 7:00 and 9:00 p.m.?
   Think: Altogether Steve collected $\square$ bars.
   He ate $\square$ bars before 7:00 p.m.
   That left him with $\square$ more bars of candy to eat.
   The candy he ate between 7:00 and 9:00 is the difference between $\square$ and $\square$.
   The number sentence for this is as follows:
   Rhonda solved Steve's Halloween problem with this algorithm. Explain how she did it.

A	B	C
$6\frac{1}{2}$	$6\frac{2}{4}$	$5\frac{6}{4}$
$-4\frac{3}{4}$	$-4\frac{3}{4}$	$-4\frac{3}{4}$
		$1\frac{3}{4}$

How did she get from A to B?
How did she get from B to C?
How did she find the difference between $5\frac{6}{4}$ and $4\frac{3}{4}$?
How much of a candy bar did Steve have left after 9:00 p.m.?

14.3 Multiplication of Fractions by Whole Numbers

Developmental Transitions and Scaffolds

Multiplication of fractions by whole-number operators should be presented as repeated addition of the same fraction. Using manipulatives and real materials, students should discover that, as in the addition of like fractions, the numerators are enlarged but the denominators remain the same. *1/3 repeated two whole times is 2/3, and 2/5 repeated three times is 6/5.*

Allow students to discover that just the numerators have to be multiplied, while the denominators remain the same before moving to the horizontal and vertical algorithm.

Follow this with multiplication of mixed numbers by whole numbers—changing to improper fractions.

Exemplar Problem

The running track that Lori ran on was 1½ miles long. How many miles did she run in three laps? Try this problem, but estimate your answer first.
   Allan tried to solve the running track problem with an algorithm. Explain how he got from A to B, from B to C, and then to D.

A	B	C	D

$$3 \times 1\tfrac{1}{2} \ = \ 3 \times \tfrac{3}{2} \ = \ \tfrac{9}{2} \ = \ 4\tfrac{1}{2}$$

Did you find the same answer in a different way? Explain it to your group.

14.4 Fractional Parts of Sets—Unit Fractions

Developmental Transitions and Scaffolds

The concepts of the multiplication of fractions by fractions should be addressed in three stages. Begin with a review of multiplication of a set by a unit fraction to strengthen the basic concepts that students need to discover about fractional operators:

- Multiplication by a common fraction is the same as repeating the referent value (multiplicand) less than one whole time, and therefore the product or result will have a value less than the referent.
- It is also the same as finding the fractional part of a value.
- If the operator is a unit fraction, it is the same as dividing the value by the denominator.

Exemplar Problem

Every time the clock hand goes around one whole time, twelve hours pass. Two times around covers (?) hours, but $\tfrac{1}{2}$ time around is only $\tfrac{1}{2}$ of the twelve or (?) hours. How do you find $\tfrac{1}{2}$ of 12? How do you find $\tfrac{1}{2} \times 12$?

Football games also play by the clock. The total playing time is one hour or sixty minutes. How much time is used up at halftime?

We learned that $\tfrac{1}{2}$ times 60 is the same as $\tfrac{1}{2}$ of 60, and it is the same as dividing 60 into two parts and equal to 30.

$$\tfrac{1}{2} \times 60 = 60 \div 2 = 30$$

14.5 Fractional Parts of Sets—More-Than-Unit Fractions

Developmental Transitions and Scaffolds

The next stage is to consider more than unit fractions of whole-number values. Begin to develop the algorithm for the multiplication of fractions with students by generalizing back to the concept that two times one third is 2/3 and that, therefore, 2/3 of a value is two times more than whatever 1/3 of that value is. *Once you find 1/3, then you just have to multiply the numerator by 2 in order to find 2/3.*

- If the multiplier is more than a unit fraction, the unit fraction value obtained by dividing by the denominator of the multiplier must then be multiplied by the numerator of the multiplier.

Exemplar Problem

We know how to find $\frac{1}{6}$ of 24. How do we find $\frac{5}{6}$ of 24?
$\frac{1}{6}$ of 24 is the same as $\frac{1}{6} \times 24$ and the same as dividing 24 by 6 and equal to 4, but $\frac{5}{6}$ of 24 is five times as much as 4 and equal to 20.

We find the value of the unit fraction of a number by dividing the number by the denominator; we can then find the value of more-than-unit fractions by repeating the value of the unit fraction or enlarging it the number of times given by the numerator. When you multiply by a more-than-unit fraction, you divide by the denominator and multiply by the numerator.

When we multiplied 24 by $\frac{5}{6}$, we divided by the denominator (6) and then multiplied the quotient (4) by the numerator of 5.

14.6–14.8 Multiplication of Fractions by Unit Fractions

Developmental Transitions and Scaffolds

Using the fraction tiles and referring back to the above, students can then apply their generalizations to multiplication operations involving fractional parts of fractions. Multiplying a fraction by a common fraction operator is like finding a fractional part of the referent fraction, and the resulting product is going to be less than the referent fraction. Extend this with number sense analysis. The student can easily see that 1/2 of 1/3 is going to be 1/6 and that 1/3 of 1/2 is going to be the same 1/6, and then that 1/2 of 1/6 is 1/12. The generalization can then be made that this result of the operation can be obtained by multiplying the denominators of the operator and the referent value—in effect, producing a fraction with a larger denominator and smaller value. Finding a unit fractional part of a unit fraction *value (or multiplying the value by the fraction as above)* has the same effect as dividing the unit fractional part into smaller parts. It makes the fraction a number of times smaller (the number of times is equal to the multiplier denominator).

How many times smaller is $\frac{1}{4}$ of $\frac{1}{5}$ than $\frac{1}{5}$?
   $\frac{1}{4}$ of $\frac{1}{5}$ is going to be four times smaller than $\frac{1}{5}$.
   $\frac{1}{5}$ will be divided into four smaller parts, and each part will only be $\frac{1}{20}$.
   What happened to the denominator when we divided the fraction into 4 smaller parts?

What can we say about the product of a fraction multiplied by a common fraction?
   The product of a fraction multiplied by a fraction less than one whole is always less than the multiplicand. It is the same as finding the fractional part of the fraction.

$$\frac{1}{2} \times \frac{1}{4} = \frac{1}{8} \quad \text{or} \quad \frac{1}{2} \text{ of } \frac{1}{4} = \frac{1}{8} \quad \text{and} \quad \frac{1}{2} \times \frac{1}{40} = \frac{1}{80}$$

What do you notice about the denominator of the products?
   You can see that the computed value has a denominator that is the product of the two denominators.

How do we find a unit fraction of a more-than-unit fraction?

What happens when you multiply a more-than-unit fraction by a fraction?

If $(\frac{1}{2} \times \frac{1}{6}) = \frac{1}{12}$, then $(\frac{1}{2} \times \frac{2}{6})$ has to be two times as much or $\frac{2}{12}$ or $\frac{1}{6}$.

   $\frac{1}{2} \times \frac{2}{3}$ is going to be twice as great as $\frac{1}{2} \times \frac{1}{3}$, and it is equal to $\frac{2}{6}$ or $\frac{1}{3}$.

$\frac{1}{3}$ of $\frac{3}{4}$ will be equal to $3 \times (\frac{1}{3}$ of $\frac{1}{4})$ or $\frac{3}{12}$ or $\frac{1}{4}$, and $\frac{1}{5} \times \frac{5}{6} = \frac{5}{30} = \frac{1}{6}$.

$\frac{1}{2}$ of $\frac{10}{12}$ is equal to $\frac{5}{12}$ or $\frac{10}{12} \div 2$.

What do you notice about the numerator and denominator of the products?
Encourage students to think about what they are doing as they apply the algorithm.

Exemplar Problem

Do the answers you compute by using the algorithm make sense? Can you predict some answers before doing the algorithm? Try to use your number sense to predict these answers and then prove them with the algorithm.

$$\frac{1}{2} \times \frac{6}{13} = \qquad \frac{1}{5} \times \frac{10}{12} = \qquad \frac{1}{2} \times \frac{14}{27} =$$

Look at your products. Do you see a shortcut algorithm?
The shortcut algorithm is to multiply numerators and denominators.

14.9 Multiplying Fractions—More-Than-Unit Fractions of Fractions

Developmental Transitions and Scaffolds

How do we find more than one unit fraction of fractions?
To find more than one unit fraction of fractions, you can find the smaller unit fraction value by multiplying the denominators; then, because it is more than one unit, multiply the numerators. $\frac{1}{3}$ of $\frac{1}{2} = \frac{1}{6}$, and therefore $\frac{2}{3}$ of $\frac{1}{2}$ is twice as much or $\frac{2}{3}$.

The product of $\frac{2}{3} \times \frac{1}{2}$ is less than $\frac{1}{2}$ and equal to $\frac{1}{3}$. The product of $\frac{1}{2} \times \frac{2}{3}$ is less than $\frac{2}{3}$ and equal to $\frac{2}{6}$ or $\frac{1}{3}$.

Explain how this applies the commutative property.

What if both fractions are more than single units? How do we multiply them?
$\frac{2}{3}$ of $\frac{3}{2}$ would be three times as much as $\frac{2}{3} \times \frac{1}{2}$ or $\frac{2}{6}$. It equals $\frac{6}{6}$ or one whole.

$$\frac{2}{3} \times \frac{3}{2} = \frac{6}{6} = 1$$

Look at your products. What is the shortcut algorithm?
The shortcut algorithm is to multiply numerators and denominators.

15.1 Multiplication of Fractions by Mixed Numbers

See also Chapter 2, pages 41–43, for concepts and expectations.

Developmental Transitions and Scaffolds

Multiplication of fractions by mixed numbers can be considered as an application of the distributive property. Multiplication of mixed numbers by fractions can also be considered commutatively as a similar process.

How do we multiply $2\frac{1}{2} \times \frac{1}{3}$ or $\frac{1}{3} \times 2\frac{1}{2}$?
Why do the problems below have the same answers?

$$2\frac{1}{2} \times \frac{1}{3} = 2 \times \frac{1}{3} + \frac{1}{2} \times \frac{1}{3} = \frac{2}{3} + \frac{1}{6} = \frac{5}{6}$$

$$\frac{1}{3} \times 2\frac{1}{2} = \frac{1}{3} \times 2 + \frac{1}{3} \times \frac{1}{2} = \frac{2}{3} + \frac{1}{6} = \frac{5}{6}$$

The easier way is to change the mixed numbers to improper fractions and apply the algorithm.

$$2\frac{1}{2} = \frac{5}{2}$$

$$\frac{5}{2} \times \frac{1}{3} = \frac{5}{6} \text{ and } \frac{1}{3} \times \frac{5}{2} = \frac{5}{6}$$

Exemplar Problems

Mike and Dan were on a hike. They refilled their emptied half-gallon jug with water at every spring and shared the water equally. How much water did they each drink before the jug was empty? How much water did each one drink by the time they filled and emptied the jug three times? Use your fraction tiles to help solve this problem.

Hint: First find out how much water each friend drank from each refill.

Mike and Dan each drank ____ of a $\frac{1}{2}$ gallon of water from each refill.

That is the same as ____ of a gallon for each refill.

The number sentence for this problem is $3 \times (\frac{1}{2} \times \frac{1}{2}) = ?$

By the end of the hike they each had consumed ____ of a gallon.

Think about what you did to solve the problem and think of a simple way to explain how to do it from the number sentence. There may be more than one way to do it.

Suppose they refilled a different jug with $2\frac{1}{2}$ quarts at each spring and shared the water. How much did they each drink between refills?

The number sentence for this problem is $\frac{1}{2} \times 2\frac{1}{2} = ?$

Think about what you did to solve the problem and think of a simple way to explain how to do it from the number sentence. There may be more than one way to do it.

ONE WHOLE					

1/2			1/2		

| 1/4 | | 1/4 | | 1/4 | | 1/4 | |

| 1/3 | | 1/3 | | 1/3 | |

| 1/6 | 1/6 | 1/6 | 1/6 | 1/6 | 1/6 |

Compare both problems. How are they alike and how are they different?

One day Lori fell when she was only halfway around the $1\frac{1}{2}$ mile track. How far did she run? She made up for it the next day by running $5\frac{1}{2}$ times around the track. How far did she run that day?

For each of the following incomplete number sentences, estimate whether the answer will be more or less than the value in the box.
   Then try the multiplication algorithm to find the answer.

$$\frac{1}{3} \times [4] = \quad 1\frac{1}{3} \times [4] = \quad \frac{5}{6} \times [36] = \quad \frac{7}{6} \times [36] =$$

15.2 Reducing Fractions to Lowest Terms

Developmental Transitions and Scaffolds

The process of reducing a fraction to lowest terms has some function in making work with fractions simpler and is useful in understanding ratios. However, with calculators in everyday use, most complex fraction operations should be done by converting the fraction to a decimal. In solving a problem, the unreduced fraction is not a wrong answer unless the problem specifically says: reduce to lowest terms. Refer back to understandings of equivalent fractions, multiples, and factors (see Numbers 5.1, 5.2, and 13.6) to help students generalize:

- That dividing numerator and denominator by the same factor does not change the value of a fraction
- That dividing numerator and denominator by their greatest common factor will reduce the fraction to lowest terms

Exemplar Problems

It rains in parts of Arizona on average about fifteen days a year. We were in Arizona for seventy-three days, and it rained on three of them. Was that close to average?

1. *Express the average rainfall as a fraction.*

2. *How can we make the denominator of this fraction closer to 73 (our number of days) without changing the value of the fraction?*

3. *Explain your answer and how you found it.*

15.3 Division of Fractions by Whole Numbers

Developmental Transitions and Scaffolds

Use fraction tiles to help concept development of division of fractions by whole numbers from the partition view (dividing the fraction into a given number of parts) in this sequence:

1. Begin with unit fractions and a review of the concept that the value of unit fractions decreases proportionally with the size of the denominator. 1/3 divided into two parts is 1/6.

2. Follow with more-than-unit fractions with the same denominator and numerators that can be evenly divided.

3. Students can then discover that when the numerator cannot be evenly divided by the divisor, you can change the fraction to smaller sized equivalents and divide these.

4. Refer back to the concept that dividing a value into a number of parts is the same as finding that number's unit fraction of it; $1/6 \div 5$ is the same as $1/5$ of $1/6$ and $1/5 \times 1/6$.

5. Connect this to the concept that whole numbers can be represented by fractions with the denominator of 1, and this may lead to the "invert and multiply" algorithm generalization. Practice the transfer to multiplication using problems with common and improper fractions as well as mixed numbers.

Exemplar Problem

Roger and Dean bought a large bag of chips to eat at the football game. They had eaten about half of it when they were joined by Brad at the halftime break. They then shared the rest of the bag among the three of them. What fraction of a whole bag of chips did they each have after the break? Use your fraction tiles to help.

1. *What did the boys have to do with the $\frac{1}{2}$ bag?*

2. *Complete the number sentence for their problem: $\frac{1}{2} \div ? = ?$*

3. *That is the same as finding what fractional part of $\frac{1}{2}$?*

Finding a fractional part of a value is the same as multiplying by the fraction.

4. *Then why can we think of $\frac{1}{3} \times \frac{1}{2}$ as the same as $\frac{1}{2} \div 3$?*

5. *Explain why we can think of three wholes as $\frac{3}{1}$.*

6. *Then $\frac{1}{3} \times \frac{1}{2}$, which is equal to $\frac{1}{2} \times \frac{1}{3}$, is also equal to $\frac{1}{2} \div \frac{3}{1}$.*

$\frac{1}{3} \times \frac{1}{2} = \frac{1}{6}$ is equal to $\frac{1}{2} \times \frac{1}{3}$, and $\frac{1}{2} \div \frac{3}{1} = \frac{1}{6}$.

Can you recognize an algorithm or shortcut procedure for dividing a fraction?
Does it make sense? Check it with your fraction tiles.
Try the algorithm on this number sentence: $\frac{5}{6} \div 5 = ?$
Explain how you used the algorithm to solve this.
Use your number sense to verify that your answer was correct. If you divided $\frac{5}{6}$ of a pizza pie among five friends, how much of a pie would each one get?

Division of fractions by whole numbers from the quotition view (how many groups of a given size are there in a given size) is more challenging but requires attention for its number sense impact. *The number of whole size groups in a fraction that is less than a whole is going to be less than the whole. How many whole groups of three are in 1/2? There is less than one group of three in 1/2. There is only 1/6 of a group of three in 1/2.*

$$1/2 \div 3 = \frac{1}{6}$$

Jerry had some small bags that held only 1/2 a pound of candy. What fractional part of his large 3-pound bag could he put in each small bag?

15.4–15.5 Division of Fractions by Fractions

Developmental Transitions and Scaffolds

Division of a value by a fractional divisor is a difficult to understand concept. It is frequently confused with finding a fractional part of the value. The first clarification then has to relate back to the meaning of division. The partition meaning of division does not work for division *by* a fraction because a fraction is not a counting number. You can divide a value into two parts or one part, but you cannot divide a value into 1/2 number of parts. The quotition meaning works. You can divide a value into parts that are of a size that is 1/2 of one whole. When we divide 4 by 1/2, we think: "How many parts of size 1/2 of one whole are there in 4?"

Once there is clarity in the concept of what is happening in the division of a value by a fraction, there is still the challenge of developing a true understanding of the algorithm for division by a fraction. Step-by-step interpretations of problems such as those illustrated that describe real situations will help. They can try to develop the following sequence of concepts:

- Start with division of whole values by a unit fraction. The number of unit fractions in any one whole is the same as the denominator of a fraction. One whole = 4/4. Two wholes would have twice as many units or 2 × the numerator or 8/4. The generalization here is that to find the number of unit fractions in values of more than one whole, we just multiply the whole number, which is the dividend by the denominator of the divisor. 6 ÷ 1/4 = 24 because there are four unit fractions of size 1/4 in one whole and six times as many (6 × 4) 1/4's in six wholes.
- Then proceed to mixed-number dividends and more-than-unit fraction divisors. The problem 6 ÷ 2/4 means the following: "How many 2/4's are there in 6?" Although there are four unit fractions (1/4's) in one whole, there are only half as many 2/4's. There are only half as many because 2/4 is twice as large as 1/4. There would also be only 1/3 as many 3/4's in the same whole.

If there are (24) 1/4's in 6, then there are only (12) 2/4's and only (8) 3/4's. In each case, we found the number of more-than-unit fractions in the dividend (6) by dividing the number of unit fractions in the dividend (24) by the numerator of the divisor: 2 or 3.

- The generalization to aim for is that dividing the number of unit fractions in a given dividend by the numerator of a more-than-unit fraction divisor then tells us the number of more-than-unit fractions there are in the dividend.
- The algorithm combines the two concepts: multiply the dividend by the denominator of the divisor to find the number of unit fractions in the dividend and then divide by the numerator of the divisor to find the number of more-than-unit fractions in it—or just invert the divisor and multiply by it. It repeats and confirms the algorithm as it was applied in Number 15.3 to division of a fraction by a whole number.

Exemplar Problems

Jenna wanted to make some banners for the cheering squad. She went to the material store and bought 5 yards of material. Each banner needed 1/3 of a yard. How many banners could she make? Use your fraction tiles or a diagram to help.

Write a number sentence for this problem.
   Think:

   How many banners could she make with 1 yard? or

   How many 1/3 yards are there in 1 whole yard?

   How many in 5 yards?

Jenna tried to find an algorithm to solve the material problem of dividing 5 by $\frac{1}{3}$.
First she thought about the problem as "How many $\frac{1}{3}$ yards are there in 5 yards?"
Then she listed the three steps she needed to solve the problem: A, B, and C.
Explain what she did in each step.
Why did she do step B?
Why did she do step C?

$$\text{A. 5 yards} \div \frac{1}{3} \text{ yard} = ? \text{ Banners}$$

$$\text{B. 1 yard} = 3 \text{ banners}$$

$$\text{C. } 5 \times 3 \text{ banners} = 15 \text{ banners}$$

Then she decided that $5 \div \frac{1}{3}$ was the same as $5 \times \frac{3}{1}$.
Do you agree?
Suppose she had bought 8 yards. How many banners could she make? Solve the problem in your head, and then try Jenna's algorithm to see if it works.
Then try Jenna's problem with $6\frac{1}{3}$ yards. You will have to change the mixed number to an improper fraction first.

$$6\frac{1}{3} \text{ yards} \div \frac{1}{3} \text{ yard} = ?$$

   Suppose Jenna wanted to make double-sized banners. She would need $\frac{2}{3}$ yard for each. How many could she make from 6 yards of material? Try using Jenna's algorithm.

Reggie took the same vitamin pills each morning. The pills came in a box, and each day he took two whole pills. Each pill was divided into two halves. One day he noticed that the box had only eight pills left and realized that he needed to know how long they would last if he continued to take two whole pills each day. How many days would the pills last? Reggie then decided that he would need to stretch the pills by taking one whole pill each day instead of two. How many days would they last if he only took one? How many days would they last if he only took half a pill each day? What fractional part of the normal dose would half a pill be?

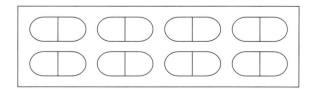

*How many groups of this size
were in the box ?*

$8 \div 2 = [\quad]$

How many groups of this size were in the box?

$8 \div 1 = [\quad]$

How many groups of this size were in the box?

$8 \div \frac{1}{2} = [\quad]$

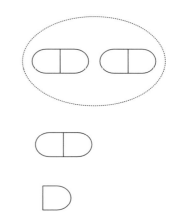

*Complete the number sentence for each of these problems.
Check the algorithm with your number sense answers.*

16.1–16.2 Fractions as Ratios

See also Chapter 2, pages 43–45, for concepts and expectations.

Developmental Transitions and Scaffolds

I often compare fractions to actors who play different roles with different costumes and settings but underneath are always the same person. Another role for fractions is the application of the fraction form as an expression of ratio. A ratio expresses the relationship between two different values. There are alternate forms for expressing ratios. In word form, we say the ratio of new toys to old ones is 1 to 3, or as a line expression, we use a colon and write 1:3. The different forms should be simultaneously introduced.

The use of the fraction notation can be confusing because we are accustomed to identifying the denominator of a fraction as the whole, and ratios can represent either a relationship between parts and the whole ("One pound of the five-pound box of chocolates is filled with nuts") or a relationship between different parts of the whole ("The ice cream cone is two parts vanilla and three parts chocolate"). Ratios can also represent both preceding relationships between groups of items: "Three out of the five girls on the team had caps on" or "For every three girls with caps on, there were two without caps." As they are with simple fractions, analyses of ratio and proportion problems should include identification of given quantities in terms of parts and wholes.

In some problems where only the parts are described, the whole may have to be computed first. Even adults frequently misinterpret this type of problem. Analyses of ratio problems should include identification *of given quantities in terms of parts and wholes.*

The fraction $\frac{2}{3}$ can represent two parts (items) out of a whole group of three parts (items). This ratio, expressed as $\frac{2}{3}$, can also be expressed in word form as 2 out of 3 or as 2 : 3.

Two out of three students at the lunch table brought their lunch to school in a paper bag.
In this case, the size of the whole is 3 and the size of the part is 2.
However, in a different form, a ratio can mean that for every two parts of one kind in a whole group, there are three parts of another kind.

There are three experienced soccer players for every two new ones on the team. Three out of every whole of five players, or 3/5 of the players, are experienced.

This ratio can also be expressed in word form as 3 is to 2, or 3 to 2, or symbolically as 3 : 2. If there were no other kinds of parts in this group, *the size of the whole would be 5 (or multiples of 5)*, and one kind of part would be $\frac{3}{5}$ of the whole, while the other would be $\frac{2}{5}$ of the whole.

For every six students who are only carrying a backpack, there are five who are carrying the backpack and another bag. *What is the size of the whole? Express the part of the whole number of students who are only carrying a backpack as a fraction, in symbol form, and in words.*

Ratios can be expressed in algebraic terms, as *a/b*, *a* out of *b*, or *a : b*. They can be used in solving problems that compare part-to-whole relationships. Some ratio problems such as the one in the figure below have no given value for the size either of the whole or parts—just the relative sizes. Eventually, these ratio problems may be described and solved symbolically as algebraic equations.

Jim's father is three times as tall as Jim.
What fractional part of his father's height is Jim's height?
Write the ratio of Jim's height to his father's height in fraction and symbol form.
Jim's brother is twice as tall as Jim.
Write the ratio of Jim's brother's height to Jim's height.
What is the ratio of Jim's brother's height to his father's height?
What fraction represents how much taller Jim's father is than his brother?
In algebraic form, this problem can be solved as follows: Jim's size (x) is $\frac{1}{3}$ of his father's size (y).

The equation for this is $x = \frac{1}{3} y$.
Jim's brother (z) is two times Jim's size ($z = 2x$).
If we substitute the value of x, we get the equation $z = 2(\frac{1}{3}y)$ or $z = \frac{2}{3}y$.
Jim's brother is therefore $\frac{2}{3}$ of his father's size.
In the inverse equation, Jim's father's size is $\frac{3}{2}$ times his brother's. $y = \frac{3}{2}z$

16.3 Proportions

Developmental Transitions and Scaffolds

When we think of equivalent fractions, we are considering the fractions as ratios. One out of six parts is the same as two out of twelve. Statements of equivalent ratios in fraction form are called proportions. The patterns of equivalent fractions or proportions can also help us compute unknown parts and wholes. Five out of ten parts is the same as one out of two parts or half the total number of parts. When the size of the denominator increases or decreases, the size of the numerator must change proportionately (by the same factor) in order for the fractions to be equivalent. As multiplicative functions, ratios and proportions can be considered either (a) from the aspect of comparing multiple units such as those above or (b) from the aspect of enlargement and shrinkage of a single unit.

Proportions can be used to compute unknown quantities based on the equivalent relationships.

There are three experienced soccer players for every two new ones on the team.
What are the parts in this ratio? What is the size of the whole?
What fraction name tells us what part of a whole of five are experienced players? Suppose there were fifteen players on the team. How many would be experienced? How many would be experienced on a team of twenty players?

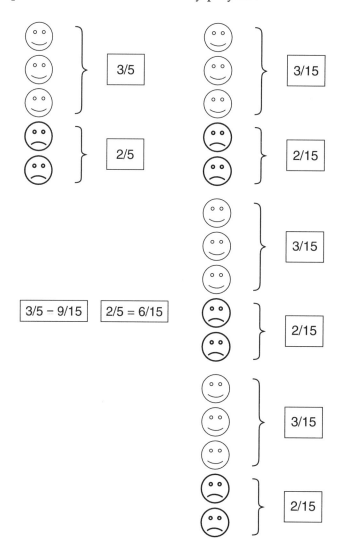

Now try these.

| 2/5 = ?/20 |

| 3/5 = ?/20 |

Pattern blocks can help you discover the relations that are true about the polygon design that follows.

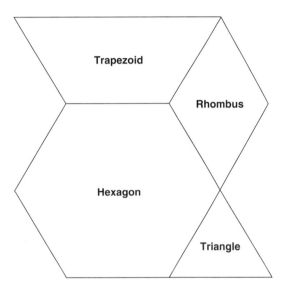

1. What is the ratio of one triangle part to the whole polygon design? Write your answer in ratio (a) symbol and (b) fraction form.

2. Write the fraction that represents the ratio of two triangle parts to the whole design.

3. What is the ratio of one rhombus to the whole design?

4. How many triangles form one rhombus?

5. Write the two equivalent fractions that represent the ratio of the two triangles to the whole design and the ratio of a single rhombus to the whole design. Now write the two equivalent ratios in symbol form.

6. What fractional part of the whole polygon design is a whole trapezoid?

7. How many triangles form the trapezoid?

8. Write the two equivalent fractions that represent the ratio of the three triangles to the whole design and the ratio of the single trapezoid to the whole design. Write the same two equivalent ratios in symbol form.

9. What is the term we use for equivalent ratios and fractions?

10. What fractional part of the whole polygon design is the hexagon?

11. Write a proportion that shows that a single hexagon and six triangles are equal parts of the whole design.

16.4 Proportions—Use of Algorithm

Developmental Transitions and Scaffolds

Use of the common algorithm for solving for missing values in proportions needs to be related to the recognition that for equivalent fractions as the size of the denominator grows, the size of the numerator must grow proportionately by the same factor. If you compare the two, the product of the number of parts (numerator) for the fraction with the larger total number of parts (A) and the denominator of the fraction with the fewer number of parts (B) equals the product of the denominator of (A) and numerator of (B). This makes sense because if a multiplier is increased, the multiplicand must be proportionately decreased to equal the same product. $4 \times 6 = 24$ and $8 \times 3 = 24$. The multiplier is $2 \times$ larger in the second equation, so the multiplicand must be reduced by a factor of 2 to equal the same value.

For any two equivalent fractions, the product of the numerator of one fraction and the denominator of the second is equal to the product of the denominator of the first fraction and the numerator of the second. This relationship is described as "the product of the means equals the product of the extremes," but more often, it is just applied as "cross-multiplication."

$$\text{If } \frac{a}{b} = \frac{c}{d}, \text{ then } ad = bc$$

The extremes are the numerator of the first stated fraction (*a*) and the denominator of the second one (*d*), while the means are the denominator of the first fraction (*b*) and the numerator of the second (*c*). The algorithm can also be used to check the equality of two fractions.

The algorithm also can be used to *compare equal and unequal relationships.*

I have six video games, and one of them is new. My friend has twelve, including two new ones. Do we both have the same ratio of new to old ones?

$$\frac{1}{6} = \frac{2}{12} \quad 1 \times 12 = 6 \times 2 \text{ and } 12 = 12$$

One out of six parts is the same as two out of twelve.

For inequalities, there is a basic concept that when you consider the same number of elements of a smaller and larger whole, that same number of elements represents a greater proportion of the smaller whole. In fraction terms, if there are two fractions with the same denominator, the one with a lower denominator represents the greatest value of the whole.

I have fifteen video games, and three of them are new. My friend has twelve, including three new ones. Who has the greatest proportion of new ones?

Three out of fifteen is going to be less than three out of twelve. To prove this, we can reduce the fractions to compare them. Three out of fifteen is the same as 1/5, but three out of twelve is equal to 1/4, which is a larger fraction.

We can also use the proportion algorithm to prove the relationship.

$$\frac{3}{15} < \frac{3}{12} \text{ If we multiply the means by the extremes, we get: } 3 \times 12 < 3 \times 15 \text{ and } 36 < 45$$

The inequality is time.

Exemplar Problems

I have fifteen video games, and three of them are new. My friend has seven games, including two new ones. I think he has the greater proportion of new ones. How can I prove who has the greatest ratio of new ones to old ones?

Is this a true inequality? $\frac{3}{15} < \frac{2}{7}$

If the means and extremes are multiplied, you get $21 < 30$, and so it is true that $\frac{3}{15}$ is less than $\frac{2}{7}$.

Which is the lesser fraction, $\frac{4}{9}$ or $\frac{2}{5}$?

Try this inequality: $\frac{4}{9} > \frac{2}{5}$ $20 > 18$ is true, so $\frac{2}{5}$ is the lesser fraction.

Check each of the following equalities and inequalities by multiplying the means by the extremes:

$$\frac{6}{8} = \frac{3}{4} \qquad \frac{7}{9} > \frac{21}{17} \qquad \frac{2}{3} > \frac{4}{7} \qquad \frac{7}{15} < \frac{10}{19}$$

16.5 Proportions in Scale Drawings

Developmental Transitions and Scaffolds

Understanding of proportions is also needed in applications to use scale drawings and maps. Here they are applied from the aspect of enlargement and shrinkage of a single unit. They may be presented from either the shrinkage or enlargement aspect. The interpretation of a scaled map represents the enlargement type, but drawing one would involve shrinkage. The value of the shrunken part size is given, and the true value is expressed in the scale as a ratio. As an example of the first type, the figure below shows a scale-drawing problem where the value or size of the part is compared as a ratio to a unit of measure in the scale, and the whole has to be measured in its scaled form and its actual size computed as a similar ratio.

Exemplar Problems

Mavis wanted to know how tall her house was. She couldn't get up to the roof to measure the height, but she had another idea. She took a picture of the house and then measured the height and width of the house on the picture using a centimeter grid. Then she measured the width of the house with a tape measure and found that it was 9 meters wide. How could she determine the height of the house? Hint: first make a scale for the picture using the given measures.

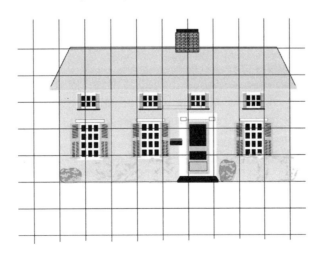

The scale on a map is 2cm : 75km. The distance on the map from Funville to Sunnyville is 5.5 cm. What is the actual distance?

This is the floor plan of Doctor Smith's office.

1. *Using the scale shown, determine the area of each of the rooms. Use the centimeter side of your ruler to complete this problem.*

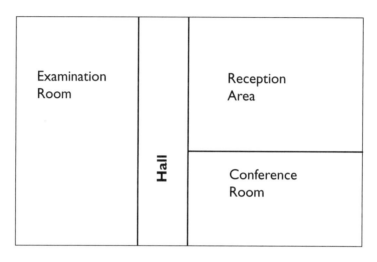

Scale: 1 cm = 5 ft.

Reception Area = _____
Hall = _____
Conference Room = _____
Examination Room = _____

2. *Dr. Robinson's office is twice the length and twice the width of Dr. Smith's. Dr. Robinson needs the same kind of rooms, although they may be in different proportion to one another.*

   A. *Construct a floor plan of Dr. Robinson's office using a different scale.*

   B. *Determine the area of each room.*

16.6 Percentage as Ratios and Proportions

Developmental Transitions and Scaffolds

The importance of understanding percentage in the everyday culture of the present cannot be overestimated. Students need to understand that percentage is based on a ratio that compares a part to a whole of 100. Although conversion of the percent to its decimal equivalent and multiplication by the decimal works well in finding a given percentage of a number, as we described in Numbers 10.6 to 10.8, proportions need to be applied when trying to find the percentage of a given whole for a given part. It is essentially the comparison of the ratios of the unknown percentage compared to the ratio of the part to the whole.

Seven out of the twenty-eight players on the two teams had hit homeruns that day. What percent of the team hit them?

The ratio that describes the relationship of the number of homerun hitters to the whole number of players is compared to the ratio of the unknown percentage or part to the total number of parts of 100. $\frac{7}{28} = \frac{x}{100}$, and using the algorithm, $700 = 28x$ and $x = 25$.

Exemplar Problems

Jose created a table and a circle graph to keep track of his personal spending for two weeks. Complete the table according to the directions below.

   A. *For each item, calculate the percent of the total amount spent. Round each percent to the nearest whole percent and enter it on the table.*

   B. *Match the letter on the graph to the expense and place it in the correct place on the table.*

Budget Items	Amount Spent	% of Total	Letter on Graph
Food	$65.75		
Clothes	$88.00		
Entertainment	$45.35		
School supplies	$15.00		
Miscellaneous items	$35.90		
Total	$250.00		

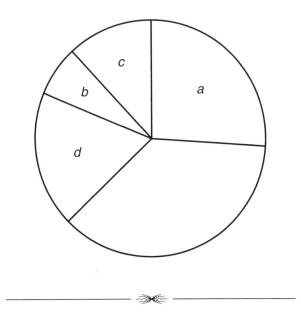

Sam bought a pair of sneakers at Sneaker World. The regular price of the sneakers was $150, but they were on sale at a 20% discount. The sales tax was 5%. How much did Sam pay in total? What percent of the original cost did he pay?

16.7 Rates

Developmental Transitions and Scaffolds

A ratio that describes rate is different from part-to-part and part-to-whole ratios in that it compares different units of measures that are related. When we look at the speedometer of a car, it is measuring miles per hour or comparing the distance traveled to the unit of time. The denominator of a fraction that describes the rate is often a standard unit of measure, such as an hour or mile, and the numerator is the related value of a different measure. We can relate a variety of measures such as distance traveled/unit time, miles/gallon, and mass/unit volume. A proportion can be used to determine the unit rate from the measured quantities. The measured ratio is compared in the proportion to the unit standard. For example, to find the speed in miles per hour, a measured distance of 80 miles traveled in two hours of time can be represented by the proportion $\frac{80}{2} = \frac{x}{1} = 80 = 2x$ and $x = 40$. Thus, the rate traveled is 40 miles per hour. Note: Although a proportion that uses distance measured to unit distance as a ratio and time measured to time unit is a comparative one, it requires a transition from the unit rate expression. Therefore, suggest to students that in setting up the proportion, it may be easier to use the standard rate expression as one ratio and the ratio of the two different measures as the other. Hint: use the unit that follows the word *per* or *for each* as the denominator in both ratios.

Exemplar Problems

Shawn rode his bicycle to school each day. He traveled the distance of 6 miles in thirty minutes. What was his rate of distance traveled in miles per hour?

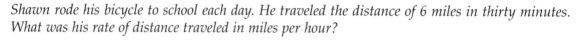

The new car bought by the Jones family used about 10 gallons of gas for a distance of 180 miles. What was the approximate gas usage per mile?

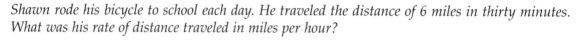

The density of water is 1 gram per cubic centimeter. What would be the weight of 10 cc of water? If a substance had twice the density of water, how much would 8 cc of the substance weigh?

16.7 Equivalent Conversions

Conversions between different-size units of measure and between different standards of measure can be done using proportions. The proportions consist of the ratios or rate of the unit standard compared to the ratio of equal measured and unknown amounts. When converting larger units into smaller ones, there will be more of the smaller ones. Also see Numbers 26.5 to 26.9 for additional approaches.

Exemplar Problems

Jenna measured the width of the room as 19.5 feet. How many yards was that?
    Rate 3 feet = 1 yard

$$\frac{3}{1} = \frac{19.5}{x} \qquad 3x = 19.5 \qquad x =$$

Manuel measured his desk using a centimeter ruler. It measured 50 cm. How many inches was that?

Rate 2.5 cm = 1 in

$$\frac{2.5}{1} = \frac{50}{x} \qquad 2.5x = 50 \qquad x =$$

———————————— ✳ ————————————

Jorge came from Spain to the United States for a visit. He needed to change his money in euros to dollars. The exchange rate was 1.6 dollars = 1 euro. He had 200 euros. How many dollars could he get for that?

16.8 Unit Costs

Developmental Transitions and Scaffolds

Proportions can also help us compare the unit cost of items. The proportion can be set up as an estimated inequality and the algorithm applied.

If you pay $62 for two pairs of shoes, is it more or less than paying $80 for three pairs?

Is $\frac{62}{2} > \frac{80}{3}$? Cross multiply and you get 186 > 160. Is this true?

Exemplar Problems

Jean earned $2,500 from his summer job. He decided to deposit 40% into his savings account and to spend the rest on a trip to New York City. If his trip to New York City will last 5 days, how much money could Jean spend on average per day?

———————————— ✳ ————————————

Diane's recipe for chocolate milk is 4 ounces of syrup for each quart of milk. How many ounces of syrup will she need for 20 ounces of milk? (Reminder: 1 quart = 32 ounces)

ALGEBRA: EXPRESSIONS AND LINEAR EQUATIONS ■

By the time today's students have reached the sixth grade, they have been applying the mathematical concepts and tenets of algebra to solve numerous problems in the form of open number sentences. They may not, however, have been exposed to the special language for communicating algebraic concepts, as well as the algorithmic procedures and understanding that give algebra its special power and efficacy as a mathematical tool. Previously developed skills in applying the processes in simplistic ways may actually be a slight hindrance to learning the procedures needed for the more complex problems. While working with sixth graders recently, I observed that they understood perfectly how to apply the inverse operations to solving algebraic equations such as $x - 12 = 38$ and $3x = 36$. They simply explained with accuracy the following: "The x equals 50 because if you take 12 away from a number and you are left with 38, then you started with 50 because when you add back the 12 you get 50." Also, "The number you have to multiply by 3 to get 36 is 12 because 3 times 12 is 36 and 36 divided by 3 is 12." They did not understand why they needed to do the algorithm of applying the inverse operation to both sides of the equation in order to isolate the variable, when they saw the answer so easily. It took the challenge of less easily solved problems and some practice with manipulatives combined with direct analysis of how their approaches reflected the algorithms to open their minds. They also needed some time to absorb the new language so that they could explain the relationship between their prior knowledge and the new formal procedures. As usual, it is also important to make the problems as close to those they will encounter in their real lives.

In response to the need to introduce the language for communication of algebraic concepts, we begin with algebraic expressions in our outline and show the developmental sequence over the grades. This is followed by a similar sequence for solving equations. However, for grade-level curricula or even for a single lesson, it will be more practical to apply the topics in tandem. For example, they should be able to identify an expression as part of an equation and then immediately apply the terminology and rules of expressions to explaining and solving an equation that contains them.

17.1–17.8 Expressions—Definitions and Forms

See also Chapter 2, pages 46–48, for concepts and expectations

Developmental Transitions and Scaffolds

The language of mathematics has a structure that provides us with the ability to communicate with shared meaning for the symbols, words, and sentences. Unlike other languages, it also has the purpose of helping us solve the complex quantitative problems of our civilized human existence. Just as words are put together to form a sentence that has meaning, words are joined in mathematics to form mathematical sentences such as equations and inequalities. As we learn the mathematics language, we have the advantage of checking our interpretations with our quantitative instincts and prior knowledge.

Just as we find to be true in the process of learning other new languages, it is helpful to keep connecting the new words and meanings to those we already know. Mathematical expressions are symbolic ways to describe a number or operation. They are words or a combination of words but not a complete sentence. For complete sentences to show relationships, we need equations and inequalities. Sometimes, it helps to put the expressions into sentences so that we can prove and understand their meaning.

The sequence of necessary concepts for defining expressions includes the following:

- A numerical expression has only numbers in it.
- An algebraic expression has both numbers and letters that represent numbers.
- The letters are called variables, and they can represent different numbers or quantities.
- The numbers are called constants because they represent a specific value.
- An expression can define an operation such as addition ($6 + n$), subtraction ($n - 6$), multiplication ($6 \times n$), or division ($6 \div n$).
- The operation of multiplication in an expression can be shown by placing a constant multiplier in front of the variable.
- The constant number that is directly in front of a variable (e.g., $3n$ or $6b$) is called a coefficient. It indicates that the variable must be multiplied by the coefficient number. $3n$ means ($3 \times n$).

- When two variables are directly next to each other or side by side, that also means that they are multiplied (or are factors of a multiple). The expression (lw) in the equation $A = lw$ means ($l \times w$). Another form for this could be $l(w)$.
- The operation of division in an expression is most often shown in its fraction form; $6 \div n$ is the same as $\frac{6}{n}$, and $\frac{a}{b}$ is translated as (a) divided by (b).
- Each separate variable or constant (or group of constants and variables within parentheses) that is separated from another individual or group by an addition or subtraction operation sign is a different term of the expression.
- The operation signs (+, −) indicate separate terms, but the multiplication and division operation may also be part of the same term. When a coefficient (with or without parentheses) is used to denote multiplication, or the fraction form shows division of a term, it is part of the term. $3n$ is a single term, and $\frac{3}{4}$ is a single term.
- A group of constants and variables within parentheses is a single term. For example, ($3 + a + b$).
- A polynomial is an expression with one term or one that shows the sum or difference between two or more terms.
- A monomial expression is a polynomial with one term.
- A binomial is a polynomial with only two terms.
- A trinomial is a polynomial with three terms.
- Any term in front of a parenthesis indicates that every term within the parenthesis must be multiplied by the term in front of it (distribution property). $6(a + b + 3) = 6a + 6b + 18$
- Any binomial in front of a parenthesis indicates that every term within the parenthesis must be multiplied by each term of the binomial (distribution property). $a + b(c + d) = ac + ad + bc + bd$

17.9 Evaluating Expressions

Developmental Transitions and Scaffolds

Some practice with just evaluating expressions may be helpful in diagnosing where the "bumps in the road of understanding" are. It can also help with embedding the term definitions. It may, however, be possible to move quickly to the equations that contain them. See Numbers 20.5 to 20.8 for suggestions for manipulatives to use in conjunction with the equation introduction.

Exemplar Problems

We need to write expressions and solve equations for many of our everyday problems. When you evaluate an expression, you substitute numbers that you know or are given for any variable terms. Then you may be able to form and solve an equation that contains an expression and identify the value of an unknown variable.

For example, consider the following real-life situation:

You purchased three jars (j) of peanut butter and had a 10¢ off coupon to use in the purchase.

1. *What is the term for the multiple variable that represents the jars of peanut butter?* (3j)

2. *What is the term for the constant of 10¢ off?* (−10)

3. *Combine the two terms in a binomial expression.* (3j −10)

4. *Now write an equation that can be used to find the total cost of the peanut butter. (x = 3j –10)*

5. *What additional variable was added to the equation? (x)*

6. *If the variable (j) = 60¢, solve the equation and find the value of (x).*

Evaluate the following expressions using the given value of the variable.

1. *If (b = 4), then 4b = ?, and 3b + 12 = ?, and 5b – 5 = ?*

2. *If (a = 24), then $\frac{1}{2}a – 4 =$*

3. *If (b = 8), then $6 + 3b – \frac{1}{2}b =$*

4. *If (a = 4, b = 2), then 3a + b(2a + 2) =*

5. *If (b = – 3), then $b^2 + 2b – 4 =$*

For each of the following examples of mathematical situations:

- *Write the expression in symbol form.*
- *Write an equation that contains the expression.*
- *Select a value for one of the variables.*
- *Solve the equation for the other unknown variable.*

1. *A distance 8 miles less than the distance (d)*

2. *Number of miles traveled on a car trip in five hours at an average speed of (n) miles per hour*

3. *Number of miles traveled at the end of seven hours at an average speed of (n) miles per hour if you took a one-hour break*

4. *Numbered pages in a book (p) if there are six chapters, each with fifteen pages of text (t), and some numbered blank pages*

Try writing and solving these equations:

1. *Lois is four times as old as her son Dan. The sum of their ages is 40. How old is Lois?*

2. *Tadd wants to limit his lunch to 500 calories. A hamburger without the roll has 320 calories, and an average single French fry has 15 calories. How many French fries can he eat if he does not eat a roll?*

18.1 Adding and Subtracting Like Monomials

See also Chapter 2, pages 48–51, for concepts and expectations.

Developmental Transitions and Scaffolds

Like terms have corresponding variables with the same exponents. (6a) and (3a) are like terms. Just asc two apples plus three apples are five apples, the sum of like terms is equal to the common variable of the terms preceded by the sum of their coefficients. Different exponential forms (powers) of the same variable are not like terms and cannot be added by adding the coefficients. The terms (a) and (a^2) are not like terms, but ($6a^2$) and ($3a^2$) are like terms. Therefore,

$$6a + 3a = 9a \text{ and } 6a^2 + 3a^2 = 9a^2$$

The difference between like terms is similarly equal to the common variable of the terms preceded by the difference between their coefficients.

$$6a - 3a = 3a \text{ and } 6a^2 - 3a^2 = 3a^2$$

Exemplar Problems

Simplify the expressions by adding or subtracting like terms:

$$2x - 3y - 5x - 8y$$
$$(x^2 - 3x + 1) \text{ and } (-2x^2 - x - 5)$$

18.2 Order of Operations

Developmental Transitions and Scaffolds

Suppose you substituted the following number values, $a = 3$, $b = 4$, $c = 8$, $d = 2$, for the variables in the expression $a + b\,(c + d)$. You could get $3 + 4\,(8 + 2) = 7(10) = 70$ if you added first—or if you multiplied first, you could get $3 + (32 + 8)$ or $3 + 40 = 43$. Which is the right answer? What did the writer of the expression mean?

The order in which the operations in an expression are performed may sometimes affect the value. Therefore, when evaluating expressions, we use a specific order of performing operations that has been agreed upon by mathematicians. This allows us to communicate mathematically. The order corresponds to the acronym PEMDAS. Operations attached to grouping symbols such as *Parentheses* and brackets are done first. *Exponents* come next. *Multiplication* and *Division* follow and are equal in status, but the operation that comes first from left to right is done first. This also holds true of the final *Addition* and *Subtraction*.

If it is possible when one grouping symbol is inside the other, you can perform the innermost operation first to make it easier. For $3b + b(5 - 2) + 8$, subtract inside the parentheses first (5–2) and then multiply by (b).

$$3b + b(5 - 2) + 8 = 3b + 5b - 2b + 8 = 6b + 8$$

or

$$3b + b(3) + 8 = 6b + 8$$

Exemplar Problems

Simplify the following expressions using the order of operations and combining like terms.

$$6t + 5(6 - t)$$
$$3x - 2(4 - x) + 2x$$
$$5x - 2x\,(3 + 4)$$

18.3 Multiplying Monomials

Developmental Transitions and Scaffolds

If there is more than one variable factor, we can just combine them in the product.

$$3a \times 4b = 12ab$$

We also just multiply the coefficients.

$$3a \times 6a = 18a^2$$

In contrast to the fact that we cannot add or subtract the unlike terms of different powers of a variable by adding the coefficients, we can show the products of both like and unlike powers of the same variable by adding the exponents. As proof that $(a^2)(a^3) = a^5$, we can substitute values.

If $a = 2$, then $a^2 = 4$ and $a^3 = 8$. And $4 \times 8 = 32$, which is equal to a^5.

The product of monomials with different variables is the product of the corresponding variables and their coefficients.

$$3a \times 6a^3 = 18a^4 \qquad\qquad 3a \times 6ab = 18a^2b$$

Exemplar Problems

Simplify the following expressions:

$$6(y + 8)$$
$$3t + 5(6 - t)$$
$$3x - 2(4 - x) + 2x$$
$$2x + 3x\,(y + x^2)$$

18.4 Multiplying Two Binomials

Developmental Transitions and Scaffolds

Since any binomial in front of a parenthesis indicates that every term within the parenthesis must be multiplied by each term of the binomial, we apply the distributive property to multiplication of two binomials.

$$(a + b)\,(c + d) = ac + ad + bc + bd$$

An algorithm we can use is a procedure called the FOIL method (first, outside, inside, and last) for multiplying two binomials. FOIL is an application of the distributive property.

If you multiply by each term of the binomial multiplier separately and then combine the two products, the sum is the same as the result of the FOIL procedure.

Distribution method: $(6 + 3) \times (6 + 3) = 6(6 + 3) + 3(6 + 3) = 36 + 18 + 18 + 9 = 81$.

FOIL method:

- Multiply first numbers in each binomial = 36.
- Multiply the two outside numbers (first and last) and the two inside (last and first) numbers (combine them if you can): 18 + 18 = 36.
- Multiply the last two numbers in each binomial = 9. And 36 + 36 + 9 = 81.

Multiplying two binomials may result either in a polynomial with three or more terms or in a binomial.

Exemplar Problems

Multiply the following binomials:

$$(a + 6)(2a + 3) \quad (3y - 4)(2y + 3) \quad (2x + 3)(2x - 3)$$

18.5–18.9 Dividing Monomials by Constants and Monomials

Developmental Transitions and Scaffolds

The division operation in algebraic expressions is usually represented by its fraction form.

$6a \div 2$ is shown as $\frac{6a}{2}$.

In its partition meaning, it simply translates into the following: "If we divide the term $6a$ into 2 parts, how big will each part be?" If six apples are divided into two parts, each part will be three apples. $\frac{6a}{2}$ is equal to $3a$.

The quotient of a monomial divided by a constant is the quotient of the coefficient of the numerator divided by the constant and has the same variable as the numerator.

In contrast, the quotient of a monomial divided by a like-term monomial is best explained from the quotitive view.

The meaning of the fraction $\frac{12a}{3a}$ can be expressed as follows: "How many units of $3a$ are there in $12a$?" There are (4) units of $3a$ in $12a$.

The quotient of like-term monomials is then the quotient of the coefficient of the numerator divided by the coefficient of the denominator, and the variable of the numerator divided by the variable of the denominator is $\frac{12a}{3a} = 4$. A shortcut algorithm is to divide the numerator and denominator by the same term or cancel the same term in the numerator and denominator because any number divided by itself is equal to 1.

$$\frac{12a \div (3a)}{3a \div (3a)} = \frac{\overset{4}{\cancel{12}a}}{\underset{1}{\cancel{3}a}} = \frac{4}{1} = 4$$

The coefficient and the variable are separate factors of a monomial. Dividing the numerator and denominator by the same factor can reduce a monomial division expression to a simpler fraction form.

$$\frac{6a}{2a} = \frac{3a}{b} \text{ and } \frac{7a}{9a} = \frac{7}{9}$$

If we think about $18a^2 \div 3a$ as how many units of $(3a)$ will there be in $(18a^2)$, we realize that there would be 6 units of 3 in 18 and (a) units of (a) in a^2 ($a \times a = a^2$), so there must be $(6a)$ units of $(3a)$ in $18a^2$.

In order to find the quotient of a monomial divided by a monomial with a lesser degree of the same variable, we put the expression into fraction form and perform the following operations:

$$18a^2 \div 3a = \frac{18a^2}{3a}$$

1. Divide the coefficient of the numerator and the coefficient of the denominator by the same factor (3). $\frac{18a^2}{3a} = \frac{6a^2}{a}$

2. Divide the variable of the numerator and the variable of the denominator by the same factor (a). $\frac{6a^2}{a} = \frac{6a}{1}$

Or, more efficiently:

We can combine the coefficient and variable and divide numerator and denominator by 3a.

$$\frac{\overset{6a}{\cancel{18a^2}}}{\underset{1}{\cancel{3a}}} = \frac{6a}{1} = 6a$$

When the numerator is a polynomial, the distributive principle applies to the division process as it did in multiplication.

When dividing polynomials by monomials, each individual term of the numerator must be divided by the monomial term of the denominator.

$$\frac{6a^3 + 9a^2 - 12a}{3a} = 2a^2 + 3a - 4$$

Exemplar Problems

Complete the following operation:

$$(24x^2 + 12x + 18) \div 6 \qquad (36a^3 + 9a^2 + 27a) \div 9a$$

19.1–19.3 Factoring Expressions

See also Chapter 2, pages 51–52, for concepts and expectations.

Developmental Transitions and Scaffolds

It may be helpful to review the numerical concepts of factors and multiples before approaching the algebraic applications (see Numbers 5.1–5.9). Factoring an expression means representing a composite (multiple) term or group of terms by their common factors. It actually involves a reversal of the operations that formed the composites. We need to do this because in order to find the value of an unknown variable, we must isolate it, and the terms in polynomial equations may need to be factored before the variable can be isolated. We can simplify a polynomial expression by dividing all the terms by the same factor and then expressing it with the divisor we used as a multiplier factor and the quotients for each divided term as the multiplicands.

What common factor do you see in the expression (3x + 5x)?

How could you express the same value and separate the common factor?

If you divide each term by x in the expression $(3x + 5x)$, the same value can then be expressed as $x(3 + 5)$ or $8x$.

How could you express (6b + 3a) in factored form?

In factored form, $6b + 3a$ is equal to $3(2b + a)$.

Sometimes there is more than one common factor.

What common factors do you see in the expression $(3x^2 + 6x)$?

Both 3 and x are common factors, so $(3x^2 + 6x)$ can be expressed as $3x(x + 2)$.

You can divide the two terms of the expression by the greatest common factor (GCF) of $3x$ and show it as a separate multiplier.

When factoring polynomials, it helps to factor groups of terms by the GCF or the largest multiple of common factors. In the equation $6a + 5a = 66$, the factors of the terms $6a + 5a$ are (a) and $(6 + 5)$, and therefore $a(6 + 5) = 66$ and $a(11) = 66$. If you then divide both sides by 11, you are left with $a = 6$.

In the expression $6a^2 + 18a$, separating the (GCF) factor of $(6a)$ simplifies the expression to $6a (a + 3)$.

When dividing a polynomial by a binomial, it may be useful to use the GCF to factor the numerator first, in order to find a factor in the numerator that is common to the denominator. The expression can then be simplified by dividing numerator and denominator by the common factor.

$$\frac{3a^2 + 6a}{a+2} = \frac{3a\ (a+2)}{a+2} = \frac{3a\ \cancel{(a+2)}}{\cancel{a+2}} = 3a$$

19.4 Factoring Trinomials in Quadratic Form

Developmental Transitions and Scaffolds

A quadratic expression or equation must have one term where the greatest power of the variable is 2. The general form of a quadratic equation is $y = ax^2 + bx + c$, where (b) and (c) are constants (see Number 23.7). The solution of most quadratic equations in this form requires factorization and is a challenge for many students. The approach is mostly trial and error, but it can have a systematic approach.

Trinomials in the quadratic forms of $(ax^2 + bx + c)$ $(ax^2 - bx + c)$ $(ax^2 + bx - c)$ and $(ax^2 - bx - c)$ may be factored into the two root binomials, by thinking of the FOIL procedure in reverse. The first term must be the product of the first terms of the binomials and the last term the product of the second terms of the binomials, while the middle term must be the sum of the product of the inside and outside terms.

One systematic approach to applying the FOIL procedure in reverse is to follow the steps below.

Factor the expression $x^2 + 2x - 15$.

Think: This form is representative of the product of two binomials.

Think: The first term has to be the product of the first two numbers of each binomial.

Think: They must be $x \times x$, so the first term of each binomial is x $(x\ ?) (x\ ?)$.

Think: The last term is -15. What factors are there in 15? (15, 1, 3, 5), and one needs to be negative and the other positive.

Think: The 1 and 15 cannot work because we could not get a sum of $2x$ for the inside and outside products from those two numbers. It must be 3 and 5 $(x\ ?\ 3) (x\ ?\ 5)$.

Think: If the sum of the inside and outside numbers is positive, which of the two factors of 15 must be positive? The greater factor of 5 must be positive.

The factors of $x^2 + 2x - 15$ are $(x - 3)(x + 5)$.

Follow this up with analyses of why other variations of the factors such as $(x - 5)(x + 3)$ and the connected generalizations, such as the following:

If the center term is positive and the final term is negative, the higher value of the second term must also be positive and vice versa.

Would that work if the first x was negative?

Exemplar Problems

Find the factors of the following expressions:

$$x^2 - 6x - 27$$

$$2x^2 - x - 6$$

If $(x - 3)$ and $(x + 7)$ are the factors of the trinomial $x^2 + ax - 21$, what is the value of a?

If $x^2 - 10x + k$ is a perfect square trinomial, what is the value of k?

19.5 Factoring Quadratic Expressions—Difference Between Two Squares

Developmental Transitions and Scaffolds

A very useful generalization is that if we multiply any two binomials in the form of $(a + b)(a - b)$, we always get a binomial of two perfect squares $(a^2 - b^2)$ because the inside numbers and outside numbers cancel each other.

Therefore, the factors of a binomial that is the difference between two perfect squares will be $(a + b)(a - b)$. For example, $(x^2 - 16) = (x + 4)(x - 4)$.

Exemplar Problems

Find the factors of the following expressions:

$$x^2 - 36$$

$$9x^4 - 25$$

19.6 Two-Step Quadratics

Developmental Transitions and Scaffolds

Trinomials may also be factored in a sequence of steps by separating the greatest common factor first and then applying the reverse FOIL method. For example, the expression $(6x^2 y - 6xy - 36y)$ may be factored first by removing the GCF of $6y$ to get the expression $6y(x^2 - x - 6)$ and then factored to $6y(x + 2)(x - 3)$.

See Number 22.5 for the exemplar problems.

20.1–20.7 Solving Equations and Inequalities

See also Chapter 2, pages 52–55, for concepts and expectations.

Developmental Transitions and Scaffolds

As previously stated, the concepts and procedural skills of solving equations should be addressed in tandem with the concepts of algebraic expression and factoring processes. They are the real-life tools we need to find the measures of the unknown quantities we cannot directly measure. Basic concepts include the following:

- An equation is a mathematical sentence that says that the expressions on each side of it are equal. Equations may have both constants and variables.
- A single variable in an equation will have a specific value that can be determined or solved for.
- When a specific value for the variable is substituted into an equation and/or inequality, it will make that equation and/or inequality either true or false. When we need to show a relationship between expressions, we use either an equality sign (=) to form an equation or an inequality sign ($>, <, \geq, \leq, \neq$) to form an inequality.
- For inequalities, a variable may have more than one value. In the expression ($b < 5$), (b) could equal any number less than (5). The inequality ($6a > 3 + a$) tells you that the expression ($6a$) is greater than the expression ($3 + a$).
- We can also use symbols to show that a variable may be equal to a range of numbers that are less than, more than, or equal to a given value. ($6b \leq 30$) means that (b) could be any number less than or equal to (5).
- We need to isolate the variable to solve the equation or inequality.
- You must combine like terms in order to solve the equation.
- If we add the same quantity to or subtract the same quantity from both sides of an equation or inequality, the sides are still equal or balanced. The equation or inequality is still true.
- If we multiply or divide both sides of an equation or inequality by the same factor, the sides are still equal or balanced. The equation or inequality is still true.

20.1 Showing Relationships Between Expressions: Algebraic Equations

Developmental Transitions and Scaffolds

When a specific value for the variable is substituted into an equation, it will make that equation either true or false.

The total cost for an item ordered online equals the cost of the item (n) and a shipping charge of $5.00. If the total cost is $30.00, write an equation that can be used to determine the cost of the item.

$$n + 5 = 30$$

Could the item cost $10.00?
Could the item cost $25.00?

20.2 Showing Relationships Between Expressions: Algebraic Inequalities

Developmental Transitions and Scaffolds

When we need to show a relationship between expressions that is not equal, we use an inequality sign to form an inequality. The different relationships are shown by the signs ($>, <, \geq, \leq, \neq$).

For inequalities, a variable may have more than one value that makes it true. In the expression $(b - 2) < 7$, $(b - 2)$ could equal any number less than (5).

Jack had only $30.00 to spend on an item he bought with an online order. He also had to pay a shipping charge of $5.00. What could the cost of his item (n) be?

$$n + 5 \leq 30$$

Could the item cost $10.00?
Could the item cost $25.00?
Could the item cost $30.00?

20.3–20.4 Isolating the Variable and Solving Equations—Using Number Sense

We previously noted that students have been solving for unknown quantities by applying inverse procedures since the early elementary grades. Their comfort with this useful number sense practice may get in the way of learning the traditional algebraic procedures of isolating the variable by performing operations that can do it while maintaining the equality. Showing them how the number sense thinking and procedures they are presently using are proven by the algorithm may be helpful.

If they are accustomed to finding an unknown minuend (the number from which a value is subtracted) by applying the inverse action of adding the given subtrahend (the subtracted value) to the given difference ($x - 12 = 8$) so that $x = 12 + 8$, show them how adding the 12 to both sides of the equations isolates the variable, maintains the equality, and gives us the value of the unknown minuend.

$$x - 12 = \quad 8 \qquad x = 20$$
$$(+\ 12) \quad (+\ 12)$$

20.5 Isolating the Variable and Solving Equations—Additive Inverse

The concept of balancing equations can be strengthened by the use of manipulatives. The ones I have found most effective are balance scales and/or boxes with the unknowns in them. Algebra tiles can also be used.

Developmental Transitions and Scaffolds

A box with an unknown number of weights was placed on side A of a balance scale. How can we discover the number of weights in the box?

- A similar box with ten equal-size weights is placed on side B of the scale.
- We needed to place three more weights on the unknown number side A in order to balance the scale.
- In algebraic equation form, we knew that $x + 3 = 10$.

If we took off three weights from both sides of the scale, would the scales still balance? How many would be left on side B? How many weights would there be in the box on side A?

In algebraic equation form, we can subtract 3 from both sides of an equation by adding the additive inverse of −3.

If $x + 3 = 10$, would $x + 3 - 3 = 10 - 3$?

If we then combine terms, $x = 7$.

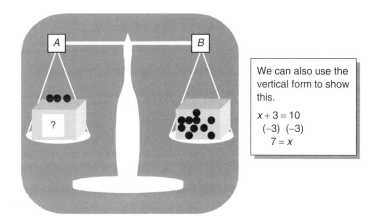

Using algebra tiles:

The total cost for an item ordered online equals the cost of the item (n) and a shipping charge of $10.00. If the total cost is $30.00, write an equation that can be used to determine the cost of the item. Solve the equation to find the cost.

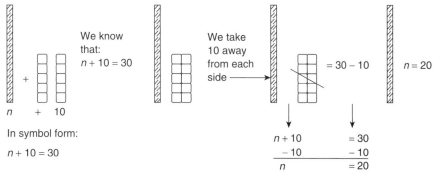

Exemplar Problems

Use your algebra tiles to help solve the following equations:

$$(c + 12 = 23) \qquad (x - 30 = 15) \qquad (a + 6 - 12 = 40)$$

20.6 Solving Equations: Combining Like Terms

Developmental Transitions and Scaffolds

For an equation with binomial or trinomial expressions, it is important to combine like terms before you isolate the variable.

$$3x + 2x + 7 - 3 = 39 \quad \longrightarrow \quad 5x + 4 = 39 \quad \longrightarrow \quad 5x = 35$$

20.7 Isolating the Variable and Solving Equations—One-Step Multiplicative Inverse

Developmental Transitions and Scaffolds

If an equation includes multiplication by a factor, we can isolate the variable by performing the inverse operation, which is division by the same factor, on both sides of the equation so that they remain equal,

$$6n = 42 \quad \frac{6n}{6} = \frac{42}{6} \qquad \frac{\cancel{6}n}{\cancel{6}} = \frac{\overset{7}{\cancel{42}}}{\cancel{6}}$$

If you divide both sides by (6), you get $n = 7$.

Exemplar Problems

Solve the following equations:

$$3n + 9 = 21$$
$$7a - 2 = 54$$

20.8 Solving Equations: Two and Three Step With Whole-Number Coefficients

Developmental Transitions and Scaffolds

Sometimes an equation requires several steps in order to isolate the variable.

When the equation includes binomial or trinomial expressions, we can begin to isolate the variable by dividing all terms on both sides by the same factor (divisor). This keeps the sides equal. We may then be able to isolate the variable by dividing by another same factor.

For the equation $3c(a + b) = 6(a + b)$, first divide both sides by the binomial $(a + b)$, and then divide both sides by the factor of 3 to isolate the variable.

$$3c \frac{\cancel{a+b}}{\cancel{a+b}} = 6 \frac{\cancel{a+b}}{\cancel{a+b}}$$

$$3c = 6 \text{ and } c = 2$$

Line segment *AB* is the same length as line segment *CD*.
Write an equation that can be used to find the value of *x*.
Solve the equation to find the value of *x*.

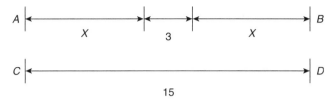

We need three steps to solve this equation

1. Combine terms $x + x + 3 = 15$ and $2x + 3 = 15$.

2. Add (−3) to both sides of the equation.

   $2x + 3 − 3 = 15 − 3 \rightarrow 2x = 12$

3. Then divide both sides by 2. $2x = 12 \rightarrow x = 6$

Additive Inverses of Variables

We can add the additive inverse of variables to both sides of the equation to help isolate the variables. If they are the same-term variables, we can just add or subtract the coefficients. In a multistep equation, $7a − 16 = 3a + 4$.

1. We can add (−3a) to both sides of the equation

   $7a − 3a − 16 = 3a − 3a + 4$.

2. Then combine terms to get $4a − 16 = 4$.

3. Then we add +16 to both sides.

   $$4a − 16 + 16 = 4 + 16 \text{ and } 4a = 20$$

4. Then we divide both sides by 4, and we get $a = 5$.

Use your algebra tiles to solve the following problem: the total cost of some books and $3 tax was $36. How much did each book (*b*) cost?

$$3b + 3 = 36$$

Isolate the variable term by subtracting 3 from each side.
Divide both sides by 3.

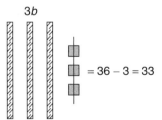

Subtract 3 from each side
$3b − 3 = 36 − 3$ and $3b = 33$

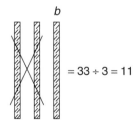

then divide each side by 3
$3b \div 3 = b$, $33 \div 3 = 11$ and $b = 11$

$3b + 3 = 36$;
$3b + 3 − 3 = 36 − 3$ and $3b = 33$
$3b = 33$; $3b \div 3 = 33 \div 3 = 11$ and $b = 11$

20.9 Solving Equations: Two Related Variables

We can solve an equation with two variables if we know of a relationship between them. The second variable is a function of the first. If you buy three pairs of socks for one price and another pair that costs twice as much and pay $10 for them, you can find the cost of the socks with this equation: $3x + 2x = 10$ or $5x = 10$ and $x = 2$. The cost of the cheaper pair is $2.00, and the other pair cost $4.00.

Exemplar Problems

The sum of two consecutive integers is 89.
Find the two integers.

———————————— ✻ ————————————

A music club wanted to raise money for new materials. They decided to sell twenty CDs they made of their performance. They sold ten of them for one price and then added $3.00 to the price for the rest. If they earned a total of $270, how much did they sell them for?

———————————— ✻ ————————————

The length of a rectangle is two times the measure of its width. If the perimeter of the rectangle is 84 cm, write and solve an equation that could be used to find the length and width of the rectangle.

We can even find the value of two unequal numbers we do not know if we know the difference between them and we know their sum. The difference is the relationship. If we subtract the difference between them from their sum, we are left with the sum of two equal values. The value of one of these is the smaller number. If (a) is the smaller number and (b) is greater by 3, then $(a + b) - 3 = 2a$. If we know that $a + b = 23$, we can substitute and solve the equation.

———————————— ✻ ————————————

Jesse bought two computer games for $36. One game cost $4 more than the other. How much did they each cost?

If (a) is the smaller number and (b) is greater by 4, then $(a + b) - 4 = 2a$. We know that $(a + b) = 36$, so we can substitute $(36 - 4 = 2a)$ and solve the equation for the cost of (a). Then we just add the difference back for the cost of (b).

21.1 Isolating the Variable and Solving Equations With Fractional Terms

See also Chapter 2, pages 55–56, for concepts and expectations.

Developmental Transitions and Scaffolds

We can isolate the variable in an equation with a fraction by multiplying both sides of the equation by the reciprocal of the denominator. If we multiply both sides of the equation by the reciprocal of the denominator of a fractional coefficient, we can change the fractional coefficient on either side of the equation to the whole number of the original numerator. What we essentially do to one side of the equation is multiply the numerator by the factor of the denominator and then divide the product of the numerator and denominator by the same factor. The shortcut is to cancel the common-terms factors in the numerator and denominator.

The bowling team bought two packages of snacks and shared them among the five members. Each member got ten snacks. How many snacks were in each package?

If a = one package of snacks, then each member got $\frac{2}{5}a$ (or) $\frac{2a}{5}$, and we know that $\frac{2a}{5} = 10$.

We can then multiply both sides of the equation by the reciprocal of the coefficient denominator.

$$\frac{2a}{5} \times \frac{5}{1} = 10 \times \frac{5}{1}$$

When we multiply the left side of the equation by the reciprocal of the coefficient denominator, we get the following for the left side:

$\frac{2a}{5} \times \frac{5}{1} = \frac{10a}{5} = 2a$ [with canceling $\frac{2a}{\cancel{5}} \times \frac{\cancel{5}}{1} = \frac{2a}{1} = 2a$]

When we multiply the right side of the equation by the reciprocal of the coefficient denominator, we get the following for the right side:

$$10 \times \frac{5}{1} = 50$$

The original equation now is $2a = 50$, and $a = 25$.

Two Step With Decimal Coefficients

Solve for u in the following equation: $0.2u + 10 = 22$.

How do we express the decimal .2 in fraction form?

$$.2 \text{ is the same as } \frac{2}{10} \text{ or } 2 \times \frac{1}{10}$$

How do we begin to solve equations with fractional coefficients or constants?
Multiply both sides of the equation by the fraction reciprocal, which is $\frac{10}{1}$ or 10.
$10(0.2u + 10) = 10(22)$ and $2u + 100 = 220$.

Exemplar Problems

Solve the following equations:

$$.5x + 8 = 48 \quad \frac{3}{4} x - 3 = 15$$

21.2 Isolating the Variable and Solving Equations Using the GCF

Developmental Transitions and Scaffolds

In the equation $12a + 36 = 84$, separating the GCF factor of 12 from the terms on the left side of the equation and then dividing both sides of the equation by 12 would solve the equation. We can also solve the equation by dividing each term on both sides by the GCF.

Method A   Method B

$$12a + 36 = 84 \text{ and } \cancel{12} (a + 3) = \overset{7}{\cancel{84}}$$
$$\cancel{\div 12} \qquad \div 12$$

$$\overset{3}{\cancel{12a}} + \overset{7}{\cancel{36}} = \overset{7}{\cancel{84}}$$
$$\cancel{\div 12} \; \cancel{\div 12} \; \cancel{\div 12}$$

$$a + 3 = 7 \text{ and } a = 4$$

The use of the GCF is most useful in a more complex equation to help get the equation into quadratic form (see Numbers 19.4 and 22.5).

For the equation $2a^3 + 4a^2 - 4a = 12a$, the common factor of $2a$ can be separated on the left side

$$2a(a^2 + 2a - 2) = 12a$$

and then both sides of the equation can be divided by $2a$ to get to the quadratic form

$$a^2 + 2a - 2 = 6 \text{ or } a^2 + 2a - 8 = 0$$

$$(a + 4)(a - 2) = 0$$

and the roots of the equation are $a = -4, +2$.

Exemplar Problems

Solve the following equations by first factoring the greatest common factor.

$$15(x - 4) = 60 \qquad 12(8 + x) = 144$$

———————— ✳ ————————

Find the roots of the following quadratic equation by first factoring both sides by the greatest common factor and then factoring the quadratic equation form.

$$12x^4 + 3x^3 - 6x^2 = 6x^2$$

21.3 Equations With Two Variables

Developmental Transitions and Scaffolds

Equations with two variables (x and y) may have a set of possible solutions. Changing the value of one variable will change the value of the other. The solutions may be expressed as ordered pairs of x and y. A possible value of x is followed by the resulting value of y. The equation $2x + 3 = y$ could include the following ordered pairs in its solution set: 2, 7; 3, 9; 4, 1; –2, –1. See Numbers 23.4 and 23.6 for graphing applications.

Exemplar Problems

Find four ordered pairs for the following equation: $y = 4x + 2$.

———————— ✳ ————————

Is the ordered pair (5,14) a correct solution for the equation $y = 3x - 1$?

———————— ✳ ————————

Write an equation with two related variables and a set of five ordered pairs that solve your equation.

21.4 Inequalities

Developmental Transitions and Scaffolds

A linear equation containing one variable will be true for just one value of the variable, whereas a linear inequality will have an infinite solution set.

You solve an inequality in the same way that you solve an equation by simplifying it and isolating the unknown quantity.

$$2a + 5 < 11 \rightarrow 2a + 5\,(-5) < 11(-5) \rightarrow 2a < 6 \rightarrow a < 3$$

The range of values for the solution set may be shown on a number line as a pointed arrow pointing in the direction of its continuing values or as an arrow with circle ends showing the range of values. Open circles indicate that the value under the arrow end is not included; in symbol form, $a < 3$ does not include 3 as a possible value. A closed circle indicates that the value under the arrow end is included. This notation is matched by the symbol $\leq$ or $\geq$. The expression $a \leq 3$ includes 3 as a possible value.

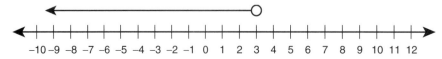

In symbol form, the range of values for a variable (n) may be represented as $3 \leq n \geq 16$. This means that the value of n is greater than or equal to 3 and less than or equal to 16.

Exemplar Problems

What values of x satisfy the inequality ($-6 < x < 3$)?

Write the inequality for the value of X that matches the line graph below in symbol form:

What is the range of values of x that satisfies both inequalities below?

$$x + 2 \geq 4 \text{ and } 2x - 4 \leq 10$$

If $x + 2 \geq 4$, then x ≥ 2. If $2x - 4 \leq 10$, then $2x \leq 14$, and x ≤ 7.
The range is $2 \leq x \leq 7$.
Show the range on the number line.

If two thirds of an integer is decreased by 4, the result is at most 6. What values of the integer satisfy the inequality?
Solve the inequality and show the range of solutions on a number line.

A high school student noticed that he spent up to twelve hours a week at his desk while working on homework assignments. Write an inequality that shows the range of time he spent at his desk.
He actually spent about 1/4 of that time at his desk answering or making phone calls. Write and solve an inequality that can be used to determine the actual range of time spent on the homework.

21.5 Number Series/Sequences (See Also Numbers 7.2–7.4)

Developmental Transitions and Scaffolds

Number sequences are sets of numbers that follow a pattern. There are relationships where successive numbers are related to the previous one or ones. Number series may be arithmetic, geometric, or neither arithmetic nor geometric.

In an arithmetic series, the next number is determined by adding a positive or negative value to the previous one (it is called the common difference between the number).

In a geometric series, the next number is determined by multiplying the previous one by a fixed (the same) multiplier (named the common ratio).

The function equation for the arithmetic number series (1, 5, 9, 13, 17) is $y = x + 4$, where y = the next number and x = the previous number.

For the geometric series of 3, 9, 27, 71, the function equation is $y = 3x$.

For the famous Fibonacci series 1, 1, 2, 3, 5, 8, each successive number is the sum of the previous two numbers in the sequence, and it is neither arithmetic nor geometric.

We can also use two forms of the variable letter in the equations for series. The capital (N) is the cardinal value of a number and an uncapitalized (n) is the ordinal value.

The fifth number (n) in the multiplication table for the multiplicand of 6 has a cardinal value of 30.

$$N = n(6) \text{ or } 30 = 5 \times 6$$

What would be the value of the eighth number in the same multiplication series (the table)?

Exemplar Problems

Identify each of the following series as arithmetic, geometric, or neither and find the next two terms. Then write the function equation.

$$3.4, 3.6, 3.8, 4.0, 4.2$$

$$\frac{1}{2}, \frac{1}{4}, \frac{1}{8}, \frac{1}{16}$$

$$2, 1, 0.5, 0.25$$

$$1.1, 1.01, 1.001, 1.0001$$

■ ALGEBRA: FUNCTIONS, QUADRATICS, AND GRAPHING

22.1 Function: Defined—A Set of Input and Output Values

See also Chapter 2, pages 56–58, for concepts and expectations.

Developmental Transitions and Scaffolds

The shift from thinking of an equation as a relationship that can be used to determine a specific value of a variable to the concept of a function may be a challenge for some students. Solutions to equations that are not functions determine the value of a specific variable. They are based on given values of another variable and constants in an equation that shows a specific relationship. That relationship, however, may not be a function and not always result in corresponding changes. For example, if an equation such as ($n + y + 6 = 18$) represents how many noncustomers (n), customers (y), and employees (6) called an office on one day, a change in the value of (n) for the next day will not predict the value of y. In contrast, if (y) in the equation $y = x + b$ represents the total number of calls for a particular day, (x) represents the sum of customer and noncustomer calls on a particular day, and (b) represents a constant value that represents the sign-in and sign-off calls made by employees, any change in the input variable (x) will cause a related change in the output variable (y). The equation $y = x + b$ is a function.

If $3x = y$ represents the average number of calls per day and y is the number of calls handled in three days, any change in (x) will cause a related change in (y). If x is doubled, then y is doubled. The equation $3x = y$ is a function or function rule. Important concepts include the following:

- Functions are two sets of related variables whose relationship can be shown as a function rule in the form of an equation.
- A function is a relationship between two variables (x and y) in which for each value of x in a set, there is only one value of y in a second set.
- We sometimes relate the function value sets as input and output. They are represented as ordered pairs of the value of x and y.

- The set of inputs or values of x that satisfy the function is called the *domain* of the function, and the outputs or values of y are called the *range* of the function corresponding.

22.2–22.4 Functions: Forms and Applications

Developmental Transitions and Scaffolds

Functions forms include the following:

$$y = x + b \text{ or } f(x) = x + b \text{ or } f(x) = mx \text{ or } f(x) = mx + b$$

$f(x)$ can be substituted for y because the value of y is a function of the value of x. A function in the form $f(x) = mx + b$ is a linear function. When the ordered pairs of the function are graphed in the coordinate plane, they form a straight line.

Number patterns and geometric sequences that depend on a specific relationship between values may be expressed as functions. Multiplication tables are an example. If the multiplier for the table is represented as the constant, the ordinal number of the series (the multiplicand) is represented by (n), and the cardinal number or product of the multiples is represented by N or $f(n)$, the function for the three times table is $3n = N$. A change in one variable will result in a corresponding and predictable change in the other.

For multiplication of exponential forms, the function expression is

$$(b^x) \times (b^y) = b^{x+y}$$

Sometimes, values may satisfy the function but not make sense in the problem. For example, negative values of measures of the length and width of a figure do not apply.

Exemplar Problems

What is the function rule for this table of time (t) and distance (d) traveled?

Input (hours) *(t)*	1	2	3	4
Output (miles) *(d)*	50	100	150	200

The owner of Steve's Ice Cream shop kept a record of the number of ice cream cones and cups sold for a week. He noticed that there was a pattern in the relationship between the number of cones and the number of cups he sold that continued through Saturday.
The table below shows the results for part of the week.

1. *Complete the table.*

2. *Write a function equation that describes the pattern of the relationship between the number of cones and the number of cups.*

Serving Type	Monday	Tuesday	Wednesday	Thursday	Friday	Saturday
Cones	24	28	32			
Cups	11	13		17		

Can you think of a real-life reason why the pattern might not continue on Sunday?

Christy made popcorn from corn kernels. The pattern for making the popcorn is shown in the table below.

    Write a function rule that represents the pattern.

    Apply the function rule to discover how many cups of kernels Christy will need to make twenty cups of popcorn.

Cups of Kernels (Input)	Cups of Popcorn (Output)
$\frac{1}{2}$	4
1	8
$1\frac{1}{2}$	12

Janelle had $100 to spend.

    A. *If the tax rate on what she bought was 5%, write a function rule that represents how much tax Janelle would pay if she spent x amount of dollars on any item.*
        Rule: _____

    B. *Janelle spent anywhere from $1 to $100. Circle the inequality that represents the domain of the function and a line through the range of the function.*

$1 \leq x \leq 100$	$.05 < f(x) < .10$	$.05 \leq f(x) \leq 5.00$	$0 < x < 100$

22.4 Quadratic Equations: Defined

Developmental Transitions and Scaffolds

A quadratic equation must have one term where the greatest power of the variable is 2. The general form of a quadratic equation is $y = ax^2 + bx + c$, where (b) and (c) are constants. Nevertheless, if $b = 1$ and $c = 0$, the resulting equation $y = ax^2$ is still quadratic. Quadratic equations can represent relationships where the square of a variable is related to another variable. For example, the area of a square is related to the square of the measure of a single side of the square. $y = x^2$, where x equals the measure of the side. If you increase the measure of a side by 2, the equation that describes the relationship is $y = (x + 2)^2$ or $y = x^2 + 4x + 4$ and an example of a quadratic equation in general form.

22.5–22.8 Quadratic Functions and Equations

Developmental Transitions and Scaffolds

What is a quadratic equation?

    An equation in the form of ($y = ax^2 + bx + c$) is a quadratic function. As in other function equations, we can substitute (y) with the term $f(x)$, and thus $f(x) = ax^2 + bx + c$. We can also reverse the substitution and name $f(x)$ as another variable (y).

Why does it usually have two roots as possible solutions?

    Standard-form quadratic equations can have two roots that represent possible solutions to the value of the variable. The fact that quadratic equations include a variable to the second degree or the power of 2 expands the set of possible solutions. The square root of any number can be either the positive or negative value of the base. Both values are parts of the set of solutions, and for each value $(+x)$ or $(-x)$, there will be a corresponding value of (y). And for each value of (y), there will be a corresponding value or values of (x).

How do we solve quadratic equations?

We can begin to solve quadratic equations by finding the possible values of x when $y = 0$. For example, the following is the sequence of steps for solving the quadratic equation $f(x) = x^2 ? 6x + 9$.

- Substitute the possible value of 0 for $f(x)$ or y. $0 = x^2 - 4x + 12$
- Factor the expression $x^2 - 4x + 12$ to the binomial factors: $(x - 6)(x + 2)$ (see Number 19.4 for factoring process).
- If $0 = (x - 6)(x + 2)$, then one of the two binomials must be equal to zero.
- Set each one separately equal to zero: $x - 6 = 0$ or $x + 2 = 0$ and $x = 6$ or $x = -2$.
- $(6, -2)$ are the roots of the equation $y = x^2 - 6x + 9$.

How do we prove that our solutions are correct?

We can prove that a root is a true solution to the equation by substituting the root value. In some equations such as $(x^2 + 2x + 1)$, there is only one possible root. Sometimes, one possible root may be eliminated as a solution to a problem because it is impossible for the problem. For example, a negative value makes no sense for the measure of the side of a plot of land. Using the ordered pairs of each root and its corresponding value of y, which is zero, and other substitutions that work in the equation, the graph representing the possible solutions can be formed.

If we set the difference between two squares as an equation $(x^2 - 16) = 0$ and factor the binomial into $(x + 4)(x - 4) = 0$, we reach the roots of $x = +4$ or -4. We can find the same possible solutions by shifting the value of the constant to form the equation $x^2 = 16$ and finding the square roots of both sides of the equation; $x = +4$ or -4.

Exemplar Problem

Danice had a small square garden in her backyard. She needed to use about 4 square feet of her garden for storing her tools. Danice wanted to know how much actual area she would have for planting when using different side (s) lengths for her square.

What is the formula and function for the area of a square?

$$A = s^2$$

What equation would represent how much area she had for planting?

$$A = s^2 - 4$$

What kind of equation is this?
It is a quadratic equation.

What are two possible solutions—the roots of the equation?

$$s = +2 \text{ or } -2$$

Do they work in the problem?

Only +2 works because the side cannot be negative. She would also not have any room for planting because the roots represent an area of zero for planting.

How can the roots help her find measures that work?

They can identify two points on the graph of the equation.

23.1–23.2 The Coordinate Plane

See also Chapter 2, pages 58–60, for concepts and expectations.

Developmental Transitions and Scaffolds

Important concepts include the following:

- A coordinate plane consists of two perpendicular reference lines intersecting at one point or origin and equally measured spaces from the reference lines that form a grid.
- The grid locates specific points in the plane. The location or value of the points is shown as an *ordered pair* of digits. The first digit shows the distance from the vertical line (y-axis) and is the value of the x coordinate. The second digit is the distance from the horizontal line (x-axis) and is the value of the y coordinate.
- Lines connecting the points form graphs on the coordinate plane that show how two variables are related (e.g., how a variable changes over time).
- The coordinate plane can show both positive and negative values of the variables. The plane is divided into four quadrants that are numbered in a counterclockwise order. Quadrant I is where a (positive x, positive y) point is located. Quadrant II is where a (negative x, positive y) point is found. Quadrant III is where a (negative x, negative y) point is located. Quadrant IV is where a (positive x, negative y) point is located.

Exemplar Problem

In which quadrant of the grid below would you find the location for each ordered pair of coordinates (2, –3) (–4, 3) (–5, –3) (4, 6)?

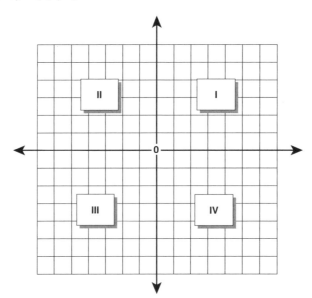

23.3 The Coordinate Plane as a Map/Calculating Distance

Developmental Transitions and Scaffolds

The coordinate plane can also be used as a map from a point of origin, with the *x*-axis representing east and west intervals and the *y*-axis representing north and south intervals. Begin with illustrations of distances parallel to the axes as the difference between the matching coordinates.

Exemplar Problem

The summer visitors to the camp needed a grid map of the campgrounds. Use the outline on the next page to create the map. Decide on a reasonable scale. The map must be arranged in four quadrants around the center of camp, which is at the grid origin. A flagpole marks the origin and center of camp, whose coordinates are (0, 0).

There were four locations that everyone had to know about immediately. The campers were taken on a tour of the four locations at the coordinate points listed in the table below. They started at the bunkhouse and traveled only in straight lines east, west, north, or south—not on diagonals. They then returned to the bunkhouse.

1. *Create and show a reasonable scale for your grid map.*

2. *Plot and label the coordinates for each listed location on the grid map.*

3. *Draw lines to trace the connecting paths between the locations.*

4. *Answer the questions.*

Point	Coordinates on Grid
A. Bunkhouse	(2, 6)
B. Bathroom	(−5, 6)
C. Dining hall	(−5, −2)
D. Director's office	(2, −2)
E.	
F.	
G.	

Questions:

1. *What polygon did the path of the campers' tour create?*

2. *Explain why they had to return to the bunkhouse to form a polygon on the coordinate grid.*

3. *Using the scale you created, determine the total distance they traveled as they completed the polygon from the bunkhouse through the other three locations and back.*

4. *In what direction did they travel from the dining hall to the director's office?*

5. *Using your scale, determine the total distance of the tour.*

Grid Map of Camp Chestnut

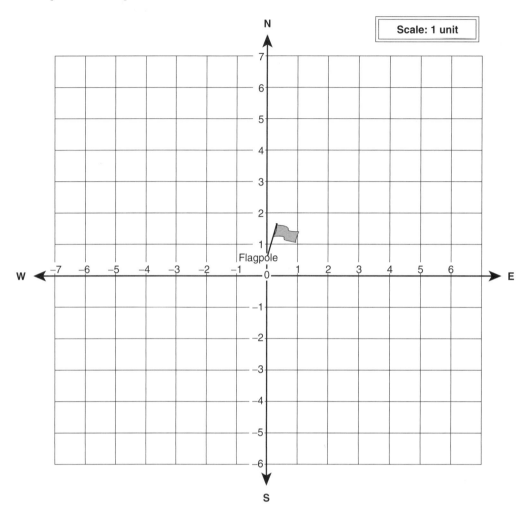

Developmental Transitions and Scaffolds

The diagonal or shortest distance between any two points on a grid map can be computed using the Pythagorean theorem. The straight line that marks the distance or difference between the values of the two x coordinate points can form one side of a right triangle, the distance between the y coordinates of the two points can form the other side of the triangle, and the hypotenuse of the triangle is the shortest (diagonal) distance between the points.

The distance formula, which incorporates the concepts and procedures into a single equation, may be also be introduced in Grade 9.

$$D = \sqrt{(x_2 - x_1)^2 + (y_2 - y_1)^2}$$

Exemplar Problem

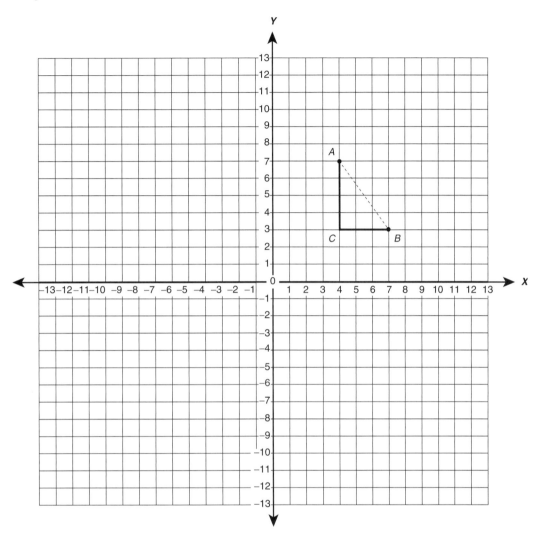

Points A and B are two points on the coordinate planes A (4, 7) and B (7, 3).
What is the difference between the x coordinate values of points B and A?

$$7 - 4 = 3$$

Name the line that shows the distance between the x coordinates.
What is the length of the line?
What is the difference between the y coordinate values of points A and B?

$$7 - 3 = 4$$

What is the length of line AC?
What is the length of the shortest distance from A to B?
Use the Pythagorean theorem or the distance formula to find it.

23.4–23.6 Linear Equations/Functions on the Coordinate Plane

Developmental Transitions and Scaffolds

Students are often not made aware of the power of mathematics. The realization of how the transfer of an equation to graphic form can reveal a whole set of possible solutions may be an eye-opening motivating factor for learning mathematics. The process of transfer to graphic form will also strengthen the concepts included below.

The ordered pairs of the possible solutions of a linear equation with two variables in the function form $y = mx + b$ may be represented in table or graph form.

The ordered pairs represent points in the coordinate plane because every value of x determines a specific value of y. The points may be connected to form a line. A graph of a linear equation forms a straight line.

- A linear equation is one whose graph is a straight line. It can be represented in the form $y = mx + b$. The terms (m) and (b) are constant values.
- Since only two points are needed to form a straight line, the solution set of a linear equation can be extended from a set of only two ordered pairs that represent possible solutions. The line is extended and passes through all the possible points that represent the set.
- Additional solutions may be determined by extending the line on the graph.
- A linear equation only has variables to the power of 1.

Exemplar Problems

Use all the integers from –2 to +2 for the values of x to complete the input/output table for the function y = 3x – 1. Find the corresponding values of y.

Input (x)	Function	Output (y)

Graph the ordered pairs of the function in the coordinate plane on the next page.
   Is y = 3x – 1 a linear function?
   Extend the line to discover additional points. Check them by substituting the ordered pair values in the equation.

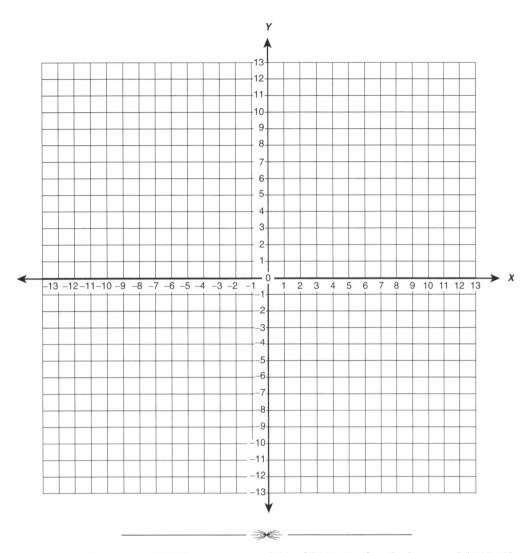

Shawna wants to buy a new TV that costs a total (t) of $420. So far, she has saved $120. Shawna earns $60 each week baby-sitting.

Write an equation that can be used to find the number of weeks (w) it will take Shawna to save enough to buy the TV.

Write an equation that can be used to find the number of weeks (w) it would it take for her to buy a laptop computer that costs a total (t) of $720.

Solve both equations to find the values of (w).

Write a function rule for the relationship between (t) and (w).

Then use the values of (t) and (w) as coordinate points to plot the graph of the function.

Use intervals of $50 on the x-axis to show the total saved and one-week intervals on the y-axis to show the weeks.

Extend the graph to find out how many weeks it would take to reach a total of $840.

Determine from the graph how much money she could have at the end of three weeks.

23.7 Horizontal and Vertical Lines

Developmental Transitions and Scaffolds

Horizontal and vertical line equations have only one variable. A graph of a vertical line does not cross the y-axis and has a constant value of x. The equation $x = 3$ is represented by a vertical line in Quadrants I and IV.

A graph of a horizontal line does not cross the x-axis and has a constant value of y. The equation $y = 3$ is represented by a horizontal line in Quadrants I and II.

The equations for horizontal and vertical lines are not functions because there is not one specific value of y for each value of x.

Exemplar Problem

Graph each of these equations and answer the following questions:

1. *In which quadrants of the coordinate plane is each graph line located?*
2. *How can you describe the line?*
3. *Are these equations functions? Explain your answer.*

$$x = 5$$
$$y = 4$$

24.1–24.3 Slope and Intercepts

See also Chapter 2, pages 60–61, for concepts and expectations.

Developmental Transitions and Scaffolds

The relationship between the variables in a linear function is the slope of the line. Slope is defined as the change in y over (or divided by) the change in x. The rate of change is a constant. If y (the numerator) changes very quickly compared to x, the slope is greater. The slope is like the steepness of a hill or staircase. The faster the rise (value of y) compared to the run (value of x), the steeper the hill.

The slope can be determined from the graph of the line or from a table of ordered pairs by finding the difference between two values of y and two values of x.

$$\frac{y_2 - y_1}{x_2 - x_1}$$

If we write a linear function in the form of $f(x) = mx + b$ or as the equation $y = mx + b$, the coefficient of $x(m)$ will be equal to the slope of the graphed line, and b will be equal to the y intercept or the y coordinate of the point where the line crosses the y-axis.

24.4 Slope and Intercepts of Horizontal and Vertical Lines

Developmental Transitions and Scaffolds

When we graph a horizontal line, the value of x changes, but there is zero change in y. Since the definition of slope is the change in y divided by the change in x, and zero divided by any number is still zero, a horizontal line has a slope of zero.

When we graph a vertical line, the value of y changes, but there is zero change in x. A vertical line has no slope. The change in the divisor (x) is zero, and any number divided by zero is undefined.

The y intercept of the graph of a straight line in the coordinate plane is the value of y, where the line crosses the y-axis and ($x = 0$). The x intercept is the value of x where the line crosses the x-axis and ($y = 0$).

If we substitute zero for the slope or coefficient (m) in the equation of a horizontal line $y = mx + b$, we get $y = b$. The equation for a horizontal line is $y = b$, and b is the y intercept.

If we examine a vertical line in the coordinate plane, it never crosses the *y*-axis and has no *y* intercept and no slope, so the equation of a vertical line is simply the value of the *x* intercept. For the vertical line equation $x = 4$, the *x* intercept is 4.

Exemplar Problems

Write the equations for the horizontal and vertical lines on the graph below.
  Identify the x and y intercepts.
  Add lines for the equations $x = (-3)$ and $y = (-3)$.

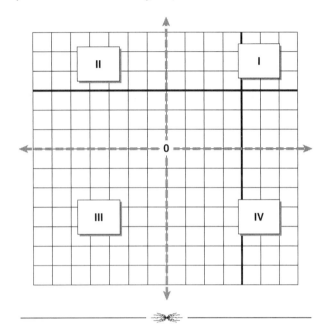

Randy's mother noticed that every time they added a new air conditioner, their electric bill increased quite a bit. New television sets didn't seem to cost as much. She decided to plot the cost of electricity against the number of each on a graph, and it looked like the one below. What does the x-axis show? What does the y-axis show?

How do the graph lines compare? Which line do you think represents the air conditioners? Draw a line that you think might represent the addition of lamps. Draw a line that might represent what would happen if they kept eliminating television sets and the time they spent watching. The angle that a line makes with the x-axis is called the slope. What ratio does it represent? What makes a slope steeper or more gradual?

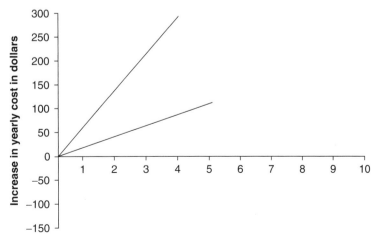

24.5–24.6 Graphs of Quadratic Functions

Developmental Transitions and Scaffolds

The graph of a quadratic function is a nonlinear open curve called a parabola. When the parabola crosses the x-axis at two points, the intersect points are the two roots of the equation.

The parabola may intersect only once or not at all. If it intersects once, it meets the x-axis at its vertex. If it does not cross the x-axis, the roots of the equation of the function are imaginary numbers.

When the coefficient of x^2 in the general equation $y = -x^2 + mx + b$ is negative, the parabola will face downward with its vertex on top.

When the ordered pairs (x, y) that satisfy a quadratic function are connected on a graph, they form a curve called a parabola. In this project, your group will be investigating how to identify the graph of a quadratic function and determine its roots from the graph. You will also investigate the application of a quadratic function to a real problem.

Exemplar Problem

Each of the functions below is followed by their four graphs: E, F, G, and H.

1. *Find the roots of each function by solving it.*

2. *Then match each function with its graph. Write the letter of the graph next to its function rule and write the function rule under the graph.*

3. *Explain how you could use the form of the graph to help match it to the equation.*

(a) $f(x) = x^2 - 1$ _____

   Roots: _____

(b) $f(x) = -x^2 + 4$ _____

   Roots: _____

(c) $f(x) = x^2 - 6x + 9$ _____

   Roots: _____

(d) $f(x) = x^2 + 2x + 1$ _____

   Roots: _____

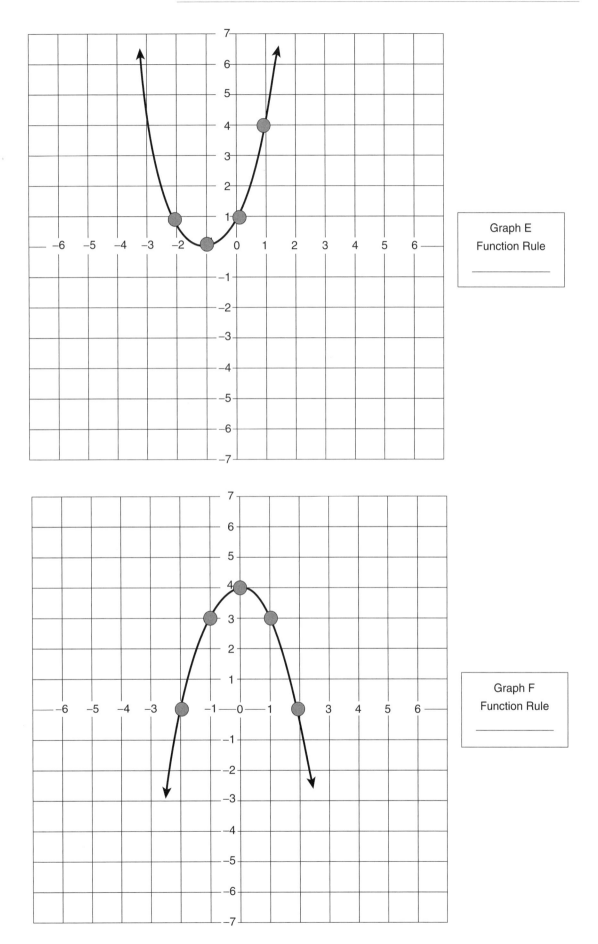

Graph E
Function Rule
_____

Graph F
Function Rule
_____

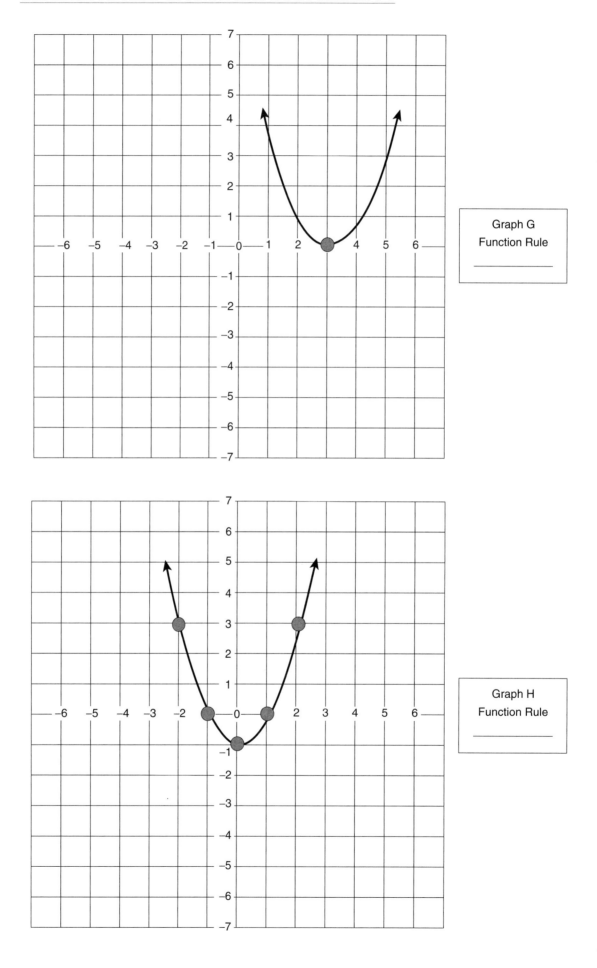

Graph G
Function Rule

_____

Graph H
Function Rule

_____

■ MEASUREMENT

Developmental Transitions and Scaffolds

Measures are the most common real-life applications in the study of mathematics and operations and should be integrated within the problems presented to develop skill in these. Because of the discrepancy in the standards, students need to learn to estimate and measure in both metrics and English (customary) standard units. Useful estimates of conversions, such as the quart/liter/gallon, inch/cm, mile/kilometer, and meter/foot, should be automatized, but use the calculator for the exact conversions.

Some general concepts cut across the various categories of measures. As teachers engage students in problem-solving opportunities to develop knowledge and skill in the more specific parameters of each separate category of measure, they should reinforce these concepts.

1. Measures are the descriptive terms for the quantitative properties or attributes of objects and the way they move through space and time.

2. An important use for measures is that they help us use what we know to tell us about what we do not know. For example, we can measure the area of a rectangle by measuring its length and width. We can tell how far a car will travel in an hour at the same speed if we measure the distance it travels in five minutes.

3. Measures allow us to communicate with each other about these properties and keep records of them. In order to communicate with each other about quantitative properties, we have to share or have a common meaning for the descriptive units of measure. We need consensus. If an inch is a unit of measure that we use to describe the length of an object, then we all have to agree on and know how long an inch is. If a paper clip is the unit of measure, then it has to be the same-size clip all the time.

4. Units of measures can be grouped into larger units. The size of the grouping also has to be by consensus. Larger units (groups of smaller ones) make it easier to measure larger sizes of properties. Smaller units and parts of units allow us to measure smaller properties and be more exact. We would not measure the length of a whole room in centimeters, but centimeters might make sense for the length of a window panel in the room.

5. The equalities of the smaller and larger units are often designed to make exchanges easy. The best example of this is the metric system, which, like our number system, is a base-10 system. There are similar reasons for other groups of units. The size of a foot actually was agreed on before the smaller inches (about the size of a king's foot). But it was decided that it would be useful to divide it into 12 inches because the number 12 has so many factors, and so fractions of the foot can easily be traded for inches.

6. When regrouping within-standard larger units into smaller ones, there will be more of the smaller ones and fewer larger ones for the same measure. A proportion with the ratio of the standard of measure compared to the ratio of the known and unknown actual measures structures the problem (see Numbers 16.1–16.5). The shortcut is to multiply (from larger unit to smaller unit) or divide (from smaller unit to larger unit) by the standard equivalent of a single unit of the measure. We can translate this process from the solution of the function equations that describe the equivalent relationship. If $y = \#$ of oz and $x = \#$ of lbs, then $y = 16x$, and $x = y \div 16$. Any remainders for the division would be the extra numbers of the smaller unit.

7. Measuring instruments help us make accurate measures, but it is always helpful to estimate first.

8. Measures help us make better models of the real thing.

Note: See Numbers 35.1 to 35.6 and 36.2 to 36.4 for measures of perimeter, area and volume.

25.1–25.3 Standard Units

See also Chapter 2, pages 62–63, for concepts and expectations.

Developmental Transitions and Scaffolds

Most of our units of measure are standard units. Standard units or systems of units are decided on by governments—or in primitive societies by agreements between individuals. Government standards are based on carefully maintained representations of the measures in places such as Paris and Washington, D.C. Different governments have different systems of measures. The U.S. customary system differs from the metric system used in much of the rest of the world. Many units of measure are based on multiples that have many factors so that they can be evenly divided. For example, mathematicians decided on the 360 degrees in a circle because the multiple 360 has many factors, and this allows the circle to be easily divided into fractional parts that are a whole number of degrees.

Exemplar Problems

Explain why humans decided that they would divide the day, or the time it takes the Earth to rotate on its axis, into twenty-four hours and the measures of longitude into 360°.

The number of days in a year (365) is a multiple with few factors. It actually takes 365¼ days for the Earth to rotate around the sun, but we make up for it at leap year.
   Explain why we can't use a multiple with more factors for the number of days of the year, but we can divide the year into twelve months, a multiple that has a number of factors.

25.2 Customary Standards: Linear Measures

Developmental Transitions and Scaffolds

The customary units of the length of lines (or distance between points) are the inch, foot, yard, and mile. The multiples of the units within the customary system are usually based on their utility for the measurement process and containment of factors. The foot is divided into 12 inches because the number 12 has factors of 1, 2, 3, 4, 6, and 12. There are 36 inches in the 3 feet of a yard. The number (36) has factors of 1, 2, 3, 4, 6, 9, 12, 18, and 36. Three inches are therefore exactly $\frac{1}{4}$ of a foot and $\frac{1}{12}$ of a yard.

Exemplar Problem

The cheerleaders made some banners for the parade. They discovered that they needed to buy about 3 square yards of material for each banner. About $\frac{1}{6}$ of this was wasted for each one because of the shaping. How many square feet of waste material would they have if they made eight banners?

25.3 Metric Standards: Linear Measure

Developmental Transitions and Scaffolds

The advantage to the metric system is its relationship to the place value system and the consistent vocabulary for unit subdivisions. The prefixes describe the sizes. A decimeter is one tenth of the meter, a centimeter is one hundredth, and a millimeter one thousandth. The same prefixes apply to the gram and liter. The kilometer is 1,000 meters, and the kilogram is 1,000 grams. See Number 25.6 below.

25.4 Accuracy and Precision in Measurement

Developmental Transitions and Scaffolds

Measures are sometimes not precise. The accuracy of measures is dependent on the measurement instrument and the recorder of the measures. The necessary precision in measurement depends on what is being measured. The weight of a truck of garbage demands less precision than the size of a needle hole or the eye of an insect. The smaller the size of the unit is, the greater the need for precision. Measurement instruments with smaller units are used to measure more precise quantities.

Exemplar Problem

Brian and Ian measured their desks with blocks and with two different rulers. Brian measured 14½ inches. Ian measured 15 inches. What may have caused their measures to be different?
   Choose a unit of measure for each of the following and explain your choice:

1. *The amount of rainfall in one day*

2. *The size of the head of a pin*

3. *The weight of a large truck filled with garbage*

4. *The amount of water a plastic soda pop cover can hold*

5. *The amount of water in the pop bottle*

6. *The weight of an ant*

7. *The amount of sugar in a candy bar*

8. *The total weight of a candy bar*

25.5 Significant Digits

Developmental Transitions and Scaffolds

Significant digits represent actual measures.
   All the digits in positive integers except zeros between the actual measured digit and the decimal point (the placeholders) are considered significant. All decimal digits except

zeros used as placeholders that precede them are significant. Zeros following the decimal digit are also significant. If the length is reported as 230.050 meters, only the last zero representing zero hundred thousandths of a meter and the nonzero digits are significant.

Exemplar Problem

How many significant digits are in each of the following measurements?

0.046 mm   2,340 km   126.004 lbs   0.260 oz

25.6 Within-Standard Metric Conversions

Developmental Transitions and Scaffolds

Metric conversions can be made by multiplying or dividing the measured unit by the factor of 10 that represents the unit equivalent. Remainders are the smaller unit. There are 10 millimeters in 1 centimeter, and therefore the number of millimeters in 2.3 cm is 23 or 10×2.3 cm = 23 mm. In a reverse conversion, 345 mm = 3.45 cm or 345 mm ÷10 = 3.45 cm.

1 kg = 1,000 g, and therefore 2 kg = $2 \times 1,000$ = 2,000 g and 2.2 kg = 2,200 g. In the opposite conversion, 2,002 g = 2,002 ÷ 1,000 = 2.002 kg.

Exemplar Problems

Use the conversion chart below to help you complete the equalities.

×10						
Kilometer (km)	Hectometer (hm)	Dekameter (dam)	Meter (m)	Decimeter (dm)	Centimeter (cm)	Millimeter (mm)

÷10

(a) *672.4 km = _____ hm*

(b) *23 mm = _____ cm*

(c) *.0035 m = _____ mm*

26.1–26. 3 Equivalent Measures: Conversions Across Common Systems

See also Chapter 2, page 64, for concepts and expectations.

Developmental Transitions and Scaffolds

Because we live in a time of globalization and constant communication among nations using different standard systems, some basic estimation of cross-system conversions needs to be automatized. A meter is a little more than 3 feet. There are about 2½ cm in an inch and a little less than 2 km in a mile. As described above for conversions within systems, proportions and function equations can be used for precise conversions, and calculators and even cell phones are capable assistants once the estimates have been made. A good source for across-system conversion units either way is the U.S. government Web site at http://ts.nist.gov/ts/htdocs/200/202/mpo_home.htm.

Single-unit equivalents across standards are based on calculated tables of unit equalities. For example, a single kilogram is equal to about 2.2 pounds. The easiest way to make approximate conversions from one standard unit to another is by multiplying the number of the larger standard units by the number of smaller units in a single larger one. The single-unit equivalent of the kilogram is approximately 2.2 pounds. Therefore, 5 kilograms would equal about 5×2.2 pounds.

For multiple units, we can use proportions, which compare the ratio of the unit equivalent to the measures and unknown quantity. A kilogram is a little more than 2.2 lbs. The ratio of lbs to kilograms is $(\frac{2.2 \text{ lbs}}{1 \text{ kg}})$.

Exemplar Problem

A customary scale measured the weight of the baby as 8.8 lbs. How many kilograms did the baby weigh?

$$\frac{2.2}{1} = \frac{8.8}{x} \quad \rightarrow \quad 2.2x = 8.8 \quad \rightarrow \quad x = 8.8 \div 2.2 \quad \rightarrow \quad x = 4 \text{ kg}$$

Express the following as their equivalents:

- *$3\frac{3}{4}$ tons in pounds*
- *54 ounces in pounds*
- *2,553 centimeters as meters*
- *16.6 kilograms as grams*

27.1–27.5 Mass/Weight

See also Chapter 2, pages 64–66, for concepts and expectations.

Developmental Transitions and Scaffolds

Measures in units of mass are good applications for developing the general concepts listed above. For example, it makes no sense to measure vitamin pills in pounds or truckloads of gravel in ounces. The definitions and understanding of the concepts of mass and weight are sometimes confusing for students. Even scientists sometimes disagree on exactly what weight is. Mass is a clearly and consistently accepted measure of the amount of matter in an object. Measuring the amount of matter is not easy, however, and it is done by measuring its weight. Gravity exerts a force on mass that varies directly with the amount of mass. This force is what is considered as its weight. We ordinarily measure mass by measuring the force of gravity on the mass or its weight. The force of gravity and weight increases with increases in mass. The difficulty in understanding lies in the fact that although the mass never changes, the force of gravity does. Gravity will be different on the moon, in space, and perhaps even slightly different at different altitudes on Earth. We therefore measure mass by balancing an unknown mass with the standard measure that has been determined by the government. The standard of measure for mass is the force of gravity on a given amount of matter, as represented by the stored government sample. For most purposes, the measures of mass and weight are used interchangeably even though they have different meanings because our standards for mass are based on their weight on Earth. One pound of mass is equal to the force of gravity on the one pound of sample matter kept at the government-managed National Institute of Standards and Technology.

Students should have opportunities to measure mass/weight in both metric and English (customary) units. They should also be able to estimate the feel of a pound of weight as opposed to an ounce, a gram, or a kilogram. The units are the pound (lb) or kilogram (kg); 2.2 lbs of mass will measure about the same as 1 kg of the sample. Conversion estimates that should be automatized include that the kilogram is a little more than 2 lbs, and there are about 28 grams in an ounce. The consequence of this is that their weight in kilograms is less than half the number of pounds they weigh. It also explains why medicine doses are measured in grams rather than ounces.

When using a balance scale, we balance the unknown quantity with a known one on a fulcrum. This can be done on a simple balance. We can also measure mass by seeing how much force it exerts on a spring. The standard is actually in the resilience of the spring. The greater the mass, the more the spring gives. Many commonly used scales have springs inside of them. Spring scales measure weight based on the pull on a spring and a scale that measures the pull. Modern spring scales have computer chips in them that measure the pull and then translate it into visible number values. They are easier to use but may not be as accurate as a balance. Standard units of mass can be combined into larger units. The equivalent heavier units are better for measuring heavier objects; 1 lb = 16 oz, 1 ton = 2,000 lbs, and 1 kg = 1,000 g.

A good activity for students is to use loose sand in plastic bags and a spring scale to make their own standard equivalents for the pound, ounce, gram, and kilogram.

These can then be used on a simple balance.

Exemplar Problems

Jerry wanted to weigh his big history book on a balance. He had made bags of sand to use as standards. He needed a 1-kg bag, one ½-kg bag, and seven 1-gram bags to balance the book. How much did his book weigh? About how much did it weigh in English (customary) standard measures?

———————————— ✂ ————————————

On a visit to Italy, Sara got on a kilogram unit scale to see how much she weighed. If her actual weight was unchanged, would the number on the scale be the same, more, or less?

———————————— ✂ ————————————

A scientist needed to use exactly .3 g of a substance for an experiment. What kind of instrument would be the best to use? Explain your choice.

    a. A spring scale with grams marked

    b. A balance with 1-gram weights

    c. A milliliter flask

    d. A balance with .1-gram weights

———————————— ✂ ————————————

Chester wanted to know how much a clock weighed. He first measured a block with the spring scale that measured pounds. Then he put the clock and the block on a balance scale. How much does the clock weigh? Explain how you found the answer. Explain how the two instruments to measure mass and weight work. Would the clock weigh the same amount on the moon? Would the mass of the clock and block be the same on the moon?

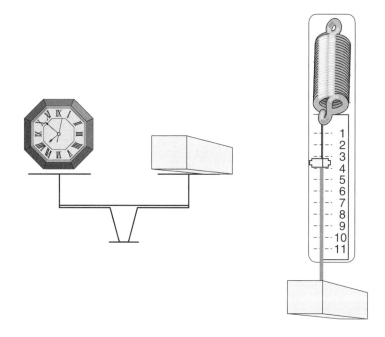

27.6 Density

Developmental Transitions and Scaffolds

The measures of density are sometimes omitted from the mathematics classroom, but an understanding of the relationship between mass and volume, which determines density, is an important mathematical concept. The standard for density is the amount of matter in comparison to a given volume of water. It is based on the mass of the matter in 1 cubic centimeter of water. One cubic centimeter (cc) of water weighs 1 g. The grams per cc are given a standard density of 1.0 or (1 g/cc). A substance with a density of 2.0 would be twice as dense as water, and 1 cubic centimeter of it would weigh 2 g. The closer the molecules are, the greater the density. Gases have a lesser density than liquids or solids.

Exemplar Problem

Discuss the measures of mass, volume, and density of the two blocks of equal size shown in the diagram with your group. One block (A) is made of Styrofoam, and the other (B) is solid metal. Discuss the diagram and your answers to the questions before writing them below.

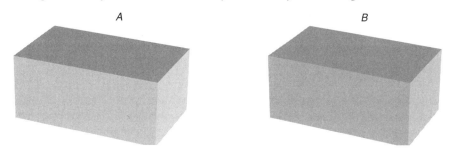

1. *Which of the two blocks (A) and (B) do you think has the greater mass? Use a definition of mass to explain your answer.*

2. *Which of the two blocks (A) and (B) do you think has the greater density? Explain your answer.*

3. *Write a general rule that describes the relationship between density, mass, and volume.*

4. *If the density of the metal block (B) is 2 g per cubic centimeter and the volume of the block is 100 cc, what is the mass of the block?*

5. *If the volume of block (A) is 100 cc and its mass is 10 g, what is the density of the Styrofoam?*

6. *Two blocks of Styrofoam (A) are put together in (C). Describe the mass, volume, and density of (C) as compared to the single block (A).*

27.7–27.8 Capacity/Volume

Developmental Transitions and Scaffolds

Although capacity and volume are related, they use different measures. Volume is applied to solid objects that have firm and measurable dimensions. Capacity is applied to liquids and small grains that assume the shape of their containers. It follows, therefore, that we measure capacity by filling a standard measure and not with a ruler. The relationship between metric capacity and volume is that 1 milliliter of liquid would fit into a container that has a volume of 1 cubic centimeter. There is no such rational relationship between capacity and volume for the English (customary) standards. There is even a difference between the dry measuring cup for small-grained flour and the liquid cup.

Students often have difficulty distinguishing between the two measures and describe volume with the capacity definition as "how much something can hold." That, of course, is not an irrational idea, but a solid object that has volume may not have the capacity to hold anything at all. Volume should be defined, in relationship to area, as the amount of space an object occupies in three dimensions rather than just on a surface.

Proportions and function equations can be used to determine conversions.

The within-standard unit equivalents that need to be automatized are the following: 1 cup = 16 fluid ounces, 2 cups = 1 pint, 4 quarts = 1 gallon, 2 pints = 1 quart = 4 half pints, 2 quarts = 1 half gallon, and 1 liter = 1,000 ml.

Cross-standard approximations that are useful include the following: a quart is just a little less than a liter. A half-gallon or 2-quart milk container is slightly less than a 2-liter soda.

Exemplar Problems

Could these two containers possibly hold the same amount of liquid when they are full?

―――――――――― ❋ ――――――――――

How could you measure the exact amount of liquid in each container to prove your answer?

―――――――――― ❋ ――――――――――

If the measure of the liquid was 60 milliliters, and it filled container A, what would be the volume of the container?

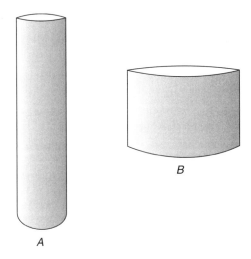

27.9 Money

Developmental Transitions and Scaffolds

Problem-solving activities with money support the concepts of decimals and should be an introduction, a major application of, and reinforcement for decimal operations. Perhaps the most real-life measurement unit conversion challenge that Americans face is the need to convert the ever-changing value of the dollar to the standard units of other countries. Part of the problem is that the conversion standard changes on a daily basis and is based on market economy conditions. Daily newspapers will show the most current rates, and it may be a good experience to graph the daily rates on a line graph to show trends over time. The euro is the common standard unit used in most of Europe. We can use proportions and the published current rate equivalents to find the values we need to know (see Number 16.7).

Exemplar Problem

On a particular day, the rate equivalent for the euro versus the dollar was 1.28, or each 1.0 euro was worth 1.28 dollars. Which unit could buy more, a single euro or a single dollar?

How many dollars could you get for 50 euros? Solve the proportion.

$$\frac{1}{1.28} = \frac{50}{x}$$

How many euros could you get for $100? Write and solve the proportion.

28.1–28.3 Time

See also Chapter 2, pages 66–67, for concepts and expectations.

Developmental Transitions and Scaffolds

By the sixth grade, the basic skills of telling and measuring time are usually in place for most students. The common use of digital clocks, however, has created some gaps in the understanding of elapsed time. Some basic concepts for review include the following:

- The division of the natural day into twenty-four hour-parts and the hour into sixty minutes is a manmade standard.
- The natural day could be divided into other numbers of units that would be longer or shorter. The numbers 24 and 60 are useful because they are common multiples of many factors and therefore easily divided into parts.
- Twelve noon is the time that the sun is most directly overhead or halfway between the east and west horizons. At twelve noon, it crosses an imaginary line in the sky halfway between them called the meridian.
- The twenty-four hours are divided at noon into twelve hours each of a.m. time and p.m. time. The beginning of the first twelve hours of any day starts twelve hours before noon at midnight, so we begin to count the twenty-four hour day as a new one at every midnight.

Review of measures of elapsed time, especially across noon, may be a good opportunity to apply numeration and multiplication concepts. The challenge of solving the problem, "How many minutes pass from 10:15 a.m. until 2:45 p.m.?" could be a real-life multistep problem that reviews the elapsed time concepts and uses the ratio of minutes to hours with an improper fractional multiplier. Minutes (M) = Hours (h) × 60 (60 h), and M = 4½ (60) or (60). However, in this case, there is also the task of first calculating the total of 4½ hours. The realization that there are many alternatives for solving this problem also is a worthwhile experience.

Concepts of time differences on Earth need to be related to the Earth's rotation. The standard time of day is different at different places on Earth. Since the Earth rotates toward the east, places to the west of us are behind in the time of day as compared to places to their east. We lose time when we travel to the east faster than the Earth moves because it has taken those on the ground and not in an airplane longer to get to that place in relation to the sun. More time has passed and it is later for them. The opposite happens when we travel west. We may have traveled in a plane from New York to California for six hours, but when we arrive there, the time is only three hours later than when we left.

Standards of time depend on the lines of longitude that are drawn from the North to South Poles. There is a 15° difference between each line, and the space between two lines defines a different time zone. When it is midnight at one point on Earth, the place on the completely opposite side, or 180° of longitude away, is at noon or twelve zones different. The actual distance between each line varies, with the greatest distance at the equator and the least at the poles. A new date begins at midnight at the international date line (180° longitude), which is directly opposite the meridian of Greenwich in England at (0) degrees of longitude.

Because the Earth is tilted on its axis and the hours of daylight change, we change the clocks at different times of the year to add more daylight hours to our workday. If we did not do this, we would be sleeping longer in the daylight hours. We change back to regular time when the number of daylight hours decreases. The days grow longer from December to June in the Northern Hemisphere and grow shorter in the Southern Hemisphere. This change is reversed from June to December.

It actually takes the Earth about 365¼ days to rotate around the sun, so we have to add a day every four years. This is leap year and the reason why the calendar is different every year. Memorization of the number of days in each month can be facilitated by a variety of mnemonics, but students should also know that these are manmade standards and that, over time, there have been other calendars. There are even alternative calendars in use today. The reason for different days in different months is that, unfortunately, 365 is not evenly divisible by 12, and so calendar makers assigned different numbers of days to the twelve months.

Some students (and adults) have difficulty predicting the date or day of the week for days in advance—especially when the date passes the end of the month. A problem often arises in this kind of calculation: "If today (Thursday) is the 27th, what is next Tuesday's date?" This is a two- or three-step problem. Students have to count the number of days between Thursday and Tuesday and sometimes incorrectly include Thursday in their count. They then have to count the days until the end of the month and possibly add on the new month. Use number lines such as the one below as well as real problems to help.

Exemplar Problems

The class wanted to have a surprise party for their teacher and needed to order a cake. They ordered the cake on Thursday, June 6, for the following Wednesday. Use the number line to find out the date of the party. Count how many days ahead the party was. What day of the week were you at when you counted one day ahead to June 7? Why don't we count the day we ordered the cake?

The Earth rotates toward the east in the direction of the arrow. The globe map below shows some (but not all) of the different time zones. If is 10:00 a.m. at point A, what time is it at point B? If location (A) was at 90° longitude west of Greenwich, England, what would be the longitude of location B? Use a map of the United States or globe to find two cities between which there is the following:

1. *A three-hour time difference*

2. *A two-hour time difference*

3. *A one-hour time difference*

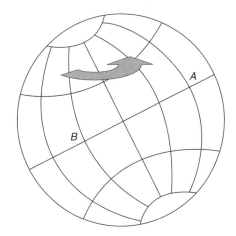

Starting on the 5th of September, the soccer team had practice on Tuesdays and Wednesdays, before their ten Saturday games. The team wanted to know the dates on which they would have practice and the dates of their games. We could use a one-year calendar for this problem, but it might not work for the next year. Explain why not. Use the table below to make a game and practice schedule for the team for two different years, one beginning with a Tuesday practice and another beginning with a Wednesday practice. Put an x next to the practice dates and an xx next to the Saturday games.

Do you see any patterns that would help you make schedules in other years? If the second year is 2007, will the same pattern continue for 2008?

Year1 Date	Year1 Day	Practice (x) Game (xx)	Year 2 Date	Year 2 Day	Practice (x) Game (xx)
Sept 5	Tuesday				

28.4 Temperature

Developmental Transitions and Scaffolds

Measures of temperature should be related to perceptions of how warm or cold it is. Activities can relate a particular Fahrenheit temperature to whether or not a jacket is needed—and whether or not it will snow. Room, body, freezing, and boiling temperatures are significant benchmarks with which to become familiar. Students should also become aware of their own *normal* body temperature and how to read a thermometer. "Normal," then, can be related to the concept of range and average. Investigations of temperature ranges can use original data retrieved over the Internet from all over the world and related to seasons and latitude. An important science-related concept in reference to the thermometer, as an instrument, is that its use depends on the characteristic of materials to expand with increasing temperature and contract with decreasing temperature. The customary standard in the United States is again different from most other places, but both standards use the term *degree*. The temperatures at which water freezes and boils are benchmarks for both the Celsius and Fahrenheit scale. An important concept to extract from the much larger range of degrees between freezing and boiling of Fahrenheit temperature (32°–212°) is that each degree Fahrenheit must be smaller than each degree Celsius (where the range is only 100). The Fahrenheit scale has smaller degree units because the range between freezing and boiling (32°–212°) is 180° wide. The Celsius range of 0° to 100° between the benchmarks makes better sense, but because each Fahrenheit degree is slightly more than half as much, conversions between the two are difficult. Students should be able to distinguish the important benchmarks of each standard and learn to use proportions that compare specific measured temperatures in either form to the standard conversion rate. Calculators can be used once the concept of the procedure is clear.

Standard units of measure for temperature are degrees Fahrenheit (F) or Celsius (C). Water freezes at 32°F (0°C) and boils at 212°F (l00°C).

Room temperature is about 70°F (21°C).

Each degree Fahrenheit is about $\frac{5}{9}$ of a degree Celsius. This can be estimated as a little more than half. The standard formulas for conversion are

$$F = 9/5 \ (C) + 32$$

$$C = 5/9 \ (F{-}32)$$

Exemplar Problems

Two equal-sized balloons were filled with the same amount of air. One was placed in water that was filled with ice and the other in almost boiling water. A centigrade thermometer was used to measure the temperature of the water.

1. *Label each thermometer reading (A) or (B) to match the balloon label that shows what happened to the ballon at that water temperature.*

2. *Put the approximate centigrade temperature of the ice-filled water and the almost boiling water under the thermometer that shows it best.*

3. *Put the approximate Fahrenheit temperature under the centigrade temperature.*

4. *Explain the similarity between what happened to the density of the substances in the thermometers and the balloons.*

5. *If the thermometers measured Fahrenheit temperature, what would be true of the difference in the total numbers of degrees for each reading? What would be true of the size of each degree of difference?*

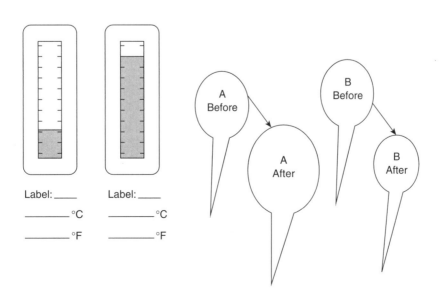

The temperature at sea level when Ed and Joe left their camp for a mountain hike was 60°F. When they got to the top of the mountain, they realized that they only had a Centigrade thermometer. It measured 9°C. What was the difference in temperature in both Centigrade and Fahrenheit measures?

■ GEOMETRY

29.1–29.4 Defining Geometrical Terms/Symbolic Notations

See also Chapter 2, pages 68–69, for concepts and expectations.

Developmental Transitions and Scaffolds

Whole cultures in the ancient world were built around the study and applications of geometry. The power bestowed on ordinary people such as the Freemasons of Rome by their ability to apply their skills and knowledge in building magnificent structures of lasting existence gave them reason to learn more. We are still learning and revising our knowledge. Consequently, mathematicians do not always agree on the exact definitions of some terms. We can, however, use common meanings for terms such as point, line curve, and plane that help us understand and describe them. *They are best learned in a combination of spoken words, written symbols, and the observation and construction of graphic images and real objects.* The objects can also include manipulatives such as pattern blocks, attribute blocks, tangrams, and geoboards, which will help students see and feel the differences and the patterns. In addition to increasing their skill in using graph paper for constructions, students should now develop skills in using the protractor and the compass for making measurements and for constructing figures. Computer drawing programs that allow students to copy figures and rotate figures are excellent for demonstrating transformations and proving congruence as well as for measures of perimeter and area. For example, students can even use the drawing program for Microsoft Word with an exact grid shown to construct and measure a specific area.

Just the experience of constructing different patterns is helpful, but teachers need to scaffold the important concepts that can be derived from them. In a triad, the manipulatives should be connected to real objects in the environment and to the pictures on paper as both two- and three-dimensional representations. What do we know about the shape of the Pentagon building in Washington, D.C.? What is the shape of the skating rink? Why does it have that shape? Why are some places called Squares—like Washington Square? Have you ever seen an intersection that forms a triangular corner?

The consensus of written definitions includes the following:

- A *point* is a particular location in space. We usually label a point with a letter.

- A *line* is determined by connected points that follow a straight path and go on infinitely (endlessly) in only two opposite (mirror image) directions. A line can be determined by any two points. We can show that it goes on endlessly by drawing arrows in its continuing direction.

The symbol for a line is a notation of two points with a double-pointed arrow over it: $\overleftrightarrow{AB}$.

- Points on the same line are *collinear.*

How can we describe points *A* and *B*?

- A *ray* is the part of the line that is going in one direction from one point on the line. The point where it begins is the *endpoint.* A ray is denoted with an overbar of a single arrow pointed in the direction in which it continues: $\overrightarrow{AB}$.

- Describe the ray above in words and symbol form.
- Describe point *D* in words.
- A *line segment* is part of a line between two particular points. It includes all the points in between the two particular ones. The symbolic notation for a line segment is the letters of the points with a straight-line overbar: $\overline{AB}$.

$\overline{AB}$ is a line segment of the line shown above

When a line with just two endpoints labeled is shown, it is a line segment.

Describe the line segment above in words and write a symbol for it.

29.5–29.6 Different Kinds of Lines

Developmental Transitions and Scaffolds

A review of the classification of forms of lines that is normally addressed in the earlier grades should include these definitions:

- Horizontal lines are like the horizon; they go from left to right or right to left.
- Vertical lines go up and down from the horizon.
- When two lines meet and form a right angle (see below), we say the lines are *perpendicular.*
- Parallel lines are two separate lines that go in the same directions in the same plane and never intersect.

A possibly new addition to this list is the following:

- When two lines meet, the point at which they meet is the intersection, and the lines are *intersecting lines.*

Exemplar Problems

Look at the picture, find the places and lines, and then match them to the letters. Write the letter for each one you find.

Find the horizon on the picture of a skyline. _____

Find a horizontal line on the building that follows the same direction. _____

Find a vertical line. _____

Find a place where a vertical line and horizontal line are perpendicular to each other. _____

Draw a line that intersects with the longest vertical line.

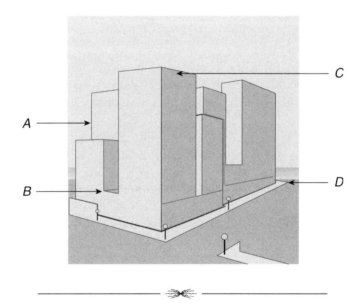

Look at the figures on the next page. Write the letters that label the following:

1. *A ray* ___

2. *A line* ___

3. *A line segment* ___

4. *Perpendicular lines* ___

5. *Intersecting lines* ___

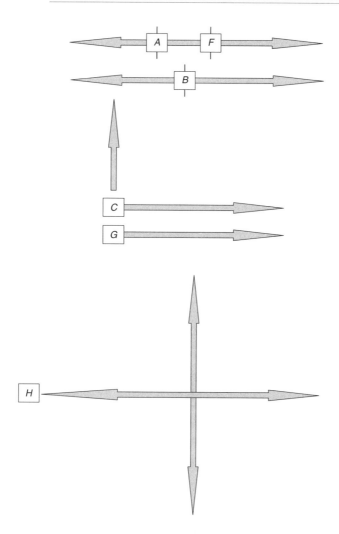

29.7 Midpoint/Perpendicular Bisector

Developmental Transitions and Scaffolds

The midpoint of a line segment is the point halfway from either point of the segment. The midpoint of a line segment can be located by drawing two equal arcs—one from each point—and then drawing a second line between the intersections of the arcs. The second line will be the perpendicular bisector of the first line and intersect it at the midpoint.

   In the diagram below, the two curves were constructed using a compass. The point of the compass was set apart from the pencil a distance that was estimated to be little more than half the size of the line segment *AB.* The same compass distance was used to draw a dashed curve from each endpoint of *AB*. The two curves intersected twice, and another line segment was drawn between the two intersections.

Exemplar Problem

Look at the figure of intersecting lines (on the next page). Identify each of the following:

   1. *The midpoint of* $\overline{AB}$

   2. *The perpendicular bisector of* $\overline{AB}$

   3. *The intersection of* $\overline{AB}$ *and* $\overline{DC}$

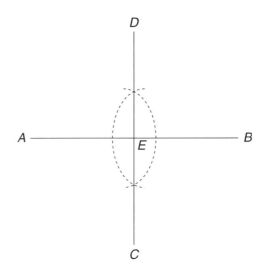

Use your ruler and safety compass to construct another line and its perpendicular bisector.

29.8 Open, Closed, and Simple Curves

Developmental Transitions and Scaffolds

A curve is determined by connected points that do not follow a straight path. If the first and last points are connected to each other, it is a closed curve—otherwise, it is described as an open curve. If the path of the points does not cross over itself, it is a simple curve.

Exemplar Problem

Identify each of the curve figures below using a pair of two terms: either open or closed and either simple or not simple.

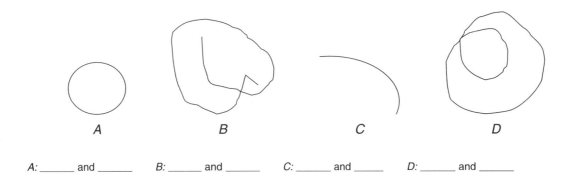

A: _____ and _____   B: _____ and _____   C: _____ and _____   D: _____ and _____

29.9 Planes

Developmental Transitions and Scaffolds

A *plane* is a surface determined by three points on that surface that are not on the same straight line. A line between any two points on the determined plane will be on that surface. A tabletop is often thought of as a plane surface, but the plane on which it lies goes on infinitely. The legs of the table are on different planes.

Parallel planes are two separate planes that never intersect.

Exemplar Problem

Jimmy thought about cutting the muffin through two different planes: ABC and EFD. What would the top of his sliced muffin look like if he cut through each of these planes? Decide between pictures 1, 2, and 3.

   Plane ABC will look like picture _____.

   Plane EFD will look like picture _____.

   Cut the muffin through a parallel plane and draw what it might look like.

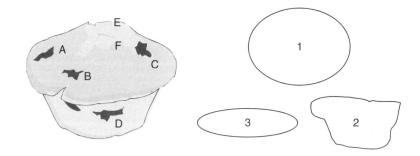

30.1 Angles: Defined

See also Chapter 2, pages 70–71, for concepts and expectations.

Developmental Transitions and Scaffolds

When two (rays) come from the same end point, they form an *angle*. The point where they meet is called the vertex. The rays are the *sides* of the angle. The larger the opening between the rays, the larger the angle. Larger angles will have a greater difference between the rays than smaller angles at the same distance from their endpoint. The size of the angle determines the direction from the endpoint. We can name in three different ways. For the first angle below, we can just name the vertex as $\angle A$, or we can name the angle by enclosing the common point of the vertex between the two other ray endpoints as either $\angle ABC$ or $\angle CBA$.

Exemplar Problem

In the angle $\angle ABC$ below, the vertex is at point B for the two rays, $\overrightarrow{BA}$ and $\overrightarrow{BC}$.

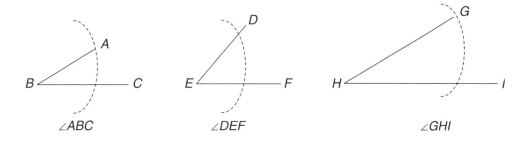

Compare the angles above. Two of them are the same size, and one is larger.
Which one do you estimate as the larger angle? Explain your answer.
Name the two sides of the larger angle.
Use your protractor to measure the angles and check your estimate.

30.2 Adjacent Angles

When two angles share a vertex (come from the same endpoint), have a common side (share a side), but have no interior points in common, they are called adjacent angles.

Exemplar Problem

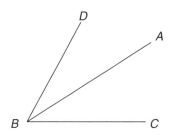

Name the two adjacent angles.
Name the common side.
Name the common endpoint.
Draw another angle from the same endpoint.
Name the new angle and the one it is adjacent to.

30.3–30.6 Measures of Angles and Circles

Developmental Transitions and Scaffolds

Measures of circles and angles are related. The standard decided by mathematicians for the total rotation of a ray to form a circle is 360 units, called degrees. A symbol for the unit (°) is used for both angles and circles (360°). The number 360 has many factors, which makes it easy to describe fractional parts of a circle. Critical concepts include the following:

- The total measure of a circle is 360°.
- If you make a duplicate of a ray and rotate it from a common endpoint away from the original, you form angles of increasing size. The more you rotate the second ray, the larger the angle.
- If you keep rotating the ray to return to where you started, a point on the ray has described a set of points on the plane that are equally distant from the center and form a circle.
- The rotation endpoint is the center of the circle, and the radius of the circle is equal to the length of the ray.
- The measure of an angle is the same as the part of the circle the ray has described. We therefore measure the size of angles or the opening between the rays in degrees

like a circle. The higher the number of degrees in the angle, the greater the distance between the rays.

- If you rotate a duplicate of a ray halfway around, a point on the ray has described a semicircle, and the duplicate ray and the original have formed a straight line or straight angle. A straight line or angle measures 180° or half the total distance of 360° that, when rotated, would form the circle.

- If you rotate a point on the ray a quarter of the way around, you form a quarter circle of 90° and a right angle. The largest angle can be any measure less than 360°.

The compass allows you to follow the path of a rotating ray and construct a set of points all equally distant from the center, which forms a circle. It can also be used to construct an angle and to divide an angle into two equal parts or bisect an angle. A protractor can be used to draw angles and measure the rotation and size of the angle.

Note: Precise construction of angles and circles requires a compass. Modern safety compasses are available for classroom use.

Exemplar Problems

Draw an angle with your protractor.

1. *Draw a straight horizontal line by tracing the bottom edge of the protractor or using a ruler.*

2. *Add two endpoint names to your line and extend it past the protractor edge on each side.*

3. *Place the hole over a point on the line in between the endpoints. Make sure it is in line with the endpoints.*

4. *Mark the point through the hole with a pencil.*

5. *Mark another point on the outside curve of the protractor that matches the size of the angle you want to draw.*

6. *Remove the protractor and use the bottom edge to draw a straight line between the two marked points.*

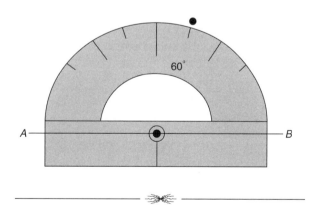

In the figure below, the ray $\overrightarrow{BA}$ was duplicated as the ray $\overrightarrow{BC}$. Then $\overrightarrow{BC}$ was rotated around to form the line CBA. As it was rotated, what shape did endpoint C trace? What was the name and measure in degrees of the shape formed when it became the straight line CBA? What is the measure of the straight line or straight angle CBA? Suppose the ray continued to rotate. What shape would be formed when it got back to where it started? How many degrees would it have rotated?

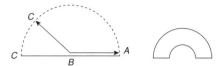

Draw a horizontal straight line on a blank piece of paper. Label the line and find the midpoint and perpendicular bisector using your compass and ruler. Put your compass on the midpoint and trace a quarter circle, semicircle, and full circle. Draw and label the angle within the circle that measures 90°. Draw and label the largest angle you can within the circle. Explain why it has to be less than 360°.

31.1–31.5 Naming Special Angles

See also Chapter 2, pages 71–72, for concepts and expectations.

Developmental Transitions and Scaffolds

The criteria for classifying the first group of special angles are related to angle size and therefore refer just to a single angle.

- A *straight angle* of 180° has two rays coming from one point in opposite directions. If we rotate one ray of the straight angle half of the way to 90°, the two rays are perpendicular and form a *right angle* of 90°.
- An angle that measures less than 90° is an acute angle.
- An angle that measures more than 90° but less than 180° is an obtuse angle.
- Two angles that form a straight angle or whose measures add up to 180° are supplementary angles.

The criteria for classifying angles in this group are based on relationships between angles. When we cannot simply say an angle is complementary, it is a complement or complementary to another angle that must be named.

- Two angles that form a right angle or whose measures add up to 90° are complementary angles.
- Angles that share a side are adjacent angles.
- The two opposite angles formed by intersecting lines are called vertical angles. They are congruent angles.

On a blank piece of paper, use your ruler to draw line segment ABC. Using a protractor, draw a right angle with its vertex at point (B) of the line segment AC below. From the same point (B), draw another line that will create an acute angle that measures 30° from AC. Name the acute, obtuse, or right angles formed, and compute their measurements. Insert your answers in the table on the next page.

Extend a line segment from point (B) to form a new angle that is vertical to one of the angles already drawn.

Name the new angle and determine its measure.

A ———————————————————— C
                    B

Type of Angle	Name of Angle	Measure of Angle
Right angle		
Acute angle		
Obtuse angle		
Vertical angle		

Look at the angles below.

Name two angles that are supplementary to each other. _____ and _____
Name two angles that are complementary to each other. _____ and _____
Name two angles that are adjacent to each other. _____ and _____

In the accompanying figure, two lines intersect and form angles 1, 2, 3, and 4.
$m \angle 3 = 6t + 30°$ and $m \angle 2 = 8t - 60°$.
Find the number of degrees in angles 2, 3, and 4.

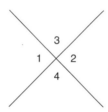

Find the angles in the batter's stance. List the angles A, B, C, and D in order of their size from smallest to largest. Can you find other angles? Add letter labels to the figure. Because the figure does not have exactly straight lines, make an approximation of the type of angle. Name each one as closest to straight, acute, obtuse, or right. Do you see a triangle? What kind of angles does it have? What name would you give it?

32.1 Congruent: Use of Term

See also Chapter 2, pages 72–73, for concepts and expectations.

Developmental Transitions and Scaffolds

Students sometimes do not understand why the term *congruent* is used in geometry if congruent figures have the same size and shape. We use the term *congruent* instead of *equal* because figures of equal size and shape may be in different positions on a surface or in space, and in that sense, they are not equal. Individual sides or angles in the same figure may also be congruent.

Exemplar Problems

Jerry built two triangles on his geoboard and said that they were congruent. Alan said they were different. Can you prove who was right? Build another triangle that is congruent to one of these.

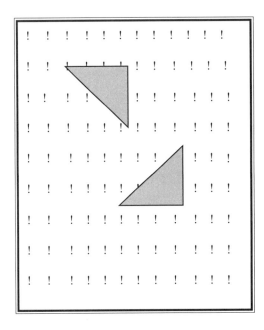

Use your geoboard or draw pictures of the figures to find the answers.
Can you put these triangles together to form a larger triangle?
Can you form a square?
Can you form a parallelogram?
If there is any symmetry in the way you put the figures together, show it with a string on your geoboard or with a line on the picture.

32.2–32.6 Definitions: Polygons

Developmental Transitions and Scaffolds

Some review of the definitions of polygons may be necessary, but most students should have had some experience with pattern blocks and the naming sequence based on the number of sides. Newly learned terms may be added to the definitions. Polygons are two-dimensional *closed* figures on a surface. They are formed by connected *line segments*, which form angles at the point of connection or *vertex*. Polygons have different numbers of segments (sides) and different-size angles. Polygons with all congruent sides and angles are called regular polygons.

Students should be able to recognize familiar items in the environment that are named after polygons (e.g., such as the Pentagon building, a traffic triangle, and a shopping square). The number of sides for each of the following should be related to the prefix and automatized: triangle, square, rectangle, pentagon, hexagon, heptagon, octagon, and nonagon. Hands-on constructions on geoboards, accompanied by their own figure drawings, are most useful in building the skills and concepts.

The difficulties that arise are in the overlapping definitions. For example, I often have to argue with adults that a square is a rectangle, as well as a quadrilateral, a parallelogram, and a rhombus. The activity below can be used to help clarify the sets and subsets. Venn diagrams also are helpful. The definitions of quadrilaterals in sequence are as follows:

- Polygons with four straight-line sides are quadrilaterals.
- If the sides are all congruent, it is a rhombus.
- If the figure has two pairs of opposite parallel sides, it is a parallelogram.
- If it is a parallelogram with four right angles, it is a rectangle.
- If it has only two opposite parallel sides, it is a trapezoid.
- A square is a quadrilateral, a rectangle, a rhombus, and a parallelogram.

There is also a need to clarify definitions of base and altitude. Although any side of a polygon can be considered the base, it is usually the bottom of the figure. The altitude (height) of the polygon is the right-angled distance (it must be perpendicular to the base) between the base and the opposite side. Students are accustomed to considering the measures of a rectangle as length and width, but they are in terms of the broader definitions equivalent to base and height. It may be helpful to recognize these alternates.

Exemplar Problems

The following road signs are part of a test given to people applying for a driver's license. Write the polygon name that describes the outside shape of each sign.

Construct a similar shape on your geoboard.

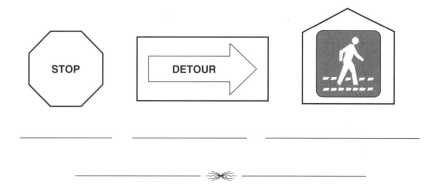

The figures below are repeated in lines A through E. Look at each line and cross out any that do not belong in the group as it is defined.

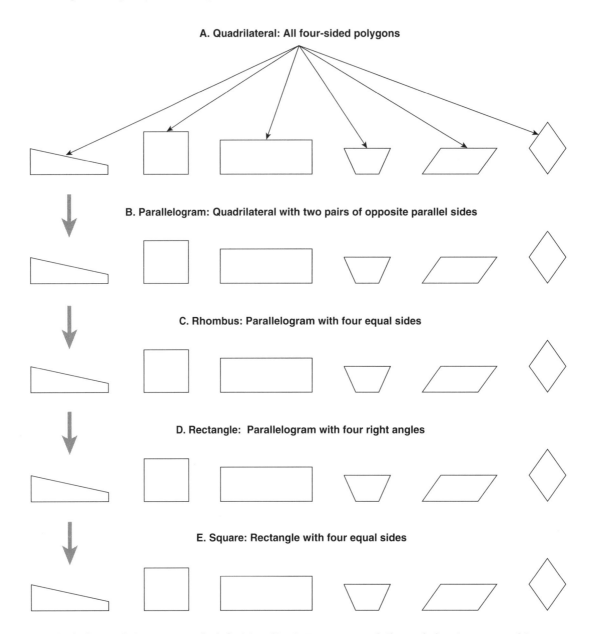

A. Quadrilateral: All four-sided polygons

B. Parallelogram: Quadrilateral with two pairs of opposite parallel sides

C. Rhombus: Parallelogram with four equal sides

D. Rectangle: Parallelogram with four right angles

E. Square: Rectangle with four equal sides

Which figure belongs in each definition line? Draw a quadrilateral that is not on this page.

32.4 Parallelograms

Developmental Transitions and Scaffolds

The parallelogram has two pairs of opposite sides that are parallel. Although any side can be considered the base, it is usually the bottom of the figure. The altitude (height) of the parallelogram is the right-angled distance (it must be perpendicular to the base) between the base and the opposite side.

Exemplar Problem

Below are two polygons: ABDC and EGHF.
What evidence proves that these are both parallelograms?
Name the base and height of each.
ABDC base:_____ Height_____
EGHF base:_____ Height_____

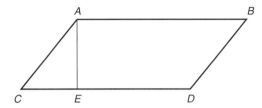 

Explain why polygon side EF is the height of the polygon, but polygon side AC is not the height.

Polygon EGHF is a special form of the parallelogram. What is its name, and what makes it different from ABDC?

32.5 Polygons: Total Measure of Angles

Developmental Transitions and Scaffolds

There is a pattern between the total number of sides of a polygon and the total measure of the interior angles. The total measure of the angles is equal to $(n - 2) \times 180°$, where (n) = the number of sides.

Exemplar Problem

Prove It—The Sum of the Angles of a Polygon

If we divide the polygons below into triangles by connecting as many vertices as we can with lines that do not cross over each other, we can see that the number of triangles formed is always a certain number less than the number of sides. The suggested formula is as follows: total measure of angles = $(n - 2) \times 180°$, where (n) = the number of sides. We can prove it.

- *We know that a square has four right angles that must add up to a sum of 360°.*
- *We can divide a square into two triangles.*
- *Does this agree with the formula for the total measure of the angles of a polygon?*

There are two triangles in the square below. They were formed when we bisected two opposite vertices.
What is the angle measure for ∠A? _____
What is the angle measure for ∠B + ∠C?_____
What is the angle measure for ∠B? _____
What is the sum of the angles of each triangle?_____
What is the sum of the angles of each triangle within the square?

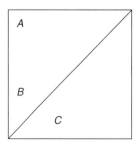

- Does this agree with the formula for the total measure of the angles of a polygon?

Now look at the pentagon.
*How many sides and angles?*_____
How many triangles can be formed? _____
What is the sum of the angles of a pentagon? _____

Now look at the hexagon.
How many sides and angles? _____
How many triangles can be formed? _____
What is the sum of the angles of a hexagon? _____
Think:

Three sides with three angles (one triangle) = 180°

Four sides with four angles (two triangles) = 360°

Five sides with five angles (three triangles) =

Six sides with six angles (four triangles) = Complete the function equation for the sum of the angles of a polygon.
N = number of degrees in the sum of angles, n = number of sides.
N = (n – ?) (180°)

Prove the formula with the octagon.

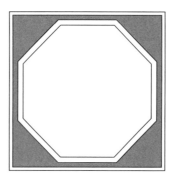

33.1–33.6 Triangles

See also Chapter 2, pages 73–75, for concepts and expectations.

Developmental Transitions and Scaffolds

A triangle is a polygon with three sides and three angles.

- Any side can be considered the base of the triangle (usually it is the side on the bottom).
- The height or altitude of the triangle is the distance from the vertex of the angle opposite the base to the base (the line of distance must be perpendicular to the base).

- The total measure of the angles of a triangle is equal to 180° (see Number 32.5 for proof activities).
- Triangles are classified according to the congruence of their sides and the measures or types of angles. The angles and sides of a triangle are in proportion to each other. The largest angle is opposite the largest side.
- The classifications or names can overlap. A right triangle can also be an isosceles triangle, and an equilateral triangle is also an isosceles triangle. In equilateral or isosceles triangles, the angles opposite the congruent sides are congruent. An isosceles triangle can also be either an acute or obtuse triangle but not a scalene triangle.
- An equilateral triangle has three congruent sides and angles. Each angle, therefore, measures 60°.
- An isosceles triangle has at least two congruent angles. If the one angle that is not congruent equals 80°, then each of the other congruent angles must equal 50°.

Exemplar Problems

Answer these questions:

1. *A right triangle has one right angle. (Why can't it have more than one right angle?)*

2. *An isosceles triangle has two congruent sides. (What would be true of the angles?)*

3. *An equilateral triangle has three congruent sides. (What would be true of the angles?)*

4. *An acute triangle has three acute angles. (Could it also be an isosceles triangle or an equilateral triangle?)*

5. *An obtuse triangle has one obtuse angle. (Why can't it have more than one obtuse angle?)*

6. *A scalene triangle has no congruent sides. (What would be true of the angles?)*

Identify the group or groups to which each of the triangles below belong. Some triangles may belong to more than one group. Write the letters of the triangles next to the group or classification name.

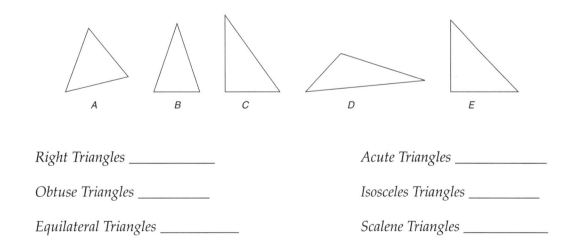

Right Triangles _____   *Acute Triangles* _____

Obtuse Triangles _____   *Isosceles Triangles* _____

Equilateral Triangles _____   *Scalene Triangles* _____

A small garden is in the shape of triangle RST. The measure of angle T is 32°, and the measure of angle R is 112°. What is the measure of ∠S?

    Name the form of ∠R.
    Name the form of ∠S.
    Name the form of triangle RST.
    Name the largest side of ΔRST.

The sides EF and EG of triangle EFG are congruent, and ∠E = 40°. What are the measures of ∠F and ∠G?

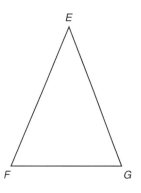

33.6–33.7 Right Triangles/Pythagorean Theorem

Developmental Transitions and Scaffolds

- A right triangle has one angle that is a right or 90° angle. The other two angles, therefore, must add up to another 90°.
- The side opposite the right angle in a right triangle is called the hypotenuse and is always the largest side.
- The other two sides are adjacent to the right angle.

The Pythagorean theorem tells us that for any right triangle, the square of the hypotenuse is equal to the sum of the squares of the other two sides. If a = hypotenuse and b and c are the other sides, then $a^2 = b^2 + c^2$. We can determine the measure of the sides of a right triangle using this formula.

This theorem is named after Pythagoras, an ancient Greek mathematician and philosopher. The theorem has enabled human beings to make important measures for building and navigation for many centuries.

Exemplar Problems

Instead of walking along two perpendicular streets on the way to school, Glen cut diagonally across an open park lawn. He wanted to know about how much less he walked when he used the diagonal. He drew a right triangle ΔABC and made the two perpendicular lines the street paths.

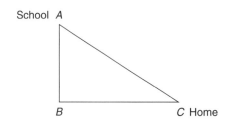

He then measured the street distance between point C and point B to be 400 feet and the distance between points B and A to be 300 feet. He said he did not have to measure his shortcut diagonal distance between points C and A because he could use the Pythagorean theorem.

Use the theorem to find the length of line segment $\overline{AC}$ and then determine about how much less distance he walked when he took the diagonal shortcut.

The measures of three sides of a triangle are 8 in, 6 in, and 10 in. Is this a right triangle?

The hypotenuse of a right triangle is equal to 5 cm, and an adjacent side is 1 cm greater than the other. Write an equation that can be used to find the measure of the sides of the triangle.
Solve the equation to find the measures.

Find the length of the diagonal (shown as a dashed line) for the rectangle shown below.

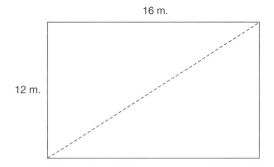

16 m.

12 m.

33. 8 Right Triangles: The Ratios (Sine, Cosine, Tangent)

Developmental Transitions and Scaffolds

We learned that for all triangles, the size of the sides and angles are proportional—the largest angle is opposite the largest side. Since we already know the measure of one angle of a right triangle, ratios that describe the relationships between the angles and sides of the right triangle can be used to determine other measures. These are very useful in determining unknown side values such as the height of a tower without climbing it if we know the measure of one other angle and one side. We can also determine the size of the angles other than the right angle using the ratio of measured sides. We identify the sides of angles other than the hypotenuse in a right triangle as opposite or adjacent to the angle.

- The ratio of the side opposite an angle to the hypotenuse is called the sine.
- The ratio of the side adjacent to an angle and the hypotenuse is called the cosine.
- The ratio of the opposite side to the adjacent side is called the tangent.

These ratios are functions of the size of the angle. If we know the sine, cosine, or tangent of an angle, we can determine the size of the angle, and if we know the size of the angle, we can determine the ratios of the sides.

$$\text{Sine } \angle = \frac{opposite}{hypotenuse} \quad \text{Cosine } \angle = \frac{adjacent}{hypotenuse} \quad \text{Tangent } \angle = \frac{opposite}{adjacent}$$

The magic of this relationship allows us to calculate the measures of any right triangle if we know the size of one other angle, one side, and the ratio for the size. Because the ratios are the same for the same-size angle, tables of the ratios were created for each size angle. Our calculators have these tables entered, and we can use them to get the ratio for any size angle. The ratios are recorded as the dividend of the numerator divided by the denominator or, for the sine, as the opposite side divided by the hypotenuse. If we form a series of right triangles by drawing increasingly larger vertical intersecting segments between the sides of the angle, we can see the proportional relationships between the ratios of the sides of the different-sized triangles with the same angles.

Exemplar Problems

In the graphed diagram below, right triangles were formed by adding vertical intersects to the angle of 45°. Study the diagram and answer the questions.

What happened to the side opposite the angle (the increase in the value of y) when the side adjacent to the angle (the increase in the value of x) was increased?

What happened to the hypotenuse when the sides were increased?

For the same angle, an increase in the opposite side *is matched by a proportional increase in the* adjacent side *and by a proportional increase in the length of the* hypotenuse.

What do we call the ratios between the sides?

$$\frac{opposite}{hypotenuse} =$$

$$\frac{adjacent}{hypotenuse} =$$

$$\frac{opposite}{adjacent} =$$

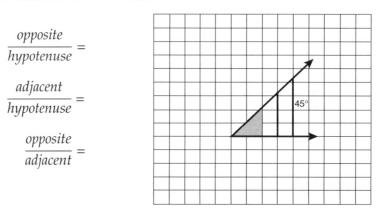

If the tangent of 45° is equal to 1, how does the graph prove the ratio?

If we know that the cosine of 45° is equal to .71, how can we find the measure of the hypotenuse of any of the triangles in the graph? Write an equation and solve it to find the measure of one hypotenuse.

Can you use a proportion and the increase in the measure of the sides to find the measures of the others?

———————— ✳ ————————

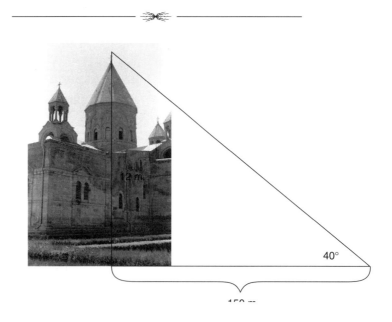

The church committee wanted to know the height of the tallest tower in the picture on the opposite page. They had an instrument that could focus on the top and show the angle it made with the ground. When they were 150 m away from the tower, the angle to the top measured 40°.

What was the height of the tower?

Use your calculator to find the ratio you need to solve the problem.

34.1–34.2 Circle Definitions

See also Chapter 2, page 75, for concepts and expectations.

Developmental Transitions and Scaffolds

A circle (closed curve) is a set of points in which all the points that form the circle are the same distance from a given point that is the *center* of the circle. The distance around the closed curve is the *circumference* of the circle. The distance from the center to any point on the curve is the *radius,* and the distance from any point on the circle through the center to the opposite point is the *diameter.* The length of the diameter is always twice the length of the radius.

An arc is part of a curve or part of the closed curve that is the circumference of a circle. Because two points describing an arc can go either way on a circle, three points on the circumference are used to identify it.

An angle whose vertex is at the center of a circle and whose sides are radii is a central angle. A central angle defines an arc.

Exemplar Problem

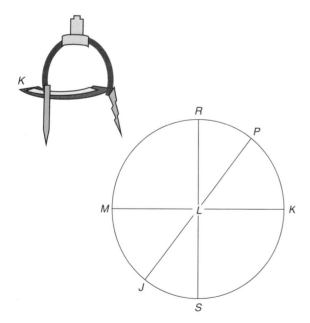

Cindy drew a circle with her compass
Write the labels that show:
    The center of the circle _____
    A central angle _____
    An arc _____
    The diameter _____
    The radius _____

Complete the equations:
    JL =
    JL + LP =

What is the measure of the angle MLS?
Name an arc with the same measure.

34.3 Value of Pi

Developmental Transitions and Scaffolds

Why is the relationship between the circumference and the diameter the same value (pi) for every circle?

- All circles are similar and are dilations or transformations of each other.
- The measures of corresponding sides of similar figures are in proportion to each other.
- The ratios of the circumference to the diameter for all circles are in proportion to each other.
- The ratio of the circumference to the diameter *for every circle* is equal to 3.14 . . . or pi.

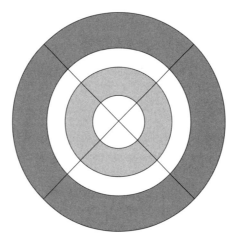

If we measure the diameters and circumferences of several circles and look for the relationship between the measures, we discover that the circumference of a circle is always about 3.14 times larger than the diameter. It is a constant value represented by a Greek letter called pi (π). The circumference of a circle is therefore expressed as $C = \pi d$, where C represents the size of the circumference and d the size of the diameter of the circle.

The rounded pi value of 3.14 that is obtained by dividing the circumference of a circle by the diameter is an *irrational* number. The division always leaves a remainder that can be regrouped into smaller units. The value of each successive digit to the right gets *smaller and smaller* because each added digit is in the next smaller place. The pi value 3.1415926 . . . can also be expressed as the separate digits or in graphic form, as shown below.

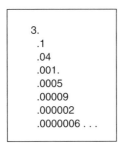

3.
.1
.04
.001.
.0005
.00009
.000002
.0000006 . . .

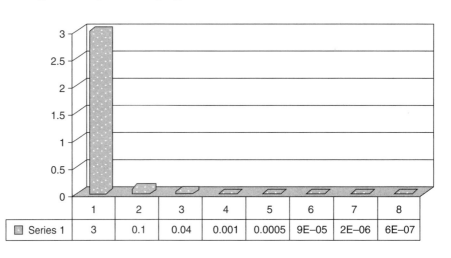

	1	2	3	4	5	6	7	8
Series 1	3	0.1	0.04	0.001	0.0005	9E–05	2E–06	6E–07

Exemplar Problem

Keshawn measured the circumference and diameter of three circles. He realized that the circumference was larger and that the relationship between the measures was a function.
    Some of his measures are shown in the following table:

Circumference	# of Times Larger	Diameter
13.2	3.14 . . .	4.21
	3.14 . . .	5.1
19.5	3.14 . . .	

1. *Explain how he determined the values in the middle column and why they are all about the same.*

2. *What do we call the constant value that shows the relationship between the diameter and circumference of a circle?*

3. *Complete the table.*

4. *Write an equation for the function that shows the relationship between the diameter and the circumference of a circle.*

35.1 Perimeter: Definitions and Applications

Developmental Transitions and Scaffolds

Definitions and applications of the measures of simple polygons are usually not difficult for students. The challenge of the irregular figures by separation into measurable parts and the computation of unknown parts via algebraic equations is more of a challenge.

- The perimeter of a figure is the total distance around it.
- The perimeter of a polygon is the sum of its sides.
- The perimeter of a circle, which is the distance around it, is called its circumference.

Exemplar Problems

Write an equation that represents the perimeter of the shaded area of the rectangle below.

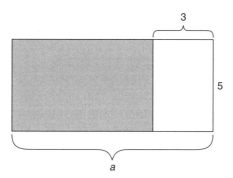

Equation:

The whole perimeter of the figure below is 40 m. Write an equation that will help you find the measure of $\overline{GH}$. Solve the equation.

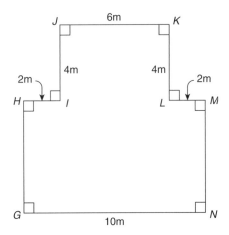

Equation:

Solution:

35.2–35.3 Area: Defined

Developmental Transitions and Scaffolds

Even adults sometimes have difficulty in expressing just what area is. It is a leap from the linear single-dimension measurement concepts to the two-dimensional measures of area. Color tiles work very well in establishing the idea of square units, but centimeter graph paper encourages the connections to actual metric units as well. Computer drawing programs, even those that are part of ordinary word-processing software, allow students to see background grids. They can measure as they draw and easily change the size of the grid unit as well. Measures of area also provide visual applications of algebraic operations.

Basic concepts requiring review include the following:

- Area is a particular space on a flat surface.
- Area is measured in square units or the number of squares with sides that are each one unit long.
- Squares and rectangles have a pattern of repeated whole square units, and the area is the product of their length (or base) and width (or height).

A new concept is the following:

- As a figure is dilated, the area increases at a much greater rate than the area. Practical observations will reveal the explanation that there is more space added in the middle and less added to the edges. Mathematically, the pattern of the relationship between perimeter and area is a practical application of the difference between arithmetic and geometric growth patterns.

Review problem applications should follow a sequence from simple to more complex, such as the one below to uncover the gaps in understanding and apply other recently acquired skills such as multiplication and division of fractions, as well as algebraic applications.

Exemplar Problems

Each side of a square is $3\frac{1}{2}$ ft. What is its area?

———————————— ✖ ————————————

The length of a rectangular space is $1\frac{1}{2}$ m and its area is 25 m². What is the width of the space?

———————————— ✖ ————————————

Robert built a larger figure using only his hexagon blocks. He compared the perimeter and area of the one hexagon with his new figure. How many times larger was the area covered by the new figure? How many times larger was the perimeter?
   Explain why the answers are different.

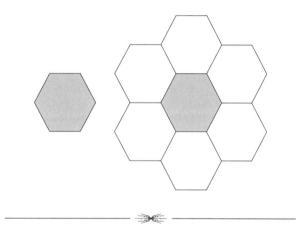

———————————— ✖ ————————————

The base of a rectangle is represented by the expression (2a + b), and its height is equal to (4). What is the equation that describes its area?

———————————— ✖ ————————————

The area of the rectangle shown below is $4(x^2 + 10x + 24)$ square feet. The width is $2(x + 4)$ ft. Express the length of the rectangle in lowest terms.

2 (x + 4) ft.

———————————— ✖ ————————————

The length of a rectangle is three times the width. If the width of the rectangle is increased by 3 inches and the length of the rectangle is decreased by 1 inch, the ratio of the width of the new rectangle to the length of the new rectangle is 4 : 7. Write an equation to find the dimensions of the original rectangle.

Equation:

Solution:

Length =   *Width =*

_____ ✂ _____

A farmer wanted to build a pen for his rabbits. The cost of fencing was about $50 for a linear foot. What would be the least he could spend and still have a pen that had an area of at least 32 square feet? Use your graph paper or the grid on your computer drawing program to find some different shapes for the pen that he could build. What shape would give him the most space for his money? How much would it cost him? Make a table record of the area and the perimeter. Look at the table and see if you can use your data to answer the following questions.

Why do builders like to build square houses?

What kind of a pen would you build for dogs?

35.3 Area of a Parallelogram

Developmental Transitions and Scaffolds

Not all areas have an exact whole number of repeated similar groups of units, but we can use our geometric knowledge to help us measure these areas. For example, by dividing a parallelogram into squares and triangles, we can prove that the area of a parallelogram is equal to the product of its base times its altitude (height).

Discover the Formula—Area of a Parallelogram

Draw a parallelogram like the one labeled, *RTVU*, on a piece of paper. Cut it out.

Draw a line like *SU* that connects point *S* and *U* to form a triangle.

Cut your parallelogram along line *SU* and put it on the other side of the parallelogram next to line *TV*.

What kind of a figure do you now have?

Have you changed the area of your original figure?

If the base *VU* = 4 in and the height *SU* = 3 in, what is the area of the rectangle *WSUV*?

Write the formula you used to get that answer. (Use base for length and height for width.)

What is the area of parallelogram *RTVU*?

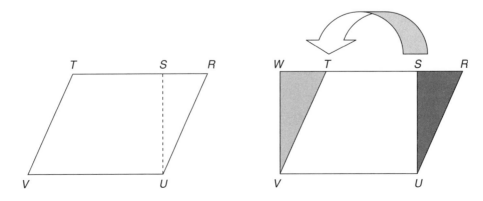

Exemplar Problems

In the diagram of parallelogram ABCD, side $\overline{BC}$ = 4 cm and the height of the parallelogram is 3 cm. What is the area of the parallelogram?

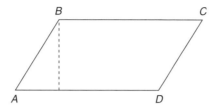

In the diagram of parallelogram ABCD, side $\overline{BC}$ = 3ft and the area = 12 ft². Write an equation and find the measure of the height $\overline{BV}$.

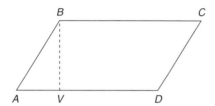

35.4 Area of a Triangle

Developmental Transitions and Scaffolds

Teachers can help students develop the algorithm for finding the area of a right triangle by constructing a diagonal for a square or rectangle and measuring the area of the two to discover that the area is half the area of the rectangle or ½ ($L \times W$). They can also reverse the procedure and construct a rectangle from two duplicate right triangles. This can also be done on the computer with a simple drawing program. Note: Any two congruent triangles can be formed into a rectangle if one of them is cut through the altitude. Students can then see that the rectangle formed has the altitude as one side and the base of the triangle as the other. This develops the algorithm for the area of any triangle as ½($b \times h$).

Discover the Formula—Area of a Triangle

1. Draw any triangle on a piece of letter-size paper. Use your ruler and make it large enough to fill at least half the page.

2. Carefully cut out the triangle with scissors.

3. Make an exact copy—a *congruent* triangle. Cut that one out.

4. Put the largest side of one triangle on the bottom (facing you) so that it becomes the *base*.

5. Draw a line perpendicular to the base that goes through the vertex of the opposite angle. This line is the *altitude* or *height* of the triangle.

6. Do the same thing to the other congruent triangle.

7. Cut only one triangle through the altitude. You now have two pieces of a triangle and the whole of the original congruent triangle.

8. Keeping the base of the whole triangle facing you, form a rectangle using the two pieces of the other triangle. You may have to turn the pieces over to do this.

9. How do the measures of the triangle and rectangle compare to each other?

10. What happened when we put two congruent triangles together to form a rectangle?

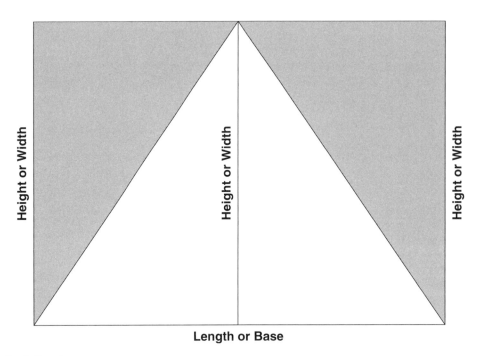

Length or Base

Notice the following measures:

We can call the length of a rectangle its base and the width its height.

Width or height of rectangle = the height of the triangle.

Length or base of the rectangle = the base of the triangle.

Area of the rectangle = (length × width), but it also equals the whole base times the height of the triangle inside—or (*bh*). It is equal to twice the area of each triangle. Therefore:

The area of each triangle = $\frac{1}{2}$ (base × height).

The area of the two triangles = the area of the rectangle.

Problem: The area of a triangle is 20 cm², and its height is 4 cm. What is the measure of its base?

We know the area of the triangle. What is the area of the rectangle that would be formed from two of the same (congruent) triangles? _____

If the area of the triangle is $\frac{1}{2}$ (*b* × *h*) = 20 cm², then the area of the rectangle (*b* × *h*) = ? _____

If (*b* × *h*) = 40 cm² and *h* = 4 cm, then *b* must equal? _____

What is the height and base of both the triangle and rectangle?

height =   base =

Remember what we learned:

The area of any rectangle is the product of its base times its height (*bh*).

(The base is the same as the length, and the height is the same as the width.)

The area of any triangle is $\frac{1}{2}$ the product of its base times its height or $\frac{1}{2}$ (*bh*).

$$A = \frac{1}{2}(bh)$$

Exemplar Problem

We cut different rectangular pieces of paper into two equal triangles.

If the area of a triangle cut from a rectangle is 32 in², the area of the rectangle from which it was cut is equal to _____.

If the area of a rectangle is 50 in², the area of each triangle cut from it is equal to _____.

35.5 Area of a Circle

Developmental Transitions and Scaffolds

It is reasonable to expect that the same ratio that exists between the diameter and circumference of a circle would also exist between the diameter and the area. However, the diameter does not divide a circle into the square units needed to measure area. The radius is just half of the diameter and, as we see below, can be used to divide the circle into four almost square units. The side of the unit is equal to (r), and the area of the unit is (r^2).

Prove It: The Formula for Area of a Circle

A. The diagram below shows a circle inscribed inside a square, *BCDE*.
The diameter of the circle $\overline{HG}$ is equal to one side of the square.
Therefore, the perimeter of the square = 4 $\overline{HG}$.
We know that the ratio of the circumference (*C*) of a circle to its diameter (*D*) is pi (π)

$$\frac{C}{D} = \pi, \text{ and } C = \pi D.$$

Therefore, the circumference of the circle = 3.146 $\overline{HG}$.
And the ratio of the circumference of the circle to the perimeter of the square = $\frac{3.146}{4}$
For every unit of size 3.146 of the circle circumference, there is a unit of size 4 for the perimeter of the square.

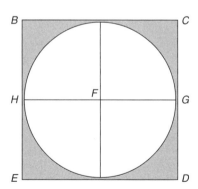

B. The square is divided into 4 equal square units, and one side of each unit is the measure of $\overline{FG}$.
Each square unit is then equal to $\overline{FG}^2$.
If there are two units of $\overline{FG}$ on each side of the whole square, then we know that the area of the whole square = 2 × 2 or 4 square units, 4$\overline{FG}^2$.
The equation for the area of the square *BCDE* is $A = 2\,\overline{FG} \times 2\,\overline{FG} = 4\,\overline{FG}^2$.

C. The circle is also divided into 4 units or central angles whose sides are equal to the radius and also equal to the side of a unit of the square. $\overline{FG} = r$.

If the same ratio exists for the area of the circle and square as we found for the perimeter and circumference, then the area of the circle = 3.146 $\overline{FG}^2$ or $\pi\,r^2$.

D. Check our conclusion:

$$\frac{\text{area of circle}}{\text{area of square}} = \frac{3.146}{4}$$

If $\overline{FG}$ = 3 in, then HG = 6 in, and the area of $BCDE$ = 36^2 in, and the area of the circle inscribed = $\pi\,(3)^2$ = 3.146 × 9 = $(28.3\ldots)^2$ in.

Are $\frac{3.146}{4}$ and $\frac{28.3}{36}$ equivalent or closely equivalent?

Exemplar Problems

What is the area of a circle whose radius is equal to 5 cm?

——————————— ✳ ———————————

If a circle is inscribed in a square with a side of 10 in, what will be the area of the circle?

35.6 Area of Regular Polygons (Five or More Sides)

Developmental Transitions and Scaffolds

The areas of regular polygons can be calculated by dividing the polygon into congruent measurable triangles.

- The regular polygon can be separated into a number of triangles that is equal to the number of sides.
- The sum of the bases of the triangles forms the perimeter of the polygon, and the vertices opposite the bases of all the triangles intersect at the center of the polygon.
- The perpendicular from the base of a triangle or side of the regular polygon to the intersect or center of the polygon is the height of each triangle. It is called the apothem (*a*).
- The area of the polygon is equal to the sum of the area of the triangles.
- The area of a regular polygon is equal to ½ *ap*, where *a* = the apothem (the height of each triangle) and *p* = the perimeter of the polygon.

The hexagon below has been divided by diagonals between the vertices into six triangles. If the base of each triangle = 4 cm and the height is 5 cm, what is the area of each triangle? One triangle has an area of *bh or* ½ (4 × 5) = 10.
What is the area of all six triangles?

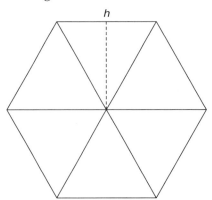

How much larger is the perimeter of the hexagon than the base of each triangle?

What is the measure of the perimeter?

If we substitute the measure of the perimeter (p) of the hexagon, which is the sum of all the bases, and use the height of each triangle, what do we find for the area of the hexagon?

$$A = ½ \, ph$$

$A = ½ (24 \times 5) = 60$. Does that match what we did above when we added the separate triangles?

Note: Mathematicians use the letter (a) to denote the perpendicular distance from a side to the center of the regular polygon, and so the formula may be seen as $A = ½ \, pa$.

35.6–35.8 Measures of Irregular Space on Surfaces

Developmental Transitions and Scaffolds

An important concept and real-life skill is that in order to measure irregular spaces, we can separate the whole space into measurable areas and combine or remove measured areas.

Exemplar Problems

The doctor's office was an irregular space. Determine the area of his office from the measures shown below.

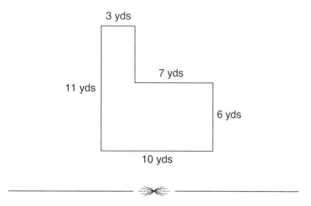

The Jaspars are buying carpeting for an irregular area of their home. They divided it into separate areas in the diagram below to help measure what they needed to buy. How many square feet of paper do they need?

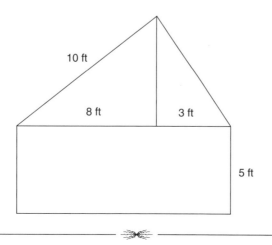

The art gallery was in the shape of an oval that was actually two congruent semicircles on either side of a rectangle. The diameter of the semicircle was 12 ft, and the longer side of the rectangle was 32 ft.
   What was the area of the gallery?

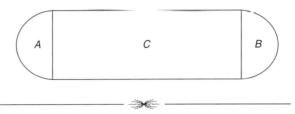

---✖---

A decorative rectangular design has an inscribed blue triangle surrounded by yellow. The whole rectangle is 10 cm wide and 18 cm high. The triangle has a height that is one third of the height of the rectangle.
   What is the area of the blue part of the design, and what is the area of the yellow part?

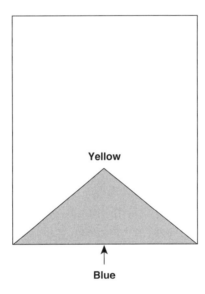

35.7 Area of a Trapezoid

Developmental Transitions and Scaffolds

One example of measures of irregular spaces is the development of the formula for the area of a trapezoid. The area of a trapezoid can be calculated by partitioning the polygon into measurable figures (triangles or triangles and a rectangle). Students will discover that it is equal to ½ the height times the sum of the parallel sides (the base b_1 and its opposite, b_2).

$$A = \tfrac{1}{2} h(b_1 + b_2)$$

Exemplar Problem

Prove It: Area of a Trapezoid = ½ $h(b_1 + b_2)$
   A trapezoid can be separated into a rectangle and two triangles when we draw a perpendicular line from the base to the endpoints of the opposite lines.

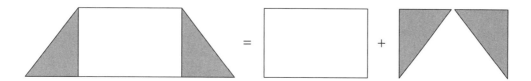

When we take two congruent trapezoids and move the triangle parts from one to join the other, we get two rectangles.

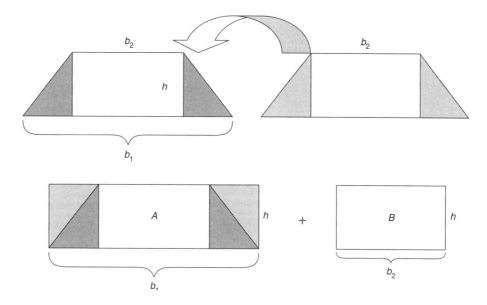

The area of the two rectangles is the sum of the area of both rectangles and equal to the area of the sum of the congruent trapezoids from which they were formed.

The area of rectangle A is equal to the base $(b_1) \times$ the height (h) of the original trapezoid.

The area of rectangle B is equal to the side opposite the base $(b_2) \times$ the height (h).

The sum of the area of the two rectangles is $h(b_1) + h(b_2)$ or $h(b_1 + b_2)$.

Because that sum is also the sum of the two original trapezoids, the area for a single trapezoid is expressed as $A = \frac{1}{2} h(b_1 + b_2)$.

36.1–36.3 Solid Forms, Three-Dimensional Figures: BasicCharacteristics

See also Chapter 2, pages 77–78, for concepts and expectations.

Developmental Transitions and Scaffolds

The shift from the concepts of two-dimensional figures on a surface to three-dimensional figures that occupy space can be helped by construction activities using real and constructed objects. Three-dimensional centimeter cubes that fit together are excellent manipulatives to help students develop volume concepts. They can, however, be supplemented by other materials. I like to use narrow sipping stirrers (straws) with connectors of wire pipe cleaners that are inserted into the ends. Toothpicks inserted into gumdrops are another alternative. Students will be amazed to find the strength of a triangle as compared to that of the cube or prism. Relating triangular strength to the real-life structures of ever-lasting pyramids, cables on bridges, and door frame supports makes the study of mathematics meaningful.

- Cubes are objects or space figures that have twelve congruent edges, six congruent faces, and eight congruent corners.
- Prisms are objects or space figures in which two of the faces are parallel and congruent. These two faces are called bases. The other lateral faces are parallelograms. The prism is named after the shape of the bases. A rectangular prism has a rectangle as a base.
- A cylinder has a two congruent circular bases and a single curved lateral face.
- A cone has a single circular base and a single curved lateral face that merges in a vertex opposite the base.
- A pyramid has a single base and is named after its polygon shape. The number of lateral faces corresponds to the number of sides of the base figure. The lateral faces merge in a vertex opposite the base.
- A three-dimensional figure that is bounded by four or more polygonal faces (faces that are polygons) is a polyhedron.

Construction of structures, such as the one below, where the area an object occupies on the surface is constant but the volume changes with the depth or height of the object, will help develop clarity in the differences of the measures. Critical concepts include the following:

- The volume measure takes the area measure into one more dimension.
- The volume of an object is the product of its three dimensions: length, width, and height.
- Area is measured in square units (multiples of the product of length times width) on a two-dimensional surface.
- Three-dimensional volume is measured in cubic units (multiples of the product of length × width × height) such as 1 cubic inch (1^3 inch) or (1^3 centimeter).
- Not all three-dimensional objects have repeated whole cubic units, but cubes and rectangular prisms do.
- Solid forms have faces, edges, and corners. Different forms have different numbers of sides (edges), faces, and corners. The size of the edges of a solid form may be the same as or different from each other.
- There are patterns between the number of faces and the number of corners.

Exemplar Problems

Jim used 1-centimeter cubes to build the object pictured below.

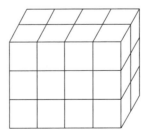

What is the volume of the object?

Figure E below shows one face of the rectangular prism labeled F.

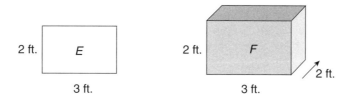

2 ft. | E
3 ft.

2 ft. | F
3 ft. 2 ft.

What is the area of the face E?
What is the volume of the rectangular prism F?

Equal-sized blocks were placed on a piece of graph paper that was measured into equal rectangles.

They are shown as arrangements A, B, and C.

- *Which arrangements of blocks occupy the same area?*
- *Which arrangements have the same volume?*

Each block has a volume of 90 cubic centimeters.

- *What is the volume of the blocks in arrangement A?*

The area occupied by each rectangle is 15 square centimeters.

- *What is the area occupied in C?*
- *Which arrangement has the same volume as C but in a smaller area?*

Each 90-cc block covers one rectangle, whose area is 15 cm.

- *Estimate how tall the block is.*

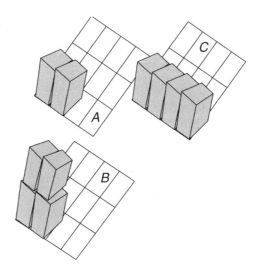

36.4–36.5 Volume of Prisms, Cylinders, Cones, and Pyramids

Developmental Transitions and Scaffolds

If we think about the area of some three-dimensional figures as extensions or repetitions of their two-dimensional bases, we can understand the formulas for finding their volume. Prisms are three-dimensional figures that have congruent and parallel bases and parallelogram faces. That makes them the same throughout their height or depth and their volume a simple number of repeats of the area of the base that is equal to their height.

- The volume of a cube, rectangular prism, or triangular prism is equal to the area of the base times its depth or height (V = area (base) × height) or ($l \times w \times h$) for the rectangular prism.
- The volume of a triangular prism is its height × 1/2 *(bh)*
- The volume of a cylinder is equal to the area of its circular base times its height or $\pi r^2 \times h$.

Cones and pyramids, on the other hand, are not simple repetitions because the faces converge in a vertex. If you experiment with filling objects with these shapes with sand and compare the amount they hold to that held by prisms or cylinders with the same base and height, you discover that they will hold one third of the amount of sand as the prism or cylinder. This explains the formula for finding the volume of pyramids and cones:

- The formula for the volume of a pyramid is $V = \frac{1}{3}$ area of base × height or $\frac{1}{3}(l \times w \times h)$.
- The formula for the volume of a pyramid is $V = \frac{1}{3}$ area of base × height or $\frac{1}{3}(\pi r^2 \times h)$.

Exemplar Problems

Write the formula and find the volume of these two prisms.

Dimensions of base: h = 5 cm, b = 4 cm
Dimension of lateral face: h = 10 cm

Dimensions of base: h = 5 cm, b = 4 cm
Dimension of lateral face: h = 10 cm

Compare the volume of the two prisms. How does it match what you know about the area of a flat surface triangle?

———————————— ✦ ————————————

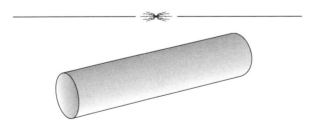

The cylinder above has a base with a diameter of 5 cm and a height of 10 cm. What is its volume?
How does it compare with the volume of the rectangular prism with a base that has an area of 5 cm × 5 cm or 25 cm² and a height of 10 cm?

———————————— ✦ ————————————

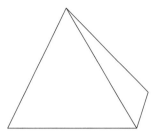

The pyramid above has a base with an area of 16 cm², and its height is 10 cm. What is its volume?
How does it compare to a rectangular prism with a base that has an area of 16 cm² and a height of 10 cm?

36.6 Surface Area of Three-Dimensional Figures

Developmental Transitions and Scaffolds

The surface area of three-dimensional figures is the sum of the areas of all planes. Different figures have different relationships of volume to surface area. A good activity to illustrate the surface area of a cylinder is to cut a paper one to show that it flattens into a rectangle with a length equal to the height of the cylinder and the width equal to the circumference of the base. Therefore, the surface area of the cylinder is equal to the sum of the height times the circumference and 2 times the area of the base.

Exemplar Problems

The triangular prism has a base with a height of 4 cm, and each face measures 2 cm by 8 cm.
Find the surface area of the prism.

Janet wanted to know the surface area of a cylinder box she was going to decorate. She took a sample box and cut it out so that it was flattened into a two-dimensional form. She had the top and bottom and then a flat piece that was the length of the height of the cylinder and the width of its circumference. How could she find the surface area of the cylinder? What would it be if the height of the cylinder was 20 inches and the diameter 3 inches?

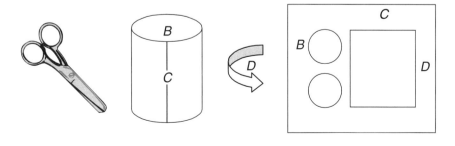

37.1–37.3 Symmetry

See also Chapter 2, pages 78–79, for concepts and expectations.

Developmental Transitions and Scaffolds

Well-developed skills in recognizing the patterns of symmetry will help students recognize the congruent relationships of geometry as well as their real-life applications, such as decorating your home and understanding the view of your face in your mirror. A manipulative called a Mira is useful for a hands-on experience with reflective symmetry, but computer drawing programs make explorations and creative constructions remarkably easy. The forms and descriptions of symmetry are as follows:

- Bilateral symmetry: the same pattern in reverse on either side of a line creates what has been classified as mirror, reflective, or bilateral symmetry.
  - Reflections can be created with a flip from right to left across a line or from top to bottom.
  - A figure that has bilateral symmetry can have a line drawn through its center that will create two reversed or reflective matching sections.
  - The line drawn is called the line of symmetry.
  - There may be more than one line of bilateral symmetry in a figure.
- Radial or rotational symmetry: if you can rotate a form in any way and it still is the same, it has radial symmetry.
  - An object with radial symmetry has an infinite number of lines of symmetry.

Exemplar Problems

Each of the objects below and on the next page has bilateral or radial symmetry or both. Discuss them with your group. Some of the figures have different symmetry in different parts. Write the name for the forms underneath and draw the lines of bilateral symmetry.

Letters of the alphabet can also have symmetry. Name the form and draw all the possible bilateral lines of symmetry for these letters.

A O X T H C

There is also symmetry in the patterns of numbers. Number tables or series objects can be constructed with symmetry and/or in shapes (e.g., triangular numbers [3, 6, 10] or square numbers [1, 4, 9, 16, 25]).

Certain numbers can form triangles and squares of individual objects. What do you notice about the number of objects in the rows and columns of square numbers? Does the pattern have rotational symmetry?

If the number of rows is seven, how many columns would there be for a square number? What is that square number?

- *Square numbers: 1, 4, 9, 16, _____ , _____*

How could you tell whether 225 is a square number?
Triangular numbers form different patterns. What kind of symmetry do they have?

- *Triangular numbers: 1, 3, 6, 10, _____ , _____*

Can you find other triangular numbers besides those shown above?
How would this help you in planning a brick wall for a pyramid-shaped structure?

37.4 Transformations

Developmental Transitions and Scaffolds

Most students have had some experience with transformations in the earlier grades. They are the practical measurable extensions of the concepts of symmetry and useful tools in geometry and in the real-life interpretation of architectural drawings—even simple floor plans. In order to be precise, however, transformations of figures need to be measured and constructed in the coordinate plane. Constructions, using either graph paper or computer software that allows you to show your figures on a grid, can be used to demonstrate and prove the congruence of transformed figures. Some important skills and concepts are the following:

- Transformed figures with the same dimensions are congruent.
- When you flip (reflect), rotate, or slide a figure, it has been transformed in its position on a plane, but the original figure and the one you transformed have the same dimensions and attributes.

Translations

- A slide is also called a translation. When you translate a figure on the coordinate plane, you move or slide each vertex point the same distance on each axis on which it is changed.
- A translation could be a change of position on the x-axis, the y-axis, or both.

Reflections

- When you reflect a figure across the x-axis, the vertex point values of x for the new figure will be the additive inverse of the original figure, but the values of y will be the same as the original.
- When you reflect a figure across the y-axis, the vertex point values of y for the new figure will be the additive inverse of the original figure, but the values of x will be the same as the original.

Rotations

- When a figure is rotated in a transformation, it turns about a *fixed* point called the "center of rotation."
- The rotations may be either clockwise or counterclockwise.
- The amount of rotation is measured in degrees.

Exemplar Problems

The graph below shows two parallelogram figures. Enter the ordered pairs of the vertex points for figures I and II, as well as the differences in the values of x and y, in the table below. Use the table to help answer the questions. Is figure II a translation of figure I? What evidence is there?

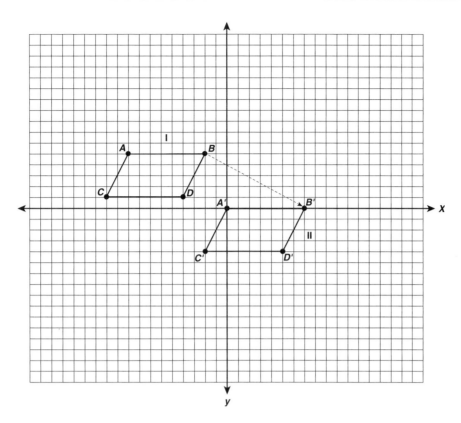

Points	I	II	Difference in x	Difference in y
A, A′	−9, 5	0, 0	+6	−5
B, B′				
C, C′				
D, D′				

Which figure (A, B, C, or D) is a 90° clockwise rotation of the figure in the box.

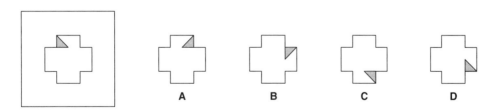

Explain why the others are not 90° clockwise rotations.
Which figure is a 270° counterclockwise rotation?

Draw a reflection of triangle B across the y-axis. What are the ordered pairs that represents the vertex of the right angle in the original and the reflection?
Original_____   Reflection_____

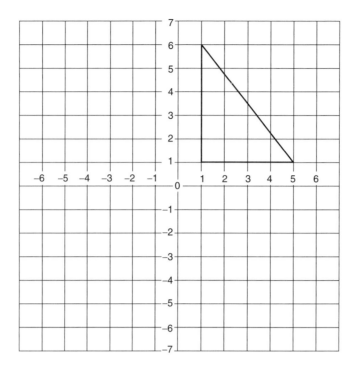

What was different? What stayed the same?

Label the other two angles ∠E and ∠F and determine the ordered pairs that represent their vertices.

    ∠E Original _____   Reflection _____
    ∠F Original _____   Reflection _____

Rotate triangle RST 90° counterclockwise around point S. List the ordered pairs for each new location for the points.

    R(   )   S(   )   T(   )

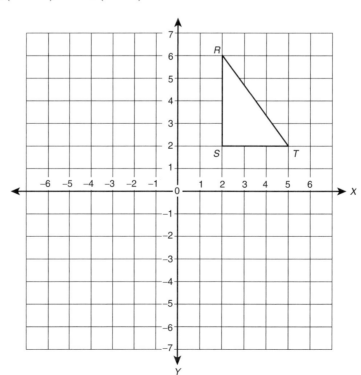

Draw a figure that is a 180° counterclockwise rotation of triangle ABC around point C. List the ordered pairs for each new location for the points.
      A(,   ) C(,   )   B(,   )

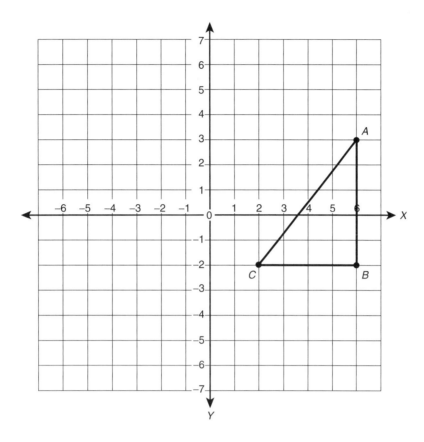

37.5 Transformations: Dilations/Similar Figures

Developmental Transitions and Scaffolds

Just as the practice and understanding of translations, reflections, and rotations can develop better and connected concepts of congruent figures, the concepts of transformations by dilation (either enlargement or reduction) are a natural lead-in to the understanding of similar figures. They include the following:

- A transformation in which a figure is proportionately enlarged or reduced is called a dilation.
- The size of the change (the factor by which the figure is enlarged or shrunken) is called the scale factor.
- All dimensions are proportionately changed by the same scale factor. The new and original figures are similar figures.
- All circles, for example, are similar to each other, and any increase in the radius is matched by a proportionate increase in circumference and area.
- The matching angles and sides of congruent figures are corresponding parts.
- The symbol $\approx$ is used to express the similarity between figures.

38.1 Similar Figures: Using Proportions to Determine Unknown Measures

See also Chapter 2, pages 79–80, for concepts and expectations.

Developmental Transitions and Scaffolds

When polygons are known to be similar, we can determine the measure of unknown dimensions by using a proportion that compares the corresponding sides of the two figures. If you know the measure of two corresponding sides or the ratio of the relationship between the sides, you can find the measure of an unknown side using the known value of a corresponding side in the proportion.

An important concept is that the perimeters of similar figures are in the same ratio as the ratio of the sides (the scale factor), but the areas of similar figures differ by the square of the scale factor. For example, if one side of two similar rectangles is greater than the other by a factor of 2, the other side and perimeter of the larger rectangle is greater by a factor of 2, but the area is greater by a factor of 4 (see Numbers 35.1–35.2).

Exemplar Problem

Rectangle EFGH is a dilation of rectangle ABCD.
   Express the relationship between the two rectangles in symbolic form:

$ABCD \approx$ _____

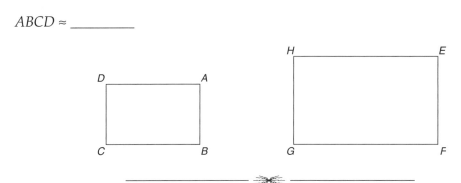

If the measure of $\overline{CB}$ = 6 cm and the measure of $\overline{GF}$ = 9 cm, what is the ratio of the two sides?
   Use the ratio in a proportion to calculate each of the following:

   The measure of $\overline{HG}$ if $\overline{DC}$ was dilated to 8 cm
   The perimeter of a rectangle similar to ABCD with a length equal to 18 cm
   The measure of the area of EFGH if the area of ABCD is 54 cm^2

38.2–38.4 Proving Congruence

Developmental Transitions and Scaffolds

An additional extension and important connection to the experiences of transformations is the concept that for some figures, it is not necessary to know all the measures to prove that all the corresponding parts of a figure are congruent and, consequently, that the figures are congruent. For example:

- Just knowing that the length and width (base and height) of two squares or rectangles are congruent proves that the figures are congruent.
- In these figures, the additional corresponding parts are determined by the ones that are known.
- We can use the symbol ≅ to show congruence.

How many different rectangles can you construct with a length of 6 in and a width of 4 in?

- Only one because the opposite sides are equal.

What about the angles? Could they be different?

- No, because they must all be right angles.

What have we proven about all rectangles with the same length and width?

- They are all congruent.

There are several options for proving that two triangles are congruent. Knowing that:

- All three sides are congruent (SSS)
- Two connected sides and the angle in between are congruent (SAS)
- Two angles and the side in between are equal (ASA)

Exemplar Problems

Prove It: What Makes Triangles Congruent?
For each of the following triangles, use the information given about another triangle to determine if it is congruent to the one shown. Use your ruler and protractor to measure and note the angles and sides for triangle ABC. Then complete the triangles ΔDEF, ΔFGH, ΔJKL, and ΔMNO using the given sides or angles that are congruent to ΔABC.

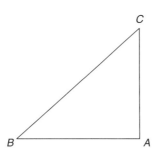

1. *Construct ΔDEF where ∠E ≅ to ∠B and $\overline{DE}$ ≅ $\overline{AB}$ and $\overline{EF}$ ≅ $\overline{BC}$. Is ΔDEF ≅ ΔABC?*

2. *Construct ΔFGH where all the sides are congruent to the sides of ΔABC. Is ΔFGH ≅ ΔABC?*

3. *Construct ΔJKL, where all the angles are congruent to the angles in ΔABC. Is ΔJKL ≅ ΔABC?*

4. *Construct ΔMNO, where ∠M ≅ ∠A, ∠N ≅ ∠B, and $\overline{MN}$ ≅ $\overline{AB}$. Is ΔMNO ≅ ΔABC?*

What congruent measures are enough to determine that two triangles are congruent?

Prove It: What Makes Parallelograms Congruent?

In order to prove that two parallelograms are congruent, we need to know that just one angle, the base, and either another side or the height are congruent. Explain why only one angle is necessary, but we need both the base and a side or the height.

Angles ABC and DEF in the figures below are congruent.

Side AB is congruent to side DE.

Side BC is congruent to side EF.

Complete the construction of a parallelogram II using sides DE and EF and ∠DEF. Draw the height as well.

How many different parallelograms could you construct with the same measures of base BC, side AB, and ∠B?

What do you need to know to prove that parallelograms I and II are congruent?

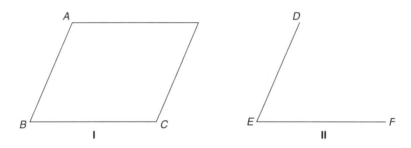

38.5–38.6 Transversals and Congruent Angles

Developmental Transitions and Scaffolds

The concepts related to the angles created by a transversal intersect of parallel lines are a critical adjunct to the study of figure congruence. They need to be connected to the experiences with the figures. For example, a parallelogram is a representation of two parallel transversals of parallel lines. The relationship between the angles of the parallelogram can then be connected to the transversal (e.g., the opposite angles are equal, and the alternating angles are supplementary).

- When a transversal intersects two parallel lines, certain congruent angles are formed.
- These are identified as corresponding and alternate interior angles.
- Corresponding angles are congruent to each other.
- Alternate interior angles are congruent to each other.
- If the corresponding or alternate interior angles formed by a transversal that connects two lines are congruent, then we know that the lines are parallel. And vice versa, if we know that the lines intersected are parallel, then we know that the corresponding or alternate interior angles are congruent.

The definitions need to be related to the figures as follows.

Exemplar Problems

∠A and ∠B, ∠1 and ∠2, ∠3 and ∠4, and ∠D and ∠C are corresponding angles. Corresponding angles are congruent.

∠1 and ∠4, as well as ∠B and ∠D, are alternate interior angles. Alternate interior angles are congruent.

∠A and ∠C, as well as ∠2 and ∠3, are alternate exterior angles. Alternate exterior angles are congruent.

Find the vertical angles. What do we know about them?

Look at ∠A and ∠1. What do we know about two adjacent angles within a vertex of a straight line?

If ∠A and ∠1 are supplementary, what do we also know about ∠1 and ∠B?

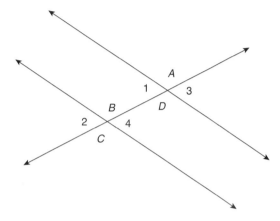

Use the diagram below to answer the questions about the angle measures.

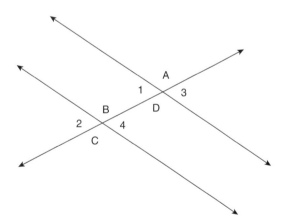

1. If m∠2 = 70°, what is the measure of ∠B?

2. If m∠1 = 80°, what is the measure of ∠4?

3. If m∠C = 100°, what is the measure of ∠A?

4. If m∠2 = 70°, what is the measure of ∠4?

5. If m∠1 = 2x + 20 and m∠4 = 3x − 10, write an equation to find the measures of ∠1 and ∠4.

■ DATA ANALYSIS, STATISTICS, AND PROBABILITY

39.1 Data: Gathering/Organization

See also Chapter 2, pages 81–82, for concepts and expectations.

Developmental Transitions and Scaffolds

Data are the collections of measures that describe the world in quantitative terms. The value of data lies in their production of records of the variations in measurements of the natural world and the effects of these phenomena on our lives, as well as the counter-vailing effects of human actions. When the records are organized and interpreted or analyzed, they can then function as a basis for life-affecting decision making. The ability to collect and organize data is a critical skill in our technological and information-rich society. Students are constantly surrounded by all kinds of data that may or may not have meaning for them: baseball statistics, tickets sold to a new movie, weather data, candy and soda sales, political polls, crime rates, and population statistics. The Internet is a source of much real data that can be retrieved and analyzed.

The usefulness of data is determined by several factors that students need to understand, which they can—even at an early age—if their attention is called to it. A number of overarching concepts bridge the construction of knowledge about the different forms of representation of data. Teachers need to address these within the context of exploring the forms. There is also a vocabulary of words and symbols that ranges from identification of interval and reference lines on a graph to the symbolic representations for permutations.

The ability to construct and interpret tables of data is a necessary basic organizational skill. Experiences should involve the collection of original data using instrumentation where appropriate and technology interfaces if possible. Students should learn how to make the necessary choices for representation and become increasingly critical in their analyses. Technology applications should follow some practice with original constructions, which may be necessary to build the concepts. The wide variety of representation choices in common spreadsheet programs makes evaluations using the appropriate forms a simple task. A data table can also be easily converted to all kinds of graphic forms.

Ordinary graphing calculators now also come with interactive temperature and other probes to take environmental measures. Although a vast amount of data can be acquired over the Internet, students should be able to evaluate data in reference to their own experiences with its collection and have the opportunity to use their own knowledge and creativity in its representation.

Important concepts include the following:

- Data are only as good as the accuracy of how they are recorded.
- The accuracy of the record is dependent on the skill and honesty of the recorder and the precision of the instrument used to measure it.

Provide students with shared experiences for collecting and recording data, such as taking the temperature of ice water as it warms and noting the differences in the records. Tables are useful organizers. Extend the data collection over time and group the data on tables to show the patterns. Identify the variables—such as different students, different times, different thermometers, or different places in the room. Poll taking is a useful and relevant way to introduce the idea of experimental probability. Important concepts include the following:

- The interpretation of data depends on its ability to show patterns clearly.
- Proper organization and representation helps. Individual measures of data may be grouped into intervals to simplify analyses and representation.
- Data may be represented in several ways—tables and graphs or combinations of both are examples.
- The kind of organization and representation of data that works best depends on the nature of the elements of the data and the information they need to provide.
- The interpretation of data must consider the many other variables that may affect them.
- Sampling polls of data may be used to make predictions of larger populations. The individual event records or measures need to be translated to fractional parts or percentages of the whole to be applied to the larger population.

Compare representations of grouped data where the interval is large to representations where the interval is smaller. If most people go to bed between 9 and 10 p.m., then a table and graph that has hourly intervals and does not show the parts of the hour between 9 and 10 doesn't tell us much. For the same reason, yearly rainfall amounts are elements that are best shown on a line graph in decimal intervals. Provide students with poll-taking experiences to demonstrate that answers are sometimes affected by who asks the questions and how they are asked.

When making records of plant growth, point out the need to control all the variables except the one you are measuring. If your measures are of the effect of light, then the water and temperature must be the same.

39.2–39.5 Measures of Central Tendency

Developmental Transitions and Scaffolds

The primary reason for looking at data is to try to understand the events of nature and the behaviors of human beings and other living things, as well as use it to predict and modify the events and behaviors when we can. There are so many variables that can affect individual events that the practical approach is to use measures of central tendency. These calculations homogenize or defuse the effects of variables by accepting them in the mixture. They look for the direction taken by the group that shows the strongest influence. Careful interpretations of data, however, need to consider the variations that may be buried in the central tendency.

Nevertheless, most of the interpretations of data focus on measures of central tendency. If we are comparing the incidence of cancer in two different populations or the number of traffic accidents on different highways, we find the mean scores, compare them, and make meaningful connections. The mean or average score is the most common and is equal to the sum of the events or scores divided by the total number of events or scores. There are also patterns of the distribution of scores or events around the mean, such as the standard deviation of the mean, that can be used to extend the data interpretation. An isolated mean score can sometimes be misleading. In addition to the mean or average, and sometimes instead of it, we need to look at the following:

- The *range* of the scores
  - The range of the data or set of scores is the difference between the highest and lowest value.

- The *outliers*
  - Sometimes, a single score that is very different (much higher or lower) can affect the mean. That event or score is called an outlier. The greater the number of scores, the less the effect of an outlier or a single additional score.
- The *median*
  - The median is the point at which half of the scores or events are above and the other half below.
  - If the total number of scores is an odd number, the median score is the specific middle score. For the group (4, 8, 11, 15, 17, 20, 21), 15 is the median.
  - If the total number of scores is an even number, the median score is the average of the two middle scores. For the group (4, 8, 11, 15, 17, 20, 21, 23), the average of 15 and 17 or 16 is the median.
- The *mode*
  - The mode is the score or event that occurs most frequently.

Basic understanding of the mean and distributions around it include the following:

- In symbolic form, the letter x with an overbar, $\overline{x}$, represents the mean; (n) represents the number of events or scores; and Σ represents the sum of the scores, and

$$\overline{x} = \frac{\Sigma}{n}$$

- In order to raise the mean of a set of scores one point, an additional score must be equal to the original mean score plus one more than the original number of scores.

There is sometimes confusion with the terms *median* and *mode*. Nevertheless, simply lining up the data in order and finding the middle of the sequence or the place where there are an equal number of items above and below works well for the median. Just identifying the largest number of single-item repeats is often enough to bring clarity to the mode. Line and stem-and-leaf plots should help. Let students discover why *outliers*, the few scores or events that are very different from most, are less significant in computations of median and mode—and have them consider the kinds of decisions where the median or mode may be better choices for looking at data.

Why is a batting average usually less than one?
Batting averages are also ratios. They tell us what proportion of the times at bat resulted in hits. Because there are only two possibilities, hit or no hit or (1) or (0), the total of the (1)s and zeros divided by the number of hits for the player, when divided by the number of times at bat, results in the average or mean. The ratio is simply the total number of hits for the player divided by the number of times at bat. The average and ratio are equal. *What other kinds of data could give us an average less than 1?*

Exemplar Problems

The weights of 12 members of the Ridge High School track team are 121, 119, 118, 115, 112, 111, 110, 108, 107, 105, 98, and 98.
Determine the range, mean, median, and mode of the team weights.
Would the mean, median, or mode give the best idea of the team's weights?
Explain your answer.
A new student who weighed 122 lbs was added to the team, and the coach said he would only change the average by slightly less than one whole pound. Was he correct? Explain your answer.

A second new student who weighed 175 lbs was added, and the average was affected. What do we call a single score that is very different from the others?

---※---

Mr. Roberts, the school director of athletics, was planning his schedule and program for the following year. He polled one class to find their favorite sports. He collected the information shown in the table below. Compute the percentage of the class that had the particular favorite sport and enter it into the table.

Favorite Sport	Number of Students	Percentage of the Class
Baseball	8	
Football	6	
Soccer	4	
Hockey	3	
Tennis	2	
Golf	1	

What factors may have affected his ability to use the data to predict his needs and plan his program?

Which of the following measures of central tendency would have the most meaning for Mr. Roberts's needs: mean, median, range, or mode? Explain your answer.

How can the percentages of the group help?

39.6–39.7 Percentiles and Quartiles

Developmental Transitions and Scaffolds

Another perspective for looking at data is to consider a particular score of the group in relation to the others. Percentiles tell us what percentage of all the scores or events was below that score or number. A score in the 90th percentile is higher than 90% of all the scores; 90% of the scores are below it. A city that is in the 90th percentile in terms of traffic accidents has more accidents than 90% of the other cities recorded.

Percentile scores can also be grouped into four quartiles. A score that is in the 75th percentile or above is in the top or first quartile. That means that 75% of the scores were below that one, and a score below the 25th percentile is in the lowest or fourth quartile. The median, which as the 50th percentile divides all the scores into equal halves, also divides the scores between the lowest and highest quartiles into the two middle second and third quartiles. (See the box-and-whiskers graph in Number 40.5.)

Exemplar Problems

Rashan was told that his score on a state test was at the 98th percentile. If 200 students took the test, how many students had scores that were lower than Rashan's?

---※---

The following table shows the normal (average) monthly precipitation for the city of Houston in inches.
Reorganize the records in descending order and then answer the questions.

Average Rainfall in Houston

Month	Inches
January	5.1
February	4.7
March	6.2
April	5.0
May	4.9
June	3.7
July	5.3
August	3.6
September	3.9
October	2.8
November	4.3
December	5.1

1. *Determine the range and median of the records.*

2. *Determine the lower (first) quartile for the yearly precipitation records.*

3. *If it rained 5.9 inches in a particular month, what would be the percentile score for the month when compared to the normal monthly average precipitation?*

40.1–40.5 Comparing Graphs

See also Chapter 2, pages 82–83, for concepts and expectations.

Developmental Transitions and Scaffolds

The variety of graphic representations allows us to share data in many ways. We need to make choices based on what we wish to communicate clearly. The ability to use and interpret the different forms of data representations is an important life skill because it can help us understand the world around us.

- Graphs can be used to show data. The choice of different graphs depends on the relationships or trends you wish to take note of or the ideas you wish to communicate.
- To make sense, graphic representations must have reference lines, beginning points from which the differences in elements are measured.
- The reference line is usually a horizontal or vertical line on which the names of the elements or measured items are found.
- Another line, perpendicular to the reference line, should show equally measured intervals from the reference line to allow for accurate reading of differences. Bar graphs sometimes do not have interval lines but show the measures on top of the bar.
- Sometimes we need the coordinate plane to show the positive and negative values (see Numbers 23.1, 23.2).

40.2 Bar Graphs and Histograms

Developmental Transitions and Scaffolds

A bar graph—or its simplistic form, the pictograph—shows the differences in the elements clearly but tells us less about the range and variations of individual results than a line graph or stem-and-leaf graph.

- Bar graphs use two perpendicular lines as labeled reference lines but differ from the coordinate plane used for line graphs in that the intervals on the axes may be different and separate from each other.
- A histogram is a special bar graph that has equal intervals without spaces.

Exemplar Problems

Mr. Edward's class was often disturbed by the loud noise of overhead planes, and so they made a daily record of the planes they heard for a week. They made a list each day and then made a graph to show the number of planes for each day.

Monday	✈✈✈✈✈✈✈✈
Tuesday	✈✈✈✈
Wednesday	✈✈✈✈✈✈
Thursday	✈✈✈✈
Friday	✈✈✈✈✈✈✈✈✈✈✈
	✈ = One plane

What could they learn from their graph about when the noise happened?
What could have affected the correctness of their data?
How can they use the data to predict when to expect noise?
How could they find out if the pattern is always the same?
Do you have any ideas about what created the pattern?

When examining data, it is sometimes important to look at the different variables that may be affecting the data. The different variables can also be shown graphically. Two different kinds of bar graphs on the next page show the results of a survey of homes to find out how many television sets were in each home. A three-dimensional graph such as the one shown can allow you to understand and analyze the different variables that may affect the data. Compare the two graphs to discover the advantage of the three dimensions.

1. *About what percentage of rural homes had three televisions?*

2. *About what percentage of suburban homes had two televisions?*

3. *What does the three-dimensional graph tell you about the difference between the numbers of televisions in different communities?*

4. *In what kind of community does almost every home included in the data have a television?*

5. *Are there any homes that do not have any televisions?*

6. *What could affect the ability to predict how many televisions there were in any particular farmhouse?*

Number of Televisions in Homes Surveyed

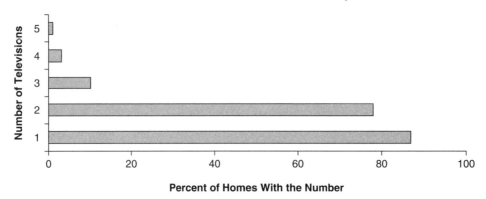

Percent of Homes With the Number

Household Televisions

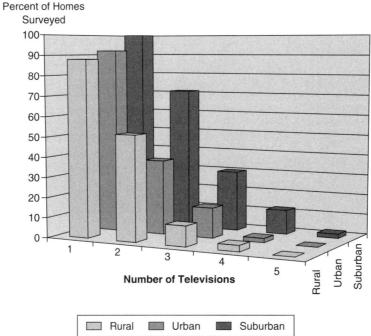

Histograms

Another kind of bar graph, called a *histogram*, has no spaces between the bars. Look at the one below to see how it is different and how it may be easier to see certain trends or changes over time.

Exemplar Problem

An appliance dealer kept a record of his sales of refrigerators from January through July and plotted the sales numbers on a histogram. What month represented the mode? Why did he choose an interval of 10 for his graph rather than 1 or 20? How could this graph help him predict his sales for the next year?

Why might the histogram be better than the bar graph for this purpose?

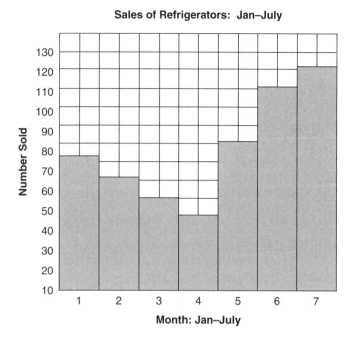

Sales of Refrigerators: Jan–July

40.3 Circle and Line Graphs

Circle graphs show the relative differences as well as the relationship to the whole. A pie or circle graph shows little of the range, but it allows us to see the relationship of the part to the whole. For example, it can show how many students in a class got between 90 and 100 on a test and compare that to how many got between 50 and 60; it can then show what part the 90–100 group is of the whole class. It is useful, for example, when we want to know not only just how many students preferred the Yankee baseball team as compared to other teams but also what fractional part or percentage of the whole class was Yankee fans.

- In a pie or circle graph, the whole circle is the reference, and the size of the arc that describes each part is the measure of the element.
- An arc of 45° is 1/8 of a whole circle, and so an element (e.g., the preference for pizza in the figure below) represented by that arc would have a measure of 1/8 of the total of fast-food selections.
- Construction of a circle graph from data requires several steps.
  - The computation of the percentage of the individual element to the whole
  - The proportionate part in degrees of a whole circle of 360° that is equivalent to the individual element percentage of a whole of 100%
  - The construction of the specific central angles in a circle
- Because of the complexity of constructing a circle graph, once students understand the process and have had the experience of doing it using a compass, we suggest the use of computer programs and graphing calculators.

Exemplar Problem: Circle Graph

Twenty students in Mr. Ashton's class made a data list of their favorite fast foods. They showed their results on a pie graph. Which fast food was the favorite? How many students liked that fast food the best?

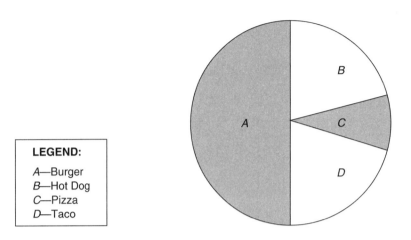

LEGEND:

A—Burger
B—Hot Dog
C—Pizza
D—Taco

Favorite Fast Foods for Students in Mr. Ashton's Class

What two fast foods tied for the second most liked? Which was the least favorite? From the pie graph, could you predict what the favorite fast food was for the whole school? What percentage of the class preferred the favorite?

If angle c = 45°, what fraction of the class preferred the pizza?

If ∠D ≅ ∠B and about 19% of the student preferred the hot dog, what percent preferred tacos?

Line Graphs

Developmental Transitions and Scaffolds

Line graphs are useful representations that clearly show the distribution of elements. Studying a line graph helps us understand the relationships and patterns in data and helps us translate the data into equations or number sentences that show the relationships as variables. For example, if we see that our germinated fast-growing plant grows 2 cm every day, with symbols for the variables, we can describe how much it will grow in any number of days as the equation $G = 2 \times D$. The G stands for the variable of total growth, and D stands for the variable of the number of days. Sometimes we have to add constants. The future height and days are related variables, but the present height is a constant, which can be used to graph the equation. To determine the exact height the plant will reach in a certain number of days from now, we also have to add it in. If the present height is 4 cm, our equation for the height that it will reach in any number of days is $G = 2 \times D + 4$ cm. We can also find the future height by extending the line of the equation on a line graph.

An extension of representations to negative quadrants will be a natural outcome of data collection that includes negative values (see Numbers 23.1, 23.2). Allow students to discover the standard possibilities and invent some of their own. Connect to the study of integers (see Numbers 1.9, 2.4). More than one line on the same graph can compare distributions of similar elements, such as the test grades of students in two different classes or the variation in monthly rainfall in three different places. Students should develop the following concepts:

- A line graph shows us how measures can change over time.
- A line graph tells us more clearly where most of the measures are and where the exceptions are. It also makes it easier to compare two sets of data, such as the amount of rain over a six-month period that happened in the daytime compared to rain that happened at night.

- • The line graph has two reference lines.
  - o The horizontal reference line, which can show different elements, often shows variations of an element over time; it is called the *x*-axis.
  - o The vertical reference line shows the intervals and is called the *y*-axis.
  - o The place where the reference lines meet is the origin.
  - o Parallel lines are drawn to both the *x*- and *y*-axes to separate the intervals and elements. The lines form a grid.
  - o The value of each different element or the same element at a different time is a point on the grid. The points are joined to form a line.

Exemplar Problems: Line Graph

The line graph below represents the number of cars sold by a dealer for the first six months of a previous year. Label the x- and y-axes of the graph. What is the size of the interval? If his sales for the year are expected to be increased by 10%, how could the dealer use his data to predict how many cars he might sell for the first six months of the following year? Complete the data table that matches the graph and make the prediction.

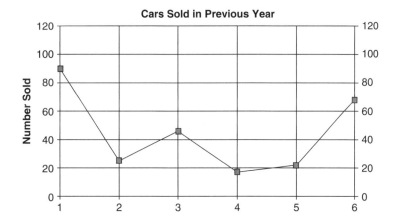

Cars Sold in Previous Year

Month	Number of Cars Sold in Previous Year	Prediction for the Following Year
January (1)	90	
February (2)		
March (3)		
April (4)		
May (5)		
June (6)		

Ellen and her sister Sue were really good at making crafts. They decided on going into business. At the end of each month, they made a record of their profits to the nearest 100 dollars and plotted it on a graph. During the fourth and fifth months, they had to buy some new materials and a machine, and so there was a loss. From their graph, can you tell how much of a loss there was over the two months? Why do you think the profits went up so much at the end of month 7? Why is this graph (see next page) better than a bar graph to show their business results?

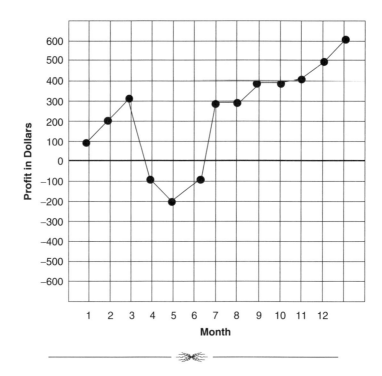

Randy's mother noticed that every time they added a new air conditioner, their electric bill increased quite a bit. New television sets didn't seem to cost as much. She decided to plot the cost of electricity against the number of each on a graph, and it looked like the one below. How do the lines compare? Which line do you think represents the air conditioners? Draw a line that you think might represent the addition of lamps. Draw a line that might represent what would happen if they kept eliminating television sets and the time they spent watching. The angle that a line makes with the x-axis is the slope. What makes slopes steeper or more gradual?

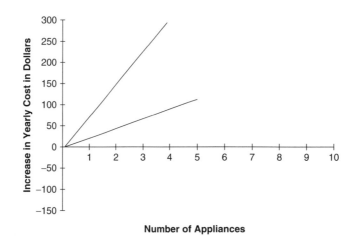

40.4 Line Plots, Stem-and-Leaf Plots, and Box-and-Whisker Plots

Developmental Transitions and Scaffolds

Other kinds of graphic representations can help us organize data and understand how data are distributed. They can also show data trends. The simple line plot in the figure below shows how the numbers of television sets in households are distributed. There is an individual marker for each household that has that number of TVs. It shows a cluster around the numbers 2 and 3. A stem-and-leaf plot is a shortcut way of showing distributions.

- Line plots and stem-and-leaf plots show groupings of data and can be used to find the measures of central tendency and distribution.
- Box-and-whisker plots show the quartile distributions and identify score clusters.
- Scatter plots show paired data and identify trends well.
- Events can be recorded on time lines in order of their occurrence, either from left to right or bottom to top. Distance between events should relate to the time between their occurrences.

Exemplar Problems

Mrs. Smith's class surveyed the number of television sets the students had in their own homes. They made a line plot to show what they found. Each X stands for one TV. Why is this a good way to show how data are spread out or distributed? Around what numbers of TVs can you find clusters of the data?

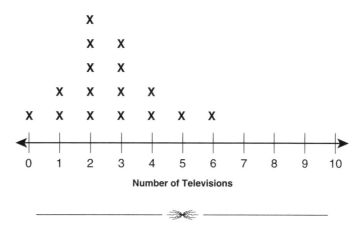

A newspaper reporter was writing an article about parties. She attended one and asked everyone how old he or she was. She then made this stem-and-leaf plot to show the ages of all the partygoers.

1	7 8 8 8 9 9 9
2	0 0 0 1 1 1 2 2 2 2 3 3 4 4
3	1 2 4 6
4	3

What was the age of the youngest person at the party? What was the age of the oldest person? What was the single partygoer age that was the most common or frequent? We call that age the mode. Which age group of partygoers was the most frequent: teens, twenties, or thirties?

A theater sold the following number of movie tickets during its matinee showings:

48 29 39 42 48 47 37 43 38 41 39 45 50 62 47 48 50 46 56

Construct a stem-and-leaf plot for the data.
What was the range and mode of the data?
What general information did the plot give the manager about matinee ticket sales?

Below is a data map similar to those that can be retrieved off the Internet from the United States Weather Service (http://www.noaa.gov.html). What is the data element it displays? Can you think of a way to group these data that would help you see patterns? What other data might a farmer need to help him or her make planting decisions for the week of June 6?

What other data might be useful in his or her planning for the year?

Make a stem-and-leaf plot to show the data.

Get a recent map off the Internet and do the same thing.

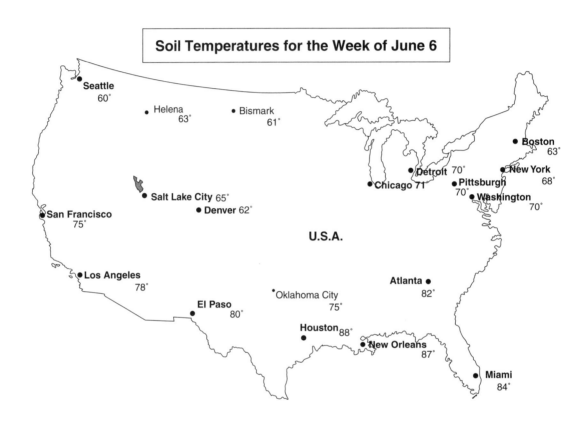

40.5 Time Lines and Scatter Plots

Developmental Transitions and Scaffolds

Time lines are simply number lines with intervals that show the passage of time in equal intervals and the events recorded in sequence. *Scatter plots* on time lines such as the one below can show how two different events may be coincidental or occur at the same time. In this case, the relationship between power blackouts and higher wind velocities in winter storms and the hurricane season is very clear, but the summer months also have a cluster of outages for different reasons.

Exemplar Problems

The local electric company kept a record of power outages over a two-year period. It recorded them by the month but also recorded the wind velocity in miles per hour (mph) at the same time. Do you notice any trends for when the outages happen? Why would there be a cluster of outages in the summertime, when the wind was not blowing so hard? What may have caused the cluster in September and October?

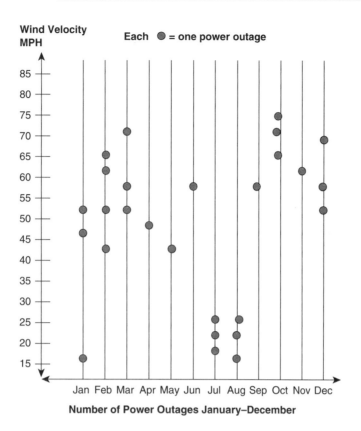

Number of Power Outages January–December

40.6 Box-and-Whisker Plots

Developmental Transitions and Scaffolds

Box-and-whisker plots can be helpful in identifying clusters of scores and recognizing outliers. They are organized into the four quartile distributions and can help students understand the applications of quartiles (see Number 39.7).

Exemplar Problem

The city school district was in the process of making plans for its high schools and needed to understand how the schools compared in their total enrollment of students. It organized the list of schools in the table on the next page and then drew a box-and-whisker plot to show the quartiles and the distribution of school enrollments within each.

1. *Identify each of the following from the graph.*
   a. *Median*
   b. *Lower (first) quartile mark*
   c. *Upper (third) quartile mark*
   d. *Range*

2. *In which quartile was Dayton located?*

3. *In which quartile was Clinton located?*

4. *Which quartile showed the greatest cluster of scores (the shortest range for 1/4 of the scores)?*

5. *Which schools were outliers?*

School	Size
Connor	510
Clinton	675
Dayton	200
Hatfield	1,311
Jefferson	780
Washington	820
Lincoln	1,000
Maybury	732
Seaside	90
Taft	715
Taylor	800

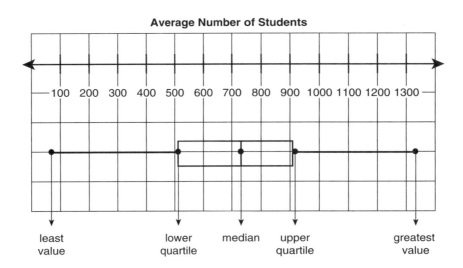

41.1 Certainty/Uncertainty

See also Chapter 2, pages 83–86, for concepts and expectations.

Developmental Transitions and Scaffolds

From the scientific, rather than religious, point of view, the nature of our human existence on Earth is a product of the fundamental laws of physics of our universe and chance. As an example, a fundamental variable identified by Einstein is time. The passage of time affects our ability to predict outcomes. Chance assumes that there are other possibilities and no certainty in the ultimate outcome. Some would argue, further, that even the fundamental laws of physics may be uncertain and limited to existing states—perhaps created by chance from other possibilities. Needless to say, chance is a critical factor in all of our existence. Even the very young can learn to discriminate between events that are more certain or uncertain. We are all interested in our chances, the probability of the occurrence of a desired or undesired event. We want to know the odds, and the odds depend on the alternative possibilities. For some reason, the two concepts are not always clearly connected in our school curriculum. The probability of the occurrence or outcome of an event is dependent on the possibility that a particular event or outcome can occur. Unless there is a major catastrophe on Earth, there is only one possibility at the equator—day follows night. It is therefore certain, and the probability of a new day is 100% because there are no other possibilities. If you consider the three possible alternatives of rain, clouds, or sunshine for most of the day, however, the probability of one of these events is not certain and is less than 100%.

Events and choices can be either certain or uncertain. A sequence of day followed by night about every twenty-four hours is certain at the equator but uncertain at the poles. If you only have white socks, it is certain that you will pick white socks, but white socks are uncertain if you have several different colors. Probability is a measure of how close an event is to being certain.

41.2 Probability/Possibility

Developmental Transitions and Scaffolds

Logically, knowing the extent of the possibilities or counting them has to come before estimating the probability of the event. This book, therefore, addresses the concepts of possibility first and pursues them from beginning concepts through the more advanced high school applications. However, just as the rest of the organization of this book dictates, teachers should address the two topics in tandem at individual grade levels—just making sure that the necessary possibility counting concepts are in place before the applications of probability.

Twenty-two hundred years ago, Archimedes was interested in the counting of alternative possibilities. Recently unearthed evidence shows that he presented a problem in the Stomachion that required the solver to compute the number of alternate possible combinations of fourteen geometric pieces that would form a square. It took a team of modern mathematicians, using their updated knowledge and computers, six weeks to come up with the answer of 17,142 possible ways to form the square from these fourteen pieces. The strategies for listing and counting the number of possibilities of an event are an aspect of what is called discrete mathematics. The development of these strategies can progress through all grade levels. Primary students, for example, might find all outfits that can be worn using two coats and three hats; middle school students might systematically list and count the number of routes from one site on a map to another—or determine the number of three-person delegations that can be selected from their class to visit the mayor. Middle and high school students can then use the counting strategies to solve problems in probability. The exemplar problems below are shown in order of difficulty.

The development of counting strategies should begin with the construction of sample spaces with actual placement of objects, pictures, or diagrams of all the possibilities, which can then be counted. Analysis of results can then lead to the application of algorithms such as the counting principle and factorial notation.

41.3–41.9 Counting Possibilities

Developmental Transitions and Scaffolds

The number of possibilities for a particular event depends on the following:

- The total number of possible alternative outcomes (including the one desired)
- Whether or not the order of the selection is significant
- Whether the alternatives are in a single category or in different categories
- The quantity selected from these alternatives or the number of choices made
- The number of possibilities for a single event in a single category is simply equal to the number of choices. There are seven possibilities for it to be a particular day of the week.

41.4–41.9 Combinations

Sometimes, choices or events are combined. If the order of selection and arrangement of events or choices from a single set does not matter, we call these events combinations. They are order-independent choices. Combinations of events and choices have more possibilities than single events. There are seven possible days of the week, but combined with the two alternative choices of rain or no rain, there are fourteen possibilities, two for each day.

- If the order of selection and arrangement does not matter, three individually selected items (A, B, and C) from a group of A, B, and C in a single category can be arranged in only one combination. For any number of events, as long as the number of choices made is equal to the total number of alternative outcomes and order does not matter, there is only one possible combination. You just pick them all and have them all. The probability of your choice is 100%.

In real-life situations, there are often instances when a specific number of choices are selected from a group of possibilities. Once you are more selective, however, of the number of choices you make from the group and do not pick them all, the possibilities for your choices are greater.

There are different ways to consider the set or sets of choices:

- As a combination of choices from a single set of different choices (1–6 different days of the week, the 1–6 possible numbers on a roll of a single die)
- As a combination of choices from more than one separate set of alternatives or events that are to be combined (a set of shoes and a set of socks, the combinations of numbers on a pair of dice)

Same Set

The number of possibilities for a particular combination of events chosen or happening from the *same set* depends on the following:

- The number of alternative choices in the set. *The greater the number of alternative choices, the greater the number of possibilities.*

- The number of choices made. *The smaller the number of choices out of a set, the greater the number of different possibilities. (Remember: if you pick them all, you have only one possibility.)*

If you have six different shirts to pick from and you chose three to take with you on vacation, the number of possibilities for your choice of three shirts is less (10) than if you only take two of them (15). (*That may be why some people take more than they need—so that they do not have to make decisions from the greater number of possibilities.*)

We can calculate the number of possible combinations of events or choices by constructing a tree diagram, a table of possible events, or filling a sample space. You need to check to make sure there are no repetitions.

Exemplar Problem

Mrs. Thaler is the adviser to the student council. She has to select two students from the four officers to attend a convention. How many ways can she select the students? Finish the tree diagram and be sure not to duplicate combinations.

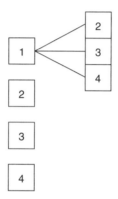

Different Sets

We can also make choices from different sets.

Sometimes, the possible combinations are restricted. In the example below, Doug cannot go bowling with Stephen.

Exemplar Problems

Doug is planning his weekend. He can hang out with Stephen and go to the movies or the mall, or he can hang out with Frank and go ice skating or bowling.

Draw a tree diagram to show his possible choices.

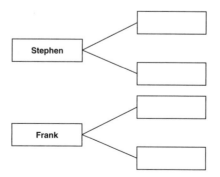

How many different choices of friends combined with activities did Doug have?

Sometimes the combinations are not restricted.

If choices are not restricted, you can combine them in any way. A tree diagram will show you that the total number of possible combinations of events or choices from two different sets is the product of the number of choices in one set multiplied by the number in the other. If you have a set of three different pairs of shoes and six different pairs of socks, there are eighteen different possible combinations of shoes and socks. The probability of choosing any one of the pairs of shoes is 1/3, and the probability of choosing any one of the pairs of socks is 1/6, but the probability of one particular match of shoes and socks is 1/18.

Shatiece is on vacation for ten days. She only has the clothes in the table below with her.

Tops	Bottoms
A beige shirt	Tan pants
A light blue polo	Brown pants
A white blouse	Blue jeans
	A green skirt

If she wears a different combination of a top and bottom each day, will she have enough clothes to wear a different outfit for the ten days?

42.1–42.4 Permutations: Order-Dependent Possibilities/Counting Principle

See also Chapter 2, pages 86–87, for concepts and expectations.

Developmental Transitions and Scaffolds

When order does matter, the possibilities are called *permutations*. There will be a greater number of possibilities. Three individually selected items (A, B, and C) can be selected (or arranged) in six different ways if the order matters. Actually recording the number of possible event orders by filling a sample space will demonstrate that after you pick your first item, the number of possibilities for the next item diminishes by one and so on until the last one is left. For this one, there is only one possibility. The counting principle can therefore be used to determine the total number of possibilities. For a group of four items, when order matters, there are 4*3*2*1 = 24 possible arrangements of the four items. The factorial notation is a way of denoting and applying the counting principle.

$$4! = 4*3*2*1 = 24$$

Calculating Possibilities:

How many total possible different orders can there be for all of a group of five unlike objects?

Number of items as a factorial: five items = 5! = 5*4*3*2*1 = 120

Exemplar Problem

Marla remembered what the last four different digits of her friend's phone number were. However, she forgot what the order of the digits was.

Use the counting principle to determine how many different combinations of the four different digits were possible.

Permutations: Selecting From a Group/Symbolic Notation Form

Again, the number of possibilities depends on whether or not order matters. For calculating reasons, it is useful to first consider permutations. Sample space records of permutations will prove that the factorial is again useful. However, for three choices of the five, we only go as far as the first three steps of the sample space. We can express the size of the group and the number of choices for the permutation in symbolic notation form using subscripts. The total size of the group precedes the letter *P*, and the number of choices from the group follows it.

All possible order-dependent arrangements
of five items
5*4*3*2*1 = 120

Only three items of the five: 5*4*3 = 60

Expressed as $_nP_r$ or $_5P_3$

Exemplar Problem

In the Sedgwick school day, there are four class periods before lunch. Next year, Jeffrey will have the following classes: English, math, science, Spanish, social studies, band, and gym. He wanted to know the number of possible schedules for the four classes before lunch. Express this problem in permutation notation.

How many different schedules before lunch are possible for Jeffrey next year?

42.5–42.6 Order-Independent Combinations: Counting Principle/Symbolic Notation

Developmental Transitions and Scaffolds

We have already seen that selections from a group when order does not matter will have fewer possibilities. Sample space examinations of combinations will show that for combinations, the total number of different possibilities is the permutation total divided by the factorial of the number of choices.

All possible order-independent selections from a group. Order does not matter, and therefore there are fewer possibilities than for permutations.

Three items of the five $\dfrac{5*4*3}{3!} = \dfrac{60}{6} = 10$

Four items of the five: $\dfrac{5*4*3*2}{4!} = \dfrac{120}{24} = 5$

Symbolically, we can write this as $_nC_r$ and recognize that

$$_nC_r = \frac{1}{r!} \times {_nP_r}$$

Notice that when using this formula for choosing five items of the five, if order does not matter, there will only be one possibility for the five items.

We can also express the size of the group and the number of choices for combinations in symbolic notation form using subscripts. The total size of the group precedes the letter C, and the number of choices from the group follows it. For the above example, it would be $_5C_3$ and $_5C_4$.

Exemplar Problem

Reggie picked three marbles from a bag containing equal numbers of five different colors.
  Express this problem in combination notation.
  How many different possible outcomes are there?

42.7 Combinations From Different Categories or Groups/Using the Counting Principle

Developmental Transitions and Scaffolds

The above combinations assume independent selections from a group of equally possible alternatives in the same category. Sometimes, in real life, we make choices that combine different categories of choices—for example, when choosing from a menu. The order in which you select the items from a menu may not matter, but you usually want at least one choice from more than one category. This constraint increases the number of possibilities. If there are four main courses, three desserts, and three beverages to choose from, filling a sample space will show that there are thirty-six different possible menu items for three separate category choices from the possible items or 4* 3* 3. The same total would apply if there were three main courses, four desserts, and three beverages. Notice that the number of possibilities for the second choice is not diminished by the first pick because they are in different categories.

Exemplar Problem

Seton Middle School is having student council elections. For the eighth-grade elections, there are five students running for president, four students running for vice president, and two students running for treasurer. The names will be placed randomly on the ballot under each office.
  How many possible arrangements are there for the names on the ballot?

For President
1. _____   2. _____   3. _____   4. _____   5. _____

For Vice President
1. _____   2. _____   3. _____   4. _____

For Treasurer
1. _____   2. _____

43.1 Defining Probability

See also Chapter 2, pages 88–89, for concepts and expectations.

Developmental Transitions and Scaffolds

Students need to understand the fundamental concepts of probability so that they can interpret weather forecasts, avoid unfair games of chance, and make informed decisions about medical treatments whose success rate is provided in terms of percentages. They should regularly be engaged in predicting and determining probabilities, often based on experiments (like flipping a coin 100 times), but eventually based on theoretical discussions of probability that make use of systematic counting strategies to determine possibilities. High school students should use probability models and solve problems involving compound events and sampling.

- Probability is a measure that helps us to predict uncertain events. The probability of the occurrence of an uncertain event is dependent on the possibility that a particular outcome can occur.
- If there are no possible alternative outcomes to the particular or desired outcome, then the event is a certainty and the probability is $\frac{1}{1}$ or 1 or 100%.
- If there is no possibility of something happening, then the probability is zero.

Discussions of examples should include comparisons such as the following: the certainty that it will be day and then night versus the uncertainty that the day will be bright and clear, as well as the certainty that it will rain sometime in a month versus the uncertainty that it will rain on a particular day. And transferring to other mathematical concepts, there is the certainty that if you walk in a circle, you will come back to where you started. Needless to say, chance is a critical factor in the existence of all of us. Chance assumes, first of all, that we have no control over an event or over choice. Looking at an assortment of shirts and purposely choosing one does not involve probability for you as the chooser. There is certainty in your choice. Your choice, however, is uncertain for the storekeeper, who does not control your choice. On the other hand, if you choose something absolutely blindly, like a particular colored marble from a hat, there are other possibilities, and the ultimate outcome is uncertain upon the possibility or the number of other possible choices. If there are only two possible choices for an event happening, then the probabilities of the events are equal; it can be either one or the other. Students need to understand, however, that although the probability of an event can be mathematically computed based on the number of choices, it is still only a probability, not a certainty. There are only two possible choices for the toss of a coin, so the probability is that you will get heads one time out of two tosses, but you can get ten heads in a row. There are over a hundred possible average temperatures for a day, and the probabilities for a particular temperature change with the seasons.

Probability tells us what the chances are that something will happen. We can predict the probability of an event based on the mathematical number of possibilities and experiments. When we calculate probability, we assume that the event we are predicting is a random event and not certain or impossible. When we pick something we cannot see, feel, or smell as different from anything else in a group, it is a random choice.

43.2–43.4 Theoretical and Experimental Probability/Expressions

Developmental Transitions and Scaffolds

The outcome of uncertain events is not guaranteed—it is only more or less likely, depending on the possibilities and the way we choose. When we calculate the probability of something happening in the future, we are predicting or theorizing what the chances for a particular outcome are. We call that *theoretical probability.*

Once you know the number of possibilities, the theoretical probability of the occurrence of the event can be calculated. For a single choice, it is the fractional part of the whole group of possibilities that the desired choice or event represents. The numerator tells us the number of probable occurrences (or parts of the total possibilities). The number of the denominator tells us the whole number of possibilities.

- If there are six choices on a die, then what is the chance for one of them to occur? What fraction describes one part out of six parts? (1/6)
- If you toss the die 360 times, and the probability is 1/6, about how many times will you toss a 6?
- What would be the probability of tossing a 6 if there were two 6s on the die and no 5?

If an event is certain, its probability is 100%. Anything less than 100% and greater than zero is uncertain. An event with zero probability is impossible.

Therefore, four red marbles out of a group of eight represents 4/8 of the whole, and the theoretical probability of picking a red marble out of a group of eight is four out of eight or 4/8. If your desired marble choice is either red or green, the probability of choosing one of your desired alternatives increases. If there are two green marbles in the group, the probability of either red or green coming up on the first choice is 6/8.

Prediction of what will happen with the toss of a coin or a die is easy because there are few possibilities. When the number of possibilities is greater, however, the predictions become more complicated. For example, the probability that today will be a Saturday is one out of seven, but the probability that we will have rain, snow, clouds, or sunshine or combinations of these on a Saturday depends on the number of possible combinations and the probability of each.

We can also determine the probability by conducting experiments or taking samples of how the events might occur. This is called *experimental probability.* Experiments to determine probability are a great opportunity to review fraction and ratio concepts. The experimental probability of a particular or desired event of the trial is equal to the *number of times the desired event occurs divided by the total number of trials.*

43.5 Probability of Single Events

Developmental Transitions and Scaffolds

If there are four possible choices or outcomes, for a single independent event, the probability of one of these occurring is 1/4 or 25%. If a set of five objects has two objects of one kind and three of another, there are only two possibilities. The probability of picking a single choice of one kind is 2/5 or 40%, and the probability of the other kind is 3/5 or 60%.

Exemplar Problems

Assume that the spinner below does not land on a line.

    A. *Write the probability of each event listed below as a fraction.*
    B. *Identify the probability of each event as an example of certainty, impossibility, or sometimes.*

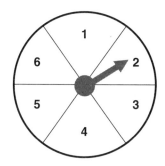

1. *Probability of landing on a 4*

2. *Probability of landing on a 7*

3. *Probability of landing either on a 2 or a 5*

4. *Probability of landing on a number between 1 and 6*

How many odd numbers and how many even numbers are on the spinner below?
    Express the probability of spinning an odd number on this spinner as a fraction and as a percent.

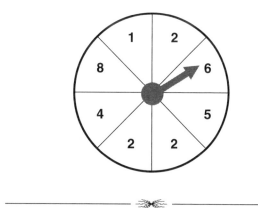

Three students tossed coins on a 36-square grid. Student A had nine coins, B had six coins, and C had fifteen. Who had the greatest chance of landing on a particular grid? What was the probability for each toss? What was the probability of tossing a heads on a particular grid?

---------------- ✄ ----------------

A bag of marbles has eight purple marbles, sixteen yellow marbles, thirty-two green marbles, and twenty-four white marbles. If you pick one marble without looking, how many possible outcomes for color of the marble are there?

Which color marble is mostly likely to be picked? Explain your answer

---------------- ✄ ----------------

Andrew flipped a coin 100 times and got fifty-two tails and forty-eight heads. What is the experimental probability of flipping tails?

---------------- ✄ ----------------

A bag contains ten marbles. There are three yellow, two red, and five blue marbles in the bag.

What is the theoretical probability of picking a yellow marble?

Express your answer as a decimal.

Diana drew one marble from the bag. Its color was recorded, and it was put back in the bag. She repeated this process twenty times. These were her results:

Yellow	Red	Blue
8	4	8

What was the experimental probability that a yellow marble was picked? Express your answer as a decimal.

Compare the theoretical and experimental probabilites of picking a yellow marble. Explain why they were the same or different.

For which color marble in the bag is the theoretical and experimental probability the same?

43.6 Probability of Multiple Events

Developmental Transitions and Scaffolds

Picking two choices, one after the other, is different from single choices. Remember that when order counts, the number of possibilities is greater, and therefore the probability of a particular sequence is less than for a single choice. The probability of picking two desired choices, one after the other, is a fractional part of the single choice. It is the product of the probability of the first choice multiplied by the probability of the second choice. When we are considering the probability of the simultaneous or attached occurrence of more than a single event or more than one of a kind in a set, we have to consider the separate probability of the occurrence of each. If you have a set of three different pairs of shoes and six different pairs of socks, there are eighteen different possible combinations of shoes and socks. The probability of choosing any one of the pairs of shoes is 1/3, and the probability of choosing any one of the pairs of socks is 1/6, but the probability of one particular match of shoes and socks is 1/18.

Notice that the probability of the combined event is equal to the product of the probabilities of each of the events combined. What is true of the size of the product of common fractions? Why are the chances of winning the lottery so small?

Exemplar Problems

Kathy will spin the spinner once and toss a coin once. What is the probability that the result will be a 4 on the spinner and tails on the coin?

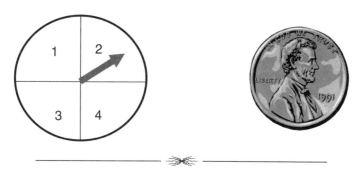

The complete breakfast menu at a local diner is seen below.

Complete Breakfast Menu (Choose one item from each column)		
Main Course	Beverages	Fruit Toppings
Omelet	Milk	Apple
Pancakes	Hot Chocolate	Banana
Hot Cereal		

Using the counting principle, how many different breakfast combinations can be ordered? Draw a tree diagram to determine the possible number of breakfasts with pancakes.

What is the theoretical probability (as a fraction) of a customer ordering pancakes, hot chocolate, and apple topping?

Jonathan has a drawer filled with single socks. There are six blue socks, nine white socks, and three black socks. Without looking, Jonathan puts his hand in the drawer and pulls out two socks. What is the probability (as a fraction) that they are both blue socks?

43.7 Probability: Replacement and Independent or Dependent Events

Developmental Transitions and Scaffolds

The probability of an event is altered if the size of the group changes. Not replacing a chosen item changes the size of the whole group and the probability. It is a dependent event and depends on how the whole group was changed. If a desired red marble has already been chosen and removed from a group of seven that originally had three red ones and a probability of $\frac{3}{7}$, the probability for another red one is now only $\frac{2}{6}$ or $\frac{1}{3}$.

If you replaced the first marble or took a marble from two separate bags, it would be an independent event, unaffected by the first pick.

Exemplar Problems

Jackie has a bag containing four red marbles, three orange marbles, and two purple marbles of the same size. Without looking, Jackie chooses an orange marble from the bag and does not replace it in the bag. Then she chooses another marble. What is the probability that the second marble will be purple?

———————— ✸ ————————

The baseball team decided that they would use a spinner to decide what the positions on the batting lineup would be. The number spun is the position assigned. If a number already assigned is spun, the player spins again until landing on an open position. What is the probability of the first player who spins for being first in the lineup? If he doesn't get the first position, what is the probability of the second player for being first in the lineup? Could the last of the players to spin be first up? How does the probability of being first change? When does it become zero?

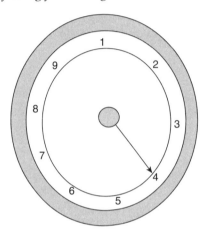

Spin your spinner twenty-four times and make a data table to show where your spinner ended. Combine your results with others in your group. What did you discover?

43.8 Experimental Probability

Developmental Transitions and Scaffolds

Theoretical probability is a mathematical assumption based on the size of the whole and on the size of the part of interest. It does not take into consideration the reality of chance. Random experiments in which events are measured or choices made are affected by chance and sometimes other affecting factors. The trick is to have enough tries or samples to overcome chance and other factors so that your experimental probability approaches the theoretical. At the middle school and high school levels, poll taking is a good experience for understanding how experimental probability can help us predict outcomes.

- Sometimes we cannot come up with a theoretical probability because we do not really know either the size of the whole population or the size of the part. We can, however, sample a population. The part of interest in the sample is then compared to the whole sample size and a probability computed. Of course, this depends on how good a sample you used. Did it represent every possibility? Does it tell us something about everyone?
- Sometimes we can limit the possibilities for our predictions with experiments. We can also prove our predictions with experiments and data collection. The weather bureau keeps a record of temperatures, and we can use its records for our prediction.

If, based on its records, we limit the choices for June, July, and August to temperatures between 50° and 105°, we have fewer possibilities and a higher probability for 90° days. The more data we collect, the closer we will come to our mathematical prediction and proof that we were correct. If you toss a coin 1,000 times, the number of heads will be close to 500.

- To help us make decisions about the reliability or representative accuracy of our polls, we can use tests of statistical significance. There are a number of these that depend on the way data are normally distributed around the mean. These tests are used not only to show whether a sample is representative of the whole possible population but, more significantly sometimes, to show a difference from the whole. That is how we learn about the many specific variables that can affect our lives—and keep us from blaming everything on chance.

Although the computation of these statistical tests may be too much for secondary students, they are accessible in computer programs such as Microsoft Excel. Students can learn their value and access them.

Exemplar Problems

The nine chips shown below are in a bag. Christina drew one chip from the bag and then replaced it and mixed it around. She did this twenty-five times and drew the number 3 chip five times. What was the experimental probability of drawing the number 3 chip? How does it compare to the theoretical probability? What might have happened if she did not mix the chips?

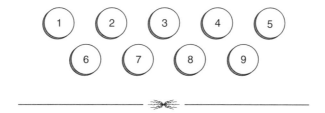

From a shipment of 500 flashlights, a sample of 25 was selected at random and tested. Two flashlights in the sample were found broken. About how many broken flashlights would be expected in the entire shipment? Would future shipments always be the same?

Tara spins the spinner 100 times. How many times must the spinner land on the shaded section in order for the experimental probability to equal the theoretical probability? Explain your answer.

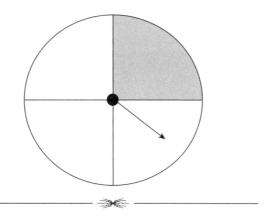

Mrs. Marshall surveyed her algebra class to find out what the students' favorite summer activities were. The following table shows the results of the survey.

Favorite Summer Activity

Swimming	
Playing baseball	
Playing video games	
Going to the movies	

Legend: = 2 students

According to the chart, what is the experimental probability that a student chosen at random from Mrs. Marshall's class will like going to the movies the most?

What factors of the survey may have affected the results?

43.9 Probability of Single Choices Combined

Developmental Transitions and Scaffolds

The probability of independent events occurring at the same time is the product of the probabilities of each occurrence. If there are three white marbles in a bag of twelve and two blue ones in the same bag, the probability that when you pick two marbles, you will get a white and blue one is $\frac{1}{4} \times \frac{1}{6}$ or $\frac{1}{24}$.

If the marbles are not replaced after the first pick, it will be a dependent event, and the probability for a second pick will change based on what the first pick was.

If the experimental probability that you will miss the school bus is one out of twenty mornings or $\frac{1}{20}$ and there are five school days in a week, then the probability that you will miss the bus on Monday is $\frac{1}{20} \times \frac{1}{5}$, which equals $\frac{1}{100}$. Of course there may be other factors that can affect the probability, such as going to bed late on Sunday nights.

Exemplar Problem

The chart below lists the number and type of soft drinks found in a cooler during the Smith family picnic.

Soft Drink	Regular	Diet
Pepsi	4	3
Mountain Dew	6	2

A. *If Clifford selects two cans at random, what is the probability that he will get one Diet Pepsi and one regular Mountain Dew?*

B. *If Clifford selects a Diet Pepsi and a Diet Mountain Dew and drinks it, what will be the probability of the next person getting one Diet Pepsi and one regular Mountain Dew?*

Resource

Assessing the Content Standards

As previously suggested, the master list of the embedded concepts and performance indicators in Chapter 2, when combined with the explications and matching figures of developmental items in Chapter 3, can be used for assessment purposes. The following represents illustrations of how these matches of standards and items can be used to create assessments and rubrics for the purpose of group or individual analyses. Assessments can be used for a variety of purposes. In the classroom, they can provide ongoing feedback to the teacher in reference to the group or individual's attainment of knowledge. When applied beyond the single classroom, they can monitor the achievement of schools and districts, as well as analyze the differences or gaps among individual groups of students. The closing of group achievement gaps has become a major educational goal for the United States, but there will always be some gaps for individual learners that teachers can expeditiously recognize and address.

Teachers can respond to individual needs or gaps in a variety of ways, but they will discover that it is most useful to first carefully identify the missing concept or lack of progress on the concept or skill. Rubrics attached to an assessed concept can be helpful benchmarks used to measure the specific levels of attainment. The following table shows how the developmental levels suggested in Chapter 2 can be translated into a general rubric. The particular concept or performance indicator can be listed using either the exact definition or a number that refers to a separate list as described below. An above-standard level (Level 4) that is not delineated by grade level in Chapter 2 may also be added for assessment purposes. For more detail on assessment and the use of rubrics, see Solomon (2002, 2003).

■ A MATCHING RUBRIC

Explanation of Mastery Levels				
Concept or Indicator	Level 1: Procedural Exploration	Level 2: Concept Mastery	Level 3: Procedural or Algorithmic Mastery	Level 4: Application Mastery
Proves or disproves congruence of two triangles by completion and measure of figures when given measures of congruent sides and/or angles Judges congruence of figures given partial corresponding measures	Solves one-step problems based on this concept when given sample patterns, figures, or concrete representative materials to follow, or by imitating the procedure, but is unable to explain the concept	Solves one-step problems and explains the concept used. May still need samples to follow.	Generalizes the concept and uses it to solve two-step problems without samples to follow	Generates an original problem using the concept or applies it in an unusual way

As the teacher implements the activities suggested in Chapter 3, the incorporated dialogue of probing questions and prompts will provide ongoing proximal assessment. Additional questions may be required, however, as missing knowledge is perceived. In a more structured or formal context, teachers can design written assessments. They can begin to develop these assessments for a grade or class by choosing those concepts and skills from Chapter 2 that are appropriate at particular time intervals. After deciding on the expected mastery level for each one, they can select matching items from Chapter 3 or develop similar ones. In some cases, the wording of the developmental Chapter 3 items may have to be slightly changed for formal measurement purposes. The necessary substance of the items is essentially described in the matching performance indicator. The assessment instrument items would be specifically matched to the list of selected concepts and indicators. It may be useful to organize the matches by creating a set of test specifications that might look like the following table.

■ TEST SPECIFICATIONS

Concept or Indicator #	Expected Mastery Level	Item(s) on Your Assessment
18.4	Level 1	34, 35, 36, 37
18.5	Level 2	36, 37, 38, 39

The assessments can provide teachers with the analytic feedback needed to guide their instruction. They may also generate feedback for students and parents. The feedback form can include a description of the individual concepts or indicators that are measured, or it can just include the number from a separately provided list that is shared among staff, parents, and students.

INDIVIDUAL STUDENT FEEDBACK ■

Individual Assessment of Levels-Student Name		
Content/Performance Standard	Expected Level for Class	Student's Level
18.4 (see standard list) 18. 5 (see standard list)	Level 1 Level 2	Level 2 Level 4

Analysis of this report would indicate that this student is achieving above the expected level and does not require group or individual remediation.

GROUP ANALYSIS ■

The following represents an analysis that can be used with a teacher-made test based on individual class or school expectations. The median expectations can be normed for an individual school population by comparison with previous grade level tests, or they can be based on a standardized test that has been normed on a large population.

Class or Grade Assessment of Achievement									
Content/Performance Standard	Median Expected Class or Grade Achievement at Each Mastery Level (in Percentage of Class That Reaches It)				Percentage of Class or Grade That Achieved Each Level				Item Number(s) on Assessment Instrument(s)
	1	2	3	4	1	2	3	4	
18.4 (see standard list in Chapter 2)	98	75	60	10	100	85	70	15	34, 35, 36, 37
18.5 (see standard list in Chapter 2)	80	50	40	5	53	37	20	0	36, 37, 38, 39

An analysis and response to the above would include the following:

- For Concept 18.4 (application of FOIL method or multiplying binomials), students in the class exceeded expectation.
- For Concept 18.5 (division of a monomial by a constant), even though the expectation was lower than that for 18.4, students did not meet it.
- This should be followed by careful analysis of the validity and reliability of item numbers 36, 37, 38, and 39.
- Individual and group score distributions should also be analyzed to make sure that a few outliers are not affecting the outcomes for a particular class.
- If the item is found to be appropriate, then teachers should analyze the materials and activities and revise them or plan additional ones for the group.
- Chapter 3 should be consulted for exemplars and scaffolds.

References

Anderson, J. R., & Douglass, S. (2001). Tower of Hanoi: Evidence of the cost of goal retrieval. *Journal of Experimental Psychology: Learning, Memory, and Cognition, 27*(6), 1331–1346.

Baltimore Public Schools. (1952). *Arithmetic in the elementary schools.* Baltimore: Author.

Cobb, P. (1990). Multiple perspectives. In L. P. Steffe & T. Wood (Eds.), *Transforming children's mathematics education: International perspectives* (pp. 200–215). Hillsdale, NJ: Lawrence Erlbaum.

Desimone, L., Smith, T., Baker, D., & Ueno, K. (2005). Assessing barriers to the reform of U.S. mathematics instruction from an international perspective. *American Educational Research Journal, 42*(3), 501–535.

Dillon, S. (2005, February 24). Report from states faults Bush's education initiative. *New York Times,* p. A18.

Greenleaf, B. (1872). *New practical arithmetic.* Boston: Robert Davis.

Herbst, P. G. (2002). Engaging students in proving: A double bind on the teacher. *Journal for Research in Mathematics Education, 33*(3), 4–46.

Hiebert, J., & Lefevre, P. (1986). Conceptual and procedural knowledge: An introductory analysis. In J. Hiebert (Ed.), *Conceptual and procedural knowledge: The case of mathematics* (pp. 21–23). Hillsdale, NJ: Lawrence Erlbaum.

Hiebert, J., & Wearne, D. (1986). Procedures over concepts: The acquisition of decimal numbers knowledge. In J. Hiebert (Ed.), *Conceptual and procedural knowledge: The case of mathematics* (pp. 199–224). Hillsdale, NJ: Lawrence Erlbaum.

Kramarski, B., & Mevarech, Z. R. (2003). Enhancing mathematical reasoning in the classroom: The effects of cooperative learning and metacognitive teaching. *American Educational Research Journal, 40*(1), 281–308.

National Council of Teachers of Mathematics, Commission on Standards for School Mathematics. (1989). *Curriculum and evaluation standards for school mathematics.* Reston, VA: Author.

National Council of Teachers of Mathematics, Commission on Standards for School Mathematics. (2000). *Curriculum and evaluation standards for school mathematics.* Reston, VA: Author.

National Council of Teachers of Mathematics, Commission on Standards for School Mathematics. (2006). *Curriculum focal points for prekindergarten through Grade 8 mathematics: A quest for coherence.* Reston, VA: Author.

No Child Left Behind Act of 2001, Pub. L. No. 107-110, 107th Cong., 1st sess. (January 8, 2002).

Schmidt, W. H. (2004). A vision for mathematics. *Educational Leadership, 61*(5), 6–11.

Schmidt, W. H., McKnight, C. C., & Raizen, S. A. (1997). *A splintered vision: An investigation of U.S. science and mathematics education.* Dordrecht, The Netherlands: Kluwer.

Solomon, P. G. (1995). *No small feat: Taking time for change.* Thousand Oaks, CA: Corwin Press.

Solomon, P. G. (2002). *The assessment bridge: Positive ways to link tests to learning, standards, and curriculum improvement.* Thousand Oaks, CA: Corwin Press.

Solomon, P. G. (2003). *The curriculum bridge: From standards to actual classroom practice* (2nd ed.). Thousand Oaks, CA: Corwin Press.

Sousa, D. A. (2000). *How the brain learns.* Thousand Oaks, CA: Corwin Press.

Usikin, Z. (1998). Paper and pencil algorithms in a calculator and computer age. In L. Morrow & M. J. Kenney (Eds.), *The teaching and learning of algorithms in school mathematics: National Council of Teachers of Mathematics 1998 yearbook* (pp. 7–19). Reston, VA: National Council of Teachers of Mathematics.

Wang, J., & Lin, E. (2005). Comparative studies on U.S. and Chinese mathematics learning and the implications for standards-based mathematics teaching reform. *Educational Researcher, 34*(5), 3–13.

Additional Reading

Ashlock, R. (1990). *Error patterns in computation: A semi-programmed approach.* Columbus, OH: Merrill.

Baroody, A. J. (1987). *Children's mathematical thinking.* New York: Teachers College Press.

Battista, M. T., & Clements, D. H. (1996). Students' understanding of three-dimensional rectangular array of cubes. *Journal for Research in Mathematics Education, 27*(3), 258–292.

Berlinghoff, W., & Washburn, R. (1990). *The mathematics of the elementary grades.* New York: Ardsley House.

Burns, M. (1987). *A collection of math lessons: From Grades 3 through 6.* White Plains, NY: Math Solutions Publications.

Carpenter, T. P. (1986). Conceptual knowledge as a foundation for procedural knowledge: Implications from research on the initial learning of arithmetic. In J. Hiebert (Ed.), *Conceptual and procedural knowledge: The case of mathematics* (pp. 113–132). Hillsdale, NJ: Lawrence Erlbaum.

Cathcart, G., & Kirkpatrick, J. (Eds.). (1979). *Organizing data and dealing with uncertainty.* Reston, VA: National Council of Teachers of Mathematics.

Chatterji, M. (2003). *Designing and using tools for educational assessment.* Boston: Allyn & Bacon.

Coburn, T. (1989). The role of computation in changing mathematics curriculum. In P. H. Trafton & A. P. Shulte (Eds.), *New directions for elementary mathematics: 1989 yearbook.* Reston, VA: National Council of Teachers of Mathematics.

Cumming, J. J., & Elkins, J. (1999). Lack of automaticity in the basic addition facts as a characteristic of arithmetic learning problems and instructional needs. *Mathematical Cognition, 5*(2), 149–180.

Fendel, D., Resek, D., Alper, L., & Fraser, S. (1996). *Baker's choice: A unit of high school mathematics* (Interactive mathematics program). Berkeley, CA: Key Curriculum Press.

Fennema, E., Carpenter, T., & Lamon, S. (1991). *Integrating research on teaching and learning mathematics.* Albany: State University of New York Press.

Fey, J. (1992). *Calculators in mathematics education.* Reston, VA: National Council of Teachers of Mathematics.

Fuson, K. (1990). Issues in place-value and multi-digit addition and subtraction: Learning and teaching. *Journal of Research in Mathematics Education, 21*(4), 273–280.

Fuson, K., & Briars, D. J. (1990). Using a base-ten blocks learning/teaching approach for first and second grade place value and multidigit addition and subtraction. *Journal for Research in Mathematics Education, 21*(3), 180–206.

Fuson, K., Wearne, D., Hiebert, J., Murray, H., Human, P., Olivier, A. L., et al. (1998). Children's conceptual structures for multi-digit numbers and methods of multi-digit addition and subtraction. *Journal for Research in Mathematics Education, 28*(2), 130–162.

Ginsburg, H. (Ed.). (1983). *The development of mathematical thinking.* New York: Academic Press.

Ginsburg, H. (1989). *Children's arithmetic: How they learn it and how you teach it.* Austin, TX: Pro-Ed.

Grossnickle, F., Perry, L., & Reckzeh, J. (1990). *Discovering meanings in elementary school mathematics.* Fort Worth, TX: Holt, Rinehart & Winston.

Grouws, D. A., Cooney, T. J., & Jones, D. (1988). *Perspectives on research on effective mathematics teaching.* Reston, VA: National Council of Teachers of Mathematics.

Haitians, J., & Speer, W. (1997). *Today's mathematics: Part 2: Activities and instructional ideas* (9th ed.). Upper Saddle River, NJ: Prentice Hall.

Harel, G., & Confrey, J. (1994). *Multiplicative reasoning in the learning of mathematics.* New York: State University of New York Press.

Hatfield, M., Edwards, N., & Bitter, G. (2005). *Mathematics methods for the elementary and middle school.* Needham Heights, MA: Allyn & Bacon.

Henderson, D. (1996). *Experiencing geometry on plane and sphere.* Upper Saddle River, NJ: Prentice Hall.

Hill, H. C., Rowan, B., & Ball, D. L. (2005). Effects of teachers' mathematical knowledge for teaching on student achievement. *American Educational Research Journal, 42*(2), 371–406.

Kellough, R. (1996). *Integrating mathematics and science: For kindergarten and primary children.* Englewood Cliffs, NJ: Prentice Hall.

Klein, D., Braams, B. J., Braden, L., Finn, C. E., Parker, T., Quirk, W., et al. (2005). *State of the state math standards.* Retrieved January 22, 2006, from http://www.edexcellence.net/foundation/global/index.cfm

Kreindler, L., & Zahm, B. (1992). *Source book: Lessons to illustrate the NCTM standards.* New York: Learning Team.

Lamon, S. (1993). Ratio and proportion: Connecting content and children's thinking. *Journal for Research in Mathematics Education, 24,* 4–46.

Lamon, S. (1996). The development of unitizing: Its role in children's partitioning strategies. *Journal for Research in Mathematics Education, 27*(2), 170–193.

Lerman, S. (1996). Intersubjectivity in mathematics learning: A challenge to the radical constructivist paradigm? *Journal for Research in Mathematics Education, 27*(2), 133–150.

Lesh, R., & Lamon, S. (1992). *Assessment of authentic performance in school mathematics.* Washington, DC: AAAS Press.

Linn, R. L., Baker, D. F., & Betebenner, D. W. (2002). Accountability systems: Implications of requirements of the No Child Left Behind Act of 2001. *Educational Researcher, 31*(6), 3–16.

Mathematical Sciences Education Board: National Research Council. (1993). *Measuring up: Prototypes for mathematics assessment.* Washington, DC: National Academy Press.

Mokros, J., & Russell, S. J. (1995). Children's concepts of average and representativeness. *Journal for Research in Mathematics Education, 26*(1), 20–39.

Morrow, L. (1998). Whither algorithms? Mathematics educators express their views. In L. Morrow & M. J. Kenney (Eds.), *The teaching and learning of algorithms in school mathematics: National Council of Teachers of Mathematics 1998 yearbook.* Reston, VA: National Council of Teachers of Mathematics.

National Center for Education Statistics. (2005). *The Trends in International Mathematics and Science Study (TIMSS).* Retrieved from http://nces.ed.gov/pubs2005/timss03/

Nesher, P. (1988). Multiplicative school word problems: Theoretical approaches and empirical findings. In J. Hiebert & M. Behr (Eds.), *Number concepts and operations in the middle grades* (pp. 19–40). Hillsdale, NJ: Lawrence Erlbaum.

Phillips, L. (2003). When flash cards are not enough. *Teaching Children Mathematics, 9*(6), 358–363.

Resnick, L. B. (1983). A developmental theory of number understanding. In H. Ginsburg (Ed.), *The development of mathematical thinking* (pp. 110–149). New York: Academic Press.

Reys, R., Suydam, M., & Lindquist, M. (1995). *Helping children learn mathematics.* New York: John Wiley.

Riedesel, A., Schwartz, J., & Clements, D. (1996). *Teaching elementary school mathematics.* Needham Heights, MA: Allyn & Bacon.

Riley, M. S., Greeno, J. G., & Heller, J. I. (1983). The development of children's problem solving abilities in arithmetic. In H. Ginsburg (Ed.), *The development of mathematical thinking* (pp. 115–200). New York: Academic Press.

Ross, S. (1989). Parts, wholes, and place value: A developmental view. *Arithmetic Teacher, 36*(6), 47–51.

Schonfeld, A. H. (1986). On having and using geometric knowledge. In J. Hiebert (Ed.), *Conceptual and procedural knowledge: The case of mathematics* (pp. 225–264). Hillsdale, NJ: Lawrence Erlbaum.

Silver, E. (1986). Using conceptual and procedural knowledge. In J. Hiebert (Ed.), *Conceptual and procedural knowledge: The case of mathematics* (pp. 181–198). Hillsdale, NJ: Lawrence Erlbaum.

Solomon, P. G. (2005, April). *Closing the achievement gap: A systemic model.* Paper presented at the American Educational Research Association conference, Montreal, Quebec, Canada.

Souviney, R. (1994). *Learning to teach mathematics* (2nd ed.). New York: Macmillan.

Sovchik, R. (1996). *Teaching mathematics to children.* New York: HarperCollins.

Troutman, A., & Lichtenberg, B. (1991). *Mathematics, a good beginning: Strategies for teaching children.* Pacific Grove, CA: Brooks/Cole.

University of the State of New York. (1989). *Teaching math with computers: K–8.* Albany, NY: State Education Department.

University of the State of New York. (1989). *Suggestions for teaching mathematics using laboratory approaches: Grades 1–6: Operations.* Albany, NY: State Education Department.

University of the State of New York. (1990). *Suggestions for teaching mathematics using laboratory approaches: Grades 1–6: Probability.* Albany, NY: State Education Department.

University of the State of New York. (2005). *Mathematics Standards Committee recommendations.* Albany, NY: State Education Department. Available online at http://www.emsc.nysed.gov/3-8/mathoverview.htm

U.S. Department of Education. (2001, August 2). *Prepared remarks of U.S. Secretary of Education Rod Paige: The nation's report card—mathematics 2000.* Retrieved February 2, 2002, from http://www.ed.gov/news/pressreleases/2001/08/08022001.html

Van de Walle, J. (1998). *Elementary and middle school mathematics: Teaching developmentally.* New York: Addison-Wesley/Longman.

VanLehn, K. (1986). Arithmetic procedures are induced from examples. In J. Hiebert (Ed.), *Conceptual and procedural knowledge: The case of mathematics* (pp. 133–179). Hillsdale, NJ: Lawrence Erlbaum.

Williams, W., Blythe, T., White, N., Li, J., Sternberg, R., & Gardner, H. (1996). *Practical intelligence for school.* New York: HarperCollins.

Wood, T., & Cobb, P. (1990). The contextual nature of teaching: Mathematics and reading instruction in one second grade classroom. *Elementary School Journal, 90,* 499–502.

Index

CORWIN PRESS